THE GREEN ARCHIPELAGO

A

Philip E. Lilienthal (signature)

Book

The Philip E. Lilienthal imprint
honors special books
in commemoration of a man whose work
at the University of California Press from 1954 to 1979
was marked by dedication to young authors
and to high standards in the field of Asian Studies.
Friends, family, authors, and foundations have together
endowed the Lilienthal Fund, which enables the Press
to publish under this imprint selected books
in a way that reflects the taste and judgment
of a great and beloved editor.

THE GREEN ARCHIPELAGO

Forestry in Preindustrial Japan

CONRAD TOTMAN

UNIVERSITY OF CALIFORNIA PRESS
BERKELEY   LOS ANGELES   LONDON

University of California Press
Berkeley and Los Angeles, California

University of California Press, Ltd.
London, England

© 1989 by
The Regents of the University of California

LIBRARY OF CONGRESS
Library of Congress Cataloging-in-Publication Data

Totman, Conrad D.
  The green archipelago: forestry in preindustrial Japan/
Conrad Totman.
      p.   cm.
  Bibliography: p.
  Includes index.
  ISBN 0-520-06313-9 (alk. paper)
  1. Forests and forestry—Japan.   2. Forest policy—Japan.
I. Title.
SD225.T67 1989
333.75′15′0952—dc 19   88-17504
                                                        CIP

Printed in the United States of America

1   2   3   4   5   6   7   8   9

For
Kathy and Chris
who have so enriched my days on
This Beautiful Planet

Contents

Illustrations

Maps

Figures

Preface

More and more our choices on this planet appear to be fire or ice: the fire of nuclear holocaust or the ice of environmental catastrophe. In both choices the heart of the problem is our continued domination by anachronistic attitudes that blind us to an essential truth: the multibillion-year history of life on earth reached a watershed in the twentieth century. The old history of our ecosystem has ended; a new history has begun. Whether it will be the history of a planet whose living face is much like that of former eons, or the history of a planet with a dramatically new face, is yet to be decided.

In either case it will be a new history. For billions of years the earth's ecosystem was immune to the depredations of any of its own. External forces could visit disaster upon it. Particular species could grievously wound one another, but none could threaten life as a whole. Because this condition provided each species or symbiotic group with a secure field of action, each could pursue its own immediate interests, utterly indifferent to the general well-being, confident that the system was self-correcting, self-perpetuating, safe from abuse by any of its members.

Today that is all changed. Now one species—our own—can ravage the whole extraordinary structure of life on earth. And we seem determined to do it. We direct our highest skills and our most elaborately organized powers to the pursuit of enterprises that will most assuredly accomplish that pathetic end: we devise ever more destructive explosives and equip them with increasingly intricate and unmanageable triggering devices; we create ever more deadly chemicals and spew out more and more poisonous wastes; and we exploit ever vaster reaches of the ecosystem and its physical foundation with little serious attention to the broader ramifications of our conduct. While doing these things, we produce endless streams of rhetoric and information that divert our attention from critical matters to secondary and tertiary issues arising from parochial prejudice and short-term, selfish interest.

This performance cannot long continue. Technological romantics may see salvation in flight to another planet, but that is not the solution. We humans are the problem: wherever we go, the problem goes with us. To cope with the problem, we must change. And if we change appropriately, there will be no need to flee anywhere. Our home here on earth will be quite sufficient for us.

Like it or not, as our planet enters a new era we humans must relinquish a forty-thousand-year legacy of thought and behavior that is no longer adequate. We must now learn more about how the ecosystem works to understand how we properly fit into it. We must learn how to manage ourselves and how to deal with our environment so that it may endure, thereby enabling our own species to endure. Or we shall ruin everything.

Historians cannot ignore the implications of our dilemma. Unless we are content to be part of the problem rather than part of the solution, we too must rethink where we stand and what we do. This study constitutes an effort by one historian—a historian who previously spent twenty years happily reconstructing a political history that is of no consequence to any living creature—to look anew at the human record in hopes of saying something worth hearing.

This examination of forestry in preindustrial Japan focuses on human interaction with the environment. From an ecologist's perspective the work will surely be disappointing. It employs a homocentric autecological approach rather than a synecological one; that is, instead of looking at the operation of the ecosystem as a whole, with the human component treated as but one of myriad variables, it focuses explicitly on the relationship of humans to environment. It does so in part because the historical record is radically skewed in that direction: preindustrial Japanese, and the present-day historians who study them, have paid great attention to human affairs but little to the rest of the archipelago's history. In addition, this approach has been used because it maximizes common ground with nonecological studies and because my own understanding of environmental history is still embryonic.

Despite its shortcomings, I hope this inquiry into the record of Japan's preindustrial use of forests will in its own small way help us understand the dynamics of ecological relationships as they have worked in historical practice. This understanding may in turn assist us in determining which traditional behaviors we must or must not abandon if we are to keep the surface of our little, green planet alive.

This study was made possible by a grant from the Japan Foundation, which sustained me during a year of research in Japan in 1981–82. Thanks to Professor Ōishi Shinzaburō, I was able to spend that year affiliated with the Tokugawa Institute for the History of Forestry (Tokugawa Rinseishi Kenkyūjo) in Mejiro. There I had the pleasure of meeting Tokoro Mitsuo, Iioka Masatake, and other scholars and staff of the institute. I thank them for their friendship, patience, and helpfulness as I learned the basics of Japanese forest history, and I thank Professor Kanai Madoka for helping arrange that year of study. I am grateful to Northwestern University for facilitating my year of leave and to the Yale University Library for providing additional research materials. I appreciate the warm interest that many colleagues have shown in my work, and, of course, I thank Michiko for continuing to bear with my puzzlements.

A Brief Chronology

Years	Epochs in Forestry	General Historical Periods	Periods and Capitals	Estimated Population	Notable Historical Entries
					agriculture spreads **2500 B.C.–A.D. 500**
					smelting **A.D. 200–**
					political consolidation **A.D. 300–**
A.D. 600					
700	ancient predation **600–850**		Nara: Heijō-kyō **710–794**	5 million **700**	Tōdaiji built **740s**
800		ancient			Heian-kyō built **790s**
900			Heian: Heian-kyō **794–1185**		Heian-kyō decays ca. **950ff.**
1000				6.5 million **1000**	
1100	exploitation forestry				Tōdaiji rebuilt **1180s**
1200			Kamakura: Kamakura **1185–1337**		Kamakura burns **1219**
1300		medieval			
1400			Muromachi: Kyoto **1337–1600**		*iriai* proliferate ca. **1400ff.**
1500	early modern predation **1570–1670**				Hideyoshi builds **1590s**
1600		early modern	Tokugawa: Edo **1603–1868**	12 million **1600**	Meireki fire **1657**
1700				31 million **1720**	*bakufu* seizes Hida **1692**
	regenerative forestry				*Nōgyō zensho* **1697**
					buwakebayashi appear **1720s**
1800			modern: Tokyo **1868–**	33 million **1870**	*nenkiyama* proliferate **1760s**
					essays by Satō Shin'en **1809–1844**
1900		modern			national forests established **1880s**

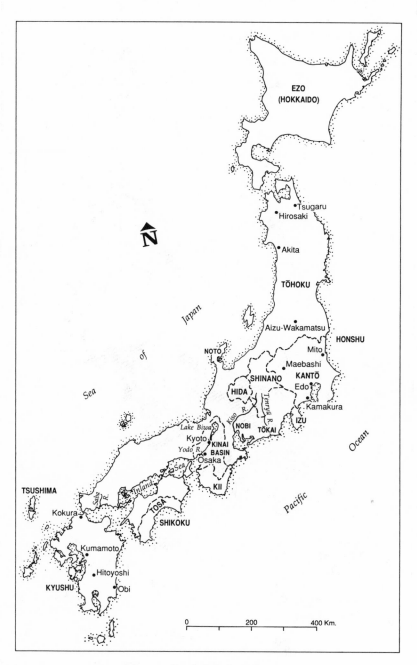

Map 1. Early Modern Japan

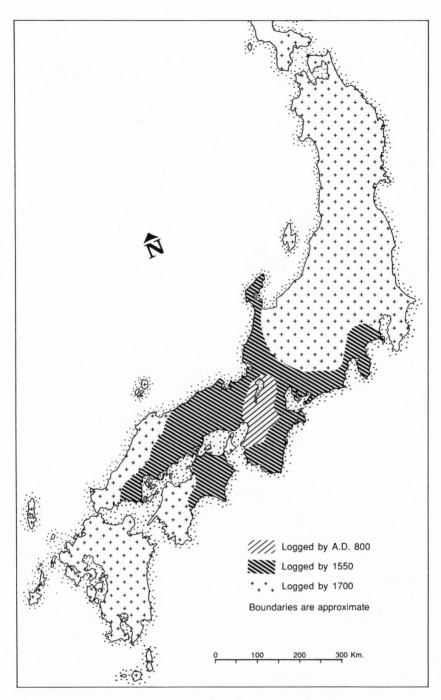

Map 2. Areas Logged by Monumental Builders

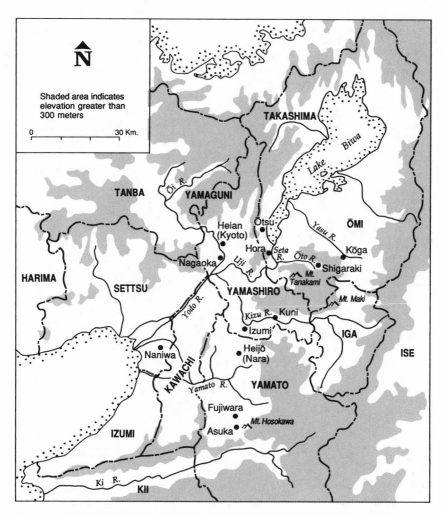

Map 3. The Kinai Basin. Based on *Nihon rekishi chizu* (map volume of *Nihon rekishi daijiten*; Tokyo: Kawade Shobō Shinsha, 1961), 7.

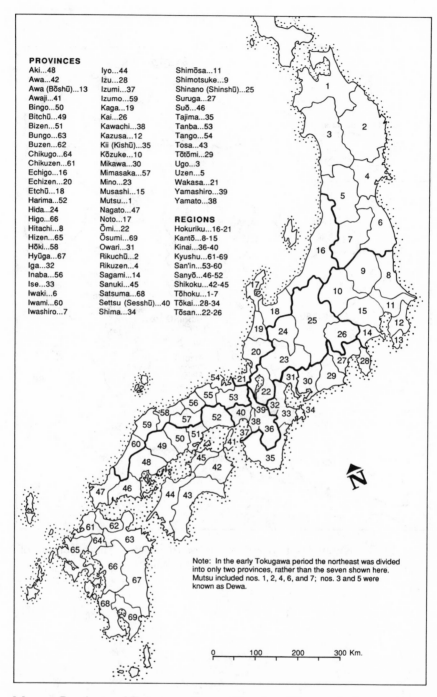

PROVINCES

Aki...48	Iyo...44	Shimōsa...11
Awa...42	Izu...28	Shimotsuke...9
Awa (Bōshū)...13	Izumi...37	Shinano (Shinshū)...25
Awaji...41	Izumo...59	Suruga...27
Bingo...50	Kaga...19	Suō...46
Bitchū...49	Kai...26	Tajima...35
Bizen...51	Kawachi...38	Tanba...53
Bungo...63	Kazusa...12	Tango...54
Buzen...62	Kii (Kishū)...35	Tosa...43
Chikugo...64	Kōzuke...10	Tōtōmi...29
Chikuzen...61	Mikawa...30	Ugo...3
Echigo...16	Mimasaka...57	Uzen...5
Echizen...20	Mino...23	Wakasa...21
Etchū...18	Musashi...15	Yamashiro...39
Harima...52	Mutsu...1	Yamato...38
Hida...24	Nagato...47	
Higo...66	Noto...17	**REGIONS**
Hitachi...8	Ōmi...22	Hokuriku...16-21
Hizen...65	Ōsumi...69	Kantō...8-15
Hōki...58	Owari...31	Kinai...36-40
Hyūga...67	Rikuchū...2	Kyushu...61-69
Iga...32	Rikuzen...4	San'in...53-60
Inaba...56	Sagami...14	Sanyō...46-52
Ise...33	Sanuki...45	Shikoku...42-45
Iwaki...6	Satsuma...68	Tōhoku...1-7
Iwami...60	Settsu (Sesshū)...40	Tōkai...28-34
Iwashiro...7	Shima...34	Tōsan...22-26

Note: In the early Tokugawa period the northeast was divided into only two provinces, rather than the seven shown here. Mutsu included nos. 1, 2, 4, 6, and 7; nos. 3 and 5 were known as Dewa.

0   100   200   300 Km.

Map 4. Provinces of Tokugawa Japan. Based on Thomas C. Smith, *Native Sources of Japanese Industrialization, 1750–1920* (Berkeley and Los Angeles: University of California Press, 1988).

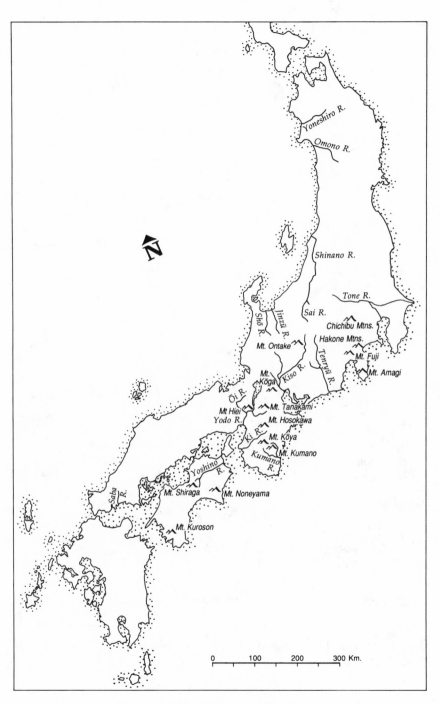

Map 5. Major Rivers and Mountains

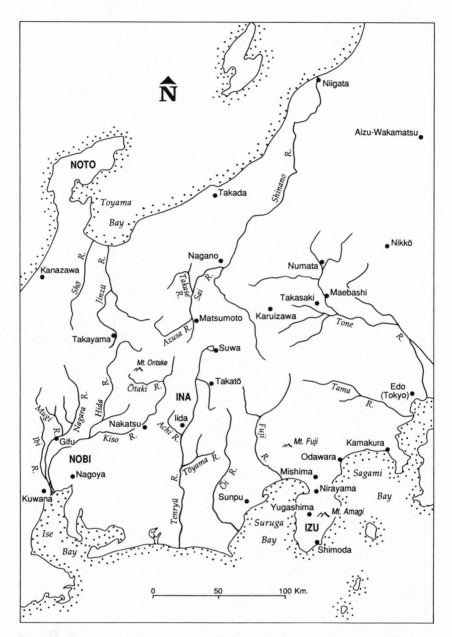

Map 6. Central Japan. Based on *Teikoku's Complete Atlas of Japan* (Tokyo: Teikoku-Shoin, 1977), 29–30.

Map 7. Cities and Towns

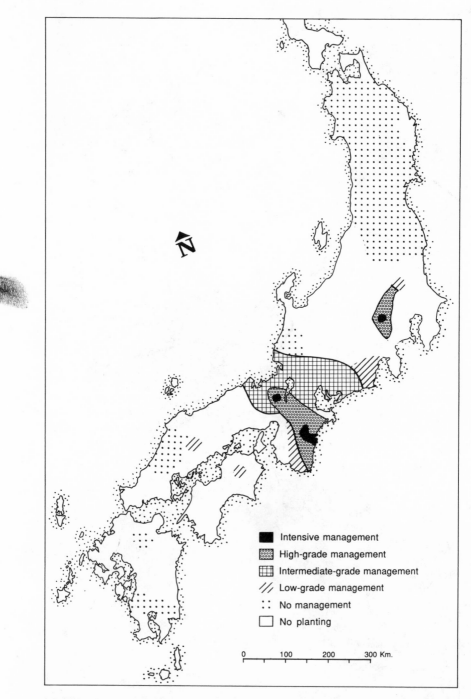

Intensive management
High-grade management
Intermediate-grade management
Low-grade management
No management
No planting

0   100   200   300 Km.

Map 8. Geographical Distribution of Late Edo-Period Afforestation (on private land). Based on Fujita Yoshihisa, "Kinsei ni okeru ikurin gijutsu taikei no chiikisei," *Tokugawa Rinseishi Kenkyūjo Kenkyū kiyō* 55 (1980): 120.

Introduction:
An Overview of Preindustrial
Japanese Forest History

Every foreign traveler in Japan is delighted by the verdant forest-shrouded mountains that thrust skyward from one end of the island chain to the other.[1] The Japanese themselves are conscious of the lush green of their homeland, which they sometimes refer to as *midori no rettō*, "the green archipelago." At first glance Japan seems to be a world of primeval forests, a gorgeous natural creation reflecting that frequently mentioned Japanese love of nature. In fact, the abundant verdure is not a monument to nature's benevolence and Japanese aesthetic sensibilities but the hard-earned result of generations of human toil that have converted the archipelago into one great forest preserve.

To put the issue directly, Japan today should be an impoverished, slum-ridden, peasant society subsisting on a barren, eroded moonscape characterized by bald mountains and debris-strewn lowlands. Instead, it is a highly industrialized society living in a luxuriantly green realm. Despite intense pressure on a vulnerable topography, the people of Japan have done less to ravage their land and bring ruin upon it than have many other societies past and present that have been favored by a less dense population and more benign terrain. We can look at the heaths and bogs of northwest Europe; the barren littoral of the Mediterranean; the ravaged mountains of south-central Korea and China; the dying Sahel region of Africa; or the disasters now unfolding in Latin America and

Southeast Asia as forests there are ripped out with no effective thought for the morrow.

Japan should be a ruined land because of the particular interaction there of geography and history. Geologically, the Japanese archipelago is an unstable complex of acutely inclined upthrust arcs and nodes.[2] These convoluted, quake-prone mountains tower above narrow valleys whose swift-running streams debouch onto small deposition plains that mostly front the ocean. The steep mountainsides are covered by a thin, coarse, immature soil that is continually being leached of the few nutrients it has. Periodically, patches slide, exposing raw bedrock. This sliding frequently results from heavy deluges that occur during the early summer monsoons and autumn typhoons. Upland and riverine surfaces facing the Sea of Japan are also threatened by heavy spring-snow runoff.

When left untouched by humans, the island chain's dense and varied natural vegetation can usually hold its soil in place, with only sporadic avalanches and surface damage occurring after volcanic activity, earthquakes, or forest fires. However, humans have not left those mountains untouched. For centuries the island chain has supported on its limited arable land an extremely dense population that has consumed great quantities of forest products obtained directly from the mountains.[3]

Such heavy consumption could easily have led to the denuding of mountainsides, permitting regolith to thunder down into valleys, whence it would surge out across once-fertile plains, repeatedly covering them with debris and exposing them to chronic and unpredictable drought, flood, and erosion. It is this sequence of events, resulting from a dense population pressing for centuries against an easily destabilized forest terrain, that long ago should have turned Japan into a zone of ecological desolation and human misery. But that did not happen, and we can wonder why.

In broadest terms the history of Japan's human-forest relationship has consisted of two phases.[4] First was a thirty-thousand-year preagricultural phase, during which *Homo sapiens sapiens* used puny wood, bone, and stone tools to exploit a wooded landscape whose essential character he could not alter. Second has been a far shorter phase encompassing the past twenty-five hundred years, during which a swelling human population, equipped with an increasingly complex and demanding technology, has altered fundamentally the character of more and more woodland—not only bottomland but also accessible upland areas.

This second phase emerged silently, with deforestation first occurring gradually as a corollary of agricultural land clearing. During the seventh century the introduction from the Asian continent of a large-scale architecture led to a tremendous building boom that was sustained by a surge in logging. This surge, the "ancient predation," severely tested the carrying capacity of forests in the Kinai basin, the watershed on the main island of Honshu where Japan's rulers were headquartered.[5] With construction booming, forest output began to fall short of demand, and ecological despoliation became apparent near the two successive capital cities of Nara and Heian (later known as Kyoto). As these conditions developed, there were attempts to control woodland use. Institutions, notably governments and monasteries, initiated forest closure as a way to preserve timber supplies. After a few generations of splendor, however, the ruling elite that had spawned the building boom gradually lost the will and capacity to pursue monumental projects. As building slackened, the pressure on woodland eased and interest in forest closure waned.

Several centuries of wider-ranging but less intensive "medieval" forest exploitation followed, during which the realm experienced great incremental development and socioeconomic change. The demand for woodland products escalated, most notably for the green fertilizer material needed to sustain production on fields now subject to more intensive tillage. Greater agricultural dependency on woodland inspired a new, local, and often communal interest in closure of untilled land. This new impulse to restrict forest use first manifested itself in the populous Kinai region, doing so from the fourteenth century. Later the practice spread as pressure on woodland dictated. Concurrently, the ruling warrior, or samurai, elite engaged in a brutal struggle for supremacy that by the sixteenth century was prompting regional military leaders, or daimyo, to tighten control over woodland as a means of assuring resources for military use.

Before the seventeenth century, in short, there were gestures toward a human-managed forestry, but in terms of the general impact on either woodland or on human culture, they amounted to little more than gestures. For all practical purposes, therefore, we may speak of Japan's forest history prior to the seventeenth century as a stereotypical era of exploitation forestry, in which woodland users generally showed little concern for preservation of site or restoration of yield. The resolution of civil strife late in the sixteenth century ended that era, however, by giving rise to a period of unprecedented nationwide timber consumption, the "early modern predation," that willy-nilly propelled Japan into the age of regenerative forestry.[6]

During the era of exploitation forestry the general populace satisfied most of its forest needs from nearby areas, which spread the impact of this consumption throughout the islands. The impact of the rulers, by contrast, was more concentrated geographically, and its scale and locus changed as the centuries passed. Map 2 attempts to show these changes in the broadest terms: as of A.D. 800 the ruling elite was making heavy demands on woodland but in only a small part of Japan. By 1550 a substantially larger area was providing timber for rulers in Kyoto (and, for a period, Kamakura), but in much of that expanded area harvesting was spotty and selective.[7] During the early modern predation, woodland throughout the country was for the first time harvested to satisfy the appetites of central power holders.[8] Logging was so intensive that when Japan entered the twentieth century only the northern island of Hokkaido still held major areas of virgin timber. Elsewhere, save for inaccessible mountainous sites, good timber existed only in plantations or as naturally seeded and supervised replacement growth.

The transition to regenerative forestry occurred during the Edo (or Tokugawa) period (1600–1867), when the Tokugawa regime ruled Japan from its capital city of Edo, the metropolis known since 1868 as Tokyo. To foreshadow the matter, for about a century after 1570 Japan experienced extraordinarily rapid population growth and a surge in castle and temple construction and city building. The food and construction demands of this mushrooming population and its newly powerful rulers led to wholesale forest clearing, which was followed by erosion that denuded mountains and damaged lowlands. Particularly hard hit was the Kinai basin, whose forest cover was already precarious due to prior centuries of heavy use. In due course the environmental damage prompted riparian work and the development of protection forestry.

Even more than terrain deterioration, forest product scarcities caused by overconsumption generated problems. Two separate but interconnected social groups—rulers in their cities and peasants in their villages—were the principal exploiters of woodland, and even though their needs were not identical, they overlapped enough that as the population grew and forest cover deteriorated, the two groups came into severe competition for use of the land. From about the mid-seventeenth century scarcity of timber and fuel, and the conflicts and litigation that accompanied it, led to active attempts at forest regulation. Land and stand management practices were substantially tightened up, and an elaborate array of sumptuary regulations was promulgated to restrain consumption. Neither maneuvering nor legislation overcame the intense competition for scarce goods, but they do appear to have helped stop the worst of terrain degradation.

In consequence of the failure to restore forest abundance, during the eighteenth century professional agronomists, itinerant scholars, entrepreneurial woodsmen, and government forest officials developed and disseminated positive policies of afforestation. Varieties of shared-use forestry appeared that may have ameliorated ruler-villager tension and facilitated the rise of plantation forestry, although the tension itself may have been a modest boon to the forests insofar as it prevented peasants from denuding as much woodland and rulers from promoting as extensive conifer monoculture as they otherwise might have done. By the late eighteenth century plantation forestry was emerging as a widely practiced art, and although only a small portion of total woodland was hand planted, nearly all forested areas were subject to some degree of purposeful regulation and management. During the nineteenth century plantation culture spread rapidly, becoming a major source of timber.

In its entirety this early modern forest system had both protective and productive functions. It was designed to stabilize land surfaces and also to regulate and maximize the output of valued forest products, doing so by the careful formation, maintenance, and utilization of healthy stands. It was grounded in an extensive silvicultural literature and was operated by knowledgeable woodsmen, both government foresters and entrepreneurial lumbermen. The forest system that had taken shape by the nineteenth century managed not only to prevent widespread forest devastation but also to help sustain a yield that maintained the physical plant of the archipelago's densely settled, heavily woodland-dependent human civilization.

It would be misleading, of course, to leave a reader with the implication that the rich forests of contemporary Japan can be attributed directly to pre-twentieth-century policies. Today's lushness is the immediate result of the decades of forest recovery—partly purposeful, partly attributable to the international marketplace—that followed World War II. Because of these decades of planting and natural rejuvenation, much of the country is clothed in a mantle of young plantation stands and natural growth, and Japan remains more forested than nearly any other country in the temperate zone.

However, that story of postwar recovery—the most recent phase of Japan's experience with "modern" forestry, which began with the formation of national forests late in the nineteenth century—is generically familiar to readers of English as an integral part of the recent global phenomenon of forest management. So this study ends with the passing of the earlier, autochthonous phase, which is less familiar but no less important. Without the forest achievements of that phase, Japan would have no modern forest system; indeed, there might not even be a modern Japan resembling the one we know.

As those comments suggest, this story of forest usage fits into two English-language historiographical contexts: that of Japanese history and that of forest history. In the former context it introduces another dimension to the existing corpus on socioeconomic history, which has examined the early modern phase of agricultural land use and village society with care but generally not dwelt on woodland usage. In the latter it adds a major non-Western case to a literature that has focused on the European and American historical experiences. In that literature Germany is commonly viewed as the society that first developed the practices of regenerative forestry. This study shows that such practices arose independently in Japan at least as early as in Germany.

Part One

A Millennium of Exploitation Forestry

Chapter One

The Ancient Predation, 600–850

The ancient predation was the first of three periods of severe deforestation in Japan's history. The other two were the early modern,
which occurred from 1570 to 1670, and the modern, of the first half
of the twentieth century. The first predation was the least severe of
the three, with damaging deforestation largely confined to woodlands of the Kinai basin.[1]

Prior to the ancient predation, millennia of Stone Age forest
utilization had made little lasting impact on the archipelago's
woodland. Eventually, however, field crops, including most notably rice, were introduced to Japan, and by about 300 B.C. rice
culture was well established in the west. During the next several
hundred years cultivation spread across the islands as far into the
northeast as available varieties of grain would grow. The forest clearance that permitted this diffusion was humankind's first dramatic
and permanent modification of Japanese woodland.

Not long after the establishment of rice culture, both bronze and
iron appeared in Japan. Initially, metal implements were brought
from the continent, but by A.D. 200 or so smelting was practiced in
the islands. It required substantial volumes of high-quality charcoal, which was made from oak, chestnut, or other dense hardwoods.[2] The products of the blacksmith, in turn, gave the Japanese powerful new tools with which to expand their assault on the
forests.

The diffusion of iron tools proceeded slowly, as sources of ore
were located and techniques of production mastered. As villagers
accumulated wealth enough to acquire the new types of tools, stone

implements were gradually replaced. New cultivating tools, such as metal hoes and spades, enabled tillers to work appreciably greater acreages of grain. And iron adzes, axes, chisels, drills, hammers, hatchets, planes, nails, wedges, and, somewhat later, small saws allowed them to clear more brush, fell larger trees, and process the wood more rapidly and skillfully into construction timber, larger dugout boats, and household and production tools and implements. The new woodworking tools enabled tillers to split and shape wood to make walls and irrigation ditches and dams for their rice fields and to build elevated warehouses in which harvested grain could be stored, safe from rodents and mildew.

Agriculture and metallurgy were the human innovations that most dramatically affected prehistoric Japanese forests. But other developments of A.D. 300–600 added to the intensity of human-forest relations. Horse-mounted warriors armed with swords, spears, and bows and arrows; protected by metal slat armor; and commanding armies of pike-carrying foot soldiers undertook political consolidation. Their need for weapons expanded the demand for smithing charcoal, and their steeds required forage, much of which came from woodland. As leaders gained power, moreover, they erected larger, wooden-stockaded headquarters and celebrated their accomplishments by building grand residences. To facilitate military operations, they adopted shipbuilding techniques from the continent, using plank construction to form seagoing vessels each capable of carrying scores of fighting men. And after they died, they were buried in carefully constructed wooden coffins of choice water-resistant woods, preferably *kōyamaki*.[3] Each coffin, together with artifacts of the fallen leader's life, was placed in a great burial mound (*kofun*) whose size reflected its occupant's power, the greatest rivaling the pyramids of Egypt and Meso-america. The mounds were then lined with prodigious numbers of pottery cylinders and figurines, whose firing alone must have consumed great quantities of fuel.

Thus, by A.D. 600 the people of Japan were using woodland much more intensively than a millennium earlier and were establishing the basic characteristics of the archipelago's human-forest relationship as it would survive until the twentieth century. Villagers needed cleared land for tillage. They needed well-wooded uplands to assure adequate water for paddy culture. And they needed woodland to provide various types of building materials, fuel, fodder, and natural food supplies. In subsequent centuries they would add only one major forest demand: green fertilizer material, which eventually surpassed all the others in political importance. The rulers needed fodder for their steeds, fuel for forging weapons and for domestic uses, and most of all, timber for their vessels, fortifications, private and public buildings, and other implements of war and peace.

Around 600 Japan's ruling elite initiated the ancient predation, employing new principles of political and economic organization and new styles of architecture in a construction boom of extraordinary magnitude. In the process they established the character of Japanese buildings for the next 1,250 years. A rash of construction projects endowed the country with a string of small provincial headquarters and dotted the Kinai basin with a plethora of great monasteries, shrines, palaces, and mansions. Most of these were situated in or near Nara and Heian, the two successive capital cities whose back streets were lined with the crudely framed bark and wattle homes of perhaps one hundred thousand to two hundred thousand urban commoners.

The social and ecological consequences of this construction boom were profound. It appears that all the accessible old-growth stands in the mountains adjoining the Kinai basin were felled. Because technical or political limitations or both precluded the importation of large timber or great volumes of wood from more distant areas, the timber scarcity that followed the felling of Kinai woodlands led to modifications in construction practices, wood use, and forest use and management. The intensive logging, together with an escalating demand for fuel and fodder, permanently changed the vegetation in parts of Ōmi, Yamashiro, and Yamato provinces, and these changes gave rise to wildfire, flooding, and erosion, which elicited tentative measures of forest protection and rehabilitation.[4]

Monumental Construction

The most striking use of forests during the ancient predation was for monumental construction. Part was secular, for palaces and mansions of the ruling elite, and part was ecclesiastical, for Buddhist monasteries and Shintō shrines. How much timber was consumed cannot be established, but the quantity was immense and its removal altered Kinai forest composition in ways detrimental to the monumental builders themselves.

It is impossible to know with certitude what sort of woodland produced the lumber used in this building activity. However, the species and quality requirements of builders suggest that stands were probably dense and more or less monocultural in character. Furthermore, having evidence of the general location of some logging projects; bearing in mind that *hinoki* (the species of choice) prefers relatively moist, shaded, sheltered sites; and being mindful that a major secondary objective of lumbering was to open land to cultivation, it seems most probable that conifer logging occurred in dense stands on lowlands, in shallow valleys, and along the lower reaches of hillsides. In other words, it likely entailed clear-cutting of varying-sized patches of dense conifer growth situated at lower elevations within broader areas of mixed forest. After the best stands in accessible watersheds were gone, felling became more selective, moving up the slopes to take the best of whatever was available in the mixed forest. As that occurred, standards of architectural excellence had to adjust downward to accommodate changes in raw material quality.

Secular Construction

By the sixth century regional rulers in Japan had enough power to build themselves sumptuous tribal (*uji*) headquarters and residences. Periodically, they had to replace the structures because supporting pillars were set directly into the soil where termites and rot could attack them, and framing timbers were lashed together with straw rope, which gradually became brittle.[5] These characteristics made rebuilding every twenty years or so unavoidable, and even sensible. In J. Edward Kidder's words: "The flimsy nature of the architecture often made it better to build anew than to repair."[6] The hegemonial Yamato tribal rulers (*uji no kami*) of central Japan evidently made a virtue out of necessity by specifying succession to family headship as the occasion for these periodic reconstructions. Tearing down the rotten old palace and replacing it with a fresh, new one symbolized the auspicious start of a new reign, and the political value of this also practical measure was enhanced by an accompanying Shintō purification ritual that endowed the event with sacred significance.

From about A.D. 550 migrants from the continent introduced a cultural "tool kit" that included such architectural elements as raised stone foundations, mortise-and-tenon framing, and tile roofs. Builders employed the new elements in structures associated with continental culture, namely government offices and Buddhist monasteries. Indigenous (Shintō) shrines and aristocratic residences, however, continued to be built in the customary manner. Even the Yamato chiefs, who by 650 were self-proclaimed emperors, evidently continued to erect their ever more extravagant residences (*dairi*) in the old posthole manner despite the necessity of periodic reconstruction, doing so until the establishment of Heian in the 790s.[7]

Besides rebuilding their residences periodically, the Yamato rulers frequently moved their headquarters. Why they did so is a subject of scholarly debate,[8] but to some degree their choice of sites seems influenced by the need for proximity to satisfactory timber. Empress Suiko's great palace at Asuka, built circa 600, and later palaces in that vicinity, had easy access to nearby woodland in central Yamato. Naniwa, which Emperor Kōtoku first occupied in 645 and which other emperors also used later, obtained timber easily via the old Yamato and Yodo rivers.[9] In 667 Emperor Tenchi built his palace at Ōtsu on Lake Biwa, which gave him access to the still-rich forests of western Ōmi.

Around 690, government leaders, who previously had returned to Asuka, decided to build a rectangular Chinese-style capital on the open plain at the nearby site of the former Fujiwara palace. By then, however, the surrounding forests were so thoroughly depleted that builders had to haul timber over a long and tortuous route from Mount Tanakami in south Ōmi, moving it by water down the Uji and back up the Kizu river to the landing at Izumi (modern-day Kizu) and thence south by oxcart to the construction site. In 710 they transferred their headquarters northward to a more spacious location known as Nara, which placed them much nearer their timber supply. There they began constructing a capital city designated Heijō, obtaining lumber for that grand project from the forests of Tanakami and Kōga in Ōmi and from other mountains in Iga province.[10]

Even after the construction of these elaborate cities, emperors still maintained secondary palaces, in some cases because they considered it correct to have at least two capitals (*baito*), one for the sovereign and one for the heir.[11] The most notable instances occurred in the 740s and 760s. In 740–41 Emperor Shōmu built a palace at Kuni, on the Kizu river, directly downstream from the forests of Iga. Within two years he erected another, at Shigaraki, adjacent the still-verdant Kōga hills east of Tanakami. During the next two years, he dwelt briefly at Naniwa, later returning to Shigaraki, and he toyed with the idea of making one of those capitals a replacement for Heijō. The sites reportedly proved too constricted, however, which allegedly prompted him to return to Nara in the summer of 745, abandoning both Kuni and Shigaraki.[12]

In the second instance, near the end of 759, government leaders ordered construction of a palace complex for a "northern capital" at Hora. They situated it close to where Lake Biwa flows into the Seta river, thereby giving themselves easy access to the forests rimming Ōmi province. Even while that project was consuming substantial timber, the government also repaired the palace at Heijō and ordered the construction of 393 seagoing vessels to transport an army to fight the government of Silla in Korea. In hopes of assuring a successful expedition, leaders also ordered the erection of a major new monastery, the Ishiyamadera, adjacent to the new capital city. In 761 the imperial family, officials, and aristocrats moved to Hora, but less than a year later internal feuds erupted, and the rulers returned to Nara. Within two more years Hora was abandoned. The Ishiyamadera, whose twenty-eight buildings were partially constructed with lumber salvaged from Shigaraki, survived, but the palace complex was disassembled and parts of it were taken south to build the Saidaiji, a monastery near Nara.[13]

The next attempt to develop a new capital occurred in 784, when Emperor Kammu took the government northwestward, crossing the Yodo river to Nagaoka, a site he declared "convenient by water and by land."[14] Convenient for what, the surviving record does not say, but the location did give Kammu direct access to woodlands on the Yamashiro-Tanba border and indirect access via the Ōi river to other forests within Tanba. During "a six-month burst of activity, roughly 300,000 people were thrown into the project," and a new capital was erected.[15] A decade later Kammu moved again, this time to Heian, which brought his builders even closer to the rich stands of Tanba. To assure his timber supply, he seized the forests of Yamaguni, the last major old-growth area on the Kinai periphery. His loggers promptly commenced harvesting Yamaguni's great conifers, especially *sugi* but also *hinoki, sawara,* and others, floating timber down the Ōi to the construction site.[16] When they finished their work a decade or so later, Japan had a capital city that would endure for a millennium.[17]

The quest for good forests was intense because emperors were choosy about their housing. Their residences, like those of aristocrats in general, were both framed and paneled in wood, and emperors wanted *hinoki* used throughout because of its attractive scent and color, fine grain, and resistance to rot. The best *hinoki* lumber came from large, knot-free, straight-grained trees, which acquired those qualities by growing undisturbed in dense stands. The grand *hinoki* palace of Empress Suiko at Asuka, for example, was considered a marvel of construction in its day. Of particular note was its roof, which was made entirely of large shingles (*itabuki*) instead of the traditional reed thatch (*kaya*) or the *hinoki* bark (*hiwada*) that became customary for residential structures from the eighth century on.[18]

Wooden roofing went out of vogue within a few decades because it consumed an immense amount of large timber that was difficult to prepare and ever harder to find. Roofs of *hiwada*, by contrast, were easily made from long, broad strips of bark that otherwise would go to waste. Bark was also comparatively easy to transport. During the eighth century workmen felling *hinoki* cut the bark into strips about three or four feet long, bound these into bundles with three-foot pieces of rope, and transported them to the work site by hand, horse, or cart, or by piling them atop log rafts.[19]

Bark roofing was less wasteful than board, but its use still sustained pressure on high-quality *hinoki* stands because other species produced inferior roofing and good *hiwada* derived only from straight, mature trees growing in dense woods.[20] Moreover, palace construction as a whole consumed immense quantities of high-quality *hinoki* because builders used wood lavishly and selectively. Resulting demand for the best timber, together with difficult transport, prompted leaders to build where adequate supplies were still accessible. As timber became scarce, the restless moving from palace to palace and the maintenance of multiple residences compelled the imperial family to send woodsmen into ever more distant forests. One after another the woodlands of central Yamato, eastern Settsu, Iga, south Ōmi, and Tanba became inadequate for imperial needs.

The imperial family was not alone in its extravagant use of timber. Aristocrats as a whole consumed it freely. A surviving architectural record reveals the lavishness and inefficiency of their wood use. In the 740s Fujiwara Toyonari, one of Emperor Shōmu's closest advisers, built a residence at Shigaraki. His house, an unexceptional mansion of pedestrian design that was supported by pillars set in the ground, required a total of 313.4 *koku* of lumber (equivalent to more than 3,000 one-inch boards 1 foot wide by 10 feet long). This lumber, mostly used for framing timbers and floor, wall, and roof boards, yielded a house about 50 feet long, 25 feet wide, and 15 feet high at the ridgepole, with broad open porches front and rear. The amount of lumber used per unit of walled floor space (some 8.7 *koku* per *tsubo*) was about four times that of a modern Japanese house.[21] And it far exceeded the approximate 2 *koku* per *tsubo* that Tokoro Mitsuo has estimated for the dwelling represented by a clay model (*haniwa*) from the preceding tomb period.[22]

A government decree of 724 suggests how burdensome this style of building was becoming, even early in the Nara period.

The capital, where the emperor resides and every region comes to court, lacks the magnificence by which virtue is expressed. Its wood shingled roofs and thatched dwellings are relics of the building modes of antiquity, are difficult to build, easily destroyed, and exhaust the people's resources. It is requested that an order be issued that those persons of the Fifth Court Rank and above, and those commoners able to do so, should build tiled-roof houses and paint them red and white.[23]

Presumably the advantages of tile were that they replaced wood and thatch roofs, thereby saving *hinoki* and *hiwada* directly, and were nonflammable, which reduced losses from urban conflagrations. Whether the rot-resistance of paint was recognized or appreciated is not clear.

Ecclesiastical Construction

Secular construction was only one element in the ancient predation. Monastery and shrine building may have been even more extensive, and ecclesiastical builders selected only the best wood, using it fully as lavishly as their aristocratic peers. By the time of Empress Suiko's death in 628 some forty-six Buddhist monasteries had already been erected, including the original version of the Hōryūji.[24] Greater projects followed, including the Yakushiji, begun in 701; the Kōfukuji, built in the 720s; and the greatest of all, the Tōdaiji, commenced during the 740s.

The Tōdaiji required eighty-four major pillars, each nearly 4 feet in basal diameter by 100 feet long. Tokoro has calculated that in its entirety the monastery's construction required some 100,000 *koku* of processed lumber (*yōzai*),[25] a volume sufficient to build three thousand ordinary 1950s-style (18-by-24-foot) Japanese dwellings. Further, he estimates that during these centuries monastery building consumed in toto some 10,000,000 *koku* of processed lumber.[26]

In addition, immense amounts of wood went into the numerous Shintō shrines, which also required periodic replacement, originally because their pillars were set directly into the ground and later because of religious custom. The greatest shrines consumed so much lumber because they were large structures built with heavy timber. The main building of Izumo Shrine, first built by Empress Saimei in 659, was a square edifice about 40 feet on a side and 75 feet high. Its secondary shrine (*karidono*) was nearly as large. For the Ise Shrine, which has been replaced at fixed twenty-year intervals since 685, Tokoro has estimated that each reconstruction requires about 16,663 *koku* of processed lumber. Over the course of several centuries, that work consumed the nearby forests originally reserved for the purpose and in later times used timber from elsewhere around the country.[27]

Ecclesiastical construction did not, of course, stop abruptly in 850. Routine maintenance and rebuilding of shrines and monasteries continued. The greatest families, that is, the imperial and the Fujiwara, which controlled large tracts of forest as household estates (*shōen*), continued to build major temples, notably the Hōjōji (circa 1020) of Fujiwara Michinaga and the Hosshōji (1077) and Sonshōji (1102) of the imperial family. As Alexander Soper has written, however, "where the eighth century had produced such monuments with careless fecundity, the power of the Heian age to continue was limited to not more than one a generation."[28]

Consequences of Monumental Construction

Estimating the total acreage of timber consumed by the construction boom of 600–850 is impossible. But, given that a fully stocked, even-aged, monocultural stand of mature *hinoki* growing on good soil in central Japan will yield some 450 cubic meters of lumber per hectare,[29] it is possible to calculate that the Tōdaiji work alone consumed timber equivalent to at least that produced by 900 hectares (2,200 acres) of first-quality forest. Given the selectivity of monumental construction and the irregular stocking of most natural forest stands, the actual acreage was probably many times greater. If we apply that same figure of 450 to Tokoro's estimate for total monastery construction, we are talking of clear-cutting 90,000 hectares of pristine, monocultural *hinoki* forest, or selectively cutting many times that amount of natural woodland, just to satisfy the church's appetite for lumber. And that figure provides not a single board for Shintō priests, aristocrats, or emperors and their governments.

After Heian's construction monumental builders lost a major source of timber—the recycled wood from existing structures that accompanied imperial moves from site to site. We have information on Fujiwara Toyonari's mansion, for example, because twenty years after its construction, and years after Toyonari vacated it, the building was sold, disassembled, and floated downstream to become part of the Ishiyamadera. The mansion's fate, like that of Hora palace itself, illustrates how, in contrast to today's "throwaway" culture, classical builders recycled their lumber. The difficulty of obtaining new timber and the high cost of processing it into finished pieces made such reuse sensible. Doubtless, recycling helped sustain the building boom and made possible a scale of aristocratic luxury that otherwise would have been impossible, given the technological and political limitations of the age and the biological limits of the Kinai basin.

Such recycling notwithstanding, timber consumption at the eighth-century rate could not go on indefinitely. Heian required maintenance, but even that proved difficult. During the late ninth and tenth centuries the quest for satisfactory wood sent logging crews ever deeper into the Ōi river watershed, southward into the poorly accessible forests of Kii, across the Kii channel into the extensive and timber-rich watershed of the Yoshino river in Shikoku, and eastward into Japan's greatest forest area, the Mino-Hida-Shinano watershed of the Kiso river system. From the Kiso, carters hauled timber overland to Lake Biwa and floated it from there to the city. Because of the difficult transport, they chopped much of that timber into five- or six-foot lengths that they then split into six or eight pieces per log before loading onto carts. This processing into split pieces, known generically as *kure* (or *kureki*),[30] reduced the timber's utility, but builders still deemed it worth the trek. They simply had no better choice. Indeed, although the forested periphery of Ōmi continued to produce *kure*, its quality declined enough so that by the eleventh century, *kure* from the Hiroshima area enjoyed a superior repute.[31]

It thus appears that by the time Heian was erected builders had pretty well stripped the Kinai periphery of construction timber. Perhaps for that reason the imperial family made no subsequent moves to new capital cities. Moreover, during later centuries difficulty in obtaining building material may have been a major factor in the gradual deterioration of Heian itself. Timber scarcity may also explain why the better classes gradually modified their style of house construction, substantially reducing unit demand for high-quality wood. Not only were wooden roofs abandoned, but wooden walls gave way to plaster, fine wooden floors were replaced by sedge mats (*tatami*) laid over rough boarding of inferior stock, and buildings became smaller, which reduced the size of framing timbers. Finally, more and more of the large edifices that did get built were erected out in the hills nearer surviving sources of wood.

When monumental construction revived in the twelfth century, much was centered far to the east in Kamakura, among forests unravaged by the ancient predation. It was pursued, moreover, by a new ruling elite that could mobilize more power and move timber longer distances than its predecessors. By then some Kinai forests had had three centuries in which to reestablish stands of construction timber through natural regeneration, yet builders in Heian still

had to hunt far and wide to find the large pillars required by monumental construction.

Other Uses of Forest Growth

Besides erecting towering monuments and great cities, the rulers of
ancient Japan consumed forests in other ways, most notably for
firewood and charcoal, but also for maritime construction and
statuary. Commoners as well made demands on woodland, but
their needs were more diverse and geographically less concentrated.

Boats, Ships, and Statuary

For thousands of years before the ancient predation the people of
Japan fashioned dugout vessels from tree trunks. Mostly, it appears,
they made boats some fifteen feet long, but a few were much
longer.[32] By about A.D. 200, for an arbitrary date, they were sup-
plementing dugouts with vessels constructed from planking. By the
sixth century rulers in the archipelago commanded enough large
oceangoing vessels to wage war in Korea, and during the seventh
century ships bearing embassies to China each carried over one
hundred people.

For dugout construction, wrights preferred large, relatively soft,
rot-resistant trees, especially *sugi* and *kusunoki*, the latter a broadleaf
evergreen that grows to great size. For building plank ships, work-
ability, flexibility, and resistance to rot and waterlogging were the
most valued characteristics, and *sugi* emerged as the maritime wood
of choice. Armadas carried armies to Korea on several occasions
during the seventh century and prepared to do so during the
eighth. But by the ninth century accessible timber for shipbuilding
was so scarce that an imperial order of 882 forbade felling on the
western side of Noto peninsula for any purpose save naval construction. In subsequent centuries, perhaps in part because of the
difficulty of finding satisfactory naval timber, large-scale shipbuilding declined, not reviving until more powerful rulers tapped forest
resources in other areas of Japan.

One other highly visible use of wood was in sculpture, a major
Buddhist art form throughout these centuries.[33] During the decades
at Asuka (circa 550–650) much sculpting was done with *kusunoki*

wood. Easy to mold and strongly scented, it made a fit substitute for sandalwood (*byakudan*), the powerfully fragrant Southeast Asian wood preferred on the continent for Buddhist images. By the eighth century, perhaps because *kusunoki* was less available, sculptors used *hinoki* more commonly.[34] They also utilized a few other woods, with preferences varying by region in accordance with species availability.[35] Some forms of sculpture required lacquer as well, and when lacquer trees (*urushi*) became scarce during the eighth century, seedlings were planted at convenient sites to sustain production.

Sculpturing continued in following centuries. From the eleventh century, especially in the Kinai basin, artisans began employing a new technique in which they fitted separate pieces of wood together to form the great images once carved from solid logs. The adoption of this technique may reveal a dearth of logs adequate for a sculptor's needs. During the Kamakura period (1185–1333), sculpture enjoyed a new burst of popularity, but by then sculptors used *hinoki* less prevalently, and wood for carving became more diverse, perhaps because good sticks were difficult to locate and artists made do with whatever they could find.

Firewood and Charcoal

Of the several human uses of forest growth, fuel for cooking and heating has everywhere been one of the most important. Figures on fuel consumption in ancient Japan are almost nonexistent, but the volume of wood used as fuel must have been immense. In eighteenth-century Germany, for a suggestive comparison, some nine-tenths of all wood production reportedly was for fuel.[36] In Nara-Heian Japan the proportion surely was lower. Japan, being warmer than Germany, required less heating fuel per capita, and the ancient Japanese may have consumed appreciably less in industrial production, even allowing for the use of coal in Germany. In contrast, in their residential and monumental construction the Japanese used lumber far more than the Germans, who had access to workable building stone and used it extensively.

Nevertheless, fuelwood was important. Firewood was so precious to the rulers that government regulations required aristocrats living in the capital to present such wood to the imperial court on New Years. The gifts were fixed according to rank, nobles of the first rank presenting ten *tan* of firewood (twenty pieces cut in seven-foot lengths); those of the third, eight *tan*; and so on down the hierarchy.

Urban aristocrats could also buy firewood at markets. In Nara wood was provided by villagers who produced it and brought it to the city by shoulder pole. In 739 a shoulder-pole load sold for nine *mon*, which suggests that a villager would have to provide at least two pole loads per day to match the income of a woodland laborer.[37] By 760 the price had risen to twelve *mon* per load, perhaps because the fuel came from more distant sources as woodland near Nara was converted to tillage or reduced to fire-prone scrub growth. Subsequent price trends are unclear, but the move to Heian may have eased the problem for a few decades.

Charcoal as well as firewood served as fuel. Its use dated back at least to the introduction of iron smelting, which required higher temperatures than raw wood could generate. There were two types of charcoal. *Watan*, used for home cooking and heating, was generally made from such deciduous broadleafs as *nara* and *kunugi* (species of oak), and *kōtan*, used for smithing, generally came from chestnut (*kuri*).

Doubtless, mountain villagers produced some charcoal, especially *watan*, and shipped it by raft or marketed it in the city along with firewood. But project workmen produced most of the smithing charcoal for monumental construction, operating their kilns in the loggers' camp, at other sources of supply, or sometimes at the project site. In one eighth-century instance a charcoal maker, who was working a small three-bay kiln that held 1.6 *koku* of wood per bay, charred each load of wood for three to four days and produced an average of 1.3 *koku* of charcoal per day, perhaps by processing the yield from one bay daily in three-day rotations.

Monumental builders consumed huge quantities of smithing charcoal in manufacturing tools, metal accessories, and religious images, not to mention metal coinage and the perennial weapons of war. During the 740s over 16,650 *koku* (about 163,200 cubic feet) of charcoal were required to cast the great bronze Buddha image for the Tōdaiji.[38] If we assume that one workman could produce 1.3 *koku* of charcoal per day, it would have required ten men working ten three-bay kilns continuously for three and a half years simply to provide fuel for casting the image. And if 1.6 *koku* of raw chestnut yielded 1.3 *koku* of smithing charcoal, the enterprise consumed over

20,000 *koku* of chestnut. Given the usual character of chestnut stands as poorly stocked, intermediate growth present in mixed forests, this output required the gathering of chestnut wood from hundreds or, more likely, thousands of acres of forestland.

The demand for charcoal was persistent. Even after monumental building went out of style, charcoal was still essential for the manufacture of armor, swords, and other weapons of war. And it remained a valued heating fuel. Indeed, its superiority over firewood (because it is nearly smokeless and sparkless and provides a steady, focused heat) made it so popular that aristocrats used it in gift exchanges. Perhaps to satisfy increased demand, during the ninth century large kilns that could handle great quantities of charring wood were introduced from China. Their presence surely added to the pressure on Kinai forests.

Commoners' Uses of Forests

Commoners, who constituted about 98 percent of the populace, surely consumed more forest products overall than did the ruling elite, even though their demand per capita was immeasurably less. The main items they utilized were simple construction materials, firewood, brush and grass for fodder, woodland foods (such as chestnuts, mushrooms, *warabi* [a bracken], game, and freshwater fish), and water for paddy irrigation and home use.[39] And of course the peasantry consumed forests by opening them to tillage, whether permanently or intermittently.

Whereas the rulers were heavy users of construction timber, commoners had extremely modest per capita requirements, and what they used were small-sized sticks, boards, and bark. Their needs were slowly increasing, however, as traditional post-and-thatch construction began giving way, in some areas at least, to houses with heavy framing and board walls. This new style of architecture roughly doubled the wood requirement of ordinary housing and added to the pressure on timber stands.[40]

Much more significant was use of fuelwood by commoners. Although the masses probably consumed domestically almost none of the charcoal they produced and much less firewood per capita than did their rulers, in the aggregate they burned great quantities of wood in cooking and heating. Demand for fuel was particularly heavy in the Kinai region. Part of this came from villagers themselves, but near the big cities urban fuel requirements probably were greater. In addition, manufacturing, much of it on behalf of the city populace, required substantial fuel. Along the seashore, for example, salt makers burned wood under their evaporator vats. And inland, potters consumed wood in their kilns. During the ninth century, scarcity of fuelwood along the forested provincial border of Kawachi and Izumi even precipitated disputes among potters that required intervention by government officials from Heian.[41]

As those comments suggest, provisioning the metropolitan populace, most of whom were commoners, probably caused the primary drain on woodlands near the great cities. The concentrated and enduring metropolitan demand for fuel sustained so much woodcutting in the Kinai basin that major timber users, such as monasteries, tried to preserve their lumber sources by keeping woodcutters out of their forests. During the eighth century, as we note below, disputes over forest use in the Kinai became a political problem, and they commonly pitted the high-born, who were seeking to preserve timber stands, against the low-born, who were seeking fuelwood, fodder, and other woodland products. Away from the cities, however, and especially outside the Kinai, fuel demand was much less intense; peasant and ruler seem to have found current supplies adequate for their needs throughout the ancient predation.

The Consequences of Predation

Excessive deforestation usually manifests itself in two ways: as wood scarcity and as environmental deterioration. Several developments of the Nara-Heian period seem to demonstrate that both conditions were appearing.

We have cited a number of these developments already.[42] Logging areas were expanded relentlessly as builders consumed stands of *hinoki* and *sugi*, as well as the less valued *sawara*, *momi*, and *tsuga*. To note some chronological benchmarks, by 655 *hinoki* stands near Asuka were so depleted that Empress Saimei had to settle for the less-esteemed *sawara* when she built her palace. By the mid-eighth century institutional loggers were cutting off the mountain fringes of Ōmi and the upper reaches of the Kizu river and its tributaries in Iga. Mount Tanakami, which had provided so much timber for the establishment of Fujiwara and Heijō, contained by the 760s scattered trees capable of providing the Ishiyamadera with only four-inch timbers and short boards.[43] The move to Heian in the 790s led to a new burst of construction that drew heavily on Yamaguni in Tanba. In following centuries workmen laboriously brought more and more timber into the Kinai region from elsewhere to make up for what the basin no longer could produce.

In theory, of course, forests are a renewable resource, and eventually they will restock themselves. A number of factors, however, slowed or even stymied their regrowth in central Japan. Conversion of large tracts to agriculture, even intermittently, removed land from timber production while permitting an increase in the human population that further exploited surviving woodland. In untilled areas the harvesting of fuelwood totally prevented revival of conifer growth. And where needle trees were able to reseed, the natural pattern of forest succession (in which logged terrain evolves through cycles of fast-growing weeds, brush, and intermediate broadleaf growth before reestablishing heavy conifer stands) meant that two or three generations—that is, a century or two—had to pass before a new climax stand was old enough for monumental use. And finally, wildfire could delay the restocking for additional scores of years.

The upshot was that once its old-growth forests were felled, the Kinai region was unable to sustain the wooden-structured civilization it had originally made possible. In consequence, the imperial family stopped migrating, monumental construction petered out, and in due course the buildings of Heian itself decayed.

Besides these large-scale trends a number of more specific developments accompanied deforestation. We noted that in construction work there was a gradual acceptance of inferior species and smaller pieces of wood. To sum up one facet of the trend, wooden roofs gave way to *hiwada*, but by the 760s widespread use of *hinoki* bark led to its scarcity and thus reliance on poorer quality bark, which in turn necessitated thicker roofs to keep out the rain. Thicker roofs required more bark, however, and even though *hiwada* was brought from farther afield, it proved insufficient, so more and more *sugi* and other inferior types of bark had to be utilized. Enough undersized and inferior pieces were showing up in city markets that late in 796 the court complained about woodsmen in adjoining provinces providing unsatisfactory *hiwada* and ordered officials to enforce size and quality standards and prevent the sale of nonconforming bark. Although the immediate problems may have been eased, scarcity persisted, and two centuries later (in 1030) aristocrats of the sixth rank and below were simply forbidden to use *hiwada*.[44]

Other changes in architecture appeared. Monasteries became less pretentious and were built back in the mountains, closer to surviving stands of timber. Sculptors became more eclectic in their choices of wood and eventually shifted from carving single timbers to using multipiece construction in which small sticks sufficed. As logging moved deeper into the mountains, rafting and other transportation techniques grew more elaborate.[45] Scattered data suggest that wood became more expensive, and some figures indicate that the rising cost of transportation, caused by longer and more laborious supply lines, was a key factor in that trend.[46]

Finally, we noted that the government tried to preserve its shipbuilding capacity by reserving the windward forests of Noto peninsula for maritime construction. That measure, Japan's first attempt to preserve naval stores, illustrates a fundamental change taking place in social policy toward forests. That change, caused by the growing scarcity of wood in the Kinai basin, was adoption of measures of forest closure.

Forest Closure: The First Impulse

Before the ancient predation, forests had been open to general use, and reform edicts of the seventh century sought to preserve that customary practice. Whereas arable land was to be measured, allocated to tillers, and taxed, most forestland was to be kept open for general use, unsurveyed, unassigned, and unassessed. The few exceptions to the open policy were sacred groves, a few government timber preserves, some hunting grounds for officialdom, and windbreaks and erosion-control plantings.[47]

In practice, however, as the seventh century advanced, monasteries and aristocrats rapidly gained control of woodlands and tried to regulate their use. The trend threatened government attempts, especially those of Emperor Temmu, to establish solid imperial control of the realm, and early in 675 Temmu ordered princes, other aristocrats, and monasteries to restore to the throne all uncultivated lands previously granted them.[48] Similar orders were issued in later years, and government administrative codes formalized the principle of open forests.[49] The standard phrasing appeared in the Yōrō Code of 718: "The benefits of mountain, river, grove, and marsh are for government and people alike."[50] Such strictures notwithstanding, as the eighth and ninth centuries progressed, monasteries, shrines, and aristocrats acquired more and more landed estates (*shōen*), and these encompassed large tracts of woodland, whose use they tried to regulate.

Indeed, much *shōen* formation may have been pursued primarily as a means of obtaining forestland; at least the court periodically complained that woodland was being seized by aristocrats but not opened to tillage.[51] In an age when loggers were rapidly felling forests, monumental builders could best assure themselves adequate timber supplies by controlling land, government directives notwithstanding, and both ecclesiastical and secular *shōen* holders acquired ever more forestland and tried to close it to unauthorized use. By the mid-Heian period, when good Kinai woodland was a precious commodity, the great aristocratic families reserved extensive tracts of forest for maintenance of their monuments. Most notably, the dominant Fujiwara households (*sekkanke*) secured control of most woodland in western Ōmi, as well as some on the eastern border, and used it as a restricted source of *hiwada* and *sugi* lumber for their establishments.[52]

Not all peasants willingly gave up their customary access to woodland, and *shōen* holders on occasion used force to expel them. Some estate holders evidently instructed forest overseers to seize the cutting tools, such as sickles (*kama*) and axes, of anyone who entered illegally to gather wood, brush, or grass.[53] In response, a court notice of 706 denounced aristocrats who seized wild land, neglected to till it, and yet confiscated the tools of peasants gathering brush there. Five years later the court reiterated its complaint and ordered the behavior stopped.[54] Despite such edicts forest holders continued to close their lands to outsiders. The Tōdaiji, for example, forbade felling on its lands in Harima in 793 and on designated areas in Yamato in 805. When *shōen* holders did permit outsiders to gather fuel, they sometimes charged a fee for the material. In the Kinai basin, moreover, where forest scarcities were most acute, even peasants resident on a *shōen* ordinarily paid for any yield they obtained from the estate holder's woods, often by providing him with labor or a portion of the forest yield.[55]

Woodland scarcity sustained disputes over exploitation rights. In 798 Emperor Kammu repeated the official policy of unrestricted use and warned that because of abuses by estate holders he would confiscate the woodland of any secular or churchly holder who seized sickles or otherwise interfered with people gathering brush. The order went on to state, however, that anyone who reforested up to five *chōbu* (twelve acres) of land inherited from his ancestors could retain that land.[56] Whereas the court complaint of 706 had suggested that land seizure was tolerable if it resulted in more cultivation, Kammu's order indicated that woodland closure would be acceptable, at least on a modest scale, if it led to reforestation. Government priorities seemed to be changing.

Even as the court opposed unauthorized forest closure by others, it restricted access to woodland under its own control.[57] In the early summer of 676 Emperor Temmu forbade fuel and fodder cutting on Minabuchi and Hosokawa mountains near Asuka and reiterated a standing proscription on unauthorized burning of Kinai brushland. In 710, as the court pressed on with the construction of Heijō, it ordered forest wardens (*yamamori be*) to control felling on its mountain lands.[58] Later the government closed more areas in the Kinai basin and, as earlier noted, the maritime forests of western Noto peninsula.

Outside the Kinai region the pressure on forests was much less intense, which doubtless permitted peasant and power holder to share woodlands more amicably. Even in the Kinai basin, after the great surge of monumental construction had passed and former conifer forests had grown up to brush and mixed broadleafs, pressure seems to have eased enough so that substantial areas of wooded upland remained open, at least to local people. In any event, attempts at forest closure eased, the movement went into abeyance for several hundred years, and full closures did not occur until the early modern predation of the seventeenth century.

Environmental Damage and Forest Protection

Forest closure, while normally undertaken for selfish reasons, constituted a forest-protection measure. At times its protective function was made explicit. In the early ninth century, when the government issued several orders against woodcutting, it stated directly that their purpose was to protect rivers or otherwise prevent water supplies from being muddied.[59] In an order of 821 that was intended to protect agricultural land by regulating peasant woodcutting, the court put it this way:

The fundamental principle for securing water is found in the combination of rivers and trees. The vegetation on mountains should always be lush. The reason for this is that, while the origin of great rivers is always near thickly vegetated mountains, the flow of small streams comes from bald hills. We know the amount of run-off depends on mountains. If a mountain produces clouds and rain, rivers will be full for 9 *ri* [about 5 miles]. If the mountain is stripped bald, the streams in the valleys will dry up.[60]

Unquestionably, erosion and flooding were problems, but in much of the Kinai basin destruction may have been quite modest: loss of virgin stands did not necessarily mean a rape of the land. For one thing, much harvesting was selective because the quest was for large, high-quality stock. Usually, loggers left forest cover partially intact, clear-cutting only scattered natural monocultural stands. Moreover, some stands were located in lowlands, which could be safely converted to tillage after logging.

Ironically, the clear-cutting of conifers in a high forest could give rise to replacement vegetation that was more responsive to human demand than the original stand. In the natural sequence of forest succession many logged conifer areas of the Kinai probably grew back to contain much broadleaf growth, such as chestnut (*kuri*), beech (*buna*), and oak (e.g., *kunugi* and *konara*). These trees, which provide high-quality fuel, grow quite rapidly and reproduce vegetatively by sending out new shoots from stumps and roots. Consequently, they can be harvested repeatedly at intervals of only ten to fifteen years. By thus shifting forests from conifer to broadleaf growth, logging increased the volume of fuelwood being produced by that portion of Kinai woodland not converted to tillage, thereby helping it meet the most compelling need of the swelling metropolitan population.

Nor was frequent gathering of fuelwood necessarily destructive. Despite repeated cutting, coppice stumps and roots would remain alive and hold soil in place. Moreover, new growth, being fed by preexisting root systems, would push out rapidly and spread quickly over harvested areas, leaving soil much less exposed to precipitation and erosion than areas clear-cut from mature conifer stands. Finally, coppice stands permitted a more luxuriant undergrowth, and this surface vegetation also helped preserve soil stability. As long as people did not rake up all the litter and dig up roots for fuel, food, or fodder, conversion of high forest to coppice growth need not have posed basic ecological dangers.

Indeed, the opening of forest floor to sunlight and highly varied pioneer growth could have had broader ecological benefits, improving the land's capacity to support a diverse population of birds and other fauna. The conversion of high forest to young mixed growth in the Kinai region may have been a precondition for the wide range of animal pelts and similar items sold in the city of Heian. But carrying the trend too far—through conversion of ever more land to tillage and the eventual decay of surviving woodlands into sparse scrub because of excessive exploitation—may underlie the disappearance of such items from the urban marketplace in later generations.[61]

Despite its ecological merits coppice growth also has liabilities. Most especially, it is highly vulnerable to forest fire. Whereas wildfire is uncommon in climax stands whose crowns tower in the air, it runs easily through scrub brush and low coppice. If it burns too hot at ground level, moreover, it does substantial damage to the soil, making revegetation problematic. That process seems to have occurred in parts of the Kinai basin.

Ever since the ancient predation Ōmi has been plagued by wildfire, and during the Nara-Heian period destructive fires erupted throughout the Kinai area. Some ten major forest conflagrations were recorded between 703 and 803.[62] In the spring of 745 a notorious fire erupted on Mount Maki in Iga, burned across hundreds of hectares, and raced westward out of control into Yamashiro and Ōmi provinces, panicking the court at Shigaraki before rain halted its thirteen-day rampage.[63] Wildfires commonly resulted from slash-and-burn tillage, careless use of fire in opening new areas to permanent cultivation, and probably from other uses of fire in woodlands, such as feeding kilns or felling large trees. Some burns resulted from lightning or, elsewhere in Japan, from geological activity. But whether fires were ignited by natural forces or humans, the conversion of high forest to brushwood and the intensive exploitation of that growth contributed to their scale and frequency in the Kinai basin.

When forest fires did break out, they generally ran free because no organized system existed for fighting them. Prayers for divine intervention were the usual extent of human resistance. In 745, however, a few months after the major burn that started on Mount Maki, a large brushfire erupted near the recently abandoned capital of Shigaraki. It is recorded that, lest everything be lost, "several thousand men and women from the town went out to the mountains to cut [brush], and then the fire died out."[64]

In short, the conversion of Kinai forestland from conifer to broadleaf growth embodied both favorable and unfavorable possibilities. Near the cities the unfavorable possibilities seem to have been realized. Because transportation was a major factor in both lumber and fuel costs, nearby forests were ruthlessly overcut. And they remained overcut. Beginning with the ancient predation uplands in the Kōga-Tanakami area of south Ōmi were repeatedly cut and burned over, and forests there were unable to proceed through a natural process of succession to reestablish climax stands. Instead, woodlands produced generation after generation of pioneer species: grass, brush, scrub pine (*akamatsu*), and miscellaneous broadleafs. And because this growth was persistently overexploited, forestlands steadily eroded, gradually lost fertility, and shifted to ever poorer vegetation, deteriorating a millennium later during the early modern predation into infertile, bald mountains (*hageyama*).

Elsewhere in the central Kinai region soil became drier and poorer. Areas around Kyoto that in the Nara and early Heian periods produced the mushroom *hiratake*, which prefers moist, shaded sites, deteriorated by the thirteenth century to the extent that they habitually produced *matsutake*, a mushroom that grows atop the shallow roots of pine trees in dry, comparatively sunlit soil. And the pines were there because they could grow in soil so nutrient-poor it would not support vegetation capable of suppressing them.[65]

These malign consequences emerged despite modest attempts at forest protection. Closing forests to timber felling and regulating fuel gathering were the first "negative" protective measures. Contemporaneously, there were a few scattered "positive" measures of forest rehabilitation, meaning tree planting.[66] Some planting was undertaken for the yield; most was designed to form protection forests.

There are only one or two records of reforesting to produce new stands of building timber. Most noteworthy is a document of the year 866 that mentions an order to plant 5,700 *kuri* and 40,000 *sugi* seedlings in Hitachi province, far to the east of the Kinai basin. The planting was to occur on shrine land (of the Kashima *jingu*), and it was intended to enhance the scenic beauty of the area as much as to replace trees consumed in the shrine's periodic reconstructions. Whether or how the planting was done is unclear.

The protective value of forests in capturing rainfall and modulating runoff, and hence the value of afforestation in harvested areas, was clearly recognized. Two clauses in the Yōrō Code of 718 expressly prohibited cultivation in mountain areas and advocated tree planting along river banks and dams to prevent erosion and water damage to cropland, and throughout the eighth century the government promoted tree planting. Shade trees, such as *nire* and *yanagi*, were planted along national highways that the court was developing. Fruit trees, such as *biwa* (loquat), *momo* (peach), *ume* (plum), *kaki* (persimmon), and *kuri* (chestnut), were also planted, mostly around homesteads. Trees were planted around graves to benefit the spirits of the deceased and around dwellings and tilled land, usually to protect buildings, water courses, and irrigation ponds, but sometimes for ornamentation. Later the order of 821 pointed out the water-retaining capacity of woodland.

During the centuries of the ancient predation the luxurious architectural demand by rulers, together with the general needs of the metropolitan populace, subjected Kinai vegetation to unprecedented pressure, in the process exhausting the region's high-quality timber supply and changing significantly the character of its forests. The experience elicited only tentative and simple responses, however, in terms of forest enhancement and damage control. It may, therefore, be correct to infer that outside the Kinai basin forests continued to meet human demand without difficulty. And in much of the Kinai itself, forest exploitation may have had only a modestly deleterious ecological impact. Nevertheless, in those parts of Yamashiro,

Yamato, and Ōmi provinces near the cities, where human pressure was greatest, the ancient predation created serious ecological problems, problems that foreshadowed what the nation as a whole would confront a millennium later, following the seventeenth-century predation.

Chapter Two

Forests and Forestry in
Medieval Japan, 1050–1550

During the ancient predation Japan's rulers consumed woodland in central Honshu at an exorbitant rate. Subsequently, forest exploitation stabilized in less intense harvesting that continued until the late sixteenth century, when a second, far more rapacious, phase of overconsumption swept the islands. Construction projects of the social elite provided dramatic highlights in the "medieval" period's forest history. Technical and social changes in rural society, however, which sharply altered the human-forest relationship, bore greater significance for woodland and its users during both medieval and subsequent centuries.

Several developments combined to intensify agricultural pressure on the woodland. After about A.D. 1200 the human population grew more rapidly and economic development brought more people a higher standard of living, which meant they consumed more food, fuel, clothing, housing materials, and other goods that came from the land. Concurrently, expansion of arable and changes in agricultural techniques increased the need for green fertilizer material, most of which came from woodland growth. Meanwhile, changes in social and political organization shifted control of more and more arable and woodland from central authorities to local people. That shift altered the way woodland was used and fostered a new surge of forest closure late in the medieval period.

Agronomic Change and
Woodland Consumption

Japan's estimated population of 6,500,000 souls in A.D. 1000 doubled by 1600.[1] This multiplication of mouths affected woodland directly by fostering land clearance, most especially on alluvial flatland, on geologically older, less fertile terrace deposits, and on lower reaches of bedrock mountains—areas that had supported the most lush woodland vegetation.

More was changing than mere numbers, however. Modifications in agricultural practice also increased village use of forest products.[2] Widespread adoption of plows and other iron implements, double cropping, irrigation, and abandonment of fallowing increased sharply the need for regular and timely fertilizing lest soil become so depleted as to lose agricultural value.[3] The fertilizer consisted primarily of natural grasses, scrub growth, and forest litter (leaves, bark, and twigs), which cultivators accumulated and worked into the soil or more commonly burned and stirred in as ash. It came from forests and wasteland (*gen'ya*).

These tillage practices also increased the use of draft animals, namely, oxen and horses, which provided comparatively rich fertilizer. Large animals are inefficient producers of fertilizer, however, yielding little manure from a great deal of fodder. Because most fodder, like green fertilizer, came from woods and wasteland, the use of draft animals increased village demand on upland natural production. The swelling human food needs of medieval Japan thus required not only many more acres of arable but also a much larger area of untilled land.

Besides fertilizer and fodder, villagers needed fuel, which they used in cooking and in such industries as metallurgy, ceramics production, and salt making, a portion of whose products they consumed locally. They also required building materials for houses, outbuildings, gates, walls, wells, bridges, irrigation equipment, and household and work implements. No dramatic technical changes increased consumption of fuel and building wood, but gross demand rose as the population grew and housing improved.

Slash-and-burn, or swidden, culture was another burden that villagers placed on woodland. Indeed, with its potential for wildfire, erosion, and soil depletion, it may have been their most destructive use of upland. Widely practiced in Japan from prehistoric times, swidden may have intensified during the medieval period as overall population growth exacerbated pressure on the land, forcing more and more marginal tillers to work nearby hills sporadically to sustain their families during difficult years.[4] Moreover, the endemic warfare of these centuries generated a large population of losers and displaced people, some of whom retreated into the woods to escape pursuit and eke out a living.

The ecological ramifications of these medieval agricultural developments are difficult to ascertain because evidence of the environmental condition is scarce. Doubtless, the opening of so much lowland to tillage eradicated some valley-floor biota and drove others into marginal habitats. Within the Kinai basin, soil degradation continued to spread. More and more woodland evolved from moist-soiled, mixed forest through coppice and scrub into poorly stocked pine barrens. By the latter part of the fifteenth century, *hiratake*, the mushroom that prefers a moist, dark environment, was found in the Kinai heartland only in protected monastery woodland.[5]

Outside the Kinai the situation was much less severe. Most hardpressed were the adjoining Tōkai and Inland Sea regions, which were extensively deforested. There substantial areas of mixed high forest shifted to coppice growth. The woodland was sufficiently extensive, however, that up to 1550 these regions appear by and large to have coped with agricultural expansion: forest composition changed, but species diversity and biomass production probably did not decline. They may have even increased where mixed deciduous growth replaced more purely coniferous stands. Elsewhere, in Tōhoku, in the central cordillera of Kai-Shinano-Hida provinces, and along the Kii-Shikoku-Kyushu axis to the south, much fine woodland remained.

Fortunately for the ecosystem, not all aspects of rural land use were harmful. Although doubtless much small-scale erosion occurred as imprudent or hard-pressed tillers opened hill land to cultivation, the practice of forming terraces reduced damage by spreading and slowing the movement of water, thereby cutting dramatically its capacity to erode and carry sediment and debris. In central and western Japan especially, many diluvial areas, foothills of bedrock mountains, and small alluvial fans and upland valleys were successfully opened to cultivation, both as elaborately terraced paddy land and as semiterraced dry fields.

Furthermore, the timber requirements of rural people were relatively benign. They needed few large, high-quality conifers. Trees of sapling or small-pole size met most construction needs, and these generally could be obtained from coppice stands after one or two decades of growth, thus allowing for frequent recutting. Moreover, some rural construction needs could be met by bamboo, which grows densely and rapidly (attaining full height in a single season), and is admirably durable even though it is a tropical grass and not a tree at all. As an additional virtue, bamboo can be cut to the ground, where it retains a thriving root mass that holds soil in place. It will then send up new shoots in another growing season even more readily than beech.

In short, population growth and agronomic change increased the rural pressure on woodland in much of central Japan. However, certain aspects of rural forest use ameliorated the environmental impact of this pressure, enabling forests to sustain themselves even while satisfying the expanded human demand.

Social Change and Forest Control

Socioeconomic developments of the medieval period also influenced forest affairs by shifting control of woodland into local hands. That control was exercised in various ways: powerful local families enjoyed a preeminent role in some places, while villagers, acting more or less communally, regulated upland use in others.

The macro political history of these centuries can fruitfully be viewed as a process of decentralization in which the governing system of early Heian rulers slowly disintegrated, until the last vestiges of *shōen*, imperial tax land, and delegated imperial authority finally disappeared around 1500–1550. As Heian rule dissolved, power devolved into the hands of regional and local leaders, mostly military men, or samurai. They established two consecutive regimes, the Kamakura (1185–1333) and Muromachi (1336–1573) shogunates (*bakufu*). The former was headquartered in the newly erected town of Kamakura and the latter in the Muromachi district of Kyoto, as Heian was called by the fourteenth century.

This broader weakening of central control was reflected in the handling of forests. Rulers in Heian had relaxed their supervision of woodland by the eleventh century, and their shogunal successors paid little attention to it. The shogunates appear occasionally to have designated a timber superintendent (*zaimoku bugyō*), but the appointee's tasks apparently were limited to overseeing lumber marketing or a temporary logging project. What interest medieval rulers did show in forests pertained to taxing them or laying down guidelines for settling disputes over use rights. Thus, the Kamakura regime reiterated classical anticlosure policy: where irrigation water, fuel supplies, or other common-use resources were found, access was to remain unrestricted.[6] Otherwise, it evidently did little beyond issuing occasional restraining orders of uncertain effect to samurai accused of stealing timber from temple forests.[7] And the Muromachi shogunate seems to have given woodland even less attention.[8]

In contrast to central secular authorities, some monasteries and shrines retained active control of their *shōen* forests. More and more they imposed rental fees (variously called *yamate*, *yamayaku*, *yama nengu*, and so on) on users, charging them for the brush, timber, or other goods they took. As tillage intensified, moreover, some *shōen* holders tried to maintain the productivity of their own fields by forbidding outsiders to remove fertilizer material from their woodland.[9]

Increasingly, however, *shōen* holders, whether churchly or aristocratic, lost wooded terrain to influential local figures, who often were military leaders. This was especially true outside the Kinai region in areas where holders had rarely asserted firm control of woodland, probably because they had little incentive to claim distant timber. From the late thirteenth century the most successful of these military men developed into regional barons, or daimyo as they eventually were called, and during the fifteenth and sixteenth centuries rebellious daimyo crippled and finally toppled the Muromachi regime. Most barons paid little heed to silvicultural matters, ordinarily obtaining forest products locally by purchase or levy. Not until the mid-sixteenth century, as the scale of warfare expanded and the medieval period hastened to a close, did some daimyo begin directly controlling forests for strategic military reasons, as noted in the next chapter.[10]

Despite the medieval elite's disregard of forests, intensifying exploitation was creating the need for some sort of woodland governance. In the absence of effective forest policy by emperor, shogun, *shōen* holder, or daimyo, woodland management became a local matter. At the village level extremely convoluted processes of social change were occurring that determined how local people exercised their control of the woods. The salient changes may be summarized as follows.[11]

During the early medieval period most villages were small clusters of human dwellings situated on *shōen* or imperial tax land. The major landholders in a locality were formally responsible for affairs there, in particular for assuring *shōen* holders their legally stipulated rental income. As intensifying warfare and disorder undermined the rent-collecting power of *shōen* holders and the central government, these local landholders established more autonomous roles as community leaders. Some used military power to dominate their localities. Some expanded their influence by promoting land-clearing operations that government and *shōen* holders no longer pursued, in the process acquiring rights to more land. Others, especially in the Kinai, where they faced stronger residual rule by the elite, relied on the support of fellow villagers.

The villages themselves were developing into more densely and compactly settled entities. This may have occurred in response to escalating warfare, or it may have resulted from the adoption of intensive cultivation. The increase in output per acre, by enabling tillers to live on smaller plots of arable and hence closer together, certainly permitted given localities to support larger villages. More positively, the new agronomy also bound cultivators more closely to their land, both the nearby woodland on which they depended so greatly and the arable itself, which required such continuous and careful attention that it acquired value as a capital investment. These developments laid a foundation upon which a sense of village identification and commitment could establish itself.

Whatever its cause, the increase in size and density of villages made them stronger power bases for any local leaders who could dominate them. Especially in the Kinai region, however, villages were able to resist local hegemons and instead control affairs communally. As communal procedures matured, villages became more self-conscious political units in which people thought of themselves as members of such and such a village rather than of such and such a *shōen*. Even where they looked to local notables for guidance, they organized their lives in terms of village rather than *shōen*.

Medieval social change thus created new patterns of local leadership and, in some cases, increased interdependence among village leaders and their neighbors. These patterns manifested themselves in the handling of forests. At one extreme, powerful local families controlled woodland, using their positions to dominate lesser neighbors who depended on them for green fertilizer and other forest produce.[12] At the other extreme, villages worked out communal patterns of shared use. Most villages probably encompassed both patterns, with powerful families exploiting their own woodlands more or less autonomously while villagers as a group controlled communal lands.

Some locally powerful families acquired forests by having wooded areas included in real estate deeds of purchase.[13] They subsequently used these patents to justify denying others use of the areas. Other local magnates were, or claimed to be, descended from professional loggers (*soma*) who had worked on *shōen* during the decades when Nara and Heian were built.[14] Later, as timber became depleted and construction petered out, these *soma* evolved into landholding peasants who gained legal title to their land as freeholders (*myōshu*). Often they retained a special claim to designated forestland through the hereditary woodcutting and provisioning duties (*soma yaku*) that originally required them to pay part of their rent to the *shōen* holder in the form of timber or fuelwood. In later generations, even after *shōen* holders disappeared, such *myōshu* frequently claimed that their family's old *soma yaku* titles gave them exclusive rights to continue exploiting the woodland as of old.

Some of these restricted forest sites eventually came to be known as *tateyama* or *tatebayashi*, literally standing or stocked forests. The terms may have been adopted because the visual appearance of these sites as high forest contrasted so sharply with the communally used coppice and scrub areas that were becoming prevalent in more densely inhabited districts. Coppice and scrub were proliferating because of increasing local demand, particularly for green fertilizer. As centuries passed, villagers opened more and more hillsides to cultivation and laboriously terraced them into workable fields. Exceptionally heavy applications of mulch were needed to restore fertility to such sites because they generally had had poor soil to begin with and had been severely disrupted by the terracing. As more intensive tillage practices spread, moreover, all cultivators required fertilizer and fodder at crucial moments in the cropping cycle. Where woodland was ample there was no problem, but in more densely settled areas the growing need for fertilizer pitted villagers against those landholders who claimed *soma yaku* privileges or other exclusive rights to woodland usufruct. Hence, the visual contrast between the village coppice and the local magnate's *tatebayashi* was symptomatic of the growing pressure on woodland and, as a corollary, of the growing tension between powerful local families and villagers in general.

The competition for usufruct that set large landholders against villagers was partially obscured by dissimilarities in their priorities and hence in their preferences among vegetation. *Soma yaku* holders were particularly interested in controlling well-wooded sites, while villagers generally valued areas of grass, scrub, and coppice growth, which best met their most essential needs. Timbered areas usually grew some brush, however, so the woodlands of *soma yaku* holders had at least modest value for others, as revealed by a dispute that arose in the hills of Yamaguni north of Kyoto. There in 1497 two village officials who were *soma yaku* holders sold their felling rights to some city merchants. The sale threatened to deprive village residents of forest understory and emergency supplies that they considered theirs by customary right. They protested vigorously, contending that the sale constituted abandonment of *soma yaku* responsibility because the office was part of an old *shōen* post that was inseparable from *myōshu* status and duty within the village. After carrying their protest to authorities in Kyoto, they finally succeeded in having the *soma yaku* authority revested in the original local officials.[15]

The capacity of villagers acting conjointly to influence the disposition of woodland, as in the Yamaguni case, points toward the other major pattern of local forest control, that of the village acting as a community. In establishing communal control over woodland, villagers were not perpetuating the ancient principle of open forests. Rather, they were articulating a new principle of exclusive communal usage. Identifying communal lands after the thirteenth century by such words as *iriai* (which they wrote in various ways), villagers defined who within and without the village had what use rights to which areas and under what conditions.[16]

This communal control of woodland developed as the larger polity decayed, emerging with communal arrangements for self-defense and local administration. It was prompted by the adoption of more intensive tillage, which gave villagers a shared need for effective control of scarce fertilizer and fodder material. They evidently found communal management effective for excluding outside competitors, regulating allocation to insiders, and preventing abuses that might precipitate erosion, wildfire, or other damaging outcomes.

Surviving documents from the village of Imabori in Ōmi province provide clues to the operation of communal forest control. Late in the year 1448, when people were about to start gathering fuel for the winter, the villagers met, discussed the problem of damage that wood gatherers had inflicted on forests in the past, and agreed on a policy to prevent it in future. They posted regulations specifying the punishment for anyone who cut trees without proper authorization, whether on village land or their own. There was to be a large fine of five hundred *mon* for anyone convicted of cutting forest trees or seedlings, a fine of one hundred *mon* for cutting mulberry trees or taking litter, and a separate fifty *mon* fee for second offenders. The effectiveness of the policy is unclear, but it may have proven inadequate after the generation that established it died off, because a half century later, in 1502, the villagers posted a new and stiffer schedule of fines not only for actually harvesting illicitly but for even being caught in the forest with harvesting tools. Those regulations stated that on either village or individually held lands, one would be fined eight hundred *mon* if caught breaking off branches by hand, or if one was apprehended with a sickle, a hatchet, or a heavy ax one would be fined two hundred, three hundred, or five hundred *mon*, respectively.[17]

As demand rose, villagers found it more difficult to work out mutually acceptable forest-use practices.[18] To settle disputes, they might appeal to community leaders. Or villages as a whole took their grievances to a higher authority, such as it was, whether monastery, shrine, aristocratic landholder, daimyo, shogun, or representative thereof. No doubt many disputes were settled in favor of the stronger party by simple abuse of position or resort to main force. If secular methods of settlement failed, villages might invoke religious authority, subjecting the disputants to trial by ordeal. In cases of illegal brush cutting or logging, for example, the accused parties might have to handle red-hot sickles or axes, and their burns determined their guilt or innocence. Many a guilty soul surely confessed before being put to the test, inadvertently sparing the hand of a falsely accused neighbor. Such instances notwithstanding, the technique of forest-use regulation most commonly visible in the surviving record is a process of litigation and rule making. It usually was undertaken to resolve disputes over the boundaries of forests and scrubland or to define the conditions of access to *iriai* (communal land) for gathering fuel, fodder, and fertilizer.

Whatever the particulars of specific settlements, cumulatively local forest management served to exclude outsiders, allocate woodland resources internally, and assure that villagers abided by any restrictions the communal leadership established on the cutting of grass, brush, bamboo, and trees; the use of water; and the grazing of animals. Forest closure was reviving. But whereas closure during the ancient predation had been initiated by the elite primarily to prevent unapproved extraction of construction timber, this was closure by commoners to guard a variety of agriculture-related products. The process of closure was giving rise to a human-forest relationship very unlike that of the early Nara period, when an abundance of resources had obviated the need for close management by anyone.

Urban Fuel and Timber Use

Not all village woodcutting was for home consumption. The urban populace also required forest products, and upland villagers spent considerable time getting them out and sending them downstream. Urban demand contributed to the general pressure on woodland and thus to the changing human-forest relationship.

The medieval period witnessed a great increase in demand for hardwood charcoal. Only it could generate the intense heat that forged swords for the flourishing armies of samurai. The manufacture of other weapons—armor, spear points, arrowheads, daggers, and eventually arquebuses and cannons—the iron tools and equipment of commoner life, and the cast bells, lanterns, and other implements of monumental architecture also consumed charcoal. Moreover, changes in urban and upper-class housing, notably the use of paper-covered sliding doors and sedge mats (*tatami*) for flooring, made spark-free, smoke-free fuel highly desirable. Charcoal replaced firewood in urban heating and cooking not only among the aristocratic few but also among samurai and well-to-do urban commoners. In consequence, charcoal production boomed around the major cities and towns, consuming the wood production of countless hillsides and providing by-employment for peasants and business for kiln operators, which often were forest-holding monasteries.[19]

In earlier centuries urban demand for fuel had damaged woodland near Nara and Heian, and during the medieval period it continued to exceed the reproductive capacity of nearby coppice stands, compelling providers to bring fuel from afar and raise fees accordingly. As Kamakura developed into a major city during the thirteenth century, its fuel needs expanded commensurately. Price increases in the city led the shogunate in 1253 to complain of recent excesses and to post guidelines for both charcoal and firewood prices.[20]

Builders continued to use construction timber in great quantities. A substantial amount was even exported to China after Sino-Japanese trade revived during the twelfth century. China's forests had become depleted by then, and a demand for large, high-quality *hinoki*, *sugi*, and *matsu* developed. Lumber exports flourished, most shiploads originating in western Japan and consisting of logs that measured some fifteen feet in length and up to four feet in diameter. Both rulers and monasteries despatched timber-laden ships to China, and by the 1220s the shogunate was sending as many as forty to fifty shiploads of lumber annually in large, oceangoing vessels.[21]

Timber exports were minor, however, compared to medieval domestic consumption. Erecting the new city of Kamakura, with its great monasteries and shrines, required vast quantities of timber. Many private residences also were elegant wooden structures surrounded by wooden walls and equipped with handsome wooden gates. Less pretentious houses utilized simpler timber construction and had shingle or thatch roofs.[22] Forests of the Tōkai and Kantō regions, notably those in Izu and Suruga, and of the lower reaches of the Tenryū river valley, provided much of the city's lumber, but the great forests of the Kiso also contributed, with timber from there, for example, going to Kamakura to build the Enkakuji.[23]

Furthermore, rebuilding the city after periodic fires sustained demand. An entry in the *Azuma kagami* for the year 1219 says, "On the twenty-second the center of Kamakura was destroyed by fire. It erupted north of the harbor residence of Kōno Shirō. Wind was blowing fiercely from the south, and fires spread up as far as the gates of Eifukuji and down to the front of the harbor warehouses."[24] Burning from the harbor in the south to Eifukuji on the northeast edge of town, the fire consumed the heart of the city. Its reconstruction must have required immense amounts of material. How much is not recorded, but when the Enkakuji burned in 1421, its reconstruction required one hundred raft loads (about two thousand logs) of timber.[25]

By the mid-thirteenth century Kamakura leaders found it difficult to obtain satisfactory timber. The notice of 1253 that set charcoal prices also complained about the sale of undersized construction lumber. "As of old," it stated, logs for split timber (*kureki*) must measure eight feet, or a minimum of seven feet, in length. It instructed supervisors to impound any undersized *kureki* and bring it to the attention of the proper authorities.[26]

Kamakura's political importance during the thirteenth century notwithstanding, the Kinai basin remained the center of Japanese civilization throughout the medieval period. As a corollary, it remained the area of the most persistent lumber consumption.[27] Insofar as nearby forests in Tanba, Ōmi, Iga, and the Yoshino mountains produced usable, new timber, it was utilized: not only *sugi* and *hinoki* were consumed but also less valued conifers such as *momi*, *tsuga*, *togasawara*, and *akamatsu*. On the Kinai periphery, moreover, cutters pushed farther back into valleys previously regarded as too difficult to harvest. Nonetheless, for many purposes the volume of timber was insufficient, stick size inadequate, or quality unsatisfactory. So cutting for Kinai consumption spread into southern Kii; over into Ise; westward into Mimasaka, Inaba, and Aki; and across the straits into Shikoku, where loggers pressed farther inland across Awa and Tosa. Most especially, logging to meet Kinai needs penetrated deeper into the Kiso watershed in Hida and Mino provinces.[28]

The quest for great timbers even sent Kinai builders to the far western end of Honshu and into Kyushu. One of the most well-documented projects was rebuilding the Tōdaiji, which had burned during a battle in 1180.[29] Records of that effort suggest the magnitude and difficulty of the provisioning. After considerable searching, project directors located timber of sufficient size for the main pillars along the upper reaches of the Saba river near the western tip of Honshu. The stand was well past its prime, but logging crews commenced felling anyway. Many trees were found to be hollow, knotty, or untrue, and workmen had to fell several hundred to obtain the few score required for pillars. The chosen trunks measured eighty to ninety feet in length and about five feet in butt diameter.[30] Supervisors stamped the monsters "Tōdaiji" and prepared them for removal.

To reach the Saba, work crews leveled a narrow valley floor to form a twenty-mile roadway and laboriously winched the tree trunks along it, probably on skid-mounted rollers. The river proved too shallow to float the trees, so transporters built 118 temporary dams along a seventeen-mile stretch to raise the water level sufficiently. A few miles from the river's mouth they dredged a sea-level channel to float the trunks on the tide. At the coast they aligned them, bound them together with vines to form rafts, and attached four ships to each raft to pull it along the Inland Sea and up the Yodo to the Kizu river. There laborers lashed the trunks directly to shallow-draft boats, which buoyed them enough to float to the landing. Workmen dragged them ashore and hoisted them onto huge carts, which 120-ox teams drew to the construction site at Nara.[31]

All that effort merely produced the main pillars. Except for some smaller pieces extracted from Saba rejects, Tōdaiji builders obtained the rest of their material elsewhere: from Settsu, Iga, Bitchū, and about nine other provinces. Reconstruction was completed during the 1190s, but it still yielded a main hall only half as spacious as the original.

The old grandeur was proving difficult to maintain, but people kept trying. The imperial court still harvested its forests, notably the stands remaining in the upper reaches of Yamaguni in Tanba, using some timber and selling the rest.[32] Similarly, aristocratic families, monasteries, and shrines continued to cut away at their holdings. Two major instances of such consumption involved Zen monasteries that burned and were rebuilt. To restore the Tōfukuji in 1442, packhorse operators transported some six thousand horse loads of Mino lumber overland from the Nagara river to Lake Biwa, from whence they were rafted to the city. Five years later eight-horse teams hauled one thousand cartloads of Mino and Hida timber from the Nagara to Biwa and Kyoto to rebuild the Buddha Hall of the Nanzenji.[33]

As these instances suggest, for the medieval age, as for the ancient, great construction projects are what remain most visible to the historian. They reveal a continuation of earlier trends: the spreading quest for large, high-quality lumber, the development of more elaborate transportation techniques, and the acceptance of smaller pieces and less treasured species. One result of these trends was that new edifices tended to be less grandiose and made with smaller timber. Perhaps as a by-product modesty of scale rather than grandeur became a common measure of aesthetic sophistication.[34]

A Recapitulation

Following the ancient predation, Japan settled into several centuries of slowly growing forest exploitation. Agriculturists became more dependent on woodland yield to sustain tillage, which prompted them to strengthen control of accessible woodland. Their efforts were facilitated by a decline in the control that higher-status groups exercised over rural areas. Not until the sixteenth century, as daimyo warred for supremacy, did the ruling elite gradually assert control over woodland in a manner reminiscent of the Nara period.

During the centuries to 1550 the forest arts themselves, those of both exploitation and rehabilitation, made only modest advances. In general, the equipment and techniques of felling, splitting, measuring, marking, squaring, sawing, hewing, and finishing wood appear to have changed very little. Bigger saws were developed, but they still lacked temper enough for heavy-duty use. The need to move logs longer distances and through more difficult terrain did lead to advances in transportation: workmen devised more sophisticated methods of chuting and winching, refined river damming and channeling techniques, and practiced log rafting more widely. Ocean transport, which originally meant carrying small pieces aboard ship, came to include both towing rafts and escorting logs strapped to the sides of the propelling vessel.

Changes in forest-preservation measures were no greater than those of exploitation. Woodland received only modest protection during the ancient predation and even less during the medieval period, probably because no interested authority had sufficient control to enforce any conservation rules. Not until the latter part of the medieval period did signs appear of villagers acting effectively to protect their forest areas or, later yet, of daimyo taking measures to protect theirs. And, needless to say, these signs, when they did appear, were signs of closure designed to protect human interests, not the interests of forest biota per se.

Afforestation had yet to acquire quantitative significance. Scattered records indicate occasional tree planting, mostly for protection forests to hold riverbanks or shores in place, or for windbreaks around buildings, highways, and villages, or for aesthetic purposes. The government occasionally admonished peasants to establish woodlots and plant useful trees such as chestnut.[35] Afforestation for the purpose of timber production, however, consisted essentially of measures to protect naturally seeded areas from human wear and tear so that seedlings could mature safely.

A very few documents of the Heian and medieval periods mention instances of *sugi* planting, commonly by use of cuttings (slips), which root well under properly humid conditions. Most notable are instances in the Kitayama area north of Kyoto, where *sugi* were started on imperial *shōen* in about 1460 to provide poles for teahouse construction.[36] Still, clear evidence of extensive afforestation, *sugi* or otherwise, dates only from the the sixteenth century, when use of *sugi* cuttings appeared in southern Kyushu and Shikoku and artificial planting of *hinoki*, *sugi*, and other timber stock began to be practiced elsewhere.[37]

The condition of forests changed substantially in some areas, very little in others. In the Kinai region original stands in accessible areas were cut off, to be replaced by natural growth whose fate depended primarily on its proximity to a city and tilled land.[38] Where not opened to tillage, the most exploitable areas became permanent sources of fuel and green fertilizer, surviving as more or less infertile areas of grass, brush, miscellaneous scrub hardwood, and hardy pine. Whereas Ōmi and Yamato, for example, had once been praised for their great stands of *sugi* and *hinoki*, by the medieval period the products of scrub forest—"the firewood of Ōhara" and "the charcoal of Ono"—enjoyed prestige.[39] Often located on diluvial deposits and foothills, these overworked areas became known as *gen'ya*, or wasteland.

Farther from the cities, wooded areas that were readily accessible to villages commonly survived as better managed coppice stands useful for fuel, fertilizer, small-dimension lumber, and foodstuffs, notably chestnuts. And scattered about in some monastery precincts and *myōshu* woodlands were groves of good-quality timber. Deeper in the mountains, cutover areas seem gradually to have grown up to all-age, mixed forests. If allowed enough time, these would again provide large timber of reasonably high quality. And finally, inaccessible and more distant areas in Tōhoku and the deeper valleys of central Honshu and Shikoku remained almost untouched prior to the seventeenth century.

Some Kinai areas deteriorated biologically; elsewhere forest composition changed, but serious biosphere decline appears to have been negligible. That the forests of Japan survived as well as they did the intensive harvesting of the ancient predation and then the escalating demand and persistent neglect of the medieval age seems to be primarily attributable to the following factors. First, because of the types of need and level of demand that commoners placed on the forests during these centuries, their impact was relatively benign. Second, the social elite, who pursued most of the high forest logging, lacked the power to harvest all of the archipelago's woodland, and the logging it did undertake was usually selective and probably left considerable cover on hillsides. Third, the mountains most vulnerable to damage were so difficult to penetrate and harvest that cutting proceeded slowly, which gave them sufficient time to repair the wounds they suffered at the hands of loggers and thus maintain their basic biological vitality. Finally, the islands of Japan were not forced to support a population of domesticated meat- and milch-producing animals, whose grazing could so easily have destroyed the undergrowth and root systems that held mountainsides in place. And so, when the rains fell and the snow melted, the woodland could still perform its great historic role, holding the billions of tons of regolith in place, and permitting the humans down on their valley floors to get on with their eternal business of working, fighting, loving, fearing, birthing, and dying, unaware of the catastrophe that would befall them should the forests ever fail at their task.

Chapter Three

Timber Depletion during
the Early Modern Predation,
1570–1670

The early modern predation was essentially the ancient predation writ large. Once again a ruling elite launched a vast construction boom that produced great monuments and cities. This time, however, the elite spanned the realm and in pursuit of its objectives had power enough to exploit human and natural resources throughout Japan. Within a century its enthusiasm for building had stripped the archipelago of nearly all its high forest.

The documentation on this surge of forest exploitation, while superior to that of earlier centuries, is still spotty and yields no satisfying series of general statistics. Cumulatively, however, the scattered records of elite timber consumption are considerable. They reveal how the archipelago lost its high forest during the seventeenth century and suggest how that process led to the creation of a "negative regimen," or pervasive attempts to regulate timber and forest use as a way to preserve and rejuvenate wood supplies. They also show that these processes of nationwide deforestation and consequent resource control were foreshadowed by actions of daimyo warring for survival and supremacy during the latter half of the sixteenth century.

The surge in elite timber consumption was accompanied by a tremendous expansion in villagers' use of woodland, primarily because of rapid population growth. Much forest was converted to tillage, and much that remained uncultivated was exploited intensively for fertilizer, fuel, fodder, and domestic construction needs. By the late seventeenth century the combined demand of ruler and ruled had consumed most of the accessible biomass reserves and exceeded current woodland production. That situation precipitated more conflicts over use rights and fostered attempts to resolve problems of overexploitation and scarcity. Many villages attacked the problems by expanding their control over woodland use, essentially extending the forest closure practices that first emerged during the fifteenth century.

Forest closure by villages collided with closure by higher authority when the latter revived during the late sixteenth century. In a sense this collision of rulers and ruled over woodland use threw Japan into a long, drawn-out social struggle for control of uplands, a struggle that in various forms continued to the mid-twentieth century. We must qualify this bipolar ruler-versus-ruled perspective, however, because intra- and intervillage conflicts over woodland use were probably much more common and central to the problem of resource scarcity and its social ramifications. Nor will it do to assert that quarrels arose among villagers because rulers deprived them of access to woodland. The rulers did so, certainly, but even if villagers had enjoyed unrestricted use of everything available, they would in due course have consumed it all, at which point they would have faced the problem of scarcity anyway.

Reconstruction of the broader story of environmental despoliation is difficult because records of commoner forest use in general, and of fuel use in particular, are few. Such records of fuel use as do exist mostly relate to the rulers, although total commoner consumption surely was greater. Figures on fodder and fertilizer use are almost nil even though the considerable record of village disputes over land-use rights suggests that these needs were one of the most common causes of village conflict. Moreover, while much woodland was converted to arable, a clear picture of what land was converted and how that process affected remaining forest has yet to emerge. Finally, the story of ecological deterioration—erosion, flooding, and denuding of hillsides—that stemmed from these several forms of exploitation is recorded only sporadically in legislation and in writings of contemporary observers. Consequently, the scale, dynamics, and social ramifications of environmental decay are poorly articulated and await further study.

Forest Use by the Rulers

The disaster that befell Japan's forests in the century after 1570 began almost surreptitiously in the scattered activities of warring daimyo. Deforestation accelerated sharply after 1590 when an almighty Toyotomi Hideyoshi, having pacified the turbulent realm, commenced monumental construction projects that required high-grade lumber from throughout Japan. After Hideyoshi's death in 1598, Tokugawa Ieyasu defeated rivals, established a shogunate (*bakufu*) in Edo, and launched an even greater series of projects. His ventures ultimately consumed more lumber than Hideyoshi's, even if many were less demanding of fine wood or giant timbers. After Ieyasu's death in 1616, the rate of monumental construction slackened but continued, and urban growth and maintenance sustained the pressure on woodland. In the rest of Japan, meanwhile, leaders of daimyo domains (*han*) pursued their own construction projects: castles, mansions, temples, shrines, and towns.[1] By 1670 the cumulative effect of this nationwide surge in building was massive deforestation from Kyushu to northern Honshu.

A Foreshadowing

The rulers who consumed Japan's high forest during the seventeenth century had to gain power before they could exercise it. They did so during the latter half of the sixteenth century, with the most successful daimyo bargaining and bludgeoning neighbors and subordinates into alliance and submission until a stable political hierarchy emerged under Hideyoshi and his Tokugawa successors.

Whether warring daimyo more often built to destroy or destroyed to build is an open question, but both their constructive and destructive undertakings were burdensome to woodland. Before the 1570s, daimyo fortresses, whether headquarters or perimeter forts, were modest affairs, often little more than stockades built of sapling- and pole-sized trees, bamboo, or crudely split logs of larger size, depending on what was available. Defense works were many, however, because brawling lords ceaselessly erected, tore down, and torched forts and barricades as battle lines advanced and retreated.

During the last decades of the century, castles became more elaborate. Lords added immense moats and stone walled foundations, but wood remained the basic building material. More elaborate gates, towers, parapets, barracks, residences, and storage facilities required both larger-sized timbers and greater quantities of wood for framing and paneling. A dramatic instance occurred in 1576 when Oda Nobunaga, the master of central Japan, erected a towering 138-foot tall, seven-story wooden keep (*tenshukaku*) within his great castle at Azuchi on the shore of Lake Biwa.[2]

To protect bastions against incendiary attack, builders concealed much woodwork under layers of plaster and tile roofs. That practice enabled them to continue using wood indiscriminately; they put better pieces where they were visible, inferior pieces elsewhere.[3] Cracked and twisted sticks; scraps and remnants; *matsu, sawara,* and *hinoki*; and even hardwoods could be used: indeed, *keyaki* was prized for load-bearing beams and pillars. This architectural style increased the efficiency of timber use, but it also meant that fellers need not be choosy and thereby encouraged clear-cutting, which could more easily lead to erosion and environmental damage than the more selective logging of earlier centuries.

During the 1570s and 1580s lords built a number of large castles, most notably Kitanoshō, Kameyama, Himeji, Okayama, and Hiroshima. Around these and lesser bastions were fostered the growth of towns, which served as centers of domains in which the rulers encouraged road and bridge building and economic development. Those activities consumed vast quantities of lumber; their scale can be inferred from the figures below, which reveal the surge in late sixteenth-century urban development.[4]

Period	No. of Towns Established	Rate per Decade
To A.D. 1192	7	0.1
1192–1333 (141 years)	2	0.1
1334–1466 (132 years)	19	1.4
1467–1571 (104 years)	111	10.6
1572–1590 (18 years)	90	50.0

Another way that daimyo consumed lumber was by building and restoring temples. Ieyasu, for example, as an ambitious young lord in the Mikawa-Tōtōmi area, repeatedly cultivated the goodwill of local Buddhist leaders by assuring them control of their temple lands and encouraging them to restore their buildings and attend to peaceable religious affairs.[5] In the 1580s the lord of Sendai built a large temple (the Zuiganji) at Matsushima. To do so in properly elegant fashion, he obtained his lumber from the Kumano watershed in Kii.[6]

In other ways as well daimyo consumed the forest. Most notably, their armies required fodder for cavalry mounts, fuelwood for cooking and heating, charcoal for iron mongering, construction timber for fortifications, and bamboo for arrows, spears, temporary defense palisades, and other field engineering projects. Warring lords also consumed the forest by fire, both accidental and incendiary. Ōmi province, whose woodland was particularly vulnerable due to centuries of overuse, was the scene of much fighting. Conflagrations touched off by armies in the field repeatedly ravaged it, exacerbating erosion and desolation and making later repair of Ōmi all the more imperative and difficult.[7]

The timber needs of daimyo kept growing, and deforestation of accessible areas forced them to seize more woodland and strengthen control of the timber and bamboo stands they already held. They valued bamboo not only for its products but also for its cover. The density and toughness of bamboo groves made them excellent defensive barriers against attacking armies. They could stymie cavalry and slow foot soldiers to a tortuous walk, during which they were vulnerable to archers and musketeers and hindered in their response. Standing timber was less valuable for defense but more generally useful for construction. And wood was indispensable for fuel.

During the last decades of the sixteenth century many daimyo strengthened their control of woodland. Some measures were designed merely to extract income, but others sought to protect scarce resources or cope with environmental damage. Some lords assigned officials the title of forest warden (*sanrin bugyō, yama bugyō*, or *yamamori*) and ordered them to assure that timber and bamboo groves were properly maintained. Some enacted regulations to control forest use. Date Masamune of Sendai, whose domain was not richly forested, required vassals to obtain official permission before cutting bamboo, even on land assigned to them. Sendai farmers were forbidden to cut trees, even around their homesteads, save with official permission. Masamune's predecessor had tried to preserve forests by delineating boundaries and forbidding the opening of more woodland to tillage; his success is unclear.[8]

The Hōjō at Odawara were particularly active in managing their forest land. Lumbering had been pursued on Izu peninsula from 1208 to build the shogunal headquarters at Kamakura, across Sagami bay, and within decades the easily extracted timber was gone. Nevertheless, exploitation continued during succeeding centuries, and when the Hōjō gained control of Izu, they inherited well-used woodland. During the 1550s Hōjō forbade unauthorized cutting of designated bamboo groves. He also appointed a timber magistrate (*hinoki bugyō*), whose task was to assure that fellers paid all required taxes and did not abuse the forest. In addition, the magistrate had to report the number of trees felled annually. In 1564 Hōjō placed Mount Amagi, the heart of Izu's forests, under direct administrative control, forbidding all but authorized cutting of *sugi* and *hinoki*. To prevent abuse by authorized loggers, moreover, he required all lumber felled on government order to be properly marked by a supervising official.[9]

Other lords also attempted to control forest use. During the 1560s and 1570s Takeda Shingen and his successor, the dominant lords in mountainous Kai province in central Honshu, forbade tree cutting on temple and shrine lands and in areas of tall timber that he designated "lord's forest" (*ohayashi*).[10] Not far away, in Shinano, the daimyo of Takatō *han* surveyed his domain in 1590, designated six areas of high-quality timber as reserved stands (*otateyama*), and closed them to entry. In following decades the number of Takatō's forest reserves expanded.[11] Elsewhere, the Imagawa of Suruga and Tōtōmi, the Rokkaku in Ōmi, the Mōri in Bingo and Bitchū farther west, and the Chosokabe of Tosa on Shikoku all took measures to preserve bamboo and timber supplies.[12]

Daimyo fostered protection forests as well as timber stands, seeking thereby to prevent erosion and riverine damage. They discouraged slash-and-burn cultivation, ordered trees planted, constructed dikes, and forbade cutting on levees and riverbanks. At least one enterprising lord ordered shrines built atop important dikes to encourage people to frequent the areas, thereby keeping the soil packed down, while assuring that newly planted trees would not be neglected or treated irreverently.[13] The lord of Sendai *han*, seeking to stabilize shorelines and safeguard productive land, ordered black pine (*kuromatsu*) and other trees planted along coasts endangered by tidal erosion.[14]

In sum, by 1590 many daimyo were already adopting policies of woodland management that presaged the negative regimen. Whatever their purposes, and they normally were pragmatic and immediate, they were setting precedents that would later gain nationwide application as first steps in a long-term effort to rebuild a squandered forest inheritance.

Hideyoshi and the Onset of National Forest Exploitation

Toyotomi Hideyoshi was the first person in Japanese history able to demand and receive massive contributions of timber from all parts of the country. Following the murder of his lord, Oda Nobunaga, in 1582, Hideyoshi seized the Oda domain in central Japan and shortly turned to subjugating rival forces. By decade's end he held suzerain power west of the Hakone mountain barrier, and by 1592 he dominated the entire realm.

Hideyoshi's interest in monumental construction grew with his spreading dominion. His first great project was Osaka castle, which he erected during 1582–83. From the late eighties until his death in 1598 he promoted a vast array of other works. To cite some famous instances, he built two armadas of troop transports for the conquest of Korea and China and a castle in western Kyushu to serve as headquarters for the venture. He erected an immense bastion at Fushimi just south of Kyoto. He promoted reconstruction of Kyoto itself, building there the Jurakutei, a mansion of unparalleled opulence, and a huge temple, the Hōkōji, whose Buddha hall (*daibutsuden*) was to house a giant 160-foot Buddha image. The hall measured some 270 by 168 feet in area and 200 feet in height, exceeding the Tōdaiji in Nara. He supported reconstruction of the Tendai

temple community on Mount Hiei and the Shingon temple complex at Mount Kōya south of Nara. And he lavished wealth on
numerous other temples and shrines to help them rebuild.[15]

These projects required immense quantities of wood. Moreover,
much was luxury construction, for which Hideyoshi demanded the
highest grades of timber. As a practical matter, that meant loggers
must cut new stands in previously untouched forests. They could
clear-cut, however, because there was plenty of demand for any
leftover lumber.

Hideyoshi obtained the material he wanted by requisitioning it
from all parts of the realm. He commandeered what he could from
surviving nearby forests, most notably those of Yoshino, but they
offered nothing compared to what he needed, so he despatched
officials elsewhere to find more.[16] Timber poured into the Kinai region from throughout Japan, most notably from Kumano in Kii;
from Hida, Mino, and Suruga to the east; from the provinces west
of Kyoto; from deep in the mountains of Tosa; from Hyūga in
Kyushu; and from Akita in the far north.[17]

The daimyo who furnished timber in response to Hideyoshi's
direct demands also contributed special pieces as gifts, sometimes at
tremendous expense. For example, in 1586, when Hideyoshi commenced work on the Hōkōji, Tokugawa Ieyasu, then daimyo of the
Tōkai area, undertook to provide the ridgepole, one of the largest
and most esteemed timbers in a temple. His loggers finally found a
tree of sufficient size and quality growing at the foot of Mount Fuji.
They felled it, cut it to form a timber exceeding eighty feet in
length, and carefully worked it downriver to Suruga bay, from
where crewmen hauled it by ship around to Osaka and up the Yodo
river to Kyoto. The project required three months of effort, fifty
thousand man-days of corvée labor, and 1,000 *ryō* in gold. An earthquake destroyed the temple before completion, and when Hideyoshi's heir started rebuilding it in 1608, he hunted three years
before finding an acceptable ridgepole in south Kyushu, for which
he paid 90 *kan* of silver, or about 1,440 *ryō*.[18]

Because Hideyoshi was highly selective, his levies on daimyo
varied with the resources and accessibility of an area. Thus, the fine
stands of Mount Shiraga in Tosa yielded masts for his China fleet
and *hinoki* pillars and *hiwada* roofing for the Hōkōji. Noneyama

near the southeast tip of Tosa provided material for thin ceiling sheets (*usuita*).[19]

He accepted smaller pieces from the Tenryū river valley. For years the valley had yielded wood for local temple and shrine construction,[20] but it still held exceptionally fine stands of untouched timber, particularly *sawara*, a species considered excellent for roofing because of its resistance to rot. The river itself was so badly cluttered with boulders, lodged tree trunks, and sandbars, however, that it could float only small pieces of wood. Consequently, despite the size and quality of Tenryū timber, when Hideyoshi ordered his daimyo there to bring lumber to Fushimi during the 1590s, he instructed them to reduce it to small pieces for use as shingles (*kawaragi*), planking (*itago*), and roofing or cooperage material (*kureki*). These were floated down to Kakezuka, loaded on ships, and sent round to Osaka and upriver to Fushimi.[21]

From Akita Sanesue, his vassal at Kubota castle in northeast Japan, Hideyoshi requisitioned *sugi*, the region's best timber, for use in Fushimi castle and in the boats handling shipping on the Yodo river. Good stands of *sugi* still lined branches of the Yoneshiro river, which was more passable than the Tenryū, so Hideyoshi required substantially larger pieces. He could not afford to ship much waste, however, because the lumber had to be brought to Kyoto via the Sea of Japan, overland from Tsuruga to Lake Biwa, by boat the length of the lake, and then as rafts down the Seta-Uji river to the city—a trip that was long and required much labor. Accordingly, he instructed Akita to provide high-grade *sugi* cut to specified dimensions. After the pieces reached Kyoto, his carpenters could cut them with a minimum of waste to make ships' planking of standard measure and castle floor, wall, and roof planking that was both durable and attractive.[22]

Nationwide forest exploitation could not be achieved by whim alone, and Hideyoshi brought to the task the attentiveness that characterized his rule as a whole. His levies on Akita Sanesue, given below, reveal the gradual systematization of his timber-gathering policy.[23] At first he called for arbitrary and imprecise amounts of wood. After four years, however, he began requiring Akita to furnish fixed quantities of timber proportional to the assessed valuation (*kokudaka*) of his domain, the wood being regarded as one form of a vassal's regular military obligation (*gun'yaku*).

Year	Quantity (sugi)	Purpose	Dimensions
1593	One boatload	China fleet	Unclear
1594	Thirty boatloads	Yodo river boats	Unclear
1595	820 *ken* (linear)	Fushimi castle	Pieces $6\frac{1}{2}'$ to $17'$ long
1596	225 *ken* (cubic)	Fushimi castle	Pieces $23' \times 4''$, full width
1597	350 *ken* (cubic)	Fushimi castle	Pieces $14' \times 5''$, full width
1598	350 *ken* (cubic)	Fushimi castle	Pieces $14' \times 5''$, full width
1599	350 *ken* (cubic)	Fushimi castle	Pieces $14' \times 5''$, full width

The crude requirements of the first two years gave way in 1595 to an imprecise linear measure, in which one *ken* was to mean one piece of lumber at least six and a half feet (six *shaku* six *sun*) long. In filling that order, Akita provided 750 pieces of timber, of which some 70 were over sixteen feet long, so that he double-counted them, thus reaching his 820 *ken* total. Most pieces were about seven to nine feet long, eighteen to twenty-one inches wide, and five inches thick. Certainly he had not tried to shortchange his lord and customer.

A year later Hideyoshi refined his measure, employing a primitive form of cubic *ken* that revealed his appreciation of the difficulties inherent in the logger's art. Woodsmen were to cut pieces to a designated length and thickness (twenty-three feet by four inches) and a "full width," which probably meant whatever the tree would yield. "Full width" pieces were to average eighteen inches (one *shaku* six *sun*) wide, so that four of them laid side by side would yield a total width of over six feet.[24] This six-foot width by the specified length and thickness constituted one *ken*. In his first use of that new measure, Hideyoshi called for very long pieces, but in his last three annual orders he specified a greater number of shorter, thicker pieces.

As his systematizing suggests, Hideyoshi, like other lords, recognized the importance of timber for his plans. Although he com-

mandeered most of his wood from daimyo, he also brought major
forests under direct control. In 1586, when commencing work on
the Hōkōji, he took charge of the Yoshino region south of Nara, ordering mountain villages there to make regular tax payments (*unjō*)
in lumber. Nine years later, when erecting Fushimi castle, he despatched an intendant (*daikan*) to survey Yoshino, supervise logging,
and assure that his timber levies were fulfilled. It appears that he
tightened control that year because the construction boom had induced merchant lumbermen to buy and ship to the public market
in Osaka *sugi* and *hinoki* timber that he wanted for his own projects.[25]

A richer prize than Yoshino was the upper reaches of the Kiso
river in Shinano and the mountain rim of eastern Mino. In its de-
scent through Shinano the Kiso follows a narrow valley containing
almost no sedimentary plains or agricultural land. In 1590 the
valley contained twenty-eight small villages that survived through
upland dry field and forest production. That year Hideyoshi
claimed the area, despatched a trusted vassal to supervise it, and
abolished river toll stations at which previous lords had taxed
village timber production. In their place he instructed the villages
to produce for his use 4,350 horse loads of *doi* (short pieces of wood
for shingles) and 268,000 pieces of *kureki* (larger split pieces).[26] On
the nearby Nagara river he retained existing toll stations but cut
the tax from as much as one piece in three to a flat rate of one in
sixteen. He offset the reduction by ordering an increase in total
output.[27]

To recapitulate, during his brief span as national hegemon,
Hideyoshi launched a series of construction projects that consumed
immense amounts of wood. He established precedents for collecting
timber from all over Japan and improved the administration of
such provisioning. He brought under direct control some of the
most valuable and famous forests in Japan, including those of
Yoshino and Kiso, and he placed minor lords loyal to himself in
other valuable forest areas, notably the Tenryū river valley and
Akita. His successors would not disregard these precedents.

Ieyasu's National Forest Exploitation

Tokugawa Ieyasu was less an innovator than an implementer. His
approach to forest control and exploitation was similar to Hide-

yoshi's. Like his predecessor, he built energetically, called on daimyo to furnish large quantities of wood and other resources, and brought valuable forests under direct control to assure himself enduring sources of high-quality construction timber.

In one important way, however, Ieyasu went beyond Hideyoshi. He strove to improve transportation, the single most costly element in lumbering. Loggers found sufficient accessible timber to meet Hideyoshi's demands, but by Ieyasu's day they evidently were cutting far enough into the mountains so that improving transportation seemed worth the effort.

Some timber went out on horseback. The sticks were small, however, mostly board stock (*itago*) or split pieces for use as roofing and cooperage (*kawaragi, doi, kureki*). For projects in Edo, Ieyasu had daimyo in northern Shinano bring pieces overland via the Nakasendō to Takasaki, from where they were rafted down the Tone river to the city. The overland route from Kiso to Lake Biwa was more important historically. First used during the ancient predation and extensively thereafter, it was still employed in Hideyoshi's day because many considered the sea route around Kii peninsula too treacherous.[28]

Such land transport required vast amounts of corvée labor and horsepower, and in any case, it could not accommodate large timbers because intercity wheeled vehicles were prohibited. Heavy pieces had to go by river or sea, and during Ieyasu's years major improvements in water transport facilitated timber shipping. The official merchant (*goyō shōnin*) Suminokura Ryōi and his son Yoichi were key agents in Ieyasu's river-improvement efforts. They cleared the Ōi in Tanba and the Fuji and Tenryū rivers in the Tōkai region, making them passable for log rafts and other craft. Yoichi played a prominent role in Ieyasu's logging on the Kiso and there too may have pursued riparian repair.[29] Villagers, when they benefited enough from lumber marketing to undertake the work, also carried out local river-improvement projects.[30]

Ieyasu also gave attention to other segments of the transport system. With his encouragement Suminokura and other lumbermen built ships that coasted the length of Japan, safely navigating such dangerous headlands as those of the Kii and Bōsō peninsulas. In consequence, whereas Hideyoshi brought lumber from Akita to Tsuruga and then overland to Biwa and the Kinai, from Ieyasu's time the route looped westward by sea, reaching the Kinai via Shimonoseki strait. And while Kiso lumber had been hauled overland by Hideyoshi, in Ieyasu's day it began circling the Kii peninsula.[31] At the point of destination, also, Ieyasu made significant improvements. Most notably, in 1611 he had Suminokura dig a new river, the twelve-kilometer Takase, on the east side of Kyoto to facilitate construction of a new imperial palace.[32]

Ieyasu made lavish use of the wood he received. His three greatest monuments were the castles at Edo, Sunpu, and Nagoya, but he has also been credited with castles at Hikone and Zeze in Ōmi, Sasayama and Kameyama in Tanba, Nijō in Kyoto, and Takada in Echigo.[33] Of his many nonmilitary monuments, the most noteworthy perhaps were situated in Kyoto, where he restored some of the imperial court's ancient splendor by erecting a new palace and mansions for the nobility, including the architecturally distinguished Katsura Detached Palace (Katsura *rikyū*). He also fostered the construction of many temples, shrines, and other buildings. In Edo he built a family temple, the great Zōjōji, which survived until 1944. Near his castle at Sunpu, he built two notable but short-lived residences.[34]

Ieyasu's monumental construction, like Hideyoshi's, consumed vast quantities of high-quality lumber. Tokoro Mitsuo has calculated that Nagoya castle contained about two hundred thousand *koku* of lumber (*yōzai*) and Chiyoda castle in Edo over five hundred thousand *koku*.[35] Sunpu castle probably required at least as much as Nagoya because a few months after it was built, it burned and was promptly reconstructed. Assuming that the three consumed about one million *koku*, or 280,000 cubic meters, of lumber, which would require about 1,100,000 cubic meters of stumpage (*tachiki*), and assuming that well-stocked conifer stands averaged 400 cubic meters of stumpage per hectare of forest, these three castles alone would have consumed about 2,750 hectares (6,800 acres) of prime forest or many times that area of natural woodland.

Much of this lumber came from *han* forests. In 1606, for example, Ieyasu requisitioned shingling wood (*kawaragi*) from lords in Shinano. Between spring and year's end seven daimyo produced 43,000 pieces and sent them overland by horse. The task required 490 people working a total of 144,550 days for pay totaling 722,750 *fuchimai* (130,095 liters of rice).[36] The following year the lord of

Tosa sent ten thousand logs to Sunpu, and in 1608, when the fire-wasted castle was rebuilt, he provided another twelve hundred.[37]

Like Hideyoshi, moreover, Ieyasu brought valuable forestland under direct control. Within weeks of his military victory in 1600, he took over Hideyoshi's lands in Yoshino and the Kiso valley. Shortly thereafter he added most of the Tenryū watershed, which was nearer Edo and still largely uncut. He secured that area by evicting all but two of the daimyo whom Hideyoshi had installed there a decade earlier. One survivor remained at Iida, where his *han* consisted almost entirely of valley bottom. The other, at Takatō, was situated on a branch of the upper Tenryū in one of the least accessible parts of the watershed.[38] The most desirable portions of Tenryū woodland thus came into Ieyasu's hands. Between 1604 and 1613, intendants supervising the area removed some 3,060,000 split pieces (*kureki*), 48,600 pieces of board stock (*itago*), and 270 heavier timbers one *ken* (seven feet) long, mostly for use in Edo and Sunpu. During Ieyasu's final years he was obtaining the equivalent of about one million split pieces of *sawara* from the Tenryū valley annually, a scale of provisioning made possible by Suminokura's riparian work.[39]

During those years, the Kiso valley was generating even more government timber (*goyōki*). Tokoro has estimated that its production fluctuated between one million and two million *koku* annually.[40] Assuming that this figure is for *genboku*, or timber prepared for rafting, it indicates logging at a rate equivalent to clear-cutting 1,500 to 3,000 hectares of well-stocked conifer forest each year, or harvesting less intensively a much larger area of natural woodland.[41]

In sum, following the precedents of Hideyoshi's day, Ieyasu accelerated the consumption of Japan's forests. Daimyo continued to be key providers of lumber, but Ieyasu also took over large areas of high-quality timber and improved access thereto, evidently to assure his regime sources of wood sufficient to maintain the monuments he was building.

Forest Use by Other Rulers After 1590

During the decades when Hideyoshi and Ieyasu were making inroads on woodland, daimyo were doing their share to consume nature's largesse. Deforestation of their domains sprang in part from the daimyo's entanglement in the schemes of central power holders. That entanglement became routinized in the *sankin kōtai* ("alternate attendance") system of hostages, which required each daimyo to maintain his wife and heir in a properly elegant mansion adjacent to Chiyoda castle. Lords tended to fulfill the requirement lavishly in arrant displays of glory, and by the late 1630s they all had homes of appropriate splendor in Edo, commonly maintaining two or three residences there, as well as warehouses.[42]

In addition, all *han* consumed immense amounts of wood domestically. In the early 1590s, for example, lords built large bastions at Kanazawa on the Sea of Japan and Aizu-Wakamatsu in the mountains north of Edo. In the late 1590s and 1600s, lords in Sendai, Kumamoto, and Hagi all erected great castles.[43] Scores of others built smaller bastions or enlarged major ones already standing at such locations as Kōchi, Hiroshima, and Kagoshima. Daimyo also celebrated their glory in other ways, building castle towns and constructing temples, shrines, mansions, and other monumental works. The lord of Tsugaru built Hirosaki castle in 1610, and that enterprise, together with construction of the adjoining town, stripped the nearby mountains Ishikawa and Kuratate.[44]

Records of Matsumoto *han* illustrate local timber consumption more fully.[45] Little of the *han*'s timber flowed into national markets despite its location midway between Kyoto and Edo. As the crow flies, the castle was only 245 kilometers from Kyoto and 170 from Edo, but crows rarely carry timber. Matsumoto is encircled by mountains and situated on the Shinano river, which flows northward, almost directly away from Kyoto, traveling some 285 kilometers before emptying into the Sea of Japan at Niigata. Furthermore, in crossing a geological fault on the Shinano-Echigo border, the river thunders down falls and rapids of such harshness that pieces of wood survive the passage very poorly. In consequence, the Shinano watershed was effectively closed to the national timber market, and save for small goods carried overland, not much Matsumoto lumber entered it. Because of that geographical constraint, deforestation in Matsumoto can be attributed primarily to local consumption.

The Shinano river valley had been settled for hundreds of years before the late sixteenth century, and much lowland was already in tillage. Major temples such as Zenkōji at Nagano long antedated the Edo period, and their construction may well have consumed the best stands of building timber. Sustained pressure on high forest, however, dates from castle-building efforts that began in the 1570s and dotted the valley with small bastions by 1600. By then the hills nearest Matsumoto, those immediately to the east, already lacked timber suitable for castle construction, so the daimyo obtained most of his timber from stands to the west, bringing pieces down the Azusa and Takase rivers to the Shinano and then hauling them upstream to the construction site.

Tokoro Mitsuo reports that construction of the relatively small central keep of Matsumoto castle in the 1590s required 2,514 *koku* of processed lumber (*yōzai*), which would have necessitated some 10,000 *koku* of stumpage (*tachiki*). Adding an estimate of lumber to build other parts of the castle—parapets, gate houses, barracks, and other buildings—he derives a total lumber volume that would have required 30,000 *koku* of stumpage. Further, he calculates that construction of some twelve hundred dwellings in the town of Matsumoto consumed another 72,000 *koku* of *yōzai* by 1600. Figuring in requirements for other buildings and bridges, as well as scaffolding and other timber needs of the construction process itself, he concludes that at least 200,000 *koku* of semiprocessed timber (or 400,000 *koku* of stumpage) were required to build the castle and town. And that amount was enough, he observes, to denude the surrounding mountains.[46]

Daimyo thus consumed great quantities of construction timber in establishing their regimes. After the towns, cities, and monuments were built, moreover, reconstruction following fire repeatedly took great amounts of lumber. Furthermore, lords sold wood to generate government income. Records from Tosa illustrate that practice.

The fine wood of Tosa drew praise from aristocrats at court as early as the thirteenth century. Later both Hideyoshi and Ieyasu requisitioned timber from Tosa, and the daimyo, Yamanouchi, marketed wood for income. In 1601 he instructed a merchant then serving him as quartermaster (*goyō shōnin*) to forward timber, bamboo, rice, and other bulk goods to his storage and garrison facilities in Osaka and Fushimi. By 1609 Yamanouchi was logging Mount Kuroson in the far southwest corner of his domain and selling the timber to a Kyoto merchant. After 1615 Tosa enlarged its processing facilities at Osaka and dredged a canal to bring timber-laden vessels directly to its warehouse and timber storage. Some lumber was stored for *han* use; some was marketed. In 1621 the *han* faced a financial crisis and arranged to substitute timber for its customary money gifts to the *bakufu* (shogunate). It also raised emergency income that year by marketing accumulated supplies of lumber. Yamanouchi ordered his officials to sell the wood or turn it over to a moneylender, explaining that he planned no construction work for the next year or two and the lumber would deteriorate and lose value if not sold soon. Pieces earmarked for the *bakufu*, however, were not to be released.[47]

Still strapped for funds a year later, Yamanouchi negotiated a three-year debt moratorium and despatched officials to Mount Shiraga to get out more good lumber for sale. He kept his logging costs down by ordering a unit of 100 foot soldiers (*teppō ashigaru*) to provide the labor. The five- to six-foot logs that they cut and floated down the Yoshino river went by ship to the *han* lumberyard at Shiragachō in Osaka. There Yamanouchi sold them for enough money to pay off the *han* debt and put cash in his treasury.[48]

In 1624 Yamanouchi ordered a canal dug at Kōchi, his castle town, to aid in the anchoring, unloading, regulating, and taxing of vessels carrying lumber, bamboo, and firewood. Three years of work by Kōchi residents completed the task, and then Yamanouchi allocated lots along the canal to local merchants. He issued regulations for the new merchant area, and it became known as Zaimoku-chō, or "Lumber Neighborhood," a name given to lumberyard areas in many towns and cities.[49] In following decades Tosa vigorously harvested lumber for use in Kōchi, for presentation to the *bakufu*, and for sale by the *han*. Paper and lacquer also became major market products,[50] gaining importance as logging changed forest composition, enlarging the acreage of paper mulberry (*kōzo*) and lacquer (*urushi*) trees. The great forests of Tosa were thus a valuable asset to the *han* during the seventeenth century, helping to sustain a treasury that, like all daimyo treasuries, faced chronic shortages of income.

After Ieyasu's death monumental construction slowed sharply. But it did not stop. Daimyo continued to build, mostly replacing structures that had rotted or been destroyed. At the center, Ieyasu's successors, Hidetada and his son, Iemitsu, kept on building. They expanded Chiyoda castle and rebuilt Osaka castle after its destruction by fire and fighting in 1615. Their most famous creation was the Tōshōgū, a shrine complex at Nikkō in the mountains north of Edo that they built to honor the Tokugawa founder. Numerous smaller shrines in Ieyasu's honor were erected elsewhere. Even modest projects such as those consumed substantial quantities of high-grade lumber. Thus in 1634, when Iemitsu returned to Edo from a grand progress to Kyoto, he ordered that a shrine, the Asama *jinja*, be erected at Sunpu, the site of Ieyasu's childhood, retirement and death. To build it, workmen logged the Ōi river on the Tōtōmi-Suruga border. They rafted some sixty thousand pieces of *hinoki, tsuki, kashiwa,* and miscellaneous other kinds of wood down to the sea, eastward along the coast to the town of Shimizu and then upriver to the construction site at Sunpu.[51]

Shipbuilding also consumed timber. Hideyoshi built his large oceangoing fleets for the conquest of China, and after he died Ieyasu promoted foreign trade. At his behest shipwrights built seaworthy junks (measuring 120 feet stem to stern and 45 feet at the beam) capable of carrying nearly four hundred people.[52] Hidetada and Iemitsu restricted and finally halted foreign trade in Japanese bottoms, but the coasting trade flourished, requiring constant production of smaller vessels. At the port of Shimoda alone, which furnished ships for use in Nagoya-to-Edo trade, fifty wrights built and repaired vessels during the 1620s, and as many as sixty-three worked there in later years.[53]

After Ieyasu's death, however, the greatest demand for building timber derived from neither shipwrights nor creators of monuments. Rather, it came from a diverse urban public whose houses, mansions, and places of business were repeatedly destroyed by fire.

To note the case of Edo briefly, "the flowers of Edo," as people called the terrifyingly beautiful urban conflagrations, repeatedly ravaged the city, sustaining almost ceaseless reconstruction. By one calculation major fires, meaning fires laying waste to at least ten blocks, occurred ninety-three times between 1601 and 1866, averaging one every two years and nine months. Uncountable others destroyed smaller areas.[54] The first of these major fires erupted near year's end in 1601, when Edo was still a modest castle town of five thousand houses. Driven by brisk winds and fed by the thatch roofs of densely packed buildings, it swept through the entire town, within hours undoing a decade of work. If we assume that most of the five thousand houses burned, then at 60 *koku* of lumber per house (the figure Tokoro used for Matsumoto), the loss was 300,000 *koku* of *yōzai* or some 1,200,000 *koku* (333,600 cubic meters) of stumpage.

Ieyasu's officials promptly set people to work rebuilding the town. Thatch roofs were forbidden and wood shingles (*itabuki*) required in their stead.[55] A year later, in early 1603, Ieyasu took the title of shogun and began transforming his small castle town into a proper headquarters for a hegemonial regime. In subsequent decades the town grew into a vast, intensely crowded, extremely fire-prone city.

Of Edo's many conflagrations the two worst occurred in 1657 and 1772, each consuming over half the city. The Meireki fire of 1657 was especially notorious. Starting in a temple in the Hongō district north of Surugadai shortly after New Year's, it rapidly spread in all directions. Before dying down three days later, it had consumed the major buildings of Chiyoda castle, 500 daimyo mansions—meaning almost all of them—779 residences of lesser shogunal retainers (*hatamoto*), 350 temples and shrines, and 400 blocks in the concentrated plebian sections of town. It killed about 100,000 people, nearly as many as the earthquake of 1923 and the great firebomb raid of 1945.[56] And it dealt a severe blow to the forests of Japan. Assuming that before the fire Edo had a population of 150,000 commoners living in thirty thousand small houses that averaged twenty-four by thirty feet, the reconstruction of half their houses alone would have required some 3,600,000 *koku* (1,000,800 cubic meters) of stumpage, which might have constituted twenty-five hundred hectares of prime forest. The rest of the city—commercial establishments, bridges, wharves, temples and shrines, barracks and domiciles of minor samurai, mansions and warehouses of the lordly, and the great castle itself—would have consumed several times as much lumber. And since few prime forests were still extant in the 1650s, the reconstruction of Edo meant in fact that trees were consumed from hundreds of thousands of hectares all over Japan.

Evidences of Exhaustion: The End of an Era

Japan did not run out of fine timber the way a rocket runs out of fuel, suddenly and completely. The forests gave out piecemeal, stand by stand, tree by tree. Dense conifer stands might be clear-cut, but for most areas of mixed forest loggers would, stereotypically, initially take the best of desired species, whether *sugi, hinoki, sawara, kusunoki,* or *keyaki*. Later they would rework the area, taking individual trees or groves they had bypassed earlier. Later yet they would cut again, taking younger and poorer trees and trees of less desired species. This bit by bit despoliation occurred in some forests or some sections of forest long before it did in others and elicited responses accordingly. Thus we find the Hōjō of Odawara, whose woodland had been subject to harvesting ever since the Kamakura period, taking protective measures as early as the 1550s, whereas some *han* did little for another century or more.

Nevertheless, by the time the early modern predation ran its course in the 1660s, a nationwide lumber marketing industry was obtaining supplies from wherever they could be found.[57] In doing so, it erased most geographical variations in the timing of forest depletion. By then human demand had outraced nature's capacity to restock forests throughout the islands south of Ezo (Hokkaido), and thereafter responses to forest exhaustion were everywhere similar in timing and character.

The Geography of Forest Exploitation

Identifying with any degree of precision what woodland was logged at what date is currently impossible because records are spotty or yet to be studied. Nevertheless, in some areas benchmarks in the progress of deforestation can be identified. In Akita, for example, most of Hideyoshi's *sugi* came from slopes overlooking southern branches of the middle Yoneshiro river and selected branches of the lower and middle Omono.[58] The main valleys of the two streams had been cut previously; deeper forks upstream were logged in subsequent decades. In the Tenryū valley, which we examine at more length below, loggers were still working rich stands in northern Tōtōmi during Hideyoshi's day. By Ieyasu's time Tōtōmi was exhausted, and cutting had moved northward into southern Shinano, the advance expedited by Suminokura's riparian work. The great stands of Tōyama valley went down, along with timber in the Tenryū valley proper and other forks as far north as the Achi, which loops northwestward around Iida.[59] In following decades lumbermen pushed into the Tenryū's remaining branches. To the west, along the Kiso, Hideyoshi's lumber had come from forests on the Mino-Shinano border near Nakatsu. By the 1620s loggers had ascended the Kiso to its most richly endowed branch, the Ōtaki, which drains 3,063-meter-high Mount Ontake. By the 1660s they had consumed all accessible stands in the Kiso watershed.[60]

In other *bakufu* lands, and in daimyo domains as well, logging was pursued relentlessly. By the late seventeenth century harvesting of natural stands had consumed nearly all the valuable timber on Japan's three main islands and was reaching into Ezo, prompting Kumazawa Banzan, the noted Confucian scholar, to lament that "eight out of ten mountains of the realm have been denuded."[61]

Forest Depletion in Matsumoto

The seventeenth-century experience of Matsumoto *han* illustrates some of the ways in which timber scarcity manifested itself.[62] As noted earlier, Matsumoto provided some roofing material for Ieyasu but consumed most lumber in its own castle and town construction. The daimyo initially obtained some timber as tax payments, specifying in tax levies on forested villages the quantities of wood to be provided. As timber became scarce and more costly to extract, however, villages substituted rice, soybeans, coins, silver, or other goods, which they evidently could obtain more easily than lumber. To offset those losses, the *han* resorted to logging with corvée labor, supporting the work crews with per diem payments (*fuchimai*). The paid corvée system posed difficulties, however, because laborers had to be fed and paid as they worked, whereas income from marketed lumber did not materialize until months later. Lacking funds to capitalize logging projects, the *han* tried farming its woodland, inviting merchants to log and sell the yield in return for a specified contract fee (*unjō*).

Local merchants began contract logging in about 1617, and during the 1620s large-scale lumber merchants from Edo and Osaka also commenced participating. For about twenty years both local and city merchants logged, but during the 1640s the latter dropped out. They withdrew, it appears, because forests had become so depleted that the increased cost of producing inferior lumber made the work unprofitable. The last city merchant to participate was an Edo man identified by his shop name as Norimonoya. He was still involved, presumably, because, as his name indicates, he was buying long sapling and small pole stock of the type used in palanquins (*norimono*), and these were still available even though large lumber-producing trees were not.

The rapidly deteriorating state of Matsumoto's forests is suggested not only by the changing pattern of logging but also by the evolution of *han* forest management. As early as 1595, while castle work was still in progress, the daimyo began designating exceptionally fine individual trees as *goyōki* ("lord's tree"), which were not to be touched except with government approval. A half century later, in 1642, the *han* established forest preserves (*ohayashi* and *tomeyama*), trying to conserve what timber remained by closing several mountains around the city that previously had been open to public harvesting. In following decades Matsumoto set aside more and more areas as preserves, imposed more elaborate restrictions, and established patrols to assure that forests were not illegally entered.

Forest Depletion in the Tenryū Valley

Evidence of timber depletion shows up clearly in records of the Tenryū river valley. Logging operations moved upstream, as mentioned earlier. At the same time, lumbermen substituted inferior species as preferred stock became scarce. *Sawara* was the species of choice for *kureki*, or split pieces, the major product of Tenryū woodland, and Tenryū *kureki* originally had been pure *sawara*. However, by 1700 it included *hinoki, kurobe,* and *karamatsu*.[63]

The size of timber also changed. During Ieyasu's day the Tenryū valley in southern Shinano had boasted many *sawara* six to seven feet in circumference, and loggers found it easy to get out *kureki* pieces six feet long by one foot in "three side" (*sanbō*) face measure. A century later trees of that size were rarities found only in inaccessible canyons.[64] As Tenryū woodland shrank and the size of *kureki* declined, it became necessary to establish minimal dimensions. The *bakufu* issued standards in 1649, but perhaps because fellers continued to produce substandard pieces, it established a second, smaller size of *kureki* in 1678. Matters continued to worsen, and from about 1688 the *bakufu* began accepting *kureki* from trees standing dead on the stump and from smaller trees that loggers split into halves or quarters rather than the traditional "*mikanwari*" sixths and eighths.[65] In 1718 Edo reduced yet again the minimal measurements for *kureki* to make smaller pieces acceptable.[66] That change helped extend the valley's productive life, no doubt, but only by a few years, as is suggested by the statistics below for lumber sent downstream between 1671 and 1782.[67]

Period	Pieces Shipped (annual ave.)	Raft Loads (annual ave.)	Sticks per Raft
1671–1688	165,572	4,653	35.6
1688–1715	334,640	2,823	118.5
1716–1735	231,989	1,305	177.8
1736–1763	42,061	426	98.7
1768–1782	8,954	128	69.9

The greater number of sticks per raft during 1716–35 reflects the declining size of timber. The decreased amounts thereafter may indicate a decision to use smaller rafts, perhaps to preserve employment for raftsmen who had fewer sticks to transport or perhaps because raft runs were starting farther upstream.[68]

Other evidence from the Tenryū valley reveals the same trends. In 1591 villagers in Ina district of south Shinano paid their taxes to Hideyoshi's vassals in pieces of *kureki*, but by 1645 only 29 of 203 villages had *sawara* of sufficient size to produce the wood. Hillsides in most of the others had been reduced to grass, brush, and scattered weed trees.[69] The *bakufu*, which had to keep roofs over the heads of its thousands of vassal families, tried to sustain *kureki* production by arranging tax obligations in its Tenryū mountain villages to encourage lumbering. In essence it defined the obligation so that villagers could log for pay and use *kureki* to write off tax burdens formally denominated in rice. By the eighteenth century, however, difficulty in finding acceptable timber made the labor cost of those arrangements punitive to villagers. For several years they petitioned to use substitutes for the wood requirement, and finally in 1735 the *bakufu* allowed them to replace *kureki* with money. A few years later Edo attempted to revive lumber payments, but villagers resisted, and eventually the *bakufu* abandoned its effort.[70]

As the seventeenth century advanced, timber scarcity in Ina evolved into a more general scarcity of woodland. Early in the century villagers had exploited forest freely, using it primarily for fuel, fodder, and fertilizer. As logging converted hillsides from high forest to brushland, villagers opened more acres to cultivation, with the enlarged areas of brushwood providing sufficient fertilizer and fodder material to sustain the expanded agricultural operations. By the 1660s, however, enough acreage had been opened to tillage so that brushland was largely restricted to the more acute mountain slopes. Moreover, villages were increasingly preserving their own supplies of brush by restricting the use rights of outsiders. By then, also, government was restricting access to much mountain woodland in an effort to protect seedling timber growth. The press of arable from below and political restraints from above created a scarcity of fertilizer-providing brushland, which led to a slowing and eventual cessation of land opening by the end of the century, despite sporadic government efforts at further reclamation.[71]

The story is similar in Takatō *han*, the one daimyo domain that Ieyasu left in possession of substantial Tenryū valley forest. There the woods gave out between 1690 and 1730, and despite the substitution of inferior species, a reduction in size requirements, and adjustments in the arrangements for land use and control, by mid-century the *han* was unable to exploit its woodland.[72]

A final, indirect expression of the growing scarcity of lumber in the Tenryū valley was revealed in attempts to reduce the loss of lumber en route from mountain to mansion, most notably by the adoption of rafting techniques.[73] Initially, when timber was plentiful, laborers dropped pieces individually into the river, letting them float down to a landing to be snared by an arresting cable or hooked by men standing in the water. Such free floating was the least labor-intensive way to move wood down the river, and Hideyoshi and Ieyasu both used it. On the Tenryū, loggers originally dropped pieces of *bakufu kureki* into the river one at a time as rapidly as fellers got them out, and the pieces floated to a government storage site in Tōtōmi. Losses were extensive, however, because wood got stranded, stolen en route, and washed out to sea during freshets. In the last month of 1608, for example, some 12,500 of 101,000 pieces were lost on the river.[74]

After a few years the *bakufu* abandoned the free float in favor of periodic, carefully supervised floats. In that method the yield from about three years worth of cutting accumulated at upriver sites, and during the winter, when streamflow was low and farmers were not using water for irrigation, workmen tossed all the sticks in together, and they drifted downstream en masse. Villagers manning riverbanks under the watchful eyes of local officials kept them moving along to the storage site. There workmen snared and stacked them pending distribution orders from Edo. These periodic mass floats reduced river losses and complications, but holding pieces upriver and then in storage for several years resulted in severe losses from rot. Consequently, the *bakufu* later discontinued periodic mass floats, replacing them with rafts. Because *kureki* pieces were small, rafts were fragile and their construction a complex, laborious task. Given the scarcity of lumber, however, Edo evidently found the costs acceptable, and rafts prevailed on the Tenryū for the rest of the Edo period.[75]

Other Evidence of Overcutting

Records from Matsumoto and the Tenryū valley thus yield evidence of declining timber stands in central Japan. Throughout the country the same general pattern appeared. In the far north, scarcity of timber prompted lumbermen in 1678 to make their first forays into Ezo.[76] By the 1660s Akita leaders were wrestling with the problems of timber and fuelwood scarcity.[77] Tsugaru *han* faced similar issues by century's end.[78] At the other end of Japan, when the Hosokawa family took over Higo *han* in 1633, the domain held rich stands of timber that the daimyo promptly began felling and selling for income. Production gradually declined, however, and in the 1750s the *han* forbade all export of Higo wood. The prohibition, though never fully effective, remained in force until the 1850s, when forest revival again permitted selective sale to other domains.[79]

On Shikoku, loggers similarly decimated the timber stands of Tosa.[80] As noted above, Hideyoshi began stripping the region's great old-growth forests, and Yamanouchi subsequently logged vigorously for income. By mid-century, timber was becoming scarce, and the *han* began relying on other types of woodland usufruct. Following the Meireki fire of 1657, which laid waste to much of Edo, the *bakufu* appealed widely for wood to rebuild the city. Yamanouchi's answer was: "The mountains of our domain are exhausted; we have neither *sugi* nor *hinoki*. We are unable to provide good lumber as requested by the shogun."[81]

Doubtless, he was being less than candid, and Tosa did provide Edo with considerable serviceable, if inelegant, lumber. A half century later, however, in 1704, when the *bakufu* asked for six thousand pieces of *tsuga* and five thousand of *momi*, Tosa was unable to meet even that request. It had difficulty simply locating pieces of *sugi* wide enough to make one thousand of the thin sheets used in rain doors *amado*). A Tosa official responded to the *bakufu* request in writing: "We no longer have any large trees, so there are no wide boards available of the sort we have provided in the past. Henceforth, please submit requests that take this situation into account."[82]

Figures on Tosa lumber contributions to Osaka also reveal that deliveries dropped off sharply around 1670, thereafter staying at roughly one-tenth of earlier levels.

In central Japan during the early decades of the seventeenth century Owari *han* allowed private cutting of Kiso timber. Indeed, to encourage lumbering, it permitted both Kiso villagers and the official in charge of the valley to market specified quantities of tax-free wood (*shiraki*) privately. By the 1660s, however, the *han* found the size of timber declining. During the 1670s, with quality and sale value continuing to drop, Owari started tightening control of production. Finally, in 1708, in an attempt to rebuild *hinoki* stands and preserve them for government use, the *han* prohibited all unofficial cutting of that species. A year later the special tax-free cutting allotment of villagers was halved, and the government substituted money payments for the discontinued half. Thirty years later the entire allotment of the official in charge was converted from lumber to rice.[83] The relative values of lumber, rice, and money evidently had changed appreciably between 1600 and 1740.

One of the best indicators of forest exhaustion would be evidence of escalating costs of lumber and fuel. Unfortunately, helpful statistics are scarce, even though cost figures are numerous. One problem is that given the unstable, regionally variable, trimetallic monetary system, money values are difficult to correlate. Moreover, the great variety of lumber types makes piece comparison nearly impossible. Another reason for scarcity of usable figures is that over the centuries fires destroyed many lumber merchant records, and others disappeared because lumbering was such a risky enterprise that lumbermen came and went with great rapidity and failed to preserve their records. And finally, because lumbering was partly market based and partly government controlled, the real costs of production are not fully reflected in recorded market prices, and hence the significance of existing statistics is difficult to establish.

To elaborate this last point, in the early seventeenth century most logging was done on behalf of lords and was performed by corvée labor or as a tax service. When someone hired villagers to get out lumber for market, the cost of such lumber was four to six times as high as that produced as tax goods.[84] This situation enabled lords to market wood at great profit, or to depress the market by undercutting entrepreneurial prices, should they wish to do so. Later on, when timber became more difficult and costly to obtain and governments found lumbering prohibitive to finance, merchants handled more of the work and villagers could sell wood directly to them. Under these changed circumstances, those governments that did continue to log often had to pay wages to villagers who worked for them, whether employed as corvée or hired labor. That reduced the cost differential, but even then government influence on lumber prices persisted because some governments paid their village loggers by simply writing off specified village tax obligations against the yield, a practice that constituted subsidized logging and kept the final market price below real cost. Governments also used their political power or timber supplies as weapons to manipulate lumber prices. When *bakufu* and *han* marketed lumber, then, as they did in substantial amounts when not pursuing monumental construction, they were commonly selling undervalued goods, making a tidy profit perhaps, but also serving to hold down the retail price of merchant lumber.

Despite the absence of general statistical series, it is clear from a great range and variety of evidence that the decades of monumental construction, city building, and land opening had transformed a plenitude of timber into a scarcity. To cite one last idiosyncratic piece of evidence, the deterioration of Tenryū valley forest accounts for one mystery in Tokugawa political history: the *bakufu*'s arbitrary seizure in 1692 of the mountainous domain of a daimyo named Kanamori, who had rendered valuable service to the regime. During the 1660s, after the Meireki fire brought the problem of timber scarcity into sharp focus, officials at Edo wrestled with the problem of their failing Tenryū reserves. They discussed reclaiming the Kiso valley, which Ieyasu had attached to the Owari domain of one of his younger sons in 1615. Owari, however, had developed into one of the most powerful and prestigious branches of the Tokugawa family, and Edo administrators were unwilling to antagonize such an influential political force. In any case, the Kiso was no longer a richly wooded valley. So they looked elsewhere. The inner mountains of Hida province were still well forested and accessible, but they had been Kanamori's fief since the days of Hideyoshi. The *bakufu* had no legal justification for ousting him, so no action was taken. When Kanamori became a confidante of *bakufu* leaders a few years later, he was able to protect his interests. After he retired from office in 1690, however, by which time the scarcity of timber was that much more acute, *bakufu* leaders evidently found a pretext to transfer him to another domain in the northeast. Thus, they obtained Hida, the last remaining area of substantial virgin timber south of Ezo. Once they had it, however, it took them only thirty years to strip it of timber.[85]

As woodland deteriorated, officials and scholars raised their voices in alarm and admonition, lamenting the decay and asserting the importance of preserving and reviving forests. Scholars such as Yamaga Sokō argued that forests should be managed for the commonweal in such a way as to perpetuate production.[86] During the 1660s, Nobumasa, the fourth daimyo of Tsugaru *han*, identified the significance of forests in this very Confucian way when explaining the three fundamental tasks of lordship:

One must take care for the family line and for one's heir. One's third consideration is the mountains. To elaborate, man is sustained by the five elements [*gogyō*: wood, fire, water, earth, and metal]. In our world today neither high nor low can survive for a moment if any one of the five is missing. Among the five, water and fire [heat] are most important. Of the two, fire is more crucial. However, fire cannot sustain itself; it requires wood. Hence, wood is central to a person's hearth and home [*kama*]. And wood comes from the mountains. Wood is fundamental to the hearth; the hearth is central to the person. Whether one be high or low, when one lacks wood, one lacks fire and cannot exist. One must take care that wood be abundant. To assure that wood not become scarce, one cherishes the mountains. And thus, because they are the foundation of the hearth, which nurtures the lives of all people, the mountains are to be treasured.[87]

Such high-minded rhetoric notwithstanding, when rulers did take steps to protect forests, they generally did so from a much narrower concern for government finances. Their measures were many and varied, but in essence they entailed delineation of borders, restriction of entry to or use of woodland, control of transport and consumption of forest products, creation of organs to enforce the plethora of rules and regulations, and lastly, promotion of afforestation.

Predictably, these measures were accompanied by severe tension. Disputes pitted rulers against one another and against villagers and even more commonly pitted villagers against each other. Attempts to resolve disputes entailed continual adjudication and constant tinkering with relevant regulations. This strategy kept most of the tension at a tolerable level, but it never solved the basic problem, which was grounded in exhaustion of the archipelago's forests. That had been caused in the first instance by overcutting that was undertaken primarily to gratify rulers and maintain the great cities and towns surrounding their castles. Subsequently, overexploitation was perpetuated by the need to maintain that urban establishment while sustaining the much larger total human populace created by rapid population growth during the seventeenth century.

Recapitulation

Japan's first era of monumental construction stripped only the woodlands of the Kinai basin even though it lasted more than two centuries. By contrast, improvements in technology and a vast expansion of state power enabled early modern builders to commandeer timber throughout the realm. Despite this huge increase in the area exploited, the construction boom ran its course in less than a century, ending so quickly because the rate of felling consumed forests far faster than the mountains could regenerate them.

Noting the powerful impact of construction activity on the human-forest relationship may prompt us to wonder why the mighty built such large and lavish secular and religious buildings. Mindful that such construction is common practice among political and religious leaders, it may suffice to suggest that these Japanese monument builders, like their counterparts in other societies, were well aware that awe-inspiring edifices help sustain the prestige and well-being of one's cause by promoting a sense of awe, envy, and even inferiority in those one is seeking to influence. That such construction may gratify both the builder's ego and his sense of virtue surely are entangled factors.

A somewhat more perplexing point in this story, and perhaps the easiest to overlook, is that the Japanese established a tradition of architecture that was exceptionally dependent on wood. Despite the variety and abundance of stone on the islands, it did not become a major component of either monumental or daily-use structures. At no point did Japanese rulers celebrate their triumphs by building great stone and masonry edifices in the manner of Roman, Mogul, and medieval European barons and prelates. At no time did brick and mortar form the carapace of Japanese civilization.

Doubtless, occupants of the archipelago initially built with wood (and thatch) rather than stone, clay, or pounded mud because the wood was available: by its nature it could be used more easily than the alternative materials, and it provided more agreeable dwellings. Clay and mud were used eventually, primarily in the form of tile roofs and plaster walls. Even when timber became scarce, however, rock was used only for the foundations of buildings, never becoming an ingredient of masonry construction.

The frequency and severity of earthquakes may explain the absence of stone construction. Conceivably, some disastrous experience with stone structures discouraged their use, but if so, there appears to be no record of it. And it is not immediately evident that stone walls are more dangerous than tile roofs in a severe quake.[88]

A partial explanation for the absence of stone construction may lie in the geological character of the islands.[89] Rock was abundant and varied, but little was easily accessible to preindustrial builders. The alluvial plains and diluvial terrace deposits on which most communities stood were essentially rock-free and lacking in the limestone used in mortaring compounds. Streambeds held plenty of rounded stones, but in the absence of cement they were of little architectural value, and builders used them only as rock facing for earthen mounds, as in castle construction. Finally, the tectonic activity that threw up Japan's mountains left the archipelago with almost no horizontally layered sandstone or limestone for workmen to chisel into building blocks. In consequence, forest products, primarily coniferous wood, remained the most accessible building material.

The absence of suitable substitutes meant that with sufficient population growth Japanese society became an exceptionally heavy user of wood products and hence exceptionally dependent on the vitality of its forests. The implications of this situation first manifested themselves in the Kinai basin during the ancient predation. They became apparent throughout the country a millenium later.

In both their military and peaceful pursuits early modern rulers were profligate in their use of lumber. Toyotomi Hideyoshi and Tokugawa Ieyasu tower above others as the greatest of big builders, but they only epitomized the new leadership. Construction and preservation of castles, palaces, mansions, temples, and shrines ate deeply into woodland, and creation and maintenance of castle towns consumed yet more timber. The problem was compounded, of course, by population growth, which added tremendously to the demand for fuel, fertilizer, and basic construction timber, as well as foodstuffs produced on land hitherto available to grow trees.

To sustain construction activity and urban life, seventeenth-century rulers improved access to forests, strengthened lumber transport, and arranged land taxes and forest employment in ways that induced villagers to get timber out. The measures bore fruit, and from one end of Japan to the other forests fell to the chopper's axe.

Rulers recognized the value of woodland and from early on began taking ad hoc measures to prevent unauthorized logging or other use and abuse. The heart of the deforestation problem, however, lay in authorized, not unauthorized, logging. The protective measures were being taken by the principal forest predators as means of assuring their own access to forest yield, not as ways of preserving forest per se. In consequence, felling continued and woodland became ever more desolate, even as the early modern epoch of monumental construction was terminated by its own excesses.

Before the seventeenth century's end the great stands of virgin timber were gone, disputes over forest use were endemic, damage to lowland was a cause for alarm, lumber quality had declined, and scarcities had become pervasive. These multiple problems gradually prodded rulers at all levels to devise new policies of forest management and use and led to basic changes in woodland utilization and control. In toto, these changes propelled Japan from the long era of exploitation forestry into a new era of regenerative forestry.

Part Two

The Emergence of Regenerative
Forestry in Early Modern Japan

Chapter Four

The Negative Regimen: Forest Regulation

The earliest historical evidence of woodland management in Japan dates from the ancient predation. After a couple of centuries such management appears to have fallen into desuetude, however, not reviving until the 1400s and 1500s, when villagers and subsequently daimyo initiated a new era of forest regulation.

During the seventeenth century, forest management acquired urgency as widespread land clearance and overcutting precipitated both erosion with its downstream ramifications and wood scarcity with its socioeconomic consequences. As decades passed, governments and villages all over the realm adopted and elaborated measures to counter the malign effects of excess, attempting most immediately to resolve disputes arising from conflicts over forest-use rights. By century's end the Japanese had constructed an elaborate system for managing woodland and its yield.

Regulation: An Overall View

Early modern forest regulation throughout Japan encompassed similar spheres: the woodland, the transportation route linking forest to town, and the town itself, that is, the spheres of production, distribution, and consumption. Policies and organs directly regulating woodland use—specifying who could do what, where, when, how, how much, and at what price and how all that was to be enforced and what punishments would follow infractions—were the core of the negative regimen. Regulations pertaining to transport and consumption of forest products were also of enough significance to merit brief comment.

Woodland Management

In essence, early modern forest management consisted of administrative rules and arrangements for enforcing them. The rules and arrangements mostly developed as ad hoc responses to immediate problems, being produced and later maintained and modified by interaction among the *bakufu*, the *han* governments, and the thousands of villages dotting the realm. Because of their tangled provenance, woodland regulations and procedures were tremendously diverse in particulars. Nevertheless, two factors gave them a high degree of functional consistency. As indicated in chapter 3, the basic problems that produced the negative regimen were essentially the same nationwide, and the range of possible solutions varied little from place to place. In addition, the practices that emerged were patterned on administrative forms and techniques of the creating agents—governments and villages—and these were quite similar throughout the land.

Because woodland management was precipitated by forest overuse, it had two basic objectives: protection and production. "Protection forests" sheltered homesteads, villages, fields, roads, streams, or shores from damage by flood, wind, or other natural forces. "Production forests" yielded timber, fuel, or other desired products. In general, interest in protection forests emerged first, becoming widespread by the mid-seventeenth century. The rulers, whose regimes depended on rural production and whose positions forced them to deal with downstream consequences of upstream abuse, gave particular attention to protection forestry. Concern for production developed somewhat later, becoming pervasive by century's end. On many sites, needless to say, policy sought to attain both objectives.

The predominant agent of government forest policy was the Tokugawa *bakufu*, the elaborate shogunal regime headquartered in the city of Edo. It administered directly about a fourth of the realm, mostly in central Japan.[1] Subordinate to the *bakufu* were the governments of the 250-odd regional barons, or daimyo, each head-quartered in its own castle town and in charge of a semiautonomous domain (*han*). In the aggregate these *han* governments controlled the remaining three-fourths of the country.

Hereditary vassals, the samurai, who exercised administrative, police, and military authority on behalf of their lords, staffed the bureaucracies of both the *bakufu* and *han*. Heads of more distinguished vassal families held higher offices; minor families, lower posts. Most samurai, high and low, lived in their lords' castle towns, along with a large populace of merchants, artisans, manual laborers, and various other people. The bulk of the population, some 85 percent of the eighteenth century's approximately thirty million, lived in the countryside in villages usually governed by councils of elders chosen from well-to-do and influential community members.[2] These elders administered local affairs, settled disputes, and collected taxes on behalf of their lord in accord with regulations issued by that lord, whether shogun or daimyo. District administrators, usually samurai serving as regional representatives of their lord, communicated the regulations to villages and, in theory at least, assured that they were obeyed.

Forest organization reflected these larger arrangements. Shogun and daimyo administered most woodland within their respective jurisdictions, placing it under the authority of their finance ministries. Subordinate officials, who often were foresters versed in their work, oversaw logging and reforestation projects and handled the actual inspection of woodland. The assigning of forest management to finance ministries sprang from the primacy of economics in government thinking about woodland. The ruler's most notable interests were forest products: lumber in particular, but also fuelwood, charcoal, lacquer, and diverse other items. They also sought to prevent erosion and flood damage to downstream agricultural lands, which constituted their tax base.

Much woodland around villages was managed locally, either communally by villagers or individually by householders. Village officials oversaw the use and maintenance of communal forest, enforcing village regulations and implementing (or resisting) such instructions as came down from higher authority. The interest of villagers in woodland, like that of rulers, was essentially economic, but it was not identical: although villagers had some lumber needs, their primary requirements were fuelwood, fertilizer, fodder, and emergency foodstuffs.

The difference in government and village priorities was a key factor shaping forest policy. Villagers generally wanted access to nearby areas of mixed broadleaf trees and tropical grasses (the bamboos), whereas rulers generally would cede land so stocked while claiming hillsides endowed with construction timber.[3] As forest cover became more impoverished, however, local brush gathering and wood cutting drew villagers ever deeper into the mountains, pitting them against government loggers and foresters and leading to encounters with other villagers approaching from different directions.

Especially between the 1640s and 1690s the *bakufu* attempted to deal with disputes of this sort by clearly delineating domain and village boundaries.[4] Rulers also used their surveyors to locate valuable timberland and establish control over it, particularly after the Meireki fire of 1657 revealed the general inadequacy of government timber supplies. By 1700 surveyors from Tsugaru to Tsushima had designated selected woodland as *ohayashi*, or "lord's forest," which they mapped and distinguished from adjacent parcels officially recognized as subject to some form of local jurisdiction.

Despite these jurisdictional distinctions, however, and despite the assiduous surveying, the functional differences between government and local woodlands were rarely clear. Forests of rulers and ruled operated under diverse but sometimes very similar arrangements. In many localities regulations deriving from either regime or village applied to both categories of nearby forest. For example, government prohibitions against cutting certain species of trees (*tomeki*, or "reserved trees") usually applied to all specimens of size, wherever they might be growing. And village regulations on who might gather how much fertilizer material and when could be applied to nearby *ohayashi* as well as village forest. Moreover, the regulations themselves continually changed as society struggled with the intractable problems stemming from forest overuse. Finally, through various legal devices woodland shifted between village and government jurisdictions, and the proper designation of many parcels was a matter of ongoing disagreement.

Villages reproduced in miniature the larger pattern of obfuscated dualism. Throughout Japan village woodland nominally existed as parcels held by separate households (*hyakushō yama*) or as communally controlled land (*iriaichi*). In reality, however, that distinction was thoroughly compromised, with villages exercising some degree of control over use of household forest and various forms of individual privilege existing vis-à-vis common land. Moreover, parcels constantly shifted from one jurisdiction to another or existed in some intermediate status, which further obscured the distinction.

All this confusion notwithstanding, by the late seventeenth century lord's forest was the greater part of the archipelago's woodland. It included, however, high ridges and peaks bearing scant natural growth as well as lower hillsides and valleys rich with conifers and mixed vegetation. Near villages, where community and household forests predominated, slopes often were less acute and valleys broader. The original soil commonly was more fertile, natural growth more dense, and biomass production greater. These qualities made such woodland particularly valuable and hence subject to more intense exploitation. One consequence was that it deteriorated sooner and more severely than did the originally less valuable interior land. Another consequence was that it became the subject of dispute and object of regulation more quickly and commonly than did hinterlands. The disputes might pit village against government, village against village, or members of a village against one another, but government sooner or later found itself involved in resolving many of the conflicts.

Villagers generally retained great interest in nearby lord's forest because it included terrain they had utilized in the past or assumed they could use in the future if necessary.[5] As population and arable increased and the quality of nearby woodland deteriorated, future need became present necessity, and more and more villagers agitated to ease restrictions on the use of such forests. In consequence, after boundary delineation removed the possibility of villagers satisfying their needs by expanding exploitable woodland acreage, petitions and lawsuits regarding use of *ohayashi* became endemic.

Because woodland regulation grew out of these local attempts to satisfy immediately conflicting demands, the forms of restraint on access and utilization became remarkably diverse. They included restrictions on areas open to harvest, goods to be removed, sequence of access to an area, number of days or workers or size and type of tools permitted on the job, number or size of loads of produce, or number or type of pack animals for carrying the yield. To enforce the rules, villages and governments deployed guards and inspectors and elaborated punishments for varying types and degrees of violations.[6]

As these forms of restraint suggest, woodland management fundamentally entailed the defining and enforcing of use rights rather than of land ownership. No one "owned" the land; the concept did not exist in Tokugawa Japan.[7] Use rights, by contrast, were universally recognized and central to all discussions of land. These rights had four cardinal characteristics:

1. They were specific: they identified the particular rights of particular people on particular sites.
2. They were transferable: the rights of a person or of a legal entity such as a village could, through sanctioned means, be consigned to others, in whole or in part, and for varying lengths of time.
3. They were legitimate: although disputes over specific rights in specific instances were endemic, no one disputed the principle of use rights itself.
4. They were justiciable when subject to dispute: reasonably orderly judicial mechanisms for resolving disputes over use rights existed, and because rights were legitimate, those mechanisms were routinely used to resolve the innumerable disputes that arose.

As noted at greater length in chapter 6, use rights were so arranged as to produce a system of regulated, multiple-use forestry. Nearly all parcels of woodland were subject to multiple use in two senses of the term: they were to yield diverse goods, and they were to yield them to more than one recipient. These arrangements reflected the piecemeal process of rule making that formed the system. They also reflected the intricate balance of power among rulers and villagers and the particular requirements all parties brought to the transactions that produced the system.

The Transport and Consumption of Forest Products

Officialdom, armed with a substantial body of forest legislation, sought to control the transport and marketing of forest output. Transit controls helped regulate forest use; for example, guards and other officials stationed at posts along rivers and highways leading out of woodland inspected goods en route and enforced laws against the shipping of illegal yield. The main purpose of governmental transit control, however, was to sustain the fisc, either directly by taxing goods or indirectly by preventing forest work from disrupting agricultural production. Villagers used such control to protect their own roles in the purveying work.

Regulations pertaining to consumption addressed the issue of resource depletion more forthrightly. Rulers issued a stream of edicts specifying who might and might not use how much of what type of forest product. Construction work was extensively controlled, with governments specifying in varying detail the size and number of pieces and types of wood allowed for building and repairing bridges, roads, dikes, irrigation works, dams, buckets, boats, and wells.[8] Regulations on the size of buildings and the materials permitted in their construction were especially noteworthy; for example, governments generally forbade peasants to use *sugi* and *hinoki* wood and bark when building, and they placed limits on residential construction by samurai. Thus, the *bakufu* in 1668 prohibited its vassals from using a number of expensive, flammable items of luxury construction, including *sugi* doors, certain lacquered items, arched windows, and *keyaki* gates, when rebuilding houses after fires.[9]

Sumptuary regulations affected a vast array of other forest-derived items, including smaller wooden goods, firewood, charcoal, lacquer, tea, silk, and paper. In 1663 the *bakufu* had forbidden any woodworker in Edo, whether requested by a city householder, renter, or roomer, to produce small boxes from either *sugi* or *hinoki* or household utensils or stands from *sugi*. It had, however, permitted continued production of larger *sugi* boxes and *hinoki* chests. Five years later it forbade the use of *sugi* and *hinoki* or other good wood in the construction of public signboards, and in 1706 it forbade the sale of large pine trees for New Year's decorations (*kadomatsu*).[10] Daimyo generated their own restrictions, many following in line with Edo's policy but differing in particulars from domain to domain. The lord of Akita *han*, for example, who marketed *sugi* and *hinoki* for income, forbade their use for rice-drying racks and chopsticks, among other things.[11] In toto, this body of regulation constituted a vast, and moderately effective, system of rationing.

The regulators anchored this rationing system in broader social norms by linking it to the social hierarchy, permitting higher-ranking families to use more of a scarce commodity than lower-ranking ones. In 1642, in an early instance, the *bakufu* had issued a short list of sumptuary restrictions and had admonished people not to build houses inappropriate to their status. The last clause betrayed the source of Edo's concern: it urged its vassals in charge of land (*jitō* and *daikan*) to establish forests by promoting tree planting. A half century later, in 1699, the *bakufu* was more precise, specifying the dimensions of timber to be used by vassals (*hatamoto*) building new houses. It forbade those with fiefs ranked at less than one thousand *koku* of putative yield (*kokudaka*) to use beams over 2 *ken* (about twelve feet) in length, and those of one thousand to three thousand *koku* rank to use any over 2.5 *ken*.[12]

More precise formulations appeared. Kokura *han* allowed villagers to obtain enough construction lumber from government woodland to erect houses of a size deemed appropriate to their status:[13]

Status	House Size
ōjōya (headman of several villages)	2 × 15 *ken*
ōjōya heir	2 × 9 *ken*
kojōya (village headman)	2 × 6 *ken*
kumigashira (neighborhood chief)	2 × 4 *ken*
takamochi hyakushō (taxable peasant)	2 × 3 *ken*
other tillers, merchants, fishermen	2 × 2 *ken*

In Aizu a similar but more complex practice prevailed. The government designated the length of timbers a builder might use for beams and the numbers of such beams, the figures being based on the putative yield of a builder's landed holding. Thus, villagers rated at one to five *koku* could use beams of 2 to 2.5 *ken* length, totaling 6 *ken*, while at the upper extreme, those of twenty or more *koku* could use beams measuring 2.5 to 3 *ken* for a total of 20 *ken*.[14] This strategy of linking consumption scale to status, which obviously served the interests of rationers, presumably improved the likelihood that edicts on rationing would generally be obeyed.[15]

Government Administration of Forests

In retrospect, the rationing system that governments applied to the general populace may be the most visible part of forest regulation. At the time, however, intervention at the production site was a more structured and probably more effective part of policy. Like rationing, site management was largely responsive rather than initiatory. Because forest depletion developed gradually, managerial arrangements arose gradually, and because they usually were ad hoc and incremental attempts to resolve specific conflicts of interest, they were inconsistent and subject to frequent change. So every generalization is flawed, and applicability in particular instances tends to vary inversely with a statement's specificity. Nevertheless, some general comments may suggest the system as a whole.[16]

Officials of each *han* administered government forest within their domain's boundaries. Subordinate to the highest domanial officials (*karō*) and usually assigned to the finance office (*kanjōsho*) were the senior forest officials, commonly called forest or mountain magistrates (*hayashi bugyō* or *yama bugyō*). Their administrative staffs ranged from a few people to an office full of personnel who surveyed woodland, kept records, investigated problems, and supervised larger logging projects. Magistrates might implement policy through district administrators (intendants: *daikan, gundai*, or *kōri bugyō*), or they might despatch staff members to the field instead, bypassing the intendants, whose overriding interest in maximizing agricultural tax income frequently made them poor protectors of forest interests. Whether magistrates worked through intendants or staff, however, policy implementation depended on regional or local foresters (*yamamori*). These foresters, of either samurai or villager status, normally were local residents appointed to enforce policy in nearby woods. They usually had some assistants and were empowered as necessary to call upon village officials for help. Commonly the performance of these various forest officials was subject to scrutiny by comptrollers (*gimmiyaku*).

The woodland that government foresters oversaw, which scholars refer to generically as *ohayashi*, or "lord's forest," actually bore a variety of names in addition to *ohayashi* (including *oyama, ojikiyama, otateyama, ohayashiyama, omotoyama, shikakurayama, akiyama*, and *okuyama*), depending on the customs and particulars of the site.[17] However labeled, lord's forest was highly fragmented, much consisting of small parcels scattered among plots of locally controlled land. Some parcels, usually freshly logged ones, would be closed to entry long enough for a new tree crop to establish itself. Areas identified as protection forests also might be closed to cutting or other utilization. Like lord's forest in general, closed parcels, now identified by scholars as *tomeyama*, were known at the time by a variety of names. Also, governments assigned much lord's forest (parcels designated *azukariyama, ukeyama, unjōyama*, and so on) to others for administration and use, often on a fee basis. As a result of this practice, villages, temples, shrines, and local samurai and entrepreneurs exercised varying degrees of control over many parcels of *ohayashi*.

The policy of reserved trees (generically called *tomeki*) forbade a person to fell, trim, or otherwise endanger the trees so designated except with official permission. Governments usually applied *tomeki* rules only to trees exceeding a certain basal circumference, but would do so wherever the desired specimens happened to be found, whether in *ohayashi*, other woodland, or even a villager's front yard. Rulers usually reserved trees because of their economic value, with timber trees, notably *sugi* and *hinoki*, being selected most commonly. Subsequently, authorities added nontimber trees, such as lacquer, chestnut, paper, and various fruit trees, to their lists of *tomeki*.

Tomeyama and *tomeki* policies were the core of government forest administration, but a vast array of other regulations addressed particular problems.[18] Prevention of wildfire was a major concern, and regulations prescribed the establishment and maintenance of firebreaks, set up fire patrols, and spelled out community fire-fighting obligations. A plethora of rules restricted use of fire for swidden culture, forest clearing, and annual grass burning and specified punishments for wrongdoing and negligence. Other regulations sought to control practices harmful to desired trees or soil stability, notably timber theft, grubbing out of roots, and unauthorized land clearance, brush cutting, or grazing. Still others clarified procedures for logging to assure that only authorized trees or areas would be harvested. In toto, the negative regimen tried to impose political control on almost all forms of human intervention in woodland affairs. Its basic objective was to sustain the production of goods desired by its authors. A major by-product of that intent, insofar as it attained its objective, was the preservation of woodland verdure.

For a closer look at government forest management, *bakufu* policy during the seventeenth century warrants attention. It shaped affairs in the quarter of Japan directly administered by the regime and served as precedent for much daimyo legislation. This was particularly so for protection forests, less so for production stands.[19]

Bakufu *Policy on Protection Forests*

Protection forestry, known by the Chinese term *chisan chisui,* "management of mountains and waters," was of particular concern during the middle decades of the seventeenth century. By then Japan was encountering the environmental effects of a half century of rampant lumbering and land clearing. The *bakufu* was especially active in promoting *chisan chisui* because its domain included some of the country's most seriously eroded landscapes, notably the Kinai basin. Moreover, only *bakufu* authority embraced the larger watersheds of central Honshu, enabling it to enforce at upstream sites policies necessary for downstream well-being. That was particularly so not only in the long-worn Kinai but also in the Kantō and Nobi plains, where erosion exacerbated stream-control problems as the Edo period advanced. The size of its domain and the scope of its authority made the *bakufu* atypical of Edo-period governments, but those characteristics also meant that *bakufu* policy on protection forests foreshadowed and illustrated, in exaggerated form, much government policy of the day.

Thanks to Tokugawa Ieyasu's policy of seizing woodland, most famously the Kiso and Tenryū river valleys, the *bakufu* had ample timber during its first decades.[20] Insofar as leaders in Edo worried about woodland, they did so in terms of protection forests. The oldest surviving *bakufu* order relating to forest protection dates from 1609. That year two senior officials instructed subordinates in charge of a recently acquired section of Hōki province to make certain that careless cutting of trees and bamboo was prevented. Two years later, in guidelines clearly aimed at terrain preservation, a general order instructed villagers not to pasture animals on dikes and river banks and not to stray carelessly from roadways or injure seedlings and shoots. In 1613 an order from three senior officials asserted that felling had long been forbidden in the *ohayashi* at Edozaki in Hitachi but that someone was nevertheless cutting trees there. The guilty must be apprehended, identified, and firmly punished, regardless of where they came from. In that instance—the oldest surviving evidence that Edo claimed woodland as *ohayashi* and was prepared to enforce a *tomeyama*-type policy—woodland was being protected because it sheltered the castle of a son of Ieyasu.[21]

By the late 1630s much new and more marginal land was opened to tillage, and much woodland was denuded, leaving nearby valleys more exposed to climatic vagaries. During those years, weather patterns in northeastern Asia appear to have deteriorated, and Japan experienced widespread crop failure and the resulting Kan'ei famine.[22] The hardship precipitated numerous *bakufu* injunctions to preserve resources, and a common theme was advice to plant trees.[23] Two notices called for tree planting in 1642. One, which instructed vassals and intendants to plant trees and establish woodlands here and there beginning in the next spring, was included in the short list of sumptuary restrictions noted previously. The other, included in a general set of injunctions, was a more pro forma call to plant seedlings in appropriate places. The following year, in an enumeration of criminal punishments, Edo ordered any villager convicted of a minor crime on *bakufu* land to plant trees on sites needing cover, such as dikes or river banks. Two contemporaneous sets of regulations instructed intendants to assist villages by encouraging tree planting that would shelter dwelling sites or reforest appropriate uplands. One notice observed that such measures would lead to village recovery and thus improve the tax base.

In a long set of hortatory injunctions issued in 1649, Edo urged villagers to plant bamboo and trees around their houses because then they would "be able to use the undergrowth and could cease buying fuelwood."[24] By that time the famine was past, and the regime could couch its advice in terms of avoiding another. Problems of site deterioration persisted, however, and injunctions continued to advise tillers on improving arable and maintaining production. The concern to preserve the watershed clearly derived from its importance to riparian works and lowland agriculture. Thus, general instructions that Edo sent to intendants in 1652 ordered them, among other things, to have villagers care properly for stored rice, repair river dikes during the low-water months of winter, improve irrigation arrangements, and convert rough and poor terrain to forest by setting out tree seedlings.[25]

Admonitions alone failed to halt the devastation of woodland. Early in 1666 the *bakufu*'s senior councillors (*rōjū*) issued a set of regulations on woodland and river management.

> Recently, upland vegetation has been torn out by the roots. As a consequence, during rain storms soil and gravel wash into streams and obstruct the flow of water. Henceforth, such uprooting of vegetation is to be prohibited.
>
> Item: Beginning this spring, seedlings are to be planted to halt erosion on denuded sites above streams.
>
> Item: Paddy land and dry fields are not to be formed on the edges and floodplains of rivers; and areas of bamboo, trees, miscanthus, or other reeds are not to press in upon streambeds.
>
> These clauses are to be enforced. This notice is being sent to intendants who, starting this spring, must despatch investigators to ensure that its clauses are not violated.
>
> 1666/2/2   [signed by senior councillors
>   Kuse, Inaba, Abe, and Sakai][26]

Still, legislation did not solve the problem. Downstream silting continued. By the 1680s it was so bad that city magistrates (*machi bugyō*) in Osaka, at the mouth of the Yodo river, ordered that dikes not be allowed carelessly to deteriorate. Moreover, work crews were to improve streamflow by removing bamboo, trees, and grassy growth from the streambed and its islands.[27]

Leaders at Edo addressed the problem again in the spring of 1684. They revamped the 1666 edict, focusing it on the Kinai basin and rephrasing it specifically to include daimyo domains.

> In Yamashiro, Yamato, Settsu, Kawachi, and Ōmi provinces, in mountains under both *bakufu* and other jurisdictions, the roots of trees and brush are constantly being dug up so that during rain storms soil and gravel wash into streams and obstruct the flow of water. Henceforth, such digging out of tree and brush roots is strictly forbidden.
>
> Starting this coming spring, on mountainous sites adjacent to water courses where there are no standing trees and where soil and gravel wash off, seedlings and turf are to be planted to stop erosion into the streams.
>
> Tree seedlings, bamboo, reeds, miscanthus rushes, and grass are to be

planted wherever there is serious washing of soil and gravel into streams. This applies not only to long-established hill fields situated along the sides of streams and on flood plains but also to newly opened paddy land and dry fields. It also applies to paddy land and dry fields that have been registered for a long time. Absolutely no new fields are to be established on stream margins or floodplains.

Note: No swidden is to be opened in the mountains.

These clauses are to be firmly obeyed in both *bakufu* and other lands. Starting in the coming spring, tree seedlings and turf are to be planted annually to prevent silting of rivers. Officials are to inspect problem streams, and if they find anyone disobeying these rules, emergency situations will be dealt with as well as investigated.[28]

Some daimyo may have pointed out the complexity of riparian management, because later in the year the *bakufu* despatched the following order to eleven fief holders with lands lying along the Yodo and Yamato rivers.

In the hills above streams that empty into the Yodo and Yamato rivers, open fields and swidden are forbidden. All are henceforth to be reforested. In your own lands, as well as in adjoining areas under *bakufu* or other jurisdiction, you are to send vassals to investigate two or three times a year and establish forests with all due care. Inquire of finance officers about those officials handling forest duties.[29]

The silting of the Yodo river eventually led Edo to establish the Office of Erosion Control (Dosha Kata Yakusho) expressly to regulate woodcutting and supervise erosion control in the Kinai basin.[30]

During the eighteenth century, *bakufu* notices on stream protection continued to appear.[31] Little accessible land remained untilled, but governments, and probably many peasants, kept trying to open more land to cultivation.[32] Because workable land was scarce, however, the rate of opening dropped sharply. Nevertheless, erosion persisted due to excesses and abuses on tillage and woodland alike. In 1742 *bakufu* leaders notified heads of the finance office (*kanjōsho*) of reports that *ohayashi* and household woodland along rivers were being cleared for cultivation. That was forbidden, they observed, and workmen should reforest such lands. In addition, where trees on streamside *ohayashi* were too crowded, workers were to thin and trim them (to improve their vitality and avoid stream clogging). Upland *ohayashi*, however, if free of large trees, could be cleared upon a cultivator's request, unless soil and gravel from the area were washing into rivers. In the latter case, weed trees (*zōki*) were to be planted and periodically cut back to form coppice (whose root systems would expand and control erosion).[33]

Pressures from both government and village to open more land and grow more crops thus constantly compromised protection forestry. In an analysis of Yodo flooding, an informed observer of the period wrote during the summer of 1743 that villagers living along the river in Yamashiro, Settsu, and Kawachi provinces periodically petitioned for construction projects to contain the river. But, he noted, they pursued projects to protect themselves without concern for the impact on other villages. Each year silt raised the riverbed, and no matter how much it was dredged, matters worsened from year to year. Moreover, he wrote, officials had failed to handle their tasks properly and matters had become very bad. The basic task was to stop the movement of soil and gravel. But as things stood, when it poured, muddy water rushed out of the mountains and the debris formed sandbars and raised the riverbed, which exacerbated flooding. Hence, the mountains that had been cut off should be reforested. However much villagers dredged and diked, he concluded, it was to no avail if officials failed to remedy the source of the problem.[34]

The tension between the conflicting impulses to destroy forests for agricultural production and to maintain them for protection emerged during the seventeenth century. During the eighteenth the picture was complicated by intensifying concern over scarcity of forest products, notably timber and fuelwood, which led forestry officials to shift their attention to wood production. The change in priorities was evident in *bakufu* regulations, which dwelt increasingly on managing the production of timber and fuel.

Bakufu *Administration of Production Forests*

Rhetoric alone did even less to preserve timber stands than it did to stop erosion because the rhetoricians were the chief lumber consumers. Nevertheless, the *bakufu*, along with *han* governments, gradually developed administrative organs that enabled it to maximize control of whatever timber the forests did yield.

The *bakufu*'s interest in timber production derived from its control of, and responsibility for, the realm's greatest cities (Edo,

Kyoto, Osaka) and monuments (castles, mansions, palaces, shrines, temples). In its early decades, with Tenryū and Kiso watersheds producing nicely and city growth at an early stage, the regime at Edo evidently saw little need to coordinate forest policy or worry about output. It simply appointed timber magistrates (*zaimoku bugyō*) to oversee the provisioning of construction projects.[35] But in 1644, as the Kan'ei famine waned, leaders tried to determine how their Kinai and Kantō territories had fared. They ordered intendants to investigate affairs, conduct a census, and make a stem count of bamboo and tree species. That seems to have been the first of what developed into a regularized system of forest registers (*ohayashi daichō*) designed to keep Edo informed of its timber resources.[36]

For some years the regime continued to rely on intendants for implementing edicts on woodland affairs, but by the 1680s bakufu leaders felt a need to coordinate forest policy more effectively. In 1685 they designated four officials as forest magistrates (*ohayashi bugyō*), attached them to the finance office, and assigned them eight assistants (*tedai*). The original duty of these magistrates evidently was to explore woodland for good timber. Later their tasks grew more elaborate: according to a notice of 1754, *ohayashi bugyō* examined forest registers to discern gains and losses in timber supplies, solicited explanations from intendants on why matters were as reported, and assured that registers were updated and logging plans developed in accordance with available information. By then there were only two magistrates, but they were assisted by officials known as *ohayashikata*, a sort of forest overseer. A document of uncertain date describes the forest magistrate's duty as supervising forest preservation, tree planting, logging, and timber transport and surveillance.[37]

Forest magistrates thus oversaw *bakufu* woodland as a whole. In some areas they seem to have exercised their authority through the overseers, but mostly they worked through intendants, whose assistants (*tedai, tetsuki*) dealt with village officials (*kumigashira, hyakushōdai, shōya*) in implementing policy. For special investigations or patrols, the magistrates might send to the area in question subordinates temporarily titled forest ranger (*yamaban, yamamori,* or *yamamawari*).[38] At Edo this hierarchy culminated in the superintendents of finance (*kanjō bugyō*), who in turn were directly subordinate to the regime's highest officials, the senior councillors (*rōjū*).

During the seventeenth century, even when erosion problems were more pressing than timber shortages, it often was unclear from the phrasing of official admonitions and instructions whether they were addressing problems of protection or production.[39] Even at century's end formulations sometimes left ambiguous whether the issue at stake was deterioration of site, insufficiency of yield, or both. Thus, on the steep and easily eroded slopes of Mount Fuji, the *bakufu* maintained *ohayashi* for both protection and production, and in 1702 the forest magistrate sent the intendant in charge of Fuji the following edict for public posting:

1. We hear that, recently, trees on the *ohayashi* of Fuji have been chopped down and burned to make charcoal. Such charcoal making, as well as field clearing by fire, is forbidden. This charcoal making and field burning must be resolutely prohibited.

2. As in the past, felling trees and cutting them up is forbidden.

3. As in the past, unless villagers who gather firewood and so on on Fuji have prior permits, they are forbidden to cut with hatchets.

   These clauses are to be strictly enforced and violators prosecuted.[40]

The prohibitions on Mount Fuji may have aimed more at sustaining a healthy surface cover than preserving timber growth. More and more, however, instructions concentrated on wood production. In 1678, in an early expression of this focus, the forest magistrate's office sent the following notice to an intendant in Tōtōmi for posting in the mountains of Tōtōmi and Suruga provinces:

1. In [specified] *tomeyama* under the jurisdiction of the [named] intendant in Tōtōmi, standing trees, and even branches, are not to be cut.

2. In the mountains, as well as in nearby hills, the use of fire is rigorously prohibited, and travelers and their horses may not stray carelessly from the road.

3. In the mountains, bark is not to be stripped from any trees.

   These clauses are to be strictly enforced on *bakufu*, *han*, temple, and shrine lands, and violators are to be investigated and punished. If there is any secret felling, informants will be rewarded from the goods recovered.[41]

Unauthorized felling constituted timber theft or removal of excessively immature trees. Fire, trampling, foraging, and stripping of bark destroyed seedling growth and ruined potential timber trees.

These injunctions, which addressed major problems in production forestry, reappeared in subsequent decades as standard items in instruction to intendants.

The concern with construction material was more explicit in an injunction that superintendents of finance sent to sixteen intendants in 1707. It pointed out that bamboo and trees were essential to cultivators for riparian construction. If adequate supplies were unavailable in nearby *ohayashi*, intendants were to obtain enough for current needs. Furthermore, they were to establish groves to meet future needs.[42]

A *bakufu* directive of 1713 had timber production in mind when it called for greater care in maintaining *ohayashi*. It specified that in revitalizing forests, attention should be given to available wood volume, site accessibility, and transport facilities. In another general set of instructions to villagers on *bakufu* land, one clause admonished intendants to make sure that villagers did not unnecessarily cut down large trees for local construction projects. The authors added, in a specially highlighted comment, that in logged areas tree seedlings should be set out, even if the work was not done according to existing regulations. Two clauses in a general notice to intendants in 1733 instructed them to inspect both *ohayashi* and household woodland before allowing the extraction of construction wood and required them to look for desirable timber beaching areas when considering sites for possible afforestation. As these last two instances suggest, by the mid-eighteenth century, the regime was moving beyond negative regulations to advocacy of afforestation as a solution to its timber shortage.[43]

A key function of the magistrate's office was maintaining the forest registers (*ohayashi daichō*) that kept officials apprised of timber actually available. Subsequent to the tree counts of the 1640s, registers were updated during the 1660s, in the wake of the massive consumption of timber that followed the Meireki fire.[44] Edo updated its registers again in the 1680s, after establishing the magistrate's office, and periodic updates occurred thereafter. The registers vary in format and content; some of the best surviving examples date from 1762. The following portion of a comparatively detailed (and subsequently updated) report was sent to the magistrate's office in Edo by the intendant in Mino province. It informed Edo of the holdings of *ohayashi* in two villages in the spring of that year.

One Parcel of Bakufu *Forest*

Responsible Villages:
Miwa village
Miyagami village
At Miwayama (local name):
an area of steep mountains

Area

114 *ken* in length; 79 *ken* in width;
3 *chō* 6 *ho* in area [7½ acres]

Tree Count

433 trees, of which
3 trees are being culled
282 are knotty or crooked

Note

Distances:

From the site to the landing on the Mugi river: roadway, 6 *chō*
From the landing to the harbor of Kuwana in Ise: waterway, 20 *ri*
From Kuwana harbor to Edo: seaway, approximately 152 *ri*
From Kuwana harbor to Osaka: seaway, 116 *ri*
From the site to Edo: by land, 102 *ri*

Breakdown of tree count

A. Pine trees

300 trees (stem: 1–2 *ken* in length; 8 *sun* to 1 *shaku* 6 *sun* in circumference at eye level), of which

3 trees are being culled
200 trees are knotty or crooked, of which

115 were delivered last year for the construction of an enclosed, unhulled-rice warehouse at this office (removed from the register on 1764/9/4)

11 trees, standing dead, were cleared away (removed from the register on 1763/2/24)

2 trees, wind damaged in 1753 and cleared away (removed from the register in the fourth month of 1755)

B. Pine trees

56 trees (stem: 2–3½ *ken* long; 1 *shaku* 6 *sun* to 2 *shaku* 5 *sun* circumference at eye level), of which

34 trees are knotty or crooked, of which

34 trees, standing dead, were cleared away (removed from the register on 1765/4/14)

7 trees, standing dead, were cleared away (removed from the register on 1763/2/24)

C. Pine trees

 24 trees (stem: 2–3 *ken* long; 1 *shaku* 3 *sun* to 2 *shaku* 5 *sun* circumference at eye level), of which

  18 trees were delivered last year for the construction of an enclosed, unhulled-rice warehouse at this office (removed from the register on 1764/9/4)

[section omitted]

D. Other trees

 86 trees (saplings and seedlings), of which

  24 are being culled, being small or troublesome to measure

[The record continues, reporting in similar fashion on another parcel 3 *chō* in size with 299 trees, of which 245 were knotty or crooked. Pine of 8 *sun* to 1 *shaku* 8 *sun* circumference number 230, and 210 of these were knotty or crooked. Of those, 35 were standing dead and were removed, and 58 were taken out for the warehouse construction. Also, there were 25 trees too small to measure.][45]

The register entry reveals that this accessible parcel of woodland (seven hundred yards to the Mugi river streamside) in the foothills north of Gifu was severely understocked and contained few good trees (no living trees over fifteen inches diameter at breast height [dbh] and fewer than 400 of three to fourteen inches dbh on $7\frac{1}{2}$ acres of land).[46] Apart from unreported underbrush, which probably was the site's major cover, it consisted essentially of "pine," meaning *akamatsu*, or Japanese red pine.[47] Since *akamatsu* commonly takes over deteriorated, infertile sites, the location and stand composition suggest that Miwayama was a naturally restocked area that had been subjected to much previous exploitation. The sparse pine growth had yielded its characteristic stand of wolf trees, knotty and crooked, with most of the older specimens (41 of the 56 trees greater than six inches dbh) dead on the stump. The other, slightly smaller parcel had only 299 trees, mostly crooked and knotty pine, and most under seven inches dbh. In both cases, the stand seemed capable of providing little timber beyond what the intendant required to maintain his own administrative establishment.

 The intendant accompanied his statistical report with a narrative in which he explained that the parcels had been assigned to a certain person for management (as *azukaridokoro*) in 1736. Subsequently, they had been reassigned to one intendancy in 1748 and shifted to another in 1753. He went on to say that some lumber and fuelwood from the area went to Edo and Osaka, but much had been plundered, and little timber of value was visible. He observed that periodically timber had to be taken out (for intendancy use, presumably) and such needs would continue. The number of trees being extremely small, he recommended planting trees and developing the two areas into fully stocked plantations. In closing, he noted that the parcels were on steep hillsides and could not be brought into cultivation.[48]

Bakufu forest registers reveal tremendous variation in the size of *ohayashi* parcels. In addition, they commonly reveal poor quality timber stands consisting mostly of pine and miscellaneous weed trees (*zōki*), with good conifers a decided rarity. In 1715 officials surveyed *ohayashi* in the eight Kinai provinces and identified 131 parcels ranging in area from 0.2 to 781.5 *chō* (0.5 acre to 1,915 acres). Tree counts were reported for thirteen areas that consisted of 32 parcels (table 1).[49]

TABLE 1.   *Ohayashi* Parcels in Eight Kinai Provinces, 1715

No. of Parcels	Area (in *chō*)	Tree Count		
		Matsu	*Zōki*	Other
2	—	27	20	
3	21.8	73	243	a
6	2.9	1,983	2,387	
1	1.2	—	—	b
3	81.8	10,092	—	
1	7.5	—	—	c
4	1.7	—	147	d
5	151.3	57,347	111	
1	0.4	382	3	
1	5.7	2,193	22	
1	6.0	4,005	26	
3	40.4	812	642	
1	84.0	400	—	

a 218 *sugi*, 263 *kuri*, 6 *tsuki*
b 724 *matsu*, *kuri*, and *enoki*
c 26,000 bamboo
d bamboo

The impoverished quality of Kinai woodland is not surprising, and not all *bakufu* woodland was that badly run down. But even in Shinano, where one might have expected richer stands, registers reveal a very light timber cover. A register of 1773 recorded the following figures on one large parcel of *ohayashi* near Karuizawa:

Area
   780 *chō* [1,911 acres]

Trees
   4,114, of which 573 are poor (crooked or knotty)

Breakdown
   78 conifers (4–6 *ken* stems; 6–7 *shaku* circumference), 12 of them poor
   293 conifers (1–1½ *ken* stems; 4–5 *shaku* circumference), 40 of them poor
   1,474 conifers (1–3 *ken* stems; 1–3 *shaku* circumference), 130 of them poor
   255 conifers (1–3 *ken* stems; 1–3 *shaku* circumference), to be harvested in 1778
   120 ridgeline conifers (2½–3 *ken* stems; 3–4 *shaku* circumference), 16 of them poor
   320 ridgeline conifers (2–4 *ken* stems; 7 *sun*–1 *shaku* circumference), 79 of them poor
   15 ridgeline conifers (2–4 *ken* stems; 7 *sun*–1 *shaku* circumference), to be harvested in 1778
   448 oak (*nara*) (2–4 *ken* stems; 3–5 *shaku* 5 *sun* circumference), 36 of them poor
   . . . .
   100 seedlings and small trees[50]

The 1,911 acres thus contained 66 good, large conifers of about two feet dbh or more, another 253 of some one to two feet dbh, approximately 1,600 under one foot dbh, about 450 good oak of one to two feet dbh and other less valued species of unspecified sizes. Some parts of the area doubtless constituted respectable natural forest, but an average of two good-sized trees per acre is hardly a lumberman's dream, or even an environmentalist's.

In 1754 the magistrate's office reviewed the registers submitted by intendants and concluded that *ohayashi* still supporting stands of good timber could be found on only one mountain in Musashi, one in Izu, two in Sagami, two in Tōtōmi, and six in Shinano province. The reviewer noted that one of the mountains in Tōtōmi and one in Shinano were in the process of being logged. He pointedly observed that the actual state of affairs was difficult to ascertain from the registers. And he recommended that the several appropriate authorities—*ohayashi bugyō*, *fushin yaku*, *daikan*, and their assistants— go and supervise tree counts and boundary surveys to assure their reliability.[51] On *bakufu* lands, at least, although a century of the negative regimen may have sustained a minimal level of forest stability and lumber production, it certainly had not re-created a verdant, timber-rich hinterland.

The condition of *bakufu* woodland during the eighteenth century can be glimpsed from two cases that also suggest why there was a negative regimen and what it achieved. The first is the one mountain in Izu that was deemed good forest in 1754. The second is *bakufu ohayashi* in Hida, which did not even appear on that year's list, although it had been excellent forest only a few decades earlier.

Bakufu ohayashi *in Izu*

The one mountain in Izu province reputed to have good woodland in 1754 was Mount Amagi, at 1,406 meters the highest peak on the peninsula.[52] The *ohayashi*, which initially covered 41,767 *chō* and later expanded to about 47,000 *chō* (approximately 115,000 acres), sprawled across Amagi and adjoining peaks amongst a patchwork of samurai fief lands. Because of its size and accessibility by sea, it was a major source of fuel, particularly charcoal, for the city of Edo, but its yield also was crucial to the people in villages surrounding the mountain.

Amagi had been subject to extensive felling from the Kamakura period onward, and during the sixteenth century, as noted in chapter 3, the Hōjō daimyo family established control over its production. By the time the Tokugawa took over Amagi, its forests were a well-used resource. Nevertheless, for most of the seventeenth century *bakufu* leaders scarcely intervened there, allowing villagers to extract fuel, fodder, fertilizer material, and scrap wood. The villagers used some fuel themselves, but they sold a great deal, charcoal in particular, to buyers from Edo. City-bound fuel left Izu via three ports where the purveyors paid the *bakufu* a 10 percent tax (*yamateyaku* or *yamayaku*) on their goods. Amagi thus provided the regime not only fuel for its capital city but a bit of income as well.

As long as sufficient timber came from other sources, Edo had little reason to restrict peasant utilization of Amagi's *ohayashi*.

The one protection measure that Edo applied to Amagi during the seventeenth century was *tomeki* policy. Initially, it had little relevance because Edo valued the mountain primarily for fuelwood production while the five species first designated *tomeki* on Amagi all were timber producers: *hinoki*, *matsu*, *sawara*, *sugi*, and *tsuki*. As timber grew scarce, however, Edo evidently assigned Amagi more value as a potential source of lumber, and restrictions became more inclusive: *kusunoki* was added to the list in 1656 and *kashi* in 1683. Two years later the *bakufu* announced that while large *tsuga* and *momi* could still be felled, smaller ones could not.[53] In 1757, by which time large *tsuga* and *momi* must have been rareties, all specimens of the two species were reserved.

This slender record of legislation suggests that *tomeki* policy alone was failing to raise Amagi's timber production to a satisfactory level. Indeed, of the species protected, only *kashi*, an evergreen oak, flourished, and it was not particularly sought by the rulers. Its success may simply reveal its capacity for taking over areas opened up by destruction of conifer growth. However, since *kashi*, unlike reserved conifers, was especially useful to villagers as a source of fertilizer, fuel, construction wood, and mast, its proliferation may indicate that *tomeki* policy succeeded best when it coincided with village priorities.

Villagers could enforce their priorities comparatively easily on Amagi because centuries of exploitation had converted much of the mountain to broadleaf coppice, which primarily yielded charcoal and green fertilizer. Once that forest condition was attained, it became self-perpetuating: while cutting coppice growth for charring and home use, woodsmen could easily destroy any *tomeki* seedlings they encountered, thereby keeping the area free of unwelcome growth.

Doubtless, the ineffectiveness of *tomeki* policy deprived Edo of potential lumber, but it surely helped sustain the city's fuel supply by leaving woodland in coppice. Even without significant conversion of land to conifer stands, however, by the late seventeenth century demand for fuel and other coppice production was exceeding Amagi's output, and competition among villagers was generating disputes. Late in 1685 woodsmen (*soma*) and officials of three villages near Yugashima petitioned to have more trees protected against felling, evidently hoping to obtain a government order prohibiting the residents of other villages from using nearby woodland. Their petition was unsuccessful, however, and cutting and quarreling continued.

Before century's end the *bakufu* concluded it must do more to control exploitation on Amagi and resolve village disputes. In 1698 it moved beyond *tomeki* policy by ordering the 54 villages abutting the *ohayashi* to select from among their members four forest overseers (*ohayashi mamori*) to patrol the woodland. The four were also to supervise barrier points on principal streams draining the mountain, maintaining at those points signboards that displayed Amagi's forest regulations. The order promptly elicited objections from people of other villages because it prevented them from harvesting undergrowth, which many had customarily done. During subsequent decades they repeatedly initiated lawsuits, and Edo gradually modified its policy, primarily by incorporating more and more village woodland into the *ohayashi*, which eventually allowed people from 120 villages to utilize the expanded area.

Overseers continued to be appointed despite the disputes. The appointees generally were village officials who took the work as a supplemental duty. In return, they were each permitted to wear a sword and use their family name in public (*myōji taitō*). They received small stipends that totaled fourteen *koku* per year for the group of four. Their duties were sufficiently onerous, however, that by 1759 the number of overseers had grown to seven and their wages were garnished to defray travel expenses. During the nineteenth century, as afforestation and harvesting intensified, their duties and pay expanded further.

The overseers alternated at fifteen day intervals. During a man's tour of duty he hiked through a portion of the forest to check boundary markers; watch for evidence of theft or damage; inspect felling, charring, brush-cutting, and other forest production; and stamp legally produced goods. He also supervised the replacement of rotten boundary markers and attempted to settle disputes. At his office he kept records of output and prepared reports for the intendant. After tree planting began on Amagi in the late eighteenth century, he also supervised that.

Prevention of wildfire was a major concern of overseers because the coppice that covered Amagi was highly flammable, and a bad burn could prove as ruinous to the villages below as to the woodland itself. The overseers had to report all fires, appending a count of the trees lost. Every autumn corvée laborers from adjoining villages carefully burned the summer's growth in firebreaks surrounding the parcels of *ohayashi*, and they removed all brush from adjacent strips thirty feet wide. Regulations called for special care in patrolling forests during the dry months of winter and spring, and anyone caught burning fields then was to be severely punished. Not only intentional burning was punished: if negligence allowed fire from a village to penetrate *ohayashi*, both village officials and the overseer were subject to reprimand or worse.[54]

By the mid-eighteenth century, when Edo could find only six *ohayashi* that qualified as good forests, it was ready to try new measures on Mount Amagi. In 1757, as noted above, all specimens of *tsuga* and *momi* were reserved. Five years later Edo designated its Amagi woodland *tomeyama*. That radical move threatened to deprive nearby villagers of essential goods, and they protested with sufficient energy to get the order rescinded. Four years later, as a feeble substitute, the *bakufu* applied *tomeki* restrictions even to those specimens of the nine reserved trees that were windthrown or dead on the stump.[55]

These mid-century attempts to legislate improvement in Amagi's timber stock had little if any impact on stand composition. Nevertheless, the coppice growth was unable to generate charcoal enough to satisfy demand. In 1798 the *bakufu*, which hitherto had allowed charcoal makers to consume only small coppice growth, authorized the charring of larger trees, including several non-*tomeki* trees and even *kashi* up to one *shaku* five *sun* in circumference (approximately six inches dbh). In 1807, apparently in hopes of increasing charcoal production, Edo raised its size limit again, allowing the charring of trees up to two *shaku* five *sun* in circumference (approximately nine inches dbh).

As forest produce became scarcer and dearer, competition for it intensified. Overseers found themselves subject to bribery attempts, which some doubtless failed to resist with all possible vigor. To prevent abuse among the overseers, the *bakufu* despatched inspectors from both the intendancy and Edo to enforce regulations and investigate irregularities.

The forest magistrate in Edo delegated direct authority over Amagi to the intendant stationed at Mishima (later at Nirayama). The magistrate's office retained the authority, however, to specify when the intendancy was to make forest inspections, when and how it was to prepare and update registers, and what matters it was to report. Further restricting the intendant was a requirement that he obtain approval from the finance office before letting contracts for charring or felling. And the construction agency in Edo (*fushin bugyōsho*) had to approve any trees selected for government timber (*goyōki*). Finally, when afforestation was undertaken in later decades, inspectors from Edo traveled to Izu to oversee all new projects.

An overseer thus found himself under the surveillance of an intendant who, in turn, was subject to scrutiny from a number of higher officials. At the same time, the overseer had to deal with fellow villagers and the residents of other villages, most of whom claimed one or another customary right to *ohayashi* usufruct. For many of these people, life was precarious and forest yield a precious boon. The overseer's task was to reconcile as best he could the conflicts of interest among officials above and villagers below that swirled around the finite resources of Amagi. In theory, he did so by enforcing forest regulations; in practice, it appears, he did so by a politically attuned blend of enforcement and accommodation that sometimes got him into trouble.

The forest law that overseers were supposed to enforce was designed to preserve woodland growth not because its preservation was deemed a good thing in itself but because it yielded products valued by consumers, whether rulers or villagers. The instrumental character of regulations, and the conditional way in which overseers applied them, was evident in an incident of 1857. By then the Amagi *ohayashi* had experienced several decades of sporadic afforestation, mostly achieved by punitive or "gratitude" (*myōga*) plantings, and scattered stands of plantation conifers were developing.[56] In an incident that appears to have affected one such area, two overseers, both respected leaders in their villages, were charged with having allowed the illegal harvesting of 797 trees during the preceding autumn. For that crime they were jailed.

An investigation revealed that in the autumn of 1856, a typhoon had damaged many *tomeki*, including 467 *hinoki*, 122 *sugi*, 188 *matsu*, and a few *momi* and *tsuki*, totaling an estimated 632 *shakujime* (approximately 7,450 cubic feet) of stumpage. The overseers informed the investigators that after examining the area they had permitted the timber's harvesting. They had found some local people already cutting out windthrown trees for sale, and because the downed trees had no value as timber, they had allowed them to continue, requiring only that part of the proceeds be used to start a new planting in the affected area. The storm left other trees standing dead or damaged, and because these too lacked timber value, the overseers allowed them to be fed into charcoal kilns, charging a fee to pay for replacement planting. Insofar as the overseers' report was correct, the policies taken seem reasoned and appropriate. However, no harvesting had been authorized, the procedure adopted by the overseers had yielded the *bakufu* no tax income, and from long experience with forest disputes, Edo had ample reason to suspect bribery and misrepresentation. So the investigators jailed the two overseers and the seven villagers most directly involved. They punished fourteen other village officials, the five other overseers, and seven other villagers with varying grades of fines, house arrest, and formal censure. Had forest resources been sufficient, the incident probably would not have occurred.

On Amagi, then, Edo introduced and elaborated forest regulations in a long, drawn-out attempt to manipulate stand composition and expand timber and charcoal production for government use. Villagers countered to protect their own interests and successfully limited the scope of *bakufu* policy. All the maneuvering notwithstanding, however, it appears that the regulatory regimen had little effect in either shaping or expanding Amagi's output.

Bakufu ohayashi *in Hida*

Being near the coast and comparatively accessible, Mount Amagi was already well cut over when Tokugawa leaders inherited it. The woodland of Hida, by contrast, may well have been the best in Japan when the regime seized it in 1692, a century after it acquired Amagi.[57] Encompassing 415 villages in 1805, the Hida domain sprawled across two watersheds, the northern one draining via the Jinzū and Shō rivers into the Sea of Japan at Toyama bay and that to the south emptying via the Hida and Nagara rivers into the Pacific Ocean at Ise bay.

During the seventeenth century, as noted in chapter 3, the Hida uplands were held in fief by the Kanamori family headquartered at Takayama. Kanamori derived some income from logging the accessible south slope and appreciably less from the north slope, whose lower reaches mostly supplied timber to castle towns facing the Sea of Japan. From the 1660s, as *bakufu* leaders encountered worsening timber scarcity, they began eyeing Hida, but not until 1692 did they find opportunity to transfer Kanamori elsewhere and place the area under direct shogunal jurisdiction. When the intendant occupied Takayama, he inherited a substantial collection of timber that Kanamori had felled but not yet used or sent to market. He also inherited much of Kanamori's governing apparatus, retaining eighty-four of his vassals as district officials, forest supervisors, and timber inspectors.

When the *bakufu* seized Hida, it took nominal control of all forested areas claimed by Kanamori, leaving other woodland under village control as in the past.[58] Three years later, however, the intendant consolidated his control by closing all Hida woodland to "unauthorized" logging. That appears to have meant local logging operations in which villagers sold their yield, as in Kanamori's day, to lumber merchants from towns such as Takayama, Gifu, and Nagoya.

With resources assured, Edo lumbermen soon arrived to take over the timber marketing. They concentrated on the south slope because it only cost eight *ryō* to ship one hundred *koku* of timber to Edo via Ise bay, whereas it cost twenty-five *ryō* from the north slope via the Sea of Japan. Even for shipping to Osaka, the difference in cost, and hence in profit margin, was dramatic. Consequently, felling on the south slope progressed rapidly, and by 1702, of Hida's 499 surveyed woodland areas 40 had been logged and closed to use (*tomeyama*), 22 were in the process of being cut off, and 155 were set aside for future government use. Two years later local woodsmen, perhaps finding their livelihoods jeopardized by the encroachment of government lumbermen, protested the usurpation of their customary right to market wood. The *bakufu* resolved the immediate conflict by assigning the disputants fixed market quantities, but that solution failed to address the underlying issue of long-term depletion.

The rate of logging remained excessive, and by 1724 it had so denuded the south slope that the intendent launched a careful three-year survey of all Hida woodland, both north and south, to determine its physical condition and current use arrangements. The survey brought under government supervision many upland areas that villagers had previously used for slash-and-burn cultivation and other purposes, and as the survey proceeded, much resistance developed. Nevertheless, whereas the 1702 survey listed only 499 sites, the new survey, when completed in 1727, identified 4,625 parcels of woodland in terms of their vegetation. The survey recorded 605 as containing valuable timber trees (such as *tsuga, todomatsu,* and *kurobi*). Another 469 were registered as *zōki* forest, 881 as areas of small trees, and 2,670 as brush- and grassland. About 1,000 of the parcels, including the 605 well-timbered areas, were designated *tomeyama* and closed to entry as *otomebayashi* or *zōki ohayashi*.

A year earlier, while the survey was still in progress, the intendant had imposed a three-year ban on logging on the south slope. The ban threatened to deprive local people of work, however, so the following year the *bakufu* responded to their complaints by establishing a "workfare" program. Residents were paid rice and money valued at 7,500 *ryō* per year in return for providing specified quantities of government wood (*goyōki*). In 1735, as the intendant tightened control over logging and land use on the north slope, he applied the same kind of program there at the rate of 1,590 *ryō* per year. On both the north and south slopes, as upland villagers worked deteriorating woodland, the policy became permanent, with payments amounting to some 10,000 *ryō* per year later in the century.

During the 1770s and 1790s the *bakufu* twice tried to stop all felling, but both times it encountered local protests and returned to the workfare program with its regulated harvest. The policy may well have coped with the social consequences of resource depletion, but it must have generated a very expensive timber yield, and in the end it failed to restore forest verdure. By 1797 Hida was producing little more than pole timber, thin boards, and small roofing shingles. These, moreover, were not primarily *hinoki* or *sugi*, but mixed species, mostly *kurobi, hiba, tsuga, momi, kuri,* and *himekomatsu*.[59]

The surviving *hinoki* was not to be cut at all except by special order. In short, loggers had decimated even the good forests of Hida within a few decades, and *bakufu* policies of restriction had failed to restore satisfactory timber stands.

Recapitulation

The widespread deforestation of the early modern predation ended once and for all that long era during which the people of Japan managed their woodland loosely and exploited it freely. In the transformation that rulers and villagers achieved by the mid-eighteenth century, forests were carefully delineated and use rights clarified. The rule makers specified forms and limits of exploitation in great detail. And they enforced them—to dubious effect—by elaborate administrative arrangements, legal sanctions, and ethical imperatives that were firmly linked to the interests of the enforcers, whether local or national. The resulting negative regimen reached from mountain to mansion, touching the production, transportation, and consumption of a vast array of forest products.

Tokoro Mitsuo pinpoints the Kanbun era (1661–72) as the critical period when scattered admonitions and measures of forest protection and control evolved into a nationwide attempt to control forest usage, and he considers *han* financial difficulty the basic factor forcing a policy shift.[60] The immediately precipitating event seems to have been the Meireki fire of 1657, which ravaged Edo. The city's reconstruction exposed the extent of timber scarcity throughout the islands even as it imposed huge expenses on the *bakufu* and most daimyo governments.[61] Had the forests of Japan in the 1660s still held rich stands of timber, they could have been harvested to *han* advantage without major policy changes, as they had been a half century earlier. It was because timber had become scarce and because governments were competing with villagers and merchants for a more costly harvest that the rulers used their political power to establish fuller control over woodland and its yield.

At first, government policy focused on protection forests because of the seventeenth-century surge in land clearance. Ecological damage caused by intensive logging and opening of fragile areas led to prohibitions and limitations on the use of many small sites, particularly along rivers and streams. During the early eighteenth century, land opening fell off sharply, but not because of government protection policy. Quite the contrary, in hopes of enhancing tax income, many governments continued to promote reclamation of even severely marginal areas. Nevertheless, reclamation work slackened, primarily because the remaining untilled land was too steep or swampy for use, given the technology available to tillers, and because the acreage already under cultivation had expanded so much that it more than balanced the area of "wasteland" whose natural vegetation was available to fertilize the arable. Under these conditions tillers lost the incentive to open more land, which reduced the need for governments to promote protection forestry.

By then, moreover, shortages in forest yields were generating widespread interest in preserving production woodland. At the village level attention centered on fertilizer material, fuelwood, and fodder, and a plethora of local regulations developed to govern their extraction from household woodland, *iriaichi*, and nearby *ohayashi*. At the government level concern that focused on timber and fuel supplies led to the creation of bureaucratic organs and mechanisms of forest regulation. These organs and mechanisms became the core elements in Japan's early modern system of government forest management.

Assessing the effectiveness of the negative regimen is difficult. Clearly, it failed to restore woodland to earlier levels of timber production. Insofar as a revival of forest output occurred, it did so late in the Edo period, as we note in subsequent chapters, and it did so as a result of afforestation efforts that were not an essential part of this regulatory regime. Indeed, the negative regimen did not even succeed in maintaining output at a level adequate to ongoing demand, and instead society labored under continual stress produced by competition for timber, fuel, fertilizer material, and fodder.

Had there been no system of forest regulation, however, early modern Japan might have found no peaceable way to resolve the struggle over scarce goods. Without regulation, moreover, such ecological protective measures as were applied might not have been possible. That situation could have made erosion problems worse, converting that much more upland to *hageyama*, or "bald mountains," the ultimate state of biological degradation toward which the overexploitation of woodland seemed to be propelling the archipelago during the decades of the early modern predation. The negative regimen may have been, then, an essential piece of a larger policy of forest rehabilitation necessitated by the environmental effects of human behavior in early modern Japan. It "bought time," so to say, enabling the Japanese to devise other, ultimately more effective, pieces of that larger policy, most notably techniques of plantation silviculture.

Chapter Five

Silviculture:
Its Principles and Practice

The timber scarcity that emerged in seventeenth-century Japan gave rise to a negative regimen whose primary function was to keep forests producing wood for the ruling elite's cities, monuments, and treasuries. Difficulties in provisioning persisted, however, which fostered silviculture: the purposeful growing of trees through application of arboreal knowledge and insight.

The Intellectual Context of Silviculture

Most early modern silvicultural writing was imbedded in a broader agronomic literature because the shortfall in woodland output was only one aspect of a more basic problem. Tokugawa society was encountering irregular but intensifying scarcity in most types of biosystem yield, including food. Consequently, the search for ways to increase forest output occurred together with a quest for solutions to other insufficiencies of rural production. The overall problem was addressed in a wide-ranging literature known as *jikatasho* or *nōsho*, "agricultural treatises" or "farm manuals," written by itinerant scholars, village headmen, practicing farmers, minor officials, and others.[1]

Generally, the manuals attempted to be comprehensive in their treatment of rural affairs. The more elaborate ones assumed that habits of work and thought, human relationships, and patterns of village organization, as well as technology, agricultural practices, and environmental context, all influenced the process of production and hence the attainment of general well-being. In their comprehensiveness and their view that production was influenced by all pertinent factors, the writings were, at least in a primitive sense, ecological in character. More precisely, because their ultimate concern was the well-being of the human community rather than the entire ecosystem, one can describe them as homocentric autecological works. The authors directed some attention to woodland because they clearly saw its use as integral to rural life and production, which they viewed, in turn, as fundamental to the vitality of society as a whole.

During the seventeenth century, well before these farm manuals appeared, a number of political leaders and official advisers advocated tree planting and the maintenance of forest stability and productivity.[2] Around 1650, for example, Matsudaira Sadatsuna, daimyo of Kuwana domain, urged woodsmen to "plant a thousand seedlings for every tree" they cut. A decade later Yamaga Sokō, a political commentator and adviser, admonished woodsmen to log only in the proper season, not to overcut, and to replant harvested areas. In the early eighteenth century advice became more precise, with Kaibara Atsunobu, adviser to a minor daimyo, recommending in 1709 that if woodsmen "divide mountain forests into several tens of sections and cut off one section per year, the whole forest will flourish and lumber increase."

Such official advocacy of rotation cutting, as well as the promotion of other silvicultural principles, reflected the appearance of these ideas in agricultural treatises. Thus, in 1668 the author of *Jikata kikigaki*, one of the earliest manuals, wrote how to produce pine firewood:

Plant an area two *chō* square [approximately five acres] each year for ten years. During the eleventh year clear-cut the area planted the first year and set out pine seedlings in the clearing. [Repeating that practice annually], firewood will never disappear. If you plant seedlings at three-foot intervals, you will grow 57,600 trees per two *chō*. In thirteen years they will yield 3 to 4 bundles of faggots per tree, for an annual yield of 170,000 bundles.[3]

Although the advice was not without flaw, it was indicative of the practical attention to detail and performance that informed *jikatasho* in general.

The major seminal work in the genre was Miyazaki Antei's *Nōgyō zensho*, completed in 1697.[4] Cognizant of the importance of woodlots in rural life, Antei devoted the last two of his ten fascicles to trees and forests and touched on them at several other places.[5] Kanō Kyōji finds four basic themes present in Antei's discussion of woodland:

1. Forests are valuable for both farmers and the realm: they should be nurtured in the manner of field crops, with valuable trees being planted and useless ones controlled. Trees planted in forests are of value for construction, fuel, and food and thus contribute to warmer houses and better health. When planted around one's homestead, they reduce winter wind, discourage burglars, prevent extramural fires from reaching buildings, yield firewood and fertilizer materials, and through thinning provide useful lumber.

2. Sound forestry requires planning: for best results both planting and harvesting should be undertaken at proper season.

3. Optimal forest planting is related to properties of the soil: if soil quality is not maintained, trees will not flourish no matter how hard one works.

4. The value of forests is relative to the value of other upland exploitation: for example, because birds consume seed sown and produced in upland fields, such fields are of little use to farmers, so the land is better employed in growing the "four trees," that is, mulberry, paper mulberry, lacquer, and tea.

In these themes and in numerous particulars Antei foreshadowed many later *jikatasho*, in part because writers familiar with his work borrowed from it directly and in part because his advice gave shape and direction to so much of the discourse on silvicultural matters that it became incorporated in farm manuals unwittingly. In particular, although Antei wrote at length about the attributes of various trees, he identified *sugi* and *hinoki* as best for timber and *sugi* as the species of greatest consequence. He characterized it as growing rapidly and easily, being strong, thriving in dense stands, reaching great height, and living long. Moreover, *sugi* timber was not heavy, which made it easy to transport, and the wood was easy to work. Finally, it was versatile, being excellent for such diverse products as boats, bridges, buckets, coffins, and wooden walls. Accordingly, he urged its propagation by both slip and seedling wherever possible, such as around buildings and in the mountains.[6]

During the eighteenth century silvicultural writing proliferated, and in the nineteenth the encyclopedic scholar Satō Shin'en organized much of the existing corpus into eight agronomic works that he produced between 1809 and 1844.[7] Satō is best known outside Japan for his provocative essays on politics and the state, but he was basically a student of agricultural economics whose major concern was increasing production to meet the needs of society. In 1827 he wrote that the principle of *kaibutsu*, which he considered of central importance, "means to survey the realm carefully; consider well the climate; evaluate the qualities of soil; develop mountain valleys, ponds, and swamps; open plains and moors to cultivation; produce various goods; and enhance the excellence of their quality."[8] Satō's silvicultural writings were thus part of a broader treatment of rural production. In them he discussed the relative advantages of different species; the particular virtues of *sugi* and *hinoki*; the merits, mechanics, and economics of nursery work; the techniques of both seedling and slip cultures; aftercare practices; the various uses of wood; the causes of wood scarcity; methods of increasing fuelwood output; and the economics of charcoal and firewood production.[9]

Miyazaki Antei and Satō Shin'en are two of the most well-known authors of silvicultural treatises, but their works represent only a small portion of a vast outpouring of commentary and advice. The essential content of that corpus can be indicated most concisely by examining it as a whole and identifying the most widely accepted themes and specifics. Because the Tokugawa era spanned two and a half centuries and because the 250-odd baronial units of the state sustained a great deal of regional diversity, the silvicultural literature contained in its specifics many variations—and even contradictions. Consequently, while a concise summary may properly be seen as normative, it is far from being a complete statement of early modern views on any facet of the forester's art.

Major Topics in the Silvicultural Literature

Both gymnosperms and angiosperms commonly reproduce by seed, and seedling culture was a major topic in Tokugawa silvicultural writing. Trees also can propagate without seeds, however, because many species clone, reproducing the whole from a part by sending out roots from living branches and stems, or stems and branches from living roots and stumps. Some broadleafs, such as beech and oak, easily start new growth from stumps and even roots, and these species provided much fuelwood and charcoal. Woodsmen exploited this arboreal talent for vegetative reproduction by coppicing: harvesting stands and then nurturing the new sprout growth. In the Yamaguni district north of Kyoto producers of timber similarly coppiced *sugi* plantations because new growth developed more rapidly from stumps than seed and because this form of site management disturbed the sharply mountainous surface less than seedling culture.[10]

In their writings silviculturists gave some attention to coppicing, but the technique of vegetative reproduction they discussed most extensively was the use of cuttings (or slips), which are sections of needle-bearing stems that are induced to put out roots. Planters might start slips by layering, that is, by keeping a strip of a low-hanging tree branch in stationary contact with moist soil for several months until it rooted, later severing the rooted piece from its parent tree and replanting it in the desired location. Layering was not useful for large-scale propagation, however, and only a few records discuss it. Much more common was the direct use of cuttings: clipping off tips of branches and inserting them butt-first in moist soil, where, if all went well, they would root without further assistance. Slip culture was a widely usable technique, and silviculturists discussed it at length.

All these forms of tree culture required aftercare to assure that the young growth not only survived but developed into valuable stands, and writers addressed the topic in some detail. Accordingly, the major concerns of the silvicultural literature, as well as other official and unofficial guidelines on forestry, can be examined in terms of three topics: seedling culture, slip culture, and aftercare.[11]

Seedling Culture

Propagating from seed included both cultivating naturally seeded growth (with or without transplanting) and nurturing and transplanting of seedlings sprouted in specially prepared beds.[12] The first step in seedbed culture was selecting the seed. Silviculturists discussed the relative merits of mother trees, old versus young, well-shaped versus ill-formed, in the process revealing the conviction that in some way the quality of the parent shaped that of the offspring. They carefully instructed the cultivator on how to gather seed, dry it, extract it from the cone or husk, store it, and prepare it for spreading on the seedbed.

Even more extensive advice guided the cultivator in preparing his bed. The site was important: proximity to the area to be forested, proper sunlight, adequate moisture, and a friable, fertile soil were all desirable. The seedbed area was to consist of as many rectangular beds 3 feet wide by 30 to 100 feet long as the project required. The beds were to be laid beside one another with some 2 feet of work space between. Starting in the fall, workmen were to lay them out, spade them, and clean out all roots. They were to fertilize them well, thoroughly working the fertilizer into the soil. Later in the winter they should apply additional fertilizer—night soil, manure, or urine preferably—and carefully pulverize the soil. In early spring they should thoroughly stir the bed again, remove debris, and smooth the surface to receive seed.

To improve sprouting, writers advised the planter to soak his seed, especially that of *sugi, hinoki*, and *matsu*, for a few days prior to sowing. Then, with the seed softened and the bed properly smoothed, he was ready to begin. He planted large seeds, such as oak or chestnut, three to four inches apart and small seeds, such as those of conifers, either broadcast or in rows. He might then settle the seed by sprinkling it with a bamboo watering can before covering it with a fine layer of soil.

Writers also told the cultivator how to protect the seed against sun, rain, and wind by spreading straw (or other suitable material) over the seedbed and holding it in place with thin bamboo poles. He was to water, weed, and fertilize his bed carefully, and ideally the seed would sprout in ten to twelve days. He should then remove the straw cover and erect a sunshade to protect the new sprouts. During the summer, he must keep his seedbed moist and in the autumn convert the sunshade into a frost covering (or a snow screen in snowy areas). The frost covering was to prevent winter winds from freezing the seedlings and reduce frost heaving that could kill them by lifting and drying out their roots. In all these matters writers offered careful guidance on how to execute the task at hand.

When spring came, the cultivator carefully removed the frost cover, sprinkled soil on any areas that had heaved, tamped it down lightly, and sprinkled it with water to resettle the roots. Writers advised him to thin his bed and remove broken and misshapen seedlings at that time. He should transplant excess healthy ones to another bed, taking care to keep their roots intact. Then he was to reerect the sunshade and tend to the summer watering, weeding, and fertilizing. Authors recommended various strategies to discourage pests such as moles, rabbits, and insects.

To assure his seedlings sufficient growing space, at some point during the next year or two the cultivator had to transplant them again, carefully protecting their roots. The seedlings would be ready for permanent relocating three or four years after their initial sprouting. Their size at that time varied by species, of course, and also with the particulars of the bed, but authors regarded a stem length of one to three feet as normal.

The silviculture literature then proceeded to describe with equal care the optimal season for transplanting, procedures for digging up and preparing seedlings for shipment to the forest, techniques of trimming roots, methods of heeling in for temporary storage, and procedures for preparing areas to be planted and for digging holes to receive the seedlings. Writers gave much attention to selecting sites for reforestation, with weather, soil, topography, exposure to sun and wind, and accessibility to markets or users all being considered. They described *sugi* as very sensitive to wind and recommended it for sheltered sites and suggested pine and various hardwoods for exposed locations.

Writers usually advised planting the seedlings in rows or grids but varied substantially their recommendations on spacing. Some advocated dense planting and subsequent thinning; others, sparse planting and less thinning. Their advice reflected geographical, biological, and economic considerations, such as the need for replacement trees or the availability of a market for the thinnings. Often writers called for three to four seedlings per *tsubo* (approximately thirty-six square feet), but a few recommended up to ten or so per *tsubo*.

The scale of planting varied greatly; some projects yielded only several hundred seedlings, and others produced tens or hundreds of thousands. Writers were keenly aware of the factors affecting seedling survival rates and gave much attention to assuring the highest rate. They made various estimates of how much seed would ultimately cover how much acreage and stressed that careful preparation and handling were crucial to success.

Slip Culture

Seedling culture came to be practiced throughout Japan; slip culture, less widely. Whereas growers used seed to propagate many species, they employed cuttings primarily for *sugi*. In the silvicultural literature much of the advice that pertained to seedlings—regarding seedbed preparation, after-sowing procedures, field site selection, and transplanting techniques—also applied to slips. In addition, authors dwelt on the choice of the mother tree, timing of the work, and methods of slip preparation and insertion.[13]

Generally, authors recommended that slips be taken from young trees or from trees producing few or no seeds. Winter, before new growth started, was the preferred time, but a few authors advised performing the task in spring, even into the rainy season. Authors agreed that cuttings must be prepared carefully. They commonly recommended slips ten to twenty inches long, shorter ones for placement in beds, longer ones for the wild. Each slip was to consist of the head, which included the prior year's growth and a few two-year-old lateral shoots, and enough stem below the head to include two or three more lateral twigs. The workman was to remove any lower twigs, leaving for insertion in the soil a clear stem measuring four inches to about a foot, depending on the site conditions. It was especially important to cut slips cleanly and not tear any bark loose, and writers generally recommended cutting them at an angle, in a "horse's ear" or "horse's hoof" shape. After the workman prepared his slips, he had to keep them moist until placed and, if possible, soak them before insertion.

Whether the planter rooted his slips in a bed (*tokozashi*) or set them out directly at the growing site (*jikizashi*), writers firmly advised him not to injure them in the process. To avoid injury, they recommended that he thrust a stick (*suai*) into the soil to the proper depth (six inches or so in a bed; six to twenty inches for field planting) and carefully slide the cutting into the resulting hole. Then he must firmly pack the soil about the stem to assure complete slip-soil contact. A number of sources recommended balling the slip (*tamazashi*): packing a ball of heavy soil or clay about the cutting and then placing the ball in the ground. Particularly on hillsides with poor, rocky soil that technique reduced injury and assured slips an immediate environment of desirable soil. Writers dwelt at some length but with little consistency on the preferred type of soil, the variations in advice reflecting the diversity of soil materials in Japan. For example, authors might recommend "red" or "black" soil that was moist but not sticky or "yellow" soil well mixed with sand.

In the beds workers were to set the cuttings one to four inches apart, the advice varying with the author; in the field advice commonly called for three-foot intervals. After the workman had set cuttings in a bed, he was to give them the same careful treatment as seedlings. Once they rooted, they were, for all practical purposes, regarded as seedlings. Authors advised the planter to assure that slips placed in the wild received both sufficient shade and adequate exposure to sunlight. One foresighted writer recommended inserting three field cuttings where two were to stay permanently, thereby providing handy transplants a year or two later when it was clear which slips had withered.

Plantation Aftercare

Silviculturists were well aware that much work stood between the initial creation of a timber plantation and its eventual harvesting a half century later. Mikami Gennosuke, a forester from Tsugaru *han*, noted:

The art of forestry is different from that of paddy or dry field. Though one may be spared flood, drought, frost, or snow, he still must give general care to the area for about ten years before withdrawing human effort. If this is done, the forest will be as though filled with a treasure whose virtue is so immense it will reach to one's children and grandchildren. Truly, one's prosperity will be eternal.[14]

Aftercare (*teiri*, or literally, "putting one's hand in") was identified by a wonderfully rich terminology. The richness notwithstanding, it may be examined in terms of three main aspects: replacement planting to establish a fully stocked stand; protection against competing vegetation; and nurturing to develop high-grade stock.[15]

All silvicultural writers considered replacement planting essential because of seedling losses caused by climatic stress or human error. They might recommend annual replacement work for up to four years or so. Thus in *bakufu ohayashi* in Hida, where heavy snowfall was customary, guidelines of the eighteenth and nineteenth centuries instructed growers to inspect new plantations in the spring following their establishment. They were to replace—very carefully, it was stressed—all bent, broken, or withered stems. And they were to keep records of their work and file reports on stand conditions. In succeeding years as well, failed seedlings were to be replaced and the results of spring inspections reported. Where woodsmen used cuttings extensively, instructions similarly called for replacement work. In Kumamoto they specified that seedlings rather than cuttings should be utilized, perhaps to minimize lost growing time. On naturally seeded plantation sites also, seedlings were sometimes set out to fill gaps in the stand.

Once the stand was established and on its way, writers pointed out, growers must protect seedlings from competing growth that could shade, break, or strangle them to death. Grasses, annual weeds, brush, and vines all threatened to overrun new sprouts, and writers firmly advised woodsmen to weed annually, some even calling for two or three weedings per year for the first five years or so and less frequent ones thereafter. Authors often identified fall and spring as the best times for that task.

After a few years plantation stock could usually suppress or outgrow grasses and flowering annuals. But vines and fast-growing weed trees remained a problem. Especially in the late Edo period, when plantation culture was most widely practiced, writers warned against the danger of creepers and undesirable trees. Viney growth, particularly *fuji* (wisteria), *tsuzura fuji* (arrowroot), or *tsuta* (Japanese ivy), was singled out as especially bothersome. Writing in 1849, Okino Takao of Kurobane *han* advised growers to promote *sugi* and *hinoki* by cutting back any underbrush in the late spring after leaves were out. He instructed them to girdle unwanted large trees twice to assure that they died. Their roots would decay, branches rot and fall, and trunks gradually collapse, after which the area would become open to planted growth. Suckers might start, but they would pose no serious problem. Chestnut, however, had to be cut down and the roots dug out because large limbs and roots were slow to decay and the hulks would be enduring nuisances in the plantation.

Replacement planting and the suppression of competing growth gave the grower a promising young stand. To transform such a stand into a mature plantation of top quality—meaning one containing the largest possible volume of the highest-grade timber—required other measures. Silviculturists discussed two of them, thinning and limbing, at length.

Writers recognized that optimizing space allotments was crucial to maximum stem development: too much space produced wolf trees; too little, spindly growth. Thinning, which they identified by many terms, was widely recommended. The recommendations on the spacing between trees and the timing of the work varied from commentator to commentator, but almost everyone agreed on the need to thin. Thus, a village in Musashi province, which started a pine plantation during the 1790s, drew up guidelines stating that when the pine were five years old, workmen were to examine them, remove poor ones, and thin healthy ones to give each remaining tree about 36 square feet of space. When the plantation was ten years old, with the pine about twenty feet tall, workers should thin a second time to allow the trees about 70 square feet, and subsequently, when appropriate, thin again to about 100 square feet.

A century earlier Miyazaki Antei had advised that *sugi* should grow densely until they reached "small pillar" size (probably about three to four inches dbh) and then be thinned to intervals of three to four feet. Especially in richly soiled coastal valleys and where transportation was convenient, planting should be dense, he argued, to yield valuable poles at thinning time. Later writers embraced much of Antei's opinion, although they varied in some details.

Thinning was a vexatious matter, influenced, as in Antei's advice, by both biological and economic considerations. Dense planting minimized replacement work and produced faster stem growth, which yielded poles for thinning, all of which was profitable. But, writers also recognized the dangers in overcrowding. In 1712 a commentator in Tsugaru warned that densely planted pine would not produce sturdy logs and consequently that stands must be properly thinned. A *bakufu* notice of the 1740s warned villagers in the Kantō region that by the time conifers measured eighteen inches in circumference at eye level their branches would be badly entangled, fresh air would not circulate, and dry rot might set in. Accordingly, they should clear out dead and dying branches and misshapen trees. Where a stand was too thick, they should thin it, but thinning should be done in two stages because surviving trees would be vulnerable to windthrow if too many were removed at once. In 1725, by way of contrast, another writer advised against thinning pine, arguing that it increased wind damage. If thinning was not done, he argued, weak trees would die and rot naturally, leaving the strongest to flourish, which was desirable. Whatever its merits, his view did not prevail.

The sale value of poles sometimes was the decisive consideration in thinning policy. On occasion hard-pressed plantation holders thinned for income rather than stand improvement, increasing the risk of wind damage to survivors and reducing the size and value of the final yield. Governments, wanting large-sized timber, tried to control this activity, and in the process they gradually formulated more precise rules on thinning. The rules varied greatly from place to place, but generally they specified the proper age for or the frequency of thinning and the proper interval between trees. In Kurobane *han*, Okino Takao recommended "the Yoshino method": plant *sugi* at three-foot intervals; remove every other stem when they attain two to three inches in butt diameter, and five years later remove every other tree again, selling the poles profitably. The remaining trees, growing at twelve-foot intervals, would then mature to produce high-grade board stock.

Whereas commentators regarded thinning as a key factor in stem size, they believed that limbing, or the trimming of branches, had a major impact on quality. Throughout the Edo period some advised against it or at least against the removal of live branches. In 1816 a writer asserted that limbing killed trees by causing resin to flow, which permitted the tree's "essence" (*seiki*) to escape. In 1849 Okino Takao advised, "Do not cut living branches from *sugi* and *hinoki*. Even though lower branches are a nuisance when one is trimming underbrush, leave them attached. If branches are cut off, no matter how large the trees grow, when you saw them into boards and cure them, the knots will fall out, leaving low-quality lumber."[16]

One practice that prompted writers to advise against limbing was its frequent use as a way to obtain fuelwood rather than as a technique of stand improvement. That motivation led to careless and excessive limbing that in fact did injure trees, and governments repeatedly but not very effectively warned against the abuse.

That problem notwithstanding (or perhaps as a way of managing it), the view that came to predominate favored limbing. Recommended from early in the Edo period, branch trimming became widely practiced, and writers grew ever more systematic in their advice. By the nineteenth century advice was elaborate, but it varied greatly in particulars: one should limb initially when a tree is five, six, or seven inches in diameter; five, eight, or more years old; and thereafter every three, five, or ten years. Limb during the fall, or winter, or during dormancy. Limb enough but not too much: remove the two bottom whorls of branches every five years, or three whorls every three years, or all but the top three, five, or seven whorls, depending on a tree's size. Remove limbs up to head height, or two-thirds of a tree's height, or up to the large branches. Remove branches under a certain length or thickness. Within this plethora of detail, what emerged by the nineteenth century was general agreement that lower limbs should be removed during dormancy, a few whorls at a time, leaving a clear stem that would bark over to make a smooth surface and straight-grained wood.

As to how limbing should be done, one writer advised using a saw on large limbs, an ax on smaller ones; another called for a heavy knife for small branches and a hand ax for larger ones. Regarding the place to cut, in 1688 a writer advised that pine limbs be cut flush to the bark, taking care not to wound the stem. *Sugi*, however, should be cut so as to leave an inch of stub, which would form an attractive knot as it was grown over, making more interesting wood. Later commentators reiterated that policy until some nineteenth-century writers began recommending that *sugi*, too, be limbed flush with the bark to eliminate loose knots and form clean lumber.

This survey of the main lines of advice in a vast and varied literature suggests the detailed attention that Tokugawa silviculturists gave to all facets of their art. Attention to detail is also evident in the treatment of other aspects of plantation culture, such as protecting against fire, theft, and damage by snow, wind, or animals. Writers also addressed the process of harvesting: identifying trees for cutting; assessing the relative merits of clear-cutting and selective felling; determining when, where, and how to fell; how to select seed trees to be left standing; how to cut up trees for maximum use; how to remove logs from the forest; and how to transport, saw into lumber, store, market, and utilize them. The technology of charcoal making and other forest-related industries were also topics of analysis and instruction.

This silvicultural literature spread throughout Japan, becoming ever more widely available as the eighteenth and nineteenth centuries advanced. It also became increasingly detailed as writers refined and improved their advice.[17] The literature's very existence is evidence of the widespread interest that rulers and ruled alike had in the maintenance of productive forests. And its proliferation and improvement show that it was considered effective by those engaged in forestry: had it not been valued, it would have been ignored and forgotten. By increasing the prospects of success in afforestation projects and by improving the effectiveness of forest use, silviculture facilitated the development of a plantation forestry that enabled early modern Japanese to offset in part the consequences of the earlier overuse of their woodland.[18]

Chapter Six

Plantation Forestry: Economic Aspects of Its Emergence

Plantation silviculture became widespread in Japan during the latter half of the eighteenth century.[1] Following the early modern predation, demand for forest yield continued to exceed supply, and afforestation and eventually plantation silviculture developed to meet that demand by increasing the desired forest output. A sharp rise in the quality and quantity of available silvicultural knowledge showed woodland holders how to pursue plantation culture successfully, and changes in economic relationships enabled rural producers to penetrate and profit from urban markets.[2] These developments made entrepreneurial forestry a comparatively attractive investment for the woodland operator.

Plantation culture thus became possible in eighteenth-century Japan, but not equally so throughout the islands. In some places plantations rose and flourished; in others they no doubt were tried and failed; in most places they never appeared. Within broad ecological limits this spatial distribution was determined by the general economics of lumbering and the particular economics of afforestation techniques. The nurturing of forests entailed substantial costs, but it also brought economic dividends to its practitioners, and where the cost-benefit ratio was sufficiently favorable, plantation forestry developed.[3] Elsewhere woodland continued to be managed less intensively, much by rudimentary methods, and some in the classic manner of exploitation.

Those economic determinants operated for both entrepreneurial and governmental afforestation. The logic of the former may be self-evident; that of the latter requires explication. By and large *han* officials regarded woodland as a source of government income. They fostered timber production to lower maintenance costs and generate revenue. Well-wooded domains, such as Tsugaru, Akita, Owari, Tosa, Obi, and Hitoyoshi, to name some of the most notable, pursued vigorous forest policies with economic objectives uppermost in mind, and they adopted silvicultural techniques accordingly. In consequence, explaining the spatial character of plantation forestry requires an examination of its costs and benefits.

Such an examination does not yield statistically satisfying results because the forest industry consisted of numerous small enterprises whose terminology and accounting methods were highly idiosyncratic and whose surviving records are spotty and inconsistent. Moreover, the business was only partially monetized, and no stable institutions preserved records encompassing all its activities. As a result, assembling complete and integrated figures appears impossible. Scattered data do abound, however, and they yield figures that illustrate the costs and advantages of plantation forestry and suggest its underlying logic.

The Costs of Plantation Silviculture

Plantation techniques were costly. Afforestation required a heavy initial investment of labor, and stand maintenance entailed periodic expenditures for decades thereafter. Moreover, the lumber producer—whether village, villager, urban entrepreneur, government (*bakufu* or *han*), or combination thereof—had to absorb much of the harvesting and marketing costs before he could finally recover his investment.

Even under the best of conditions plantation forestry thus involved long-term, incremental capital outlays. And conditions often were not ideal. Indeed, lumbering was a risky business. In a hundred ways vagaries of weather could ruin a lumberman's enterprise at any moment between the first planting and the final sale a half century later. Disease might ruin a stand; neglect could hurt as badly. Theft and vandalism were chronic problems, particularly where land scarcity was acute. Wildfire was a perennial danger, especially from the burning done by villagers to prepare land for tillage or a new year of pasturage. And finally, the market value of a stand could fluctuate sharply: city conflagrations opened new markets for lumbermen, but their occurrence was notoriously irregular.

Even favorable conditions did not assure the rise of timber plantations. Given the scarcity of capital in early modern Japan, long-term investment in forest production was hardly the most attractive opportunity an entrepreneur might envisage. And halfway measures were possible. A woodsman could enhance a stand with minimal investment by merely assisting a forest's natural recovery after logging. However, that strategy of rudimentary nurturing tended to minimize the gain in yield.

Alternatively, the woodsman could maximize investment so as to maximize return, using elaborate and expensive measures to guide his forest from seedbed to skidway. The costs of those measures can be examined in terms of the three aspects of silviculture discussed in chapter 5: seedling and slip culture and aftercare. Of course, plantation lumbermen also incurred logging and marketing costs, but exploitative loggers did too, so we need not examine them here. Costs of transport were important, but they burdened exploitative lumbermen even more than plantation operators, and the difference constituted a significant economic advantage for the latter, as noted later on.

Rudimentary Nurturing

During the Edo period only a small percentage of Japan's woodland was ever converted to thoroughgoing plantation culture. Much more widespread were rudimentary practices designed to maximize the yield from naturally seeded stands. Even in some of the greatest logging areas, such as Tsugaru, Akita, Tosa, and the Kiso river valley, naturally seeded forests remained basic to the lumber industry.[4]

The simplest way to assist natural growth was by closing woodland to human entry. Governments, villages, and households commonly closed cut-off areas under their jurisdiction, frequently enforcing such closure by deploying forest patrols and elaborating punitive legislation for use against violators. As decades passed, woodland operators employed more positive measures. In Kiso, for instance, hillsides were so steep and the soil so shallow and immature that clear-cutting and replanting were neither economically nor biologically feasible. The forest policy that emerged there during the early eighteenth century protected residual growth primarily by the close management of selective felling.[5]

Even in Hitoyoshi *han* in Kyushu, where the government and villagers established plantations of *sugi* and *hinoki*, most wooded areas regenerated through natural reseeding or coppicing.[6] In the Yama-guni forests north of Kyoto, where entrepreneurial lumbering flour-ished, woodland holders left less accessible hillsides to natural seeding. The cost of hand planting being prohibitive, they generally sought only to protect young growth, specifying in logging contracts, for example, that trees under a certain basal circumference were not to be felled or that all trees of certain species must remain untouched.[7] In Mito, where the *han* wanted more pine forest, natural stock received greater assistance. Supervised laborers cleared weeds, such as *sasa* (a dwarf bamboo), from areas of dense natural pine seedling growth. When the seedlings were about three years old, workmen thinned them to approximately one per each three feet square. Three years later they weeded and thinned again, cutting out defective seedlings and replacing them with healthy planted ones.[8]

Depending on the situation, then, lumbermen gave more or less aid to naturally seeded stands. The simplest measures involved almost no investment; more elaborate practices, as in Mito, took on the hue of plantation silviculture, with labor costs rising commensurately.

Seedling Culture

Given the great diversity and intermixture of Japanese verdure and the cyclical pattern of normal forest succession, logged conifer areas usually grew back as mixed stands of pioneer and intermediate species, only later reestablishing the climax forests that lumbermen commonly wanted. To short-circuit these natural rhythms and accelerate the growth of new timber crops, and to establish conifers in areas previously occupied by other species, woodsmen resorted to manual planting.

Initially, they gathered seedlings from wherever they happened to sprout, a practice that spread widely and persisted throughout the Edo period. The technique had two major drawbacks: the number of

available seedlings often proved insufficient, especially as the scale of
planting expanded, and mortality rates were discouragingly high
because of damage to the straggly root systems common to such
seedlings and because of inefficiencies inherent in their transplanting.
These problems led planters to gather smaller naturally seeded stock
and grow it in beds for a couple of years before transplanting it in the
wild. And more and more tree growers turned to raising bed stock
from seed.

Seedbed culture was a technically sophisticated, labor-intensive
art, but its difficulties notwithstanding, during the latter eighteenth
and nineteenth centuries it spread throughout Japan. More and more
tree growers began sprouting their own seeds, but because "Kamikata seedlings," meaning *sugi* and *hinoki* sprouts from the Kyoto-
Osaka vicinity, were believed to yield the finest timber, commercial
nurseries that developed thereabouts were able to sell their products
throughout the country.[9]

The Ikeda district north of Osaka became an active Kamikata
nursery area and exemplifies the business.[10] The vicinity lacked sufficient water for wet rice culture but was a good location for seedbeds.
It was protected from harsh winter weather by hills to the northwest
and blessed with a cohesive loam that sprouted seeds dependably and
adhered firmly to roots during shipment. The surrounding dense
population assured operators an ample labor force, and the proximity
to transportation arteries and the Osaka warehouses of daimyo facilitated marketing. Finally, the area was under shogunal jurisdiction
and hence not subject to the political and economic restrictions
common to daimyo domains.

In this favored setting Ikeda nurserymen developed their busi-
nesses. They acquired seed and some cuttings from the nearby forests
of Tanba, Yamato, and Kii. They placed them in beds, gave them
proper attention, and raised them to seedlings of optimal size, about
one foot long in the case of *sugi*. These they sold by the tens and
hundreds of thousands to daimyo all over Japan, especially in the
southwest, where *sugi* was a prized exotic. Nursery workers lifted the
seedlings and packed them in woven baskets that probably held 100
to 200 seedlings apiece. Two such baskets made a pole load; four, a
horse load. Some went down to Amagasaki for shipment by sea.
Others went to Osaka or Kyoto for sale through commercial nurseries
or directly to *han* officials in their warehouses. By the late eighteenth

century a guild of about 135 Osaka nurserymen handled all marketing of seedlings in the city. They operated their markets six days per month and moved 50 to 150 pole loads of seedlings each business day, conceivably reaching more than 300,000 seedlings during a busy month.[11]

Ikeda nurserymen were most active late in the eighteenth century, less so during the nineteenth as seedbed culture became more widely established. In effect, they became their own best competitors, because *han* leaders, seeking to reduce the outflow of currency by raising their own seedlings, hired experts from the Osaka area to teach nursery techniques to local woodsmen, who then set up their own seedbed operations.

Records of "Kamikata seedling" prices are scarce, but it appears that during the 1790s *sugi* seedlings a foot or more in length cost roughly three silver *momme* per hundred, about equal to the price of two gallons of hulled rice.[12] Prices fluctuated sharply from year to year,[13] and they differed with the species. Paper mulberry (*kōzo*) prices were comparable to *sugi*, for example, but paulownia (*kiri*) seedlings ranged from fourteen to thirty-five *momme* per hundred. The real cost of seedbed culture in the domains was probably close to that of the Ikeda nurseries because, given the technical nature of the enterprise, most cost-cutting measures would only result in a greater failure rate. In some cases local nurserymen could realize genuine savings on transport costs or losses incurred during shipment. But most other "savings" were fictive, specifically those realized when the *han* passed labor costs on to villagers by requiring contributions of seedlings or labor, whether defined as taxes (*unjō, yama nengu,* or *yama daikin*) or "gratitude for benevolent rule" (*myōga*). Villages similarly held down their recorded nursery costs by operating beds as poorly paid, off-season by-employment.

In any case, seedlings constituted only the first in a series of costs. The next major expenses were the preparation of a planting site and the planting itself. Most commonly, seedlings were set out on recently logged plots, which generally ranged in size from less than an acre to twenty-five acres or so, and work crews were proportional to the project.

In Mito, to illustrate the procedure,[14] *han* officials visited a site, selected a species for planting, and estimated the seedling requirements and project costs. They informed local officials, and late in the fall the latter supervised the site preparation by villagers, who used hatchets and hoes to cut off standing brush and break up matted roots. A few weeks later, after winter had passed and any frost was out of the ground, planting commenced. Planters worked in five-man crews (*kumi*): three members would be digging holes while two would be setting out the seedlings, which often came from *han*-operated seedbeds and usually were two feet or more in length. Supervisors considered rainy days ideal for planting and advised crew members to set the seedlings the same day they arrived from the bed. If that were impossible, they were to store them in a shaded, water-filled hole or a running stream. They instructed the laborers to dig holes eight or nine inches deep at six-foot intervals and to clean out all loose leaves lest they keep soil away from the roots. Planters were to place each seedling carefully at the edge of its hole, crumble fine soil about the roots, and pack the soil down. Then they were to add more soil and when the hole was about full, give the seedling a tug. If it moved, it needed resetting. If it split or broke, another had to be set in its place. *Han* officials expected the crews to set out about 100 to 150 seedlings (about one basket load) per member per day and advised them not to hurry lest any carelessness result in failure. The workmen might complete the project in a day, or they might take several days, the crew size having been calculated, presumably, to assure that no one be kept too long from spring farm work.

As this description suggests, most planting was done by local people as off-season work of short duration. But it required care. That could be assured through close supervision or by giving the planter a vested interest in his work. Those who planted their own trees for eventual sale had ample reason to be careful. But government projects, such as those in Mito, commonly relied on supervision. There village leaders ordinarily supervised the planting crews (*kumi*), but for large projects requiring two or more *kumi*, delegates from the *han*'s district office took charge. The *han* secured the cooperation of these supervisory figures by paying them regular stipends and special bonuses and by granting them ceremonial privileges, such as the right to wear special clothing, bear swords, or publicly use their family names.

Throughout Japan governments initially used corvée labor in their tree planting. By the nineteenth century, however, much was done for pay, whether in money or kind. Sometimes governments paid planting crews directly; at other times they provided seedlings and required nearby villages to pay wages. They justified that burden as quid pro quo for the customary village use of undergrowth as green fertilizer, fuel, fodder, and so on. Thus, in Hida province the *bakufu* required villages to furnish seedlings, but it paid laborers three *momme* for every hundred they planted.[15] Various *han* paid planting labor at per diem rates ranging from one hundred to two hundred *mon* of *zeni* (copper coinage).[16] Where wages were denominated in silver, they ranged from 1.2 to 2.5 *momme* per day. Tsugaru *han* continued to treat planting as a corvée duty but reduced village taxes by a figure deemed equivalent to the work required of its members.[17] In other instances governments compelled entrepreneurs, such as charcoal makers, to pay for their production by replanting the areas they cut over. And planting became a common punishment for persons convicted of entering or harvesting forests illegally.[18]

Governments used these diverse methods to pay for afforestation because all were financially pressed and no strong lobby persistently supported such efforts in face of competing claims on the exchequer. Moreover, in most domains forest production was a marginal and uncertain source of income not easily advocated for its fiscal value. In Tsu *han* on Ise bay, where initial plantings cost 5 or more *momme* per hundred, forest operations during the early nineteenth century regularly resulted in a net loss, even though the *han* appears to have passed about half of its tree-planting labor cost on to villagers.[19]

Small-scale entrepreneurial woodsmen doubtless buried some of their labor costs among family members or tenant farmers, but what they saved there they might lose in higher seedling costs. In Yamaguni one planter set out 7,185 seedlings between 1785 and 1798. His total cost for the work was 1,397 *momme* (19.4 *momme* per hundred), of which 627 (8.7 per hundred) was the price of his seedlings and 333 (4.6 per hundred) his labor charge.[20]

The implication of these scattered figures on seedling culture seems to be that entrepreneurial planters, who could not defray their costs through taxing power or moral suasion, might have to pay 5 to 15 *momme* for every hundred conifers they set out. And that initial planting expense only started the seedlings on their way.

Slip Culture

Woodsmen used cuttings widely, wherever climate and species preference permitted. *Sugi* slips rooted easily in shaded, moist soil, and *sugi* was by far the most commonly rooted species. But *hinoki* and other conifers also started that way. Planters reportedly used pine cuttings in Akita, for example, and larch in the Chichibu area.[21] *Sugi* were introduced to Kyushu in the late sixteenth century, if not earlier, and from the seventeenth, cuttings were employed throughout the island to multiply the new, fast-growing exotic. From the warm, moist south, the practice spread northeastward. It was adopted in parts of Shikoku; in Honshu it advanced from the far west up along the Sea of Japan coast, into the mountains of the Kinai district, and eventually as far as the northern rim of the Kantō.[22]

As noted in chapter 5, there were two basic methods of slip culture. In the simpler one, *jikizashi*, the planter inserted cuttings one or two feet in length directly into the soil where he wished them to mature. In *tokozashi*, he initially placed shorter cuttings in a rooting bed and then transplanted them to the forest site after they were well rooted, commonly two years later.

Slip culture was somewhat less complex than seedling culture, but it was a skilled art nonetheless. In *jikizashi* the planter had to clear his site sufficiently to keep competing growth from choking out the new cuttings. But to prevent the slips from withering, he had to leave enough cover to provide shade and retain soil moisture. In Kumamoto *han* in Kyushu planters often left clumps of *sasa* for shade; in Kanazawa they inserted slips adjacent to clumps of grass, where shade and soil moisture were greater. Where site conditions were marginal, planters might use cuttings in the more moist areas and seedlings in the drier sections. Woodsmen facing poor soil or inadequate shelter might first plant a "nurse" crop to improve site conditions, adding the cuttings later. The irregular terrace land of the Sanbu district on the Bōsō peninsula east of Edo, to cite an extreme case, was actually too dry and exposed to plant cuttings, evidently because of agricultural overuse. So lumbermen trying to grow *sugi* there first planted an area in pine, which they let grow for several years and then thinned. They set *sugi* cuttings in the resulting openings, leaving the surviving stand of pine to provide optimal shade, windscreening, and soil conditions. In later years, as the *sugi* became larger, woodsmen thinned the pine again, until only a windbreak remained surrounding a pure *sugi* plantation.[23]

The *tokozashi* technique was more standardized.[24] The planter formed cuttings seven to twelve inches in length, inserted them in carefully prepared beds, shaded them against the afternoon sun, watered them until well rooted, and a year or two later transferred them to the planting site. During the eighteenth century the use of rooting beds spread all across Japan. Entrepreneurial nurserymen in several locations began shipping bundles of rooted slips about the country, their products being known and promoted by their place of origin as "Nikkō *sugi*," "Tosa *sugi*," "Kumano *sugi*," and so on. The best "mother trees" for cuttings were said to be *sugi* about ten years old. By the latter part of the Edo period some entrepreneurs maintained *sugi* stands as "slip gardens," harvesting slips annually for a few years, then letting the parent trees grow to maturity.

The cost of afforestation with cuttings is difficult to determine, in part because much was done under government auspices, which tended to conceal real costs. Additionally, once a *tokozashi* slip was rooted, it had all the qualities of a seedling and was treated as such, so that records of afforestation sometimes fail to distinguish clearly between cutting and seedling cultures. Records of Kumamoto *han*, where slip culture predominated, mention tree-planters' wages ranging from under 1 *momme* to 2.5 *momme* per day.[25] In Obi *han* in southeast Kyushu the overseers of a planting project in 1824 estimated that 12,000 man-days were needed to set out 1,025,000 *sugi* cuttings, which meant about 85 slips per planter per day, a rate well under the 100 to 150 per day commonly estimated for planters of seedlings.[26] This rate of planting, if paid at the level prevalent over the mountains in Kumamoto, would make the cost of afforestation with cuttings roughly comparable to that with seedlings and perhaps even a bit cheaper.[27]

As with seedbeds the figures are suggestive at best, serving merely to place slip-culture costs in the same general range as those of seedlings. In both cases they constituted expenses not faced by the feller of natural stands. And whichever form of new growth the planter selected, his initial outlay was only the first of many he must make before recouping his investment decades later.

Plantation Aftercare

Afforestation, whether undertaken with seedlings or cuttings, was a chancy enterprise. Mortality rates could be fearsome. They varied widely, but frequently only half the sets seemed to survive transplant-

ing: for example, there were rates of 47 percent and 56 percent in two
bakufu projects in Izu; figures ranging from 50 percent to 87 percent in
eight plantings in Kumamoto; and 40 percent survival in a Fukuoka
planting.[28]

Weather was a key factor in seedling and slip survival, but equally
important was the care taken by the planter.[29] Poorly supervised
workmen performing obligatory corvée duty—especially when working on a site they wanted kept clear of timber—could achieve almost
perfect failure. On some *bakufu* land in Izu corvée planting was done
by villagers anticipating no benefit from their work. Survival rates
for projects of the 1760s ranged from 55 to 73 percent in successful instances and from 4 to 9 percent in others. Not far away in
Suruga province, villagers on other *bakufu* land set out cuttings and
seedlings as instructed, only to report failure a year or so later: of
150 *sugi* cuttings set, 150 died; of 920 *sugi* cuttings set, 136 rooted
but died later; of 307 sumac (*hazenoki*) seedlings planted, all were
killed by snow and ice. Survival rates reported in 1771 were as
follows:

No. of Cuttings or Seedlings Set	Rooted or Started (%)	Survival Rate (%)
5,230 *sugi* cuttings	51.9 (rooted)	21.0
220 *hinoki* cuttings	37.3 (rooted)	14.5
700 pine seedlings	30.7 (started)	8.6
450 chestnut seedlings	26.7 (started)	9.3
303 sumac seedlings	82.5 (started)	6.6

Interest in reducing mortality rates led to refinements in planting
techniques. Silviculturists learned that with both seedlings and cuttings care paid off. But care meant adopting more complex techniques and investing more labor. Fewer and fewer planters set cuttings
or natural seedlings directly into the wild; more and more used seedbeds and rooting beds. Nor did care stop when the shoots were set out.
Even with the best of handling, some would die, and in anticipation of
these initial losses many planters included in their original plans replacement programs for the following year. During that crucial first
year, moreover, laborers aided the sets by keeping down competing
growth. Beyond these basic measures the extent of aftercare varied

greatly, as noted in chapter 5. The long-term trend, however, was toward greater care and thus a higher investment.[30]

The aftercare given plantations north of Kyoto was rather typical. There workmen set out seedlings at seven-foot intervals, some 2,200 per *chōbu* (2.45 acres). They replaced dead ones the following year, weeded once or twice a year for five years, and turned out to straighten stems after heavy snowfall. When the stand was twelve to fifteen years old, they carried out the first limbing, repeating the job two more times at five-year intervals.[31]

In some areas planting was more dense, and woodsmen repeatedly thinned their stands to achieve optimum spacing. In a pine plantation in Mito workmen cut competing growth twice a year for a few years, then annually for five more years.[32] They suppressed creepers such as wisteria (*fuji*) and brambles (*ibara*), which could smother and break over seedlings, and maintained a circumferential firebreak, cutting off the grass in summer and burning stubble in winter. They limbed the stand during its eighth year, removing all but the top five whorls of branches, and about fifteen years later performed a second trimming. They removed dead or downed poles and thinned the stand. By the time it was fifty years old, they had thinned it two or three times to a density of 50 to 100 trees per *chōbu*.

A ubiquitous feature of Edo-period regenerative forestry was the forest patrol. Patrols served several functions, most commonly watching for fire, theft, vandalism, or storm damage. They helped with planting, aftercare, and harvesting projects and carried out follow-up inspections to assure that laborers had performed the work properly. In Akita from the early nineteenth century village officials made carefully regulated forest patrols several times monthly, watching expressly for any signs of illegal felling.[33] In *bakufu* land on the Izu peninsula a government clerk (*tedai*) examined each new planting and reported his findings to the finance office in Edo. Thereafter local foresters oversaw the site, supervising the replacement of dead seedlings, keeping a count of growing trees, and notifying Edo of any damage.[34] Where plantations were grown for entrepreneurial purposes, the grower himself or, more commonly, hired foresters (*yamamori*) looked after the trees.

Methods and levels of pay for forest patrols varied greatly. The routine daily fire patrols that were handled as communal tasks during winter months generally went unremunerated, but periodic and

special inspection patrols were compensated. In many places higher
officials made the periodic inspections of forests planted at government behest. Villagers, who fed, housed, and entertained their distinguished visitors, might bear most costs of the inspection,[35] but the
domain treasury usually paid the inspecting officials' basic stipends.
In Mito, village officials who performed forest inspections received
their salary in rice: thirty *koku* per year for the overseers of forests in
several villages (*ōyamamori*) and ten *koku* for those who inspected only
forests in their own villages (*koyamamori*).[36] In the Yoshino mountains
merchants renting land to grow trees for sale employed skilled local
people as *yamamori* and paid them roughly 5 percent of sale income as
wages.[37] For his salary the Yoshino *yamamori* patrolled the growing
stand and hired and supervised labor crews doing the planting,
weeding, limbing, and thinning.

As with other aspects of plantation culture, data on the cost of
aftercare are scattered and difficult to assess. They are particularly
problematic because aftercare entailed a series of small labor charges
spread over decades, which might in fact go unpaid or be paid in
informal ways at idiosyncratic rates. Beyond the first two or three
years much aftercare was off-season work, but it required enough skill
that plantation operators producing high-grade timber might hire
trained personnel for the task. In Yamaguni, for instance, woodland
holders customarily hired specialists from Yamato, housing them in
the local forest bunkhouse (*koya*) during their time on the job.[38]

In many places, however, aftercare was handled as unremunerated community work. Table 2, which shows the labor requirements for a village afforestation project in Maebashi *han*, suggests the
magnitude of needed aftercare and, as a corollary, the reason for its
poor compensation.[39] In 1858 the initial site preparation and planting of 11,800 seedlings required 1,940 man-days of labor. In subsequent years a slowly declining annual commitment of some 300 to
450 man-days remained necessary, even after replacement planting
ceased. Final unit costs of the venture are impossible to establish in the
absence of information on the yield, but if labor is valued at two
momme per day, the total cost of this twenty-one-year project was
400.5 *ryō* (at sixty *momme* per *ryō*). Aftercare alone was a continuing
cost that slowly dropped from about ten to five *ryō* per year for a stand
that might yield a few thousand pole timbers plus a thousand or so
mature trees half a century later. Assuredly that yield, less logging

TABLE 2. A Maebashi Planting Project

		Man-Days of Labor		
Date	Seedlings Planted	Planters	Weeders	Field Burners
1858	11,800	700	920	60
1859	1,500	149	730	57
1860	800	120	210	30
1861	500	112	300	41
1862	300	28	290	39
1863	200	19	209	55
1864	0	0	287	63
1865			274	61
1866			154	60
1867			151	59
1868			150	70
1869			170	87
1870			169	49
1871			170	54
1872			162	62
1873			153	53
1874			151	59
1875			139	49
1876			132	51
1877			141	39
1878			140	37

NOTE: In addition, *nōbiban* (fire guards) provided 260 days of labor annually.

and shipping costs, would not have paid for the investment. But because this was a village project, probably most of the labor was contributed as slack-time community service.

Because of their diachronic and irregular nature, overall figures on aftercare costs are fugitive and perhaps nonexistent, and where available, their significance is uncertain. As a consequence, since aftercare was a major added expense in plantation culture, overall cost figures are scarce, fragmentary, and of dubious reliability. As an example of recorded costs, around 1840 one entrepreneur in Ōme set out several thousand (perhaps six thousand, for an estimate) *sugi* seedlings on rented land.[40] The stand evidently numbered about 1,200 in 1864, and in 1880 he reported a surviving wood of 645 mature trees that, he claimed, had cost him about fourteen *ryō* to grow. If our Maebashi estimate of four hundred *ryō* to plant an area to 11,800 seedlings and maintain the resulting stand for twenty years suggests the general magnitude of actual labor requirements for a project roughly twice that of the Ōme entrepreneur, then the disparity between our estimate of real labor costs and the fourteen *ryō* that he reported may highlight the scale of labor inputs that could be, and perhaps had to be, written off as noncosts. This disparity suggests the severe economic constraints that plantation forestry faced, and it also points up quite dramatically the limited utility of recorded expense figures.

In any case, regardless of whether the actual added expenses of plantation forestry appeared in the lumberman's calculations or were silently absorbed by the rural work force, most were costs that could be avoided by those logging natural stands. Entrepreneurial plantation operators could cover these additional costs and still compete with exploitative lumbermen only if other factors offset them.

Economic Advantages of Plantation Culture

Offsetting these added costs of plantation forestry were a number of economic advantages. First, the practice enabled woodsmen to maximize market opportunities. Prices of forest products varied substantially with quality and species. Whereas the exploitation lumberman had to take whatever type and quality of timber his woodland provided, the plantation grower could plant a species of choice and adopt measures to maximize the quality of his crop. In Kyoto the demand for top-grade lumber yielded Yamaguni growers much greater profits on carefully nurtured *sugi* than on field-grade timber: for example, a ninety-nine *zeni* profit per year per unit of top-grade *sugi*, compared to eighty-eight *zeni* for second-grade and seventy *zeni* for third-grade *sugi*.[41] Price variation by species is nicely revealed by the following sample prices for twelve-foot logs of about six-inch diameter sold at Nagoya.[42]

Wood	Quality	Price (momme)
hinoki	top	226
	medium	181
sawara	top	83
	medium	54
maki	standard	267
	poor	223
asunaro	standard	115
	poor	96

Insofar as areas of plantation forestry became permanently established, moreover, growers could exploit "brand name recognition" to command top prices for their goods. Certain areas became known for their special wood products: Yoshino for its *sugi* barrel staves; Obi for marine planking; Ōmi for shingles; Owase for charcoal; Ōme for poles.[43] And these reputations might be well founded. Shipbuilders rightfully esteemed *sugi* stock from Obi. *Sugi* grew sparsely and rapidly in the warm, moist forests there, developing a wide grain and many knots. Although this made it undesirable for fine work, the rapid growth produced large-celled wood that floated well. It was very resinous, resisted rot and waterlogging, and dried easily. It was tough and flexible, could handle twisting, could be shaped, and did not shatter when struck. Longitudinal cracks did not run easily through the knotty wood, and the knots were tight. In short, it nicely met requirements for ships' siding and planking and was sought by shipbuilders in Osaka and elsewhere, who paid enough to make it a profitable export for the government of Obi *han*.

Similarly, with development of the *sake* (rice wine) industry near Osaka, coopers created a substantial demand for barrel staves and stock for casks, fermenting vats, storage bins, and associated equipment. *Sugi* from Yoshino acquired a nationwide reputation as the best wood for those uses, and by the eighteenth century Yoshino lumbermen not only supplied coopers in Osaka but annually shipped between 700,000 and 800,000 pieces of four-inch barrel staving to Edo. By mid-century the market for staves was so attractive that Yoshino growers were specializing in knot-free, smooth-grained poles at the expense of both large construction timber and fuelwood.

Plantation operators also could benefit from geographical advantages. Whereas exploitation lumbermen had to work where the trees grew, plantation growers could select the most accessible, biologically suitable sites that were available.[44] By establishing stands along the arteries leading to cities, they could beat competitors to market, thereby profiting from the abrupt increases in lumber prices that followed city conflagrations. And they could do so at minimal shipping cost. Growers in the Ōme area, for instance, were only a few days from Edo on the Tama river. In 1806, after learning of a fire, they shipped 1,604 raft loads of wood within twenty-three days, commanding top prices as city dwellers started to rebuild.[45]

The plantation forester may also have enjoyed a modest comparative advantage in terms of felling costs. His carefully spaced, even-aged stand could be harvested more efficiently than trees in a natural wood, in terms of both labor cost and waste. More important, the capacity to locate stands at streamside was gainful because it enabled lumbermen to minimize the most expensive portion of the timber journey: working logs down the mountainside by hand (*yamaotoshi*). That was precisely the portion that became most burdensome for exploitative loggers as they pushed deeper into the mountains in search of timber.[46] In Yamaguni, savings in transport costs evidently enabled plantation stands to compete with upriver natural forests.[47] In Kii, the plantation foresters of Owase could compete with exploitative loggers in interior valleys because their *sugi* stands grew on mountains ringing Owase harbor, and sticks could be loaded almost directly onto ships bound for Wakayama, Osaka, and Edo.[48]

The relative advantages in product quality and reputation as well as in felling and shipping costs favored the plantation operator over the exploitation logger. In addition, he was able to minimize some real or potential disadvantages of his business. Governments generally did not regard plantation forestry as a form of agriculture and imposed no new taxes on woodland converted to plantation growth.[49] As a result, growers received the full benefit from the increased yield per acre that plantation culture assured. And finally, as earlier figures have suggested, if the planting agency was a village or government, it could pass a significant portion of its labor costs on to the work force by treating planting and aftercare as "voluntary" communal effort or off-season corvée work. Even when labor was compensated, wage rates were low because the work usually constituted by-employment for mountain villagers who had few other sources of supplemental income.

Where marketing conditions offset the added costs of plantation culture, timber production increased. Developments in the Ki and Ōi river basins are illustrative. Between 1760 and 1790 lumber output along the Ki river rose as plantations matured. In the late 1760s annual output averaged some four thousand cubic meters, during the 1770s it reached eight thousand, and by the late 1780s it was running at twenty-one thousand.[50] In Yamaguni, where plantations date from the early eighteenth century, the number of timber rafts on the Ōi river rose from 200 to 300 per year in the 1670s to 500 to 600 by about 1750–70 and to roughly 800 to 1,000 from the 1790s until the late nineteenth century.[51]

The payoff from entrepreneurial forestry, and a clue to its *raison d'être*, is suggested by these cryptic entries from the diary of a village lumberman whose stands grew at streamside in the lower Tenryū river valley. An entry of 1760 says, "Big fire in Edo. Timber sells. Gold and silver pour in." An entry dated February 1772 says, "Big fire in Edo. We fell and sell all our *sugi* and pine. Woodland holders make money. Many men earn good wages. People buy back [mortgaged] paddy fields."[52]

Recapitulation

Identifying economic cause and effect in the rise of plantation forestry is difficult because satisfactory statistics are so hard to come by. Preparatory factors were rapid population growth and extensive urban construction during the seventeenth century, which created wood product scarcities that eventually created market conditions permissive of plantation culture. Then eighteenth century changes in silvicultural knowledge and marketing arrangements enabled lumbermen in favored areas to exploit their opportunity and establish forest plantations.

Even then most Japanese woodland was not converted to plantation culture because of topography that made it inaccessible, too difficult or costly to work, or too fragile for manipulation. Various levels of rudimentary management were the extent of human intervention there. Where geography and climate did place fertile, manipulable forestland within relatively easy reach of major population centers, full-fledged plantation culture arose. And clearly it was the proximity to markets above all else that determined the sites of plantation stands. Most well known were Yamaguni near Kyoto; Yoshino near Osaka; Ōme and Nishikawa near Edo; and Owase and the lower Tenryū valley, both conveniently accessible by sea to Edo, Nagoya, and Osaka. Geographically less favored sites, such as Obi and Hitoyoshi in Kyushu, could develop flourishing plantation industries because the *han* governments used their authority to hold down labor costs, thereby making their best forest products competitive in the marketplace.

It would be nice, of course, to have complete statistical information showing just how changes in supply and demand relationships and resultant cost and price movements made possible the development of regenerative forestry in Tokugawa Japan, and without such figures a definitive analysis is impossible. What our scattered data seem to reveal is that the several costs of plantation culture—for seedlings or cuttings and their setting out and aftercare—varied considerably, depending on date, site, species of tree, and extent of care. In general terms, it appears that plantation culture entailed an initial cost for seedling or slip planting that ranged from about five to fifteen *momme* per hundred conifers set out. Aftercare costs varied greatly, depending on the degree of care given, but over the decades they might add up to several times the original planting cost, conceivably totaling 80 percent of the prefelling cost of a plantation stand. A significant portion of those labor costs appears to have been absorbed by the work force, which surely was a key factor in making plantation forestry competitive with exploitative logging. And even then the new silviculture techniques only flourished in particularly favorable locations where entrepreneurs were able to offset their added costs by exploiting their advantages in product quality, "brand name recognition," and timely and economical access to markets.

In sum, within limits the circumstances necessary for plantation forestry did arise in eighteenth century Japan, and entrepreneurial woodsmen, both governmental and private, successfully seized the opportunity to create self-sustaining lumber plantations. In doing so, they moved Japan out of the "traditional" age of exploitative logging toward the "modern" age of regenerative forestry.

Chapter Seven

Land-Use Patterns and Afforestation

During the seventeenth century, overconsumption of forest products, timber in particular, generated problems that led to the creation of the negative regimen, whose central element was an elaborate countrywide system of forest management. That system may have prevented the worst of woodland abuses, and it may have hepled maintain social order in the face of difficulties arising from scarcity, but it did not end the scarcity itself. Natural restocking failed to keep pace with society's consumption of lumber and other forest goods, so afforestation—or else exploitation of overseas areas—became essential if a brutal process of social contraction was to be avoided or at least minimzed. The former occurred: by the late eighteenth and nineteenth centuries planters were implementing afforesstation projects throughout the islands. In some cases they shifted into timber production woodlands that had formerly yielded fuel, fodder, and fertilizer, a change that might or might not constitute a net gain for society. But in other cases woodland that otherwise was of limited human value was brought into substantially greater production.

For this afforestation to happen, both intellectual and socioeconomic obstacles had to be overcome. The development and dissemination of practical silvicultural know-how and its successful application in appropriate locations, as discussed in chapters 5 and 6, overcame the former obstacle. Changes in landholding arrangements substantially overcame the latter.[1]

Modifications in woodland-control arrangements were crucial to

overcoming socioeconomic obstacles because plantation forestry required sustained stand nurturing for decades at a time. Such long-
term care was difficult in Tokugawa Japan because woodland near
villages, whose accessibility made it most desirable for afforestation,
generally was subject to several concurrent uses. The difficulty of
resolving conflicts among users sabotaged attempts at long-term site
management. This was particularly so not only on village common
land but also in woods controlled by governments and individual
households. Redefinition of customary land-use practices—in effect
shifting the basic premise of woodland management from multiple to
single use—became an essential prerequisite to most plantation development.[2] This is not to say that a given site could be used only for a
single purpose but rather that site users had to accept one purpose as
primary while all others became secondary and subject to such constraints as the primary use dictated.

Multiple-Use Woodland Control

During the seventeenth century, as noted in chapter 4, governments
and villages throughout Japan elaborated forest-use rights and restrictions. They drew formal distinctions between the categories of
lord's forest (*ohayashi*), village common land (*iriaichi*), and household
land (*hyakushō yama*), but the actual use of such areas greatly overlapped. Basic to that overlapping were agreements sanctioning
multiple use, so that a specific parcel of woodland yielded diverse
goods and yielded them to more than one recipient.

Multiple Use: Its Creation and Character

The codification of multiple use was essentially a response to growing
forest scarcity. Competition for yield pitted villages and their inhabi-
tants against one other and against their governments, prodding
rulers and ruled to hammer out mutually acceptable regulations for
woodland exploitation. The regulations that emerged represented
compromises among clashing interests because neither party could
fully impose its will on the other. The rulers depended on village
cooperation because village labor constituted their economic foundation, and effective taxation required a stable, peaceable, at least
sullenly cooperative village. Consequently, rulers accommodated vil-

lage demands sufficiently to keep the peace and perpetuate basic tax arrangements. Villagers compromised their demands for various reasons. Most obviously, the rulers had weapons of war, and they did not. In addition, when disputes between and within villages proved irreconcilable, rulers might have to be brought in as mediators. Moreover, the rulers, if not too hostile, might respond favorably to pleas for special concessions during periods of village hardship.

Because neither side could fully impose its will, when government and village attempted to settle disputes over resource utilization, their initiatives became intricately linked despite the apparent distance between them. Local difficulties frequently led rulers to promulgate regulatory measures, whether intended to enhance government authority, protect the fisc, control erosion or other damage, or simply resolve local disputes. Such measures commonly elicited village reactions, however, which led in turn to modifications of government policy. The upshot was a proliferation of more or less rigorously policed arrangements that most commonly allowed peasants to gather fertilizer material, fuelwood, and other products in lord's forest as well as in village and household woodland, while lords claimed most or all of the timber production on the same lands.

Two examples from Shinano province will illustrate how village-regime interaction led to formal regulation of multiple-use practices. During the 1660s the *bakufu* delineated *ohayashi* boundaries in a section of the Ina district in Shinano. One village adjacent to a newly designated parcel of lord's forest protested that its members had customarily taken wood from the sequestered area for housewares, tools, poles, and well casings, and they requested permission to continue doing so. The writers added that they had also pursued swidden culture in the area but would agree to cease that practice if allowed to continue extracting wood products. Their initial petition was unsuccessful, so they presented another. They protested the hardship that the loss was imposing on them, insisting they had never caused wildfire in the forest—"not even once!"—and they finally regained the right to gather grass and fuelwood for home use. The settlement stipulated, however, that they could not take any for sale and that they could cut out timber only after obtaining explicit permission.[3]

Elsewhere in Ina the expansion of arable forced cultivators to collect green fertilizer material ever more intensively from surviving brushland, even from areas formerly used for fuelwood and timber.

Residents of Ikuma village, who had customarily obtained diverse goods from brushland in the jurisdiction of Ogawa village, found their rights sharply restricted in 1647. That year the *bakufu* intendant (*daikan*) responded to a petition previously submitted by Ogawa by instructing Ikuma villagers that henceforth they could gather fuel from only one carefully delineated area and grass from another. They could take out building timber for home use only with the approval of their village headman and the countersignature of the intendant. And no trees suitable for government use could be removed. Lest Ikuma not acquiesce, the leaders of Ogawa notified the village that if its people did any collecting in unauthorized areas, the miscreants' tools would be seized, the workers driven away, and the forest completely closed to their use. How well the settlement worked is unclear.[4]

Two concise examples, those of Maebashi and Tsugaru *han*, will illustrate the general character of multiple-use arrangements. In Maebashi, a middle-sized, rather poorly forested domain north of Edo, deciduous broadleafs predominated and good conifer stands were scarce.[5] Reflecting this condition, the *han* regulations for *ohayashi* claimed all timber for the lord. Peasants were forbidden to enter lord's forest without official permits and when admitted were required to obtain explicit authorization before cutting branches to clear paths or skidways through the woods. The government required them to provide fuel as tax payment and to notify officials of any dead or windthrown trees they sighted while in the *ohayashi*. As quid pro quo they were allowed to cut out undergrowth for set fees. Only by special petition could they get out lumber for home use, for example, to construct irrigation dams or canal banks. And they could not make charcoal. The *han* farmed out charcoal making, the contractor providing charcoal and money in return for the right to sell the rest of his yield to interested buyers, which included the *han* government itself as well as samurai and commoners.

On other woodland Maebashi claimed all reserved trees (*tomeki*) but permitted villagers to fell them for home construction in case of special need. Villagers had the right to take undergrowth from village land, but *han* regulations specified how they must go about obtaining permission to make charcoal or fell timber trees for home use or sale. Permission for the latter was especially difficult to obtain.

In Tsugaru *han*, the sprawling, handsomely forested domain at the northern tip of Honshu, lord's forest was called *miteyama*.[6] The daimyo claimed most of the timber on it, but villagers could get out firewood, charcoal, and scrap wood from logging projects, and they could sell timber by special permit. After parcels of *miteyama* were logged, however, the *han* closed them to commoners until a new timber crop could establish itself. To make closure effective, from the 1680s the government placed newly logged *miteyama* in the hands of specified villages or individuals, who were ordered to reforest and manage it for several decades. In return, the rulers allowed them to get out brush and other useful materials and, for a fee, to make charcoal and take out small-sized lumber for home use. Some villagers petitioned to take over and reforest such parcels of *miteyama*, and the government allowed them to do so in accord with specific regulations.

Besides *miteyama*, Tsugaru recognized other categories of *han* forest, as well as village and household woodlands. In all of them the government allowed peasant use but restricted or taxed it or both in various ways, while identifying *tomeki* and reserving them for *han* needs. Timber remained the government's major interest, but villagers generally could obtain temporary permits to extract wood for farm tools, boats, and simple structures. Firewood and charcoal were available from all but the restricted species of trees either for a fee or with the stipulation that a portion of the yield be donated to the domain. Many varieties of undergrowth were free for the taking, and villagers could keep the yield from authorized forest-improvement projects. Should a village be destroyed, by fire for example, a special authorization would enable the residents to get out material for rebuilding, sometimes even allowing them to cut restricted species such as *sugi* or *hiba*.

Arrangements of this sort, with governments claiming large timber and villagers mostly using undergrowth, were common on all categories of woodland throughout the islands. As long as production was more or less adequate to current needs, the multiple-use system was able to function. It could do so because the basic qualities of woodland-use rights, as enumerated in chapter 4—their specificity, transferability, and legitimacy, and the existence and use of mechanisms for the orderly resolution of disputes—enabled people to define rights adequately, adjust them to the vicissitudes of life, and agree on how disputes over particulars should be resolved.

Strains on the System

In any society, as long as human wants exceed environmental capacity, no fully satisfactory system of resource allocation is possible. Either the humans must adjust their wants downward, which is unpleasant, or they must find ways to increase the environment's output of desired goods, a process that is never cost-free.

Doubtless, every system of forest utilization encounters some sort of difficulty when humans attempt to increase forest production. In early modern Japan, as yield failed to keep abreast of demand, woodland users tried to increase output by resorting to long-term forest management, especially for timber production. As they did so, they found their multiple-use system becoming inadequate. Because multiple use was rarely the best way to maximize any particular type of yield on a given site, more and more disputes arose as users sought to increase one type of biomass production at the expense of others. Disputants increasingly sought to establish single-use arrangements or at least an agreement among site users that a particular use was primary. Sometimes timber emerged as the dominant product and sometimes fuelwood, but in many instances wood was sacrificed to agricultural needs, whether green fertilizer or even arable acreage.

Governments were key players in the drama because of their wish to maximize timber output, and *tomeyama* policy was the main device they employed to that end. Frequently, as in the case of *bakufu ohayashi* on Izu, noted in chapter 4, local resistance thwarted or at least led to substantial compromises in the application of *tomeyama* policy. Sometimes, however, closure was enforced quite successfully. Prior to 1708, to cite one example, Owari *han* allowed villagers to take various goods from woodland in the Kiso valley as long as they spared *tomeki*. But that year the *han* adopted a draconian policy that forbade local people to cut any trees at all, or even to gather bark or fallen branches. In addition, the government required them to report any instances of such activities and held them accountable for any violations in forests near their homes. In following years villagers repeatedly petitioned and appealed for the restoration of their old use rights, but to no avail.[7] Rather, the *han* offered them modest money payments in lieu of forest yield, surveyed more woodland, and established more *tomeyama*. Only after a crop failure in 1738 precipitated local hardship and disorder did the *han* relax some of its harshest rules and permit some controlled woodcutting by villagers.[8]

Sometimes villagers found ways to accommodate government pressure for timber production yet safeguard their own interests. In Suwa *han* in central Japan villagers had a customary right to take green fertilizer from *ohayashi* for a fee. Because the government wished to grow timber on its land, however, it regularly sought to shut them out of harvested areas while timber growth revived. Peasants just as regularly petitioned to retain their rights. In one instance a group of villagers in 1807 petitioned for continuation of their existing use rights and, in return, shrewdly offered to plant larch (*karamatsu*) seedlings in the deforested area. In making their case they wrote, "Planting seedlings is very important for the lord's forest, but while some larch have already been planted, the number is insufficient. We request permission to plant more."[9] A forest inspector visited the area and reported seeing the larch they had planted. He agreed that if they continued the work, it would indeed improve the woodland. He reported that the village's seedbed was producing sturdy seedlings that would be good for setting out, so their petition should be granted. And it was.

The shrewdness of the villagers lay not only in the way they phrased their proposal to the lord but also in their choice of larch. Unlike the evergreen conifers that would have grown from the natural self-seeding customary on *tomeyama*, larch are deciduous. In the autumn their needles fall, providing some mediocre green fertilizer and exposing the forest floor to sunlight. Larch thus allowed more undergrowth to survive, which yielded the fodder and fertilizer material villagers desired.

At other times government attempts to favor timber growth backfired, and trees were sacrificed for village needs. Because trees are oblivious to man-made boundaries, their natural self-seeding habits insidiously extended evergreen growth well beyond *tomeyama* into village lands. That tendency was enhanced by the obscurity of most boundaries. Although governments delineated most domain and village borders during the late seventeenth century, the exact location of village and lord's forest often was poorly demarcated. As long as similar multiple-use arrangements applied to both categories of land, there was little need to locate parcels precisely, but with more governments enforcing *tomeyama* policies, villagers had greater need to keep their own areas free of timber.

Unsure of *tomeyama* boundaries, villagers were cautious in their clearing of young evergreen growth lest they run afoul of the law. Time and again they complained that sprouts from nearby seed trees or protected timber stands were overrunning areas they used for fodder, fuel, and fertilizer material. Thus, in Numata *han* in the northern Kantō villagers and *han* foresters collided over use of some woodland in early 1701. The problem, village leaders explained to investigating officials, was that *tobimatsu* ("flying pine"), meaning seedlings sprouted from seed produced on a nearby area of recently designated *ohayashi*, had obscured the borders of some fodder-producing areas, precipitating the disagreement over their use.[10]

How that dispute was resolved is unrecorded, but self-seeded reforestation of this type also created new forest growth on village land in Suwa. A serious fertilizer shortage had arisen by the 1720s, and villagers attributed it to a scarcity of land that produced grass and brush. In response to peasant petitions and evidence of hardship, officials investigated and ordered villagers to cut down the new timber growth so the areas could produce grass. It was done, but by the 1760s new forest had sprung up again, and the villagers again petitioned to reconvert it to grass. They wrote:

Before 1724 lush new forest developed, making it difficult to maintain grassland. Consequently, a petition was submitted, and [named inspectors] examined the registers and had the new growth destroyed. Both the starting of new forest and the conversion of grassland to tillage were forbidden, much to the gratitude of the petitioners. Again, however, new forest has proliferated and grassland has shrunk. Because of poor harvests, many peasants are unable to survive, and we would be grateful for your assistance [in clearing the new growth].[11]

The outcome of their petition is unclear, but presumably it was approved.

Rather similarly, in Mito from the 1720s onward, the *han* periodically issued orders instructing peasants to cut back forests, including even hand-planted stands, where they shaded any crop fields.[12] Thus, forest growth that developed in response to such government policies as *tomeyama* and *tomeki* could also be destroyed by government action if it threatened nearby peasant agricultural production and, as a corollary, government tax income.

Often, however, disputes over a particular site simply dragged on, with no specific use being accepted as primary. The dispute could be expressed as disagreement over the site's official status. Thus, in Akita in 1778 a government official complained: "*Unjō* land [i.e., untilled land subject to tax] is the lord's land. However, there are villagers who do not agree that the lord's land extends beyond evergreens and *tomeyama*. Consequently, there have been many disputes over forestland in past years."[13]

Whatever the rationale of a dispute, whether presented as a problem of boundary, land category, or use right, perhaps the most common expression of the system's inadequacy was conscious violation of woodland rules, whether they be rules of government, village, or landholder. For obvious reasons such activities are not subject to quantification, but forest officials frequently complained of villagers illegally cutting down trees for use or sale and habitually destroying protected seedlings in order to preserve or expand areas that produced green fertilizer, fodder, and fuelwood. Resentful villagers might "accidentally" cross an obscure boundary into a planted area and hack down seedlings or "accidentally" let a field fire race out of control and destroy a young plantation. Nor was government forest the only target. In Naguri village in the mountains west of Edo some woodland holders started pine and *sugi* stands on disputed land. After setting out their seedlings, they had to go on guard duty, posting themselves on a hill overlooking the planting site and flinging rocks down on uncooperative neighbors, who tried to enter the area to use it for their own purposes.[14]

In sum, as the need for woodland yield intensified, the multiple-use system came under attack and was eroded by acts of both government and village. Often the needs of agriculture prevailed, but sometimes those of timber production did. Whatever the outcome, however, in most instances the process undercut the multiple-use pattern of the seventeenth century, replacing it with woodland arrangements that gave priority to a single type of production.

Modifying Woodland Control

Not surprisingly, as scarcity enhanced the value of timber production, and as the techniques and benefits of plantation forestry became more widely known, woodland holders sought ways to turn opportunity to advantage. For that purpose they devised various rental or quasi-rental mechanisms, which scholars have identified as *shakuchi ringyō*, or "rental forestry," a term dating from about 1900.[15] Those mechanisms, which in fact embraced a range of local practices that are not always clearly distinguishable, can usefully be treated in terms of three more precisely defined arrangements: *wariyama, nenkiyama,* and *buwakebayashi.*

Wariyama

Yamawari, or "mountain dividing," is one of several terms that denote the practice of parceling out woodland, whether *iriaichi* or *ohayashi,* among the households of a village to form divided forests, or *wariyama* (literally, "divided uplands").[16] This practice, found from the fourteenth to twentieth centuries, was intended to permit a landholder freer use of his assigned parcel. Production of fertilizer and fuelwood (for home use or sale) was a more common function of *wariyama* than was production of lumber, and afforestation was rarely a purpose of its creation.[17] It requires attention, however, because landholders often applied *nenkiyama* and *buwakebayashi* arrangements to parcels of *wariyama.*

Upland division seems often to have occurred when communal arrangements failed to protect an area, reducing its value to villagers and even turning it into a liability as site degradation threatened the village with flooding, erosion, and subsequent drought. Villagers themselves might effect the division after efforts at communal management had proven futile. Thus, in Kanaizawa village in Aizu, woodland gradually deteriorated because of overuse, and in the summer of 1719 thirty-seven villagers assembled, agreed on a policy to protect the forest, and appended their names to this statement:

> ### Regulation of Pine and Zōki Forests in the Village
> Forests in our village have from the past consisted of areas for the lord's use and areas for village use. Of late there has been much carelessness in their treatment, and in council today the village decreed that standing trees shall not henceforth be felled in these woodlands. Even twigs, leaves, and undergrowth shall not be removed. In this regard, the village in council now affirms by signature of all members that there shall be no violations of this decision. Should anyone in defiance remove such materials, they shall be fined one *ryō*. Half the

fine shall go to the village, half to the person who catches the offender. Anyone who neglects to report evidence of such cutting shall be fined one *kan* ten *mon* of copper cash. The regulation is formulated in this manner to assure that there be no violations.

1719/intercalary 6   Headman of Kanaizawa village: Gorōshichi
                    Peasants of said village: [thirty-seven names][18]

Essentially, this regulation applied to village forests the restrictions already applied in law to the *ohayashi* under their jurisdiction, but in the outcome it evidently proved unenforceable. Illegal cutting continued, leading to other policy initiatives during the 1740s. Those also failed of their purpose, and during the years 1756–60 the village divided the woodland in question among its households, assigning them use rights and maintenance responsibilities for the areas they received.[19]

Wariyama arrangements varied greatly. Some settlements divided acreage equally among households; others allotted it in proportion to household arable; yet others combined the two methods. Some divisions were made for a specified period of time; others were made in perpetuity. Some hedged use rights closely; others imposed few or no restraints. In some cases upland division was linked to division of arable, the former serving as a source of fertilizer for the latter; in other cases it occurred independently. Whatever the particulars, however, the dividing of forested or forestable areas usually left individual households in substantial charge of clearly delineated parcels, which, if they chose, they could then reforest, nurture, and harvest as their own.

The diversity of *wariyama* arrangements reflects the direct impact that such division had on crucial household interests. Woodland usufruct was critical to village life, and attempts to resolve woodland disputes might generate so much mutual distrust among villagers that outside intervention was necessary before effective upland division could be achieved. In the summer of 1707 *bakufu* forest magistrates issued instructions on delineating boundaries in *yamawari* cases. One clause called for preventing further overcutting of such sites to control erosion, and another required officials to prepare maps of the parcels to assure that there be no further disagreements over particular settlements.[20]

Villagers, or at least tax-paying landholders (*honbyakushō*), usually worked out their *wariyama* agreements in some form of village assembly. The details and the extent of specificity in the documents varied greatly, but below is an example of such an agreement, dated 1693, from a village in Ōmi province. It shows a village redistributing an area of restricted-use village land (*satsuyama*) that evidently had been divided previously but not to the satisfaction of recipients, perhaps because the restrictions were imposed after the earlier division had been made.

> In Seirinin valley there has been much discontent over restricted-use areas. Therefore, in accordance with the decision by villagers in assembly, forest division there will be redone and people notified. Thenceforth, there are to be no more complaints. The areas divided may not be sold or pawned. Should a family line die out, the parcel will revert to the village. At present there are forty households; should any multiply in the future, land for the new household will be taken from that of the parent house. So be it henceforth.
>
> 1693/12/28
> [names and seals of forty villagers][21]

In some cases the formation of *wariyama* was directly linked to reforestation. Parcels being reforested were sometimes treated as village land that was being temporarily "rented out" to a villager or assigned to him for supervision. For example, in a village now absorbed into Ōtsu city on the edge of Lake Biwa, residents divided their *iriaichi* in 1839, by which time afforestation was being widely practiced. As one householder explained: "In recent years the *hinoki* and undergrowth of village forests have been recklessly slashed. As a result, we villagers discussed the problem and decided during the third month to divide the forest among village households. Each household was to receive and manage three parcels. The assigning of plots was done this winter." He then went on to list his own three parcels, noting the site name and location, the grade of forest, and the numbers of large trees on each (e.g., "contains some large trees over two feet in circumference and many over one foot. Sixty-two such trees"). He noted that one of his parcels was of respectable quality but had some open areas and that he was going to plant pine seedlings there during the coming year.[22]

In a sentence, the act of dividing upland solved problems of communal usage by clarifying use rights, eliminating disputes over types and extent of exploitation, and permitting the pursuit of a sustained, long-term policy of land use. In addition, *wariyama* arrangements linked the land clearly to a source of more willing labor or investment capital or both, thereby creating a situation more favorable to afforestation when such activity became feasible.

Nenkiyama

Nenkiyama is the land-use arrangement most central to "rental forestry." It may be thought of as a long-term (*nenki* means "fixed term") lease of forestland. It seems more correct, however, to view it as an advance sale of stands, because the buyer did not acquire unrestricted use rights to the land on which his trees stood; participants in the transactions had trees rather than land in mind when they negotiated. *Nenkiyama* was, in essence, comparable to the older practice of marketing a rice crop soon after the seedlings had been transplanted from seedbed to paddy.

Scholarly studies of *nenkiyama* in the Yoshino mountains and the lower Tenryū river valley illuminate the practice. As utilized in Yoshino, *nenkiyama* involved the advance sale of stands held by villagers, often on *wariyama*. From about 1700, a village landholder would afforest a given site and sell his young stand to a timber merchant, either local or urban. After selling the stand and receiving payment, the villager continued to nurture the trees, enjoying usufruct, notably of the underbrush, as quid pro quo. When the stand was felled, the buyer paid the village an additional small fee. Use of the land then reverted to the original holder who could, if he chose, start another crop of seedlings and repeat the rental cycle.[23]

In the lower Tenryū valley, some twenty miles from the coast, *nenkiyama* arrangements seem to have emerged during the 1760s from older practices in which smallholders placed woodland in pawn to cover debts or taxes due.[24] The holder set out seedlings, sold the stand to a timber merchant, and received his payment when the contract was signed. Thereafter the merchant was responsible for nurturing and felling the stand, after which land use reverted to the holder.

Aoyama Zen'uemon of Yokoyama village, who operated his business along the Tenryū, was particularly active in this trade. In his contracts with landholders he agreed to nurture and harvest (or resell) stands of timber, sharing the income with the man whose land he had leased. The following is a *nenkiyama* contract that Zen'uemon accepted in 1782:

A Term Contract on Sugi Forest

In re my *sugi* forest located at the place known as Yamaguchi, one parcel of land, bounded on the south by Hyōemon's property [and on other sides as specified]. Three thousand *sugi* are planted on this parcel, and I sell them to you without exception for the sum of six *ryō* two *bu*, duly received. These trees, being seedlings and small trees, will henceforth be left to grow for however many years until ready for felling to make lumber. During that term all *sugi*, and other trees as well, may be cut as you choose. Having no reservation on this matter, I agree to this contract.

1782/12
[signed and sealed by the landholder,
guarantor, and coguarantor]

To [Aoyama] Zen'uemon
Yokoyama village
This matter proceeding as stated, after thirty years or thereabouts, when all *sugi* trees have been removed, said land is to revert to [the seller].[25]

In following years the Aoyama family logged with enough success so that in a contract dated 1796 the family head agreed to rent three parcels of land on which he proposed to raise a crop of trees from seed. In this example the landholder specifies the conditions of his lease, probably in line with an earlier offer from Aoyama.

I now wish you to plant *sugi* on three parcels of mountain land in Hosokubo that have been in my family for generations. You may plant on said parcels in the manner you deem best. Upon sale of the mature *sugi*, proceeds will be divided on a forty-sixty basis with 40 percent as my share. Boundaries of the parcels are as indicated in your statement to me. Until the stand is mature, you will provide aftercare, and after felling, the land will revert to us. Duly certified.

1796/3
To Aoyama Kihei   [seals of the landholder,
Yokoyama village   guarantor, coguarantor, and *nanushi*][26]

The significance of *nenkiyama*, or advance sale of stands, seems clear enough: it defined use rights for tree lifetimes and served to link land, labor, capital, and marketplace. Villagers provided the land and labor. Merchants provided the long-term investment capital, enabling the smallholder to recover his investment quickly, and assured the producer of access to markets. Moreover, the practice evaded government prohibitions on the sale of land and sidestepped the reluctance of holders to alienate property permanently.

Buwakebayashi

The term *buwakebayashi*, or shared-yield forest, refers to a parcel of *ohayashi* or other woodland (including village and household land) that a government leased to an entrepreneurial peasant or village. The lessee planted timber trees on the parcel, nurtured the stand, and shared the harvest with the government (and any third-party landholder) in accordance with the terms of the lease.[27] In one form or another the practice spread widely through Japan during the eighteenth century, appearing under various rubrics in *han* from Tsugaru to Satsuma.[28]

Arrangements varied from place to place and changed over time. In brief, during the early eighteenth century more and more *han* leaders came to realize that *tomeyama* and *tomeki* policies were insufficient for their needs. With lumber stock continuing to be depleted, more of them advocated reforestation. To induce village participation, officials promised planters a share of the yield, and as the eighteenth century progressed, the planter's portion gradually increased from about a third to a half and eventually to two-thirds or more of the harvest.

Governments applied the sharing rules not only to *ohayashi* but also to village and household land. This policy partially nullified *tomeki* and *tomeyama* effects, creating an economic inducement to villagers that offset the counterattractions of fuelwood and green fertilizer culture (i.e., growing coppice, scrub brush, bamboo, and grass). Moreover, governments furnished some seed, seedlings, cuttings, silvicultural advice, loan funds, and occasional grants to encourage *buwakebayashi* planting.

As the eighteenth century advanced, ever more villagers found the terms of *buwakebayashi* agreements attractive, and the number of shared-yield forests multiplied. In Obi *han* in southeast Kyushu, for example, the *han* began authorizing extensive shared-yield planting from the 1780s. The planter chose a site (whether *han*, village, or household land) and obtained permission from the *han* forester (*ueki-kata*) to plant. Then he set out his *sugi* cuttings, provided replacements and aftercare, and protected the area from fire. Five to fifteen years later he had the *han* forest magistrate (*yamakata bugyō*) inspect the area, designate it a shared-yield forest, and record the stand in the forest register. At appropriate times the planter thinned his stand, keeping the yield. When it was ready for harvesting, usually sixty to seventy years after planting, the planter (or more likely his heir) petitioned to cut. The magistrate inspected and granted approval, and officials oversaw the felling. Commonly, they divided stands into three-tree clusters, designating the best one of the three a *han* tree and leaving it to grow a few more years. The other two they ordered felled. They measured the timber, recorded the yield in their forest register, and made the division between planter and *han*. The *han* took one-third, the planter got the other two-thirds. For the planter the final yield plus the intermediate benefits evidently sufficed to pay for the labor invested. For the *han* the yield was nearly clear profit, and in addition officials knew that an area of upland had been protected from abuse and had helped support the local economy, which ultimately constituted the *han*'s fiscal foundation.[29]

The planters of *buwakebayashi* might be villagers who recouped their labor investment decades later at harvest time, or they might be entrepreneurs who paid for labor and recovered their capital investment upon marketing the timber. The agreements ran for the tree generation being planted, but they could be renewed if the parties so desired.

The format of *buwakebayashi* agreements varied greatly; here is one from Akita *han* dated 1813:

> To the village:
> Katsurazawa village
> in Hatara village
> in Ogachi district

Regarding the village request to plant *sugi* on the *tomeyama* in Katsurazawa, which you submitted during my cruise of the forest this spring, it has been approved as requested, following inspection of the site. Now, devote yourself energetically to the task. When you petition [to fell] the mature stand, it will be authorized as per the standard division [of seven parts for the planter, three for the *han*]. When I make my semiannual spring and fall cruises of the area, you are to report the number of trees planted. If investigation reveals that proper attention has not been given the site, this agreement will be nullified. Take this admonition to heart.

1813/10/10
Shirazuchi Giuemon[30]

These *buwakebayashi* agreements accomplished several things. By guaranteeing a future payoff, they gave villagers an incentive to reforest government land. For people interested in reforesting village land (either in their own or another village) or woodland held by someone else, the contracts assured them a government guarantee of their undertaking. In such an instance the yield would be divided three ways between the government, planter, and registered holder of the land, whether village, temple, shrine, or household. The agreements thus bound village, entrepreneur, and regime in a mutually beneficial commitment to single-use plantation projects. They also linked land to labor and generated essential capital, not only in terms of labor and land but also in terms of government or entrepreneurial funding of the project. Finally, they assured the planter access to the market through the government, which in many cases had some control over the market as well as a compelling reason to assure that the yield be disposed of advantageously.

The Emergence of Plantation Forestry

The emergence of widely practiced afforestation during the latter half of the Edo period was neither compelled nor made successful by the institutional innovations of rental or quasi-rental forestry, specifically *wariyama*, *nenkiyama*, and *buwakebayashi*. As with the diffusion of silvicultural know-how, those innovations were permissive or conducive, not causative in that outcome. When scarcity, with its political and marketplace ramifications, induced people to pursue tree planting, those rental practices facilitated it, indeed, made it possible on many woodland sites. In differing ways they overcame institutional barriers to the effective linking of land, labor, capital, and marketplace. They expedited the rise of long-term forest management and enabled plantation culture to supplement natural rejuvenation as a method of forest production.

Plantation culture did not supplant natural replacement everywhere. In Akita most timber forest rejuvenation was accomplished without resort to artificial planting. The same was true in the great Kiso forests of Owari in central Japan. In Kiso policies of selective rotation cutting were introduced in 1779, after decades of forest rehabilitation. In subsequent years the *han* was able to sustain its annual yield at 250,000 to 280,000 pieces of lumber.[31]

For Japan as a whole, however, natural rejuvenation was insufficient. Consequently, afforestation, which had been a minor theme during the seventeenth century and then primarily as an aspect of protection forestry, emerged during the eighteenth as a major thrust of policy. Especially from about the 1760s both governments and entrepreneurs planted trees to produce timber.

Government planting became widespread. Even the *bakufu* promoted it, sometimes successfully, sometimes not.[32] As noted in chapter 4, *bakufu* forests in Hida had been largely stripped of timber by the 1740s. From that time officials began requiring villagers to plant, and by the 1850s they were being paid to set out some one hundred thousand seedlings per year. This government reforestation eventually helped restore Hida's forests to conditions approaching what had existed before they were cut over by *bakufu* loggers.[33]

Daimyo also promoted timber plantations. Little Suwa *han* in central Japan was actively encouraging afforestation by the 1780s. Initially, forest officials used natural seedlings. So many died, however, that they started buying *sugi*, *sawara*, and especially *karamatsu* seedlings from nurseries. By the late 1790s *han* foresters were promoting seedbed development, and during the nineteenth century planting activity accelerated. Annual plantings of over a thousand larch were common during the early 1800s; by mid-century the scale was far greater. In 1851 *han* officials supervised a planting of forty-two thousand larch. Twelve years later the *han* bought 10,500 nursery seedlings to set out; gathered another 50,000 naturally sprouted seedlings for placement in beds, and collected about twenty liters of seed for sowing in beds the next year.[34]

As another example, officials of Kumamoto *han* in Kyushu advocated tree planting from the 1660s, initially using corvée labor to achieve it. By the 1750s *han*-directed planting was widespread, with villages providing labor, which the *han* paid in slowly rising rates of money. According to surviving records, *sugi* and *hinoki* planting in three districts of the *han* was as follows during the nineteenth century:[35]

Period	District	Seedlings	Annual Rate
1815–1847	Kamimashiki	2,400,000	75,000
1820–1865	Kikuchi	9,327,000	207,266
1824–1829	Tamana	1,000,000	200,000

Beyond the recorded afforestation activity of governments was the private work of entrepreneurial woodsmen such as Aoyama. Because their enterprises were widely scattered and often of modest scale, instructive figures are hard to come by. However, the scholar Matsushima Yoshio has worked out a general chronology of entrepreneurial afforestation in terms of four stages:

1. 1716–63: In the Kinai basin and a few other sites small-scale timber-tree planting is practiced by a few Buddhist monks, samurai, wealthy villagers, and doctors who are pursuing local objectives of public improvement.

2. 1764–1803: Afforestation develops where transportation is convenient. Planters use seedlings and cuttings intending to market the yield, but the scale remains small.

3. 1804–43: With timber still scarce and prices high, commercial afforestation spreads even to mountain villages and inaccessible interior areas. It is widely practiced by villagers, landlords, and regional merchants. Planting techniques improve rapidly, are diffused widely, and add extensive seedbed culture to naturally seeded stock.

4. 1844–67: Commercially oriented afforestation is widespread and large in scale. Stand management is sophisticated; marketing arrangements are well developed.[36]

Another scholar, Fujita Yoshihisa, speaks of the half century after 1750 as the period in which entrepreneurial afforestation expanded greatly, and after 1803, he notes, it was found nationwide.[37] Fujita has also studied the regional distribution of such planting. His findings, represented in map 8, show that the most complex forest practices existed in central Japan, in terrain favorable to conifer growth and near the greatest population centers. Lumber constituted a significant regional market product for the cooler northeast, which was a comparatively underpopulated and underdeveloped section of the country. Woodland holders there engaged in extensive seedbed culture but gave little or no aftercare to the seedlings once they were set out.[38]

In addition to afforestation projects pursued independently by governments and entrepreneurs, *buwakebayashi* arrangements facilitated planting through the combined auspices of the two. By the nineteenth century the three forms of afforestation had created such a demand for seedlings that more and more tree growers were sprouting their own seeds, especially in such areas of entrepreneurial forestry as Owase on the Kii peninsula, the Saitama and Chichibu areas of the Kantō region, and several sites in modern Shizuoka prefecture.[39] Daimyo domains, villages, and forest-operating entrepreneurs all maintained seedbeds, primarily for starting *sugi* and *hinoki*, but also for a wide variety of other species, usually conifers. And, as noted in chapter 6, in some areas, most notably the Kyoto-Osaka vicinity, commercial seedbed operations developed that sold their products all over Japan.[40]

By the early nineteenth century Japan had moved well into the era of plantation forestry. Old-growth forests were nearly gone. Nursery culture, stand nurturing, rotation cutting, and other practices of purposeful forest management were providing sustained yields in a growing number of forests.

Solid statistics do not exist to demonstrate the magnitude of increase in timber output, but available figures suggest that the adoption of plantation culture was translating into increases in timber production, if not gross forest output. Increases in timber output along the Ki and Ōi rivers were mentioned in chapter 6. To cite some other instances, in Tsugaru, *han* forests were harvested in rotation by the late eighteenth century. Sections were cut selectively at ten- to fifteen-year intervals in a carefully managed policy designed to get out high-quality pieces with minimal injury, to protect the surviving stand from damage during the logging operation, and to provide villagers with waste wood for their own use.[41] Because of improved woodland management, Tsugaru's forest yield expanded, and by the 1820s lumber was providing the *han* with income approaching seven thousand *ryō* annually.[42] Far to the south, little Obi *han* by the 1860s was able to get out some ten thousand *koku* (2,780 cubic meters) of lumber per year.[43] Just over the mountains to the west, Kumamoto *han* was harvesting some seventy thousand *koku* (19,460 cubic meters) of timber on the stump (*tachiki*) annually.[44] In central Japan, in the Ōme district west of Edo, where lumbering was handled by local entrepreneurs, production had shifted by the nineteenth century to plantation stands that contributed most of the annual 5,500 raft loads of lumber sent downstream to the capital.[45]

In sum, by the nineteenth century seedling and cutting cultures were well advanced. A complex body of silvicultural knowledge was widely available in written form and was well known to a large number of practicing silviculturists. A plethora of large- and small-scale afforestation projects was shifting enough forest production to a plantation basis so that Japan had ceased to depend on old-growth forests and was meeting most of its timber needs from replacement stock. Much was in mixed stands of natural or semi-natural growth, but a steadily increasing proportion of the harvest came from plantation stands maintained through the practices examined here. By the 1830s, it appeared that long-term forest stability was being achieved, and sustained-yield forestry was being practiced widely throughout the archipelago. A revolution of sorts had been accomplished.

Conclusion

This study opened with the suggestion that Japan today should be an impoverished, slum-ridden, peasant society subsisting on an eroded moonscape, rather than a wealthy, dynamic, highly industrialized society living on a luxuriant, green archipelago. We would predict the former situation because this fragile chain of islands long ago should have been devastated by the demands of its extraordinarily dense human population.[1]

To develop that proposition a bit further, Japan is a "fragile chain of islands" in this sense. It is not a migrant piece of archaic continent in the manner of the British Isles, where bedrock plains merge imperceptibly with rolling hills and highlands. Rather, it is an assemblage of recently formed mountains produced by the relentless pressure of northwestward-bound oceanic plates diving beneath the eastern edge of the southeastward-bound Asian continent. Consequently, Japan has no continental flatlands, neither pre-Cambrian shields nor more recent horizontal bedrock formations. Its bedrock, having been thrust up out of coastal waters by violent tectonic activity, is all folded and broken into precipitous ridges interspersed with cones and lava mantles remaining from episodes of vulcanism. The only flatlands are unconsolidated deposits of recent sedimentary origin. They consist of new (Holocene) alluvial plains—the site of most arable land and human settlement—that formed after the last glacial maximum some fifteen thousand to twenty thousand years ago and older (Upper Pleistocene) "diluvial" terrace deposits. Most of the latter rise abruptly from the newer plains to form angular, ravaged, low hilly country.

Beyond these small sedimentary areas are the hard rock mountains that constitute 80 percent of the archipelago. They are sheathed with a thin, immature soil that is low in fertility and subject to easy destabilization. Their surface fragility, manifested in landslides and erosion, is exacerbated by continuing crustal activity, such as earthquakes and vulcanism, and by irregularly heavy precipitation, most especially typhoons and monsoons, and on the Sea of Japan littoral, sudden spring thaws and rapid snow runoff.

Because of this geological origin and character, the boundaries of safely arable land are much more clearly delineated than in most densely populated regions, such as China, India, Western Europe, and the northeastern United States. Encroachment on bedrock mountains runs the risk of precipitating erosion and landslides that may ruin not only the mountainsides but also arable land and human settlements below. When agriculturists do push beyond sedimentary boundaries, they must engage in painstaking terracing and intensive manipulation simply to create and maintain tillable soil. These conditions mean that the human carrying capacity of the archipelago is relatively inflexible. Once the biosystem's limits have been reached, under a given technological and social regime, it has little elasticity for handling further human demand. Instead, the limits quickly manifest themselves in ecological damage and human hardship.

We can speak of Japan's "extraordinarily dense population" because in terms of density per unit of total land surface, Japan is one of the world's most heavily populated societies. And in terms of density per unit of arable it is dramatically more populous than any other major society on earth. More important for this topic is that the archipelago has maintained an extremely large human population for centuries: perhaps some 5 million by A.D. 700; 7 million by 1200; 12 million around 1600; 31 million in 1720; 33 million in 1870; and 120 million today.[2]

Japan's dense preindustrial population placed great demand not only on arable land but also on forests. In part this was so because the arable was created from woodland, and every gain of the one constituted a loss of the other. More significantly it was so because Japan's forests provided most of the fertilizer that grew the crops that fed the people. During the Edo period in particular, when the population nearly tripled and pressure on the land became most acute, tillers tried to maximize their yield because every increment of output reduced their risk of hunger or increased their market income. They achieved those increments in part by opening more marginal land to cultivation. That strategy, however, placed an ever larger proportion of total yield at risk while increasing the energy inputs (labor and nutrients) required for every unit of added production.

To compensate for the scarcity and marginality of arable, early modern farmers tilled intensively and applied fertilizer liberally, mostly using grass, scrub brush, and leaf fall. Fertilizer requirements varied with soil quality and crop, but in general about five to ten times as much area was needed for fertilizer material as for the crop it grew.[3] Hence, every increase in cultivated acreage entailed a many-fold increase in acreage devoted to fertilizer production.[4] Fertilizer collection rights were so important to tillers that they became the paramount issue in disputes among them. As population growth drove preindustrial Japan to the limits of its carrying capacity, excessive demand on woodland thus manifested itself in intensifying and proliferating disputes over "rights" of exploitation.

In these disputes the interests of affected groups did not receive equal consideration. Among the human disputants, "rights" were acknowledged roughly in proportion to the power that claimants brought to the case. The "rights" of unborn human generations were represented particularistically by disputants because of the strongly hereditary character of social status and place. The "rights" of other species did not enjoy any such representation, however, and only creatures "useful" to the humans, most notably domesticated plants and animals, found their interests protected in the ongoing contest over woodland use. "Useless" biota fared well only where they could adapt to "parasitic" roles vis-à-vis the human populace or where they could escape the effects of human activity.

It is these considerations of topography, climate, population density, and intensive resource exploitation that prompt the suggestion that so many people living for so many centuries on so little land should long ago have ruined it. The problem was foreshadowed during the ancient predation of A.D. 600–850, when the introduction of continental political, economic, religious, and architectural practices gave rise in the Kinai basin to an unprecedented spasm of city and monument building. That activity reduced much of the basin's high forest to scrub, opened more marginal land to tillage, and subjected those areas most accessible from Nara and Heian to severe exploitation and consequent environmental change and deterioration.

After a few generations, however, it became apparent that the builders of this urban civilization lacked the power to extend their forest exploitation throughout the archipelago. Once they had consumed the accumulated biomass of forests in and around the Kinai basin, their wood-based civilization became dependent on the region's annual biological production. That proved insufficient to maintain their great metropolitan center, and in due course it decayed.

In the twelfth century Japan entered an era of unstable, decentralized rule during which forest consumption was spread more evenly over the archipelago and seemed to press few areas beyond carrying capacity. That situation ended late in the sixteenth century when a military dictatorship of unparalleled power reimposed order on the country and precipitated a nationwide surge of deforestation. During this early modern predation (1570–1670) the Japanese harvested most of the archipelago's forests south of Ezo (Hokkaido) and brought most remaining workable areas under the hoe. In the process they triggered widespread erosion and flooding and everywhere generated disputes over woodland-use rights. They seemed to be pressing their islands beyond endurance, driving them toward environmental catastrophe.

Disaster did not unfold, however. Instead, from late in the seventeenth century the rate of exploitation slowed and more stable patterns of forest usage emerged, producing a condition perhaps described as maximum tolerable utilization. Within another century woodland holders throughout the islands were adopting methods to increase desired woodland production, and that development marked Japan's shift from exploitation to regenerative forestry. The issues that have invited particular scrutiny in this study, therefore, are why this spasm of early modern forest overuse developed and what countermeasures it induced. Addressing those issues then prompts the further and much more complicated question, why did affairs work out as they did?

Why Did Forest Overuse Develop?

Forest overuse was a product of several trends that characterized seventeenth-century Japan. Peace had been restored, and as noted at length in chapter 3, the newly powerful rulers celebrated their attainments by constructing glorious monuments: castles, mansions, palaces, temples, and shrines. Moreover, the growth of cities and towns proceeded at an unprecedented pace, consuming additional quantities of construction lumber. A surge of population growth sharply increased demand for food, fuel, and shelter, and the associated spurt in land opening greatly expanded the area of arable, removing much land from forest production even while creating greater need for fertilizer material. Finally, intensified tillage practices added to the demand for fertilizer.

Figure 1, which depicts a hypothetical forest site, illustrates the changes in the local situation. By the late sixteenth century much of Japan's alluvial plain was under cultivation, and villagers used nearby hilly areas, especially diluvial terraces, for fuel, fertilizer, and building materials. The rulers, meanwhile, logged the areas of high-quality forest, most of which were found on unopened valley floors and the slopes of bedrock mountains. As the century passed, new villages were established and land opening brought the remaining alluvium and much diluvium under cultivation. Accordingly, villagers turned increasingly to bedrock hillsides for fuel and fertilizer. That trend not only triggered erosion and downstream damage but also pitted villagers against one another in disputes over forest-use rights. Moreover, it pitted them against their rulers, who normally wished cutover woodland left undisturbed so that seedlings could grow to maturity.

By the later 1600s the pressure on resources was evident not only in disputes over use rights but also in the growing scarcity and costliness of wood products, the serious deterioration of forestland, and the resultant erosion and damage to lowland.

What Countermeasures Did the Situation Promote?

In essence, forest overuse and its ramifications promoted sequentially two types of countermeasure, the first usually labeled negative and the second, positive. The first, the "negative regimen" of chapter 4, was a system of restrictions that affected the three spheres of production, distribution, and consumption. It developed erratically throughout the country between about 1630 and 1720 and consisted of steps taken to limit and channel forest usage, thereby slowing the

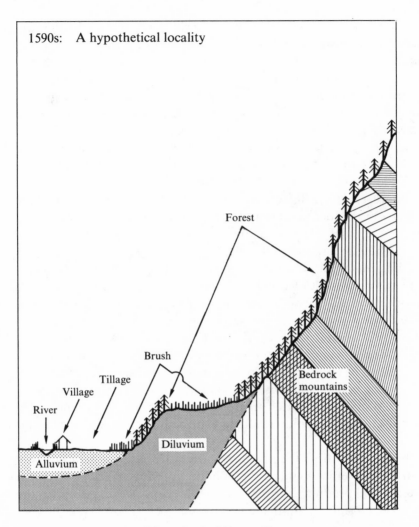

Figure 1. Changes in a Hypothetical Forest Site

From Conrad Totman, "The Forests of Tokugawa Japan: A Catastrophe That Was Avoided," *The Transactions of the Asiatic Society of Japan*, 3d ser., vol. 18 (1983): 4–5.

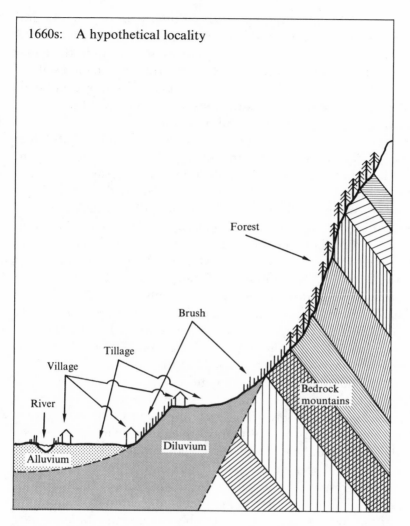

Figure 1. (*continued*)

rate of tree felling, restricting brush cutting, and assisting natural processes of forest regeneration. Those measures seem to have helped most woodland escape serious ecological abuse. Except in the Kinai and Nobi basins and the coastal areas of the Inland Sea, most soil did not become so severely degraded as to form *hageyama*, or dessicated, infertile bald mountains.[5] Rather, most uplands retained their basic biological capacity to support healthy forests.

Nevertheless, natural forest regeneration was unable to satisfy the lumber, fuel, and fertilizer demands of eighteenth-century Japan. Large trees became rare and stands, thinner, and disputes over use rights continued to flourish. In consequence, as the century advanced, governments and villagers began adopting positive policies of tree planting to produce timber stock. By century's end plantation stands could be found growing throughout the islands. And during the nineteenth century the acreage of hand-planted forest increased rapidly. By 1868 a large number of conifer plantations, mostly *sugi* and *hinoki*, were growing from Kyushu to Tōhoku.

This outcome was not cost-free. The negative regimen consistently and purposely discriminated against lower-status people by allowing them fewer and less valued goods. When plantations developed, moreover, many were on accessible land that otherwise would have produced fodder, fuel, or fertilizer material. This shift in yield, which addressed the wants of the high-status people more than the needs of the low, was commonly achieved, it appears, by depriving poorer villagers of customary use rights and forcing them to meet their needs elsewhere. Beyond these human costs, plantations presented a potential ecological danger because even-aged monocultures are notoriously species-restrictive and vulnerable biotic systems. In early modern Japan, however, the destructive potential of forest monocropping appears not to have developed, probably because plantation forests remained scattered, small in size, and a small portion of total woodland.

Despite their costs, negative and positive countermeasures were instituted and eventually proved reasonably effective in stabilizing forest use and invigorating output. To point that out does not, however, really explain why Tokugawa Japan escaped environmental calamity because it does not explain why the measures worked out as they did. The mere existence of a need, after all, does not assure a response, and to respond is not necessarily to respond effectively.

Why Did Matters Work Out as They Did?

To explain the eventual effectiveness of Edo-period forest preservation measures, it may be helpful first to note some possible explanations that do not withstand scrutiny.

Foreigners, and some Japanese as well, often speak fondly of a special Japanese "love of nature" that can be credited with this early modern forest recovery. To so argue, however, invites the tart query: did they love nature so much less during the ancient and early modern predations? More seriously, to advance this "love of nature" as an explanation would be to misconstrue terms. The "nature" of this sensibility is an aesthetic abstraction that has little relationship to the "nature" of a real ecosystem. The sensibility associated with raising *bonsai*, viewing cherry blossoms, nurturing disciplined ornamental gardens, treasuring painted landscapes, and admiring chrysanthemums is an entirely different order of things from the concerns and feelings involved in policing woodlands and planting trees. The former is quintessentially "urban"; the latter, "rural." The one is a matter of recreation and luxury; the other, of work and necessity. The one is comfortable and "indoor"; the other, uncomfortable and "outdoor." The one is delicate and refined; the other, ponderous and crude. The people who labored to salvage Japan's forests were not especially concerned with beauty or driven by any ideological sense of the aesthetics of nature. They had other matters on their minds.

Just as we do not find woodland regulators and tree growers justifying their own actions, or urging action by others, in the name of "nature," so we do not find any themes of Buddhist reverence for "sentient beings" showing up as reason or rationale in forest policy. One reason for its absence, no doubt, is that as a practical matter "sentient beings" generally meant mammals and birds. Ordinary trees, along with earthworms, grass, and almost everything else in the biosystem, lacked religious standing. Nor do other religious doctrines, such as Shintō or Shugendō, show up as motivators in the actions of forest preservers. Doubtless, a few gnarly old trees were left standing near shrines or other sacred places out of an aesthetic-religious sensibility, but such occurrences were local in application and severely limited in their environmental impact.

The one philosophical rationale that frequently appears in hortatory writings is Confucian in character. Before we conclude, however, that the "why" of early modern forest recovery can be found in "Confucian values," it would be well to remember that Confucian values had not stopped the elite from plundering Japan's forests during either the ancient or early modern predations. And it is not immediately evident that the elite predators were any less "Confucian" than their descendants of the eighteenth and nineteenth centuries. Nor should we forget that Confucian values did not save the forests of China.

Two other possible doctrine-based explanations deserve note. One is "modernization theory," an interpretive approach to Japanese history that enjoyed great popularity during the 1960s. In this view Japan "progressed" along the path of modernization during the Edo period, with society becoming more "rational" and "secular" as decades passed. In terms of forest history this view would seem to suggest that the decline in temple building, with its concomitant reduction in demand for timber, reflected a waning religious fervor and rising secularism. The difficulty with this thesis is that the early seventeenth-century spurt of temple and shrine construction was caused by rulers for reasons that had little to do with religious conviction and much to do with self-glorification and the demonstration of moral rectitude. Moreover, it is difficult to demonstrate any decline in the religiosity of their political successors.[6]

Modernization theory also might suggest that the emergence of a conservationist value system constituted the application of secular rationality to woodland management. Certainly, the writings on woodland conservation are this-worldly and pragmatic in tone, but that seems to have been as true in the early Edo period as later. The formal rhetoric often is Confucian, but much of the content could as easily be termed "practical peasant common sense" as "modern rationality." This silvicultural literature is important not because of its location in any historicist theory but because it was actually written and because many of the people who could benefit from it could read, and they did read and evidently apply it.

The other doctrine-based explanation that might be advanced posits the rise of a precocious ecological consciousness. It is a wonderfully appealing notion, but to my knowledge no one in early modern Japan argued that all living creatures have "rights." None held that biological diversity is either intrinsically good or essential to human well-being; those ideas have taken root only during the twentieth century. Rather, the concerns of those who restored woodland were emphatically "practical." They were concerned with what erosion did to road, village, and cropland. They wanted forests that would meet material human needs.

No, to seek the explanation of early modern forest recovery in formal doctrine is unhelpful. We have to get beyond simple formulations of of ideology to examine the complex questions of how people addressed their interest in human-oriented forest production and why the process of addressing that interest had the corollary effect of nurturing rather than ruining the forests of eighteenth- and nineteenth-century Japan. As that phrasing suggests, we must bear in mind that forest recovery was generally a means, not an end; a by-product more than a purposeful outcome of human effort.

To understand why human effort resulted in the by-product of forest recovery enmeshes us in multivariate analysis because we are dealing with an ecological problem that involves both human and environmental variables. The variables can be grouped into five categories—biological, technological, ideological, institutional, and ecological—each of which illuminates part of the problem. The contributions of the five can usefully be examined separately before we attempt to integrate them in an overall explanation.

1. The biological variables played their role through a pattern of socially modified forest dynamics that enabled woodland to adapt to human demand. The essential point here is that as loggers consumed old-growth stands of *sugi, hinoki, sawara, hiba,* and other conifers, those areas not converted to tillage or pasture grew up to mixed stands with a high proportion of broadleaf species. These broadleafs were deciduous in most areas but included important evergreen species along the southern littoral. The new stands provided far less lumber of the sort prized by builders of monuments, but they provided far more high-quality fuelwood and fertilizer material and often an absolute increase in biomass production per acre.

In an elemental sense this replacement of conifers with other species was a natural expression of forest dynamics. Felling removed a mature climax stand, opening the way for pioneer species to start a new cycle that would evolve through intermediate growth to a new climax forest.[7] In many places, however, this natural succession was slowed by villagers, whose repeated cutting of grass, brush, and young growth prevented the reassertion of indigenous conifers.[8] Ultimately, the Tokugawa populace, rulers included, could not survive without fertilizer to grow food and fuel to cook it, but it could get along without grand temples, mansions, and other such structures. In consequence, this change in forest composition was never fully reversed, even where governments vigorously promoted afforestation, and except in plantation stands, mixed forests came to dominate the mountains of Tokugawa Japan.

The prevalence of deciduous broadleaf growth served woodland well by enabling it to meet society's most insistent demands. This forest composition also helped preserve woodland by clothing hillsides in vegetation that gave soil exceptional protection. Whereas dense conifer stands shaded out most undergrowth, leaving a generally barren, needle-covered surface, deciduous woodland often contained substantial grass and brush. Moreover, when loggers felled conifers, the stumps died and roots decayed, permitting the barren slopes to erode easily. By contrast, when they cut down broadleafs, the stumps—especially of certain common species of oak and beech, but as well of hornbeam, chestnut, and mulberry—lived on, continuing to bind the soil in place. Moreover, these stumps rapidly pushed out new sprouts and leafy growth, forming coppice stands that soon gave soil additional protection against rain and wind.

In short, the natural process of forest succession, as modified by woodland users, enabled forests to meet the most pressing human needs while doing the best job of protecting themselves from natural damage. By themselves, of course, these biological factors cannot account for the larger pattern of forest recovery, as is evident from the severe deterioration experienced by woodlands in the Kinai and Inland Sea regions. There, biological habit notwithstanding, a longer period of human overuse achieved considerable destruction of forests and degradation of once-healthy soil.

2. Accordingly, the character of human exploitation also requires consideration. The technology of forest exploitation was a key variable, and certainly the survival of forest vitality was aided by the limitations of a primitive technology applied to impenetrable mountains. Both the felling and transport of timber required extraordinary manual effort despite the invention and widespread application of complex logging techniques. Woodsmen used slender-hafted, narrow-bladed axes and wedges to fell trees and form logs for shipping. And even though they showed great ingenuity in developing

chutes, sleds, and other devices for moving timber from felling site to river and equally great imagination in developing sluicing, rafting, snagging, and storage methods, the work remained slow, tedious, and labor-intensive. Those conditions enabled many deep mountain areas to continue providing sanctuary for both valued growth and "useless" biota that otherwise would have fallen victim to human actions. And even in more accessible areas technological considerations limited the frequency and intensity of human exploitation.

Two notable political restraints affected logging technology, one relating to wheeled vehicles and one to saws. For reasons that are not entirely clear, rulers prohibited intercity wheeled transport of goods and people.[9] In consequence, heavy wood products could not go overland, and shippers sent them by stream and coastal vessel instead. Given Japan's deeply incised topography and the extreme irregularity of streamflow, which repeatedly ruined fords and bridges, the prohibition on wheeled vehicles may have had little effect on the overall efficiency of timber transport, but in some locations it surely hampered forest exploitation and may have added to production costs.

More noteworthy was policy on crosscut saws. During the fifteenth century Japanese blacksmiths mastered the art of hammering out heavy-duty saws (*ōga*) of sufficient size, flatness, and temper to fell large trees. Woodsmen employed them in some logging projects during the rule of both Hideyoshi and Ieyasu, but for most of the Edo period governments proscribed them except for ripping timbers into planking and board stock. In some areas at least, rulers forbade felling by saw because a person could stealthily drop reserved trees with a crosscut saw, whereas the sound of ax blows carried far enough to discourage illegal woodcutting.[10] Because saws could cut much more rapidly than axes, their prohibition slowed logging and raised its labor cost appreciably.

These technological constraints on felling and moving timber to market helped keep logging an incredibly difficult and time-consuming task throughout the Edo period. By increasing labor costs, they may have helped discourage consumption. And they certainly slowed deforestation, thereby improving a forest's capacity to repair itself as felling progressed. The technical difficulty of logging did not stop it, however, and was in itself insufficient to save Japan's forests from destruction. Other factors were involved.

3. Ideology, like technology, helps shape human behavior, and the development of a conservation ethic and its effective application by rulers and villagers alike certainly influenced the forest experience. Clearly, there was such an ethic, and it began taking shape as soon as the first signs of overcutting appeared.[11] Before 1615, for example, a senior official of Akita *han* admonished his colleagues to bear in mind that "the treasure of the realm is the treasure of the mountains. When all [the trees] are cut and gone, however, their value will be nil. Before all is lost, proper care must be taken. Destitution of the mountains will result in destitution of the realm."[12]

Especially from about 1700, as noted in chapter 5, a stream of horticultural treatises (*jikatasho*); government edicts and regulations; and village, family, and business codes admonished people throughout Japan to preserve their property; nurture their resources; maximize the productivity of their lands, people, and enterprises; and bequeath a flourishing patrimony to the next generation. The writers applied this general ideal of resource preservation and output maximization to forests as well as to farmland and urban facilities. It underlay both the negative policies of use restriction and the positive policies of tree planting.

Without question, the existence of this conservation ethic was important to the survival and revival of Japan's forests. The presence of an ethic, however, does not explain why it can be applied effectively to a problem at hand. Somehow in the arrangement of its activities a society must so order affairs that people can translate an ideal into practical behavior. That requirement leads to exploration of the fourth, or institutional, set of factors that affected Tokugawa forest history.

4. An examination of institutional factors begins by noting some relevant contextual items of an institutional nature. Two items are the government policies of preserving domestic peace and minimizing foreign contact, which were largely in place by 1640 and perpetuated thereafter. One effect of these policies was to preclude a common solution to the problems caused by resource overexploitation: seizing neighboring territory to compensate for what one's own area no longer provides. The people of Tokugawa Japan, high and low alike, had to make do with what they had and what they could acquire peacefully, and they knew it. These government policies had the additional effects of preventing the introduction from abroad of

disequilibrating technology and ideas and of sustaining at home a general faith in the immutable nature of the social order. People simply took it for granted that the essential character of the future was knowable: they could prepare for it, but they must do so with the resources at hand.

Two other relevant contextual factors are these: by the mid-seventeenth century the household was established as the basic building block of society, and social status and location were strongly hereditary. Although there was in fact a great deal of geographical mobility in early modern Japan and few poor families actually maintained themselves for many generations, nevertheless a basic assumption on which villagers commonly planned the future was that ideally one's heir would inherit one's estate. Consequently, insofar as one's labor enhanced the worth of that estate, the labor would redound to the benefit of those whom one most cherished.

With these contextual matters in mind, an examination of institutional factors focuses on modifications in use rights that placed more and more real control of woodland in the hands of people with a vested interest in—and the resources to pursue—long-term forest regeneration. These modifications enabled early modern Japanese to apply their conservation ethic to woodland. The first widespread change was the formation of *tomeyama*, which governments established to prevent villagers from overcutting or destroying timber seedlings in their quest for fuel and fertilizer. This policy successfully protected large tracts of comparatively inaccessible forest, but as suggested in chapters 4 and 7, it did little to restore high-grade timber stands.

Furthermore, government policy was of limited value in woodland near villages, most of which was managed by villagers themselves, whether as communal or as household land. The quality of these woods, common land in particular, deteriorated as hard-pressed or irresponsible villagers despoiled them in defiance of protests and counterpressure from neighbors and official superiors.

In response to these problems, villages began dividing their common land, assigning designated portions (*wariyama*) to specified households for varying lengths of time and with various limitations of use, thereby giving those households greater incentive to nurture the land. Following such division, it appears, many deteriorated areas of former commons gradually regained heavier covers of grass, brush, coppice growth, and even hand-planted stands of timber trees. In contrast, in some places the conversion of commons to *wariyama* intensified the pressure on surviving communal land as poorer members of villages struggled to eke out a living by scraping together fuel and fertilizer from the patches of land still accessible to them. In consequence, the revival of some forest sites was accompanied by the spread of *hageyama* in adjoining areas.

Two other woodland arrangements that appeared in the eighteenth century—land leasing (*nenkiyama*) and yield sharing (*buwakebayashi*)—also gave interested parties reason and capacity to exercise responsible stewardship. In effect, the formation of *tomeyama*, *wariyama*, *nenkiyama*, and *buwakebayashi* shifted the basic philosophy of site utilization from multiple-use to single-use forestry, not by precluding all other uses or users but by establishing sustainable priorities on specific parcels. By facilitating this shift in the face of intensifying overconsumption of biomass, these several changes in woodland-use rights permitted orderly long-term utilization of forests and the adoption of sustained-yield policies.

5. Japan's early modern woodland experience was thus shaped by the performance of both the forests and their human exploiters. It would not do, however, to view the relationship as a simple bilateral interaction of humans and forest vegetation. The relationship was actually more complex, involving more actors whose roles are best examined from a broader ecological perspective. From this perspective the maintenance of sustained yield and, more fundamentally, the preservation of forest vitality depended on the establishment of tenable equilibria between a great array of supplies and demands. The attainment of these equilibria, and the consequent effectiveness of preservation measures, can be attributed to restraints that arose within the "homocentric biological community" of woodland exploiters, enabling it to live within the limits of its environmental context.

To explain this last sentence, the Japanese, like other human groups, were by themselves incapable of doing much damage to the ecosystem. Only after they adopted agricultural practices, forming symbiotic alliances with collaborating species of plants and animals, could they radically alter the biosystem. In forming such alliances, they not only advanced their own interests at the expense of other flora and fauna but also helped their collaborators advance their own species interest. Among plants in general, certain grains and grasses and select "vegetables" and "fruit" proved to be adaptable collaborators, with rice emerging as the primary beneficiary. Dogs, horses, chickens, and cattle proved particularly adept among the animals. Among trees, *sugi* emerged as a major winner during the Edo period. Working together, but in the service of the dominant humans, the members of this biological community established hegemony over ever larger areas of the country, primarily through systems of cultivation, pasturage, and orchardry that displaced many indigenous flora and fauna, leaving them to fare as best they could by moving elsewhere or finding "parasitic" niches.[13]

During the early modern predation, the Japanese and their biological collaborators extended their territorial sway about as far as they could on the islands south of Ezo.[14] For two reasons, however, that sway proved less damaging to other biota and to the ecosystem as a whole than it might have. First, the exploiting community did not include browsing herds of domesticated goats and sheep, such as have wreaked havoc in other parts of the world. Second, the community appears to have stabilized and perhaps even reduced its total demand on woodland during the eighteenth century, in part by restraining consumption, in part by extending its exploitation farther into the ocean, and in part by improving the efficiency of exploitation.

The human population itself nearly ceased growing after about 1720, and while the mechanisms and motivation of that numerical stabilization are topics of substantial scholarly debate, the root cause can surely be found in the intensifying constraints that the homocentric community encountered in its search for sustenance.[15] The processes of population control improved the efficiency of human exploitation of resources, it appears, by reducing the proportion of unproductive members—children, the aged, and the infirm—and, through periodic famines, by driving people out of the most vulnerable areas of the biosystem, notably interior valleys where extraction of resources was particularly difficult and where human activity could be especially destructive of the environment. Furthermore, instead of expanding consumption per capita on all fronts, the humans sorted out their priorities. They nearly abandoned monumental construction, both secular and religious, barely maintained urban establishments, and shifted woodland that once grew timber into production of more essential fertilizer, fuel, food, and other goods until the rise of plantation culture and the appearance of fertilizer substitutes allowed selective reconversion of hillsides to intensive timber production.

Gross human demand on woodland may thus have stabilized. It is possible, moreover, that some other sectors of the homocentric community shrank, enabling humans to consume directly a larger portion of the community's total woodland harvest. Most notably, where draft animals previously had pulled plows and carts, during the Edo period humans took over those tasks.[16] With those changes, and with the cessation of warfare, which eliminated the need for many cavalry mounts, horse and cattle populations may have declined, at least relative to the human population, allowing fodder-growing areas to produce green fertilizer, fuel, food, or other goods for more direct human consumption.

Trends in the population of other domestic animals are even less clear,[17] but a reduction in the overall consumption of foodstuffs by collaborating species may have left more for human use. In addition, expanded exploitation of marine products, as protein for humans and fertilizer for agriculture, meant that the human population could meet more of its needs without increasing the burden on forests. By stabilizing or even reducing its total demand on woodland, and by shifting more of the yield to direct human consumption, the homocentric biological community enabled forest production to come closer to satisfying the wants of the Japanese populace, thereby making easier the adoption of sustained-yield policies and the preservation of the terrestrial ecosystem.

In the end the historian wants to know "why" and "so what." Why did Japan's forest experience develop as it did? What were the consequences of its having done so? A sufficient explanation (the "why") and assessment (the "so what") of Tokugawa forest history must pull together these several variables of climate, geology, biology, ecology, technology, ideology, and social organization and change, to show how the result of their interaction was the survival of a stable ecosystem and vital forestland despite great and enduring human demand.

Such a formulation might read something like this. Aspects of the archipelago's geology and climate facilitated forest preservation. Because Japan was not buried under late Pleistocene glaciers, most hillsides, though geologically young and subject to easy surface destabilization, have not recently been stripped of regolith and instead have a fairly even, if thin and immature, covering of soil. Also, because glacial activity did not scour sharp ridges into rolling hills, disrupt drainage patterns, and create irregular depositional topography, and because Japan, unlike northwest Europe, has relatively rain-free winters, deforested areas are not rapidly overrun by peat moss and converted to bog and thus deprived of the capacity to reforest. Consequently, as long as deforestation is not followed by severe erosion, new woodland growth can establish itself without heroic human intervention.

Aided by these environmental qualities, and having been subjected to only moderate exploitation, most of Japan's forests outside the Kinai basin remained in generally good health until the seventeenth century. Population growth and other developments of that century, however, led to the despoliation of much woodland, giving rise to shortages of fuel, fertilizer, and construction timber and generating severe problems of flooding and erosion as well as social conflict. During the seventeenth century, these multiple pressures prodded rulers and villagers to devise new strategies of forest management. The resulting "negative regimen" of forest ordinances did little to restore high-grade timber stands, but it did mitigate the worst problems.

This policy of regulation was aided by the primitiveness of logging technology, which, given the topography of the islands, militated against rapid deforestation, and by the natural defense mechanisms of woodland, which slowed deterioration. Those factors, together with the social stability afforded by Japan's general avoidance of foreign disruptions and domestic upheaval, gave the humans more time to begin rearranging and restraining consumption within the homocentric biological community of forest users, thereby facilitating the eventual establishment of a general supply-demand equilibrium.

During the eighteenth century a body of useful silvicultural knowledge emerged. It was fostered by a basic ethic of conservation, sometimes couched in elegant Confucian terms but more commonly in terms of household or community well-being, that served the interests of the governments and village landholders who controlled most of the woodland. That silvicultural corpus, which became more sophisticated as the years passed, spelled out "positive" methods for coping with site damage and product shortages by nurturing desirable forest growth. Given the contextual factors of peace, hereditary status, and the household as the basic social unit, contemporary changes in land-control patterns made long-term forest nurturing worthwhile for those householders who managed land in economically favored locations, particularly along transportation arteries near major cities. In consequence, they were able to apply the new silvicultural knowledge to improve woodland conditions and increase timber output on selected sites, thereby easing logging pressure on other areas.

Because of this configuration of factors, by the mid-nineteenth century the Japanese had made appreciable strides in revitalizing forest production. However, the changes in woodland condition that made this possible were not achieved without cost. Within society, the broader homocentric biological community, and the ecosystem as a whole, the costs were substantial. And they were not borne equitably. Moreover, some of the gains in one type of yield were basically trade-offs achieved at the expense of other types, especially near villages, so the overall constraints on community use of woodland yield remained essentially intact. In the absence of other technological and social changes, any sharp increase in the homocentric community's total biomass consumption would produce renewed environmental deterioration and scarcities that could only disrupt long-term stability of supply.

Those caveats notwithstanding, the changes in woodland use that arose in response to the early modern predation halted much site deterioration, helped sustain species diversity, addressed with some success the social consequences of scarcity, and helped maintain valued types of forest output. In terms of the overall vitality of Japan's ecosystem, it may be appropriate to conclude that, given the scale and character of human demand on woodland during the Edo period, the social and ecological benefits of the transition from exploitation to regenerative forestry substantially outweighed the costs. That transition played a key role in enabling twentieth century Japan to survive as a luxuriant green archipelago rather than a slum-ridden, peasant society.

Bibliographical Essay: Scholarship on Preindustrial Japanese Forestry, 1880–1980

This study is the first extended report in English on preindustrial Japanese forestry.[1] Because it is a pioneer effort, some of its findings surely will be revised by subsequent scholarship. As perusers of notes will have observed, it relies heavily on the work of Japanese scholars, and this bibliographical essay attempts to summarize that work and facilitate access to it by examining the development of the field during the past century and by identifying titles pertinent to specific topics within it.[2]

Measures of forest management in Japan date back to the seventh century, but forestry experienced its most noteworthy advances during the early modern (Edo or Tokugawa) period (1600–1868). Not surprisingly, the advances in forest management, forest industry, and silviculture of the early modern period have commanded the most scholarly interest. That interest, which dates from the Meiji government's collection during the 1880s of documents on Tokugawa forestry, has been growing for a century now and has given rise to a complex and sophisticated historical sub-discipline.[3] By contrast, the study of pre-1600 woodland affairs dates only from about 1950 and is a field of study still in its infancy. Consequently, the literature on preindustrial forestry pertains over-whelmingly to the early modern period.

Studying this literature has its difficulties. There is a problem of boundaries because the topic merges imperceptibly into a host

of others, including post-1868 history; local, commercial, and
industrial history; the history of social structure and change, of
mountain-village living conditions, and of transportation; riparian
work; agricultural technology; social thought; and science. Moreover, the historiography is difficult to survey because the writings
are scattered through a vast array of journals and bulletins and
appear in books that sometimes are difficult to locate and quickly
go out of print.[4] This essay, based on works I have been able to
examine, will doubtless fail to cite some items of value.[5] Post-1980
scholarship is purposely omitted.

Major Interpretive Issues

Preindustrial forest history seems on first glance an unlikely forum
for political comment. We soon discover, however, that burning
issues are imbedded in it. Even in its genesis the discipline was
merely an academic by-product of practical efforts by the new
Meiji government to consolidate power and pursue national reform. The decision to establish a centrally controlled national forest
system led to the original compilation of documents and preparation of descriptive studies of forest organization and operation.
After the new forest system took shape, moreover, stubborn practical problems continued to sustain much of the scholarly interest
in earlier forest practices.

Other less immediate concerns also have fostered study of preindustrial forestry. Both before and after the Pacific War, some
scholars wrote on early modern silviculture, patriotically demon-
strating that Japan had an indigenous, still-serviceable tradition
of forestry. In contrast, as part of the angry postwar search for explanations of recent state policy, some forest historians produced
studies that highlighted the repressive nature of "feudal" forestry
and the exploitative nature of "capitalist" forestry, which, they
argued, paved the way for Japan's expansionist twentieth-century
"absolutism."

The issue in forest history that has most richly embodied contemporary concerns has been the state and fate of village common
land (*iriaichi*).[6] When the Meiji government rationalized forest
administration during the 1880s, it precipitated widespread rural
hardship and discontent by making sweeping changes in rights to

common land. That situation prompted scholars to study contemporary *iriai* arrangements and their historical background. During the 1930s, as parts of rural Japan wallowed in misery, *iriai* research intensified, still focusing on post-1868 developments. It was redoubled in the changed intellectual climate of the postwar years because rural suffering was seen as central to Japan's recently disastrous political experience. Concurrently, a new burst of land reform generated more disputes over common land, and these stimulated further historical study. Scholars dug deeper into the problem, and the quest for origins and determinitive experiences shifted the focus of inquiry backward to the Edo period. Since then, common-land practices have remained a focal point of research.

A broader aspect of Meiji land reform also sparked much scholarship. The creation of Japan's modern national forest system excluded many villagers not only from wooded common land but also from forestland of other types that they previously had utilized. The government's rationale for this far-reaching forest closure was that timber stands must be protected and lumber production enhanced, tasks best handled by officialdom. This perception of government as the benevolent protector of the commonweal was reflected in (and reinforced by) scholarly studies of early modern forestry, which explored carefully the extensive and presumably beneficial governmental forest policies of the Edo period.

In the wake of World War II this elitist government posture struck many scholars as dubious, and a fierce debate arose concerning the relative merits of "family forests" and "state forests." This debate promoted a considerable body of scholarship designed to reassess the contributions of early modern governments, villages, and individual entrepreneurs to forest protection, afforestation, and, by extension, the public welfare. The result has been a significant reinterpretation of how Tokugawa forestry operated. Whereas studies made earlier in the twentieth century commonly saw early modern forest policy as a desirable government effort imposed on a reluctant and unenlightened rural populace, recent works more often see government policy as exploitative and repressive, whereas private initiatives were creative and fruitful. The task of reconciling this view with that of an exploitative merchant capitalist role in Tokugawa forestry will doubtless keep scholars occupied for some time.

During the last several years, the pain of Japan's mid-century failures has been displaced by the pleasure of more recent triumphs. In keeping with this spirit, scholarship has lost some of its critical social bite. Authors have eliminated much overtly political content from their writings, transcending the issues of modern history and studying the preindustrial forest experience "objectively." The effort has generated much detailed monographic work, whose lack of explicit political purpose often makes it more accessible for interpretive use than the socially engaged scholarship. For the foreign scholar this descriptive literature can be particularly valuable.

Students of Japanese history will recognize that in addressing modern social issues, researchers in preindustrial forestry are engaged in intellectual endeavors common to the nation's historical profession as a whole. Forest history is thus an integral part of the broader historical discipline. For scholars of forest history the implication is somewhat more burdensome: it means that a general familiarity with these issues is essential to understanding the significance of the secondary literature.

The Historiography of Preindustrial Forestry

The study of forest history prior to the Edo period is difficult. The documentary base is very limited and consists largely of random bits of information scattered among records of other matters, mostly relating to the administration of political and religious institutions.

By contrast, Tokugawa forest history is based on an exceptionally rich documentation, including government archives, village records, business and family records, and the technical writings of professional agronomists of the day. Many of the government documents were assembled by Meiji officialdom during the 1880s, but rather little scholarship appeared until the 1930s, when the field experienced a burst of activity. During that decade scholars such as Endō Yasutarō, Hattori Marenobu, Toba Masao, and Tokugawa Muneyoshi produced a series of solidly researched monographs and perceptive interpretive studies of early modern forest organization, thought, and practice. Work in the field was nearly halted by the war and the hardships of the late 1940s, but during the fifties scholarship revived. It built on the achievements of the thirties and broke new ground, led by such figures as Nishikawa Zensuke, Shimada Kinzō, and Tokoro Mitsuo.

In recent decades the discipline has flowered, developing several subspecialties. They overlap, and terminology is not entirely standardized, but they can be categorized as follows:

rinseishi: the history of forest administration

ringyōshi: the history of forest industries, primarily lumbering, firewood, and charcoal

sansonshi: the history of mountain villages

sanrin shisōshi: the history of thought on forests and forestry

ringyō gijutsushi: the history of forest technology

zōrinshi: the history of afforestation

As this summary of the field suggests, the discipline can be studied in terms of source materials, prewar scholarship, scholarship during the postwar decade, and the subspecialties that have matured during the quarter century to 1980.

The Source Materials

Government documents on early modern forestry are profuse because so many governments managed woodland. Not only did the *bakufu* manage its great forests, but most of the 250 *han* also controlled woodland, maintaining administrative records and handling an endless stream of litigation relating to woodland use. Much of this corpus survived intact when the Tokugawa regime collapsed in 1868.

As Tokoro Mitsuo explains in his bibliographical essay, "Rinseishi" (**259**),[7] in June 1879 Meiji government leaders instructed the recently formed Forest Agency (Sanrinkyoku) to assemble documents that would aid in drafting legislation for a new forest system. Prefectural officials collected them, had copies transcribed, submitted the copies to Tokyo, and prepared reports detailing practices within their jurisdictions. As material flowed into the capital, agency scribes compiled it in a massive collection titled *Sanrin enkakushi* [Historical records of forestland]. On the basis of this material, plus study of European forestry, the agency prepared draft legislation and in August 1882 submitted a finished version to Meiji leaders. This document became the basis of a unified national forest system that replaced the crazy-quilt Tokugawa arrangements.

The *Sanrin enkakushi*, together with some other material, was then
stored in an agency archive in Tokyo, where it was inaccessible to
scholars. Even if it had been accessible, however, it might not have
contributed to extensive writing on early modern forestry because
the Meiji era (1868–1911) was a time when practical questions of
woodland management and development and European rather
than Japanese forest practices dominated professional interest, as is
evident in Tokugawa Muneyoshi's bibliographical essay on early
Meiji forestry (**268**).

During the first decades of the twentieth century, official
agencies, in particular prefectural governments, utilized the materials compiled in 1879–80 to publish a few volumes on forestry in
their areas. Most noteworthy are the following one-volume works:
Shinano sanrin shi (1907), *Kyōto-fu sanrin shi* (1909), *Miyagi-ken ringyō
shiryō* (1915), *Higo han rinsei enshikō* (1916), *Hitoyoshi han rinsei enkakushi* (1922), *Saga han rinsei enkakushi* (1922), and *Yamanashi-ken
rinseishi* (1922).

In 1923 matters were cruelly disrupted. Just before noon on September 1, a massive earthquake ravaged Tokyo, killing over one
hundred thousand people. One of the resulting fires consumed the
Forest Agency and its great compilation, *Sanrin enkakushi*.[8] In 1925,
after recovering from the disaster, the Ministry of Agriculture and
Forestry (Nōrinshō) ordered the entire project redone. It instructed
the prefectural governments, which by then had come into possession of many more documents than they had had during the 1880s,
to assemble and prepare copies of relevant material. They were to
send copies to a compilation office that was established in the Forest
Agency's Tokyo office and supervised by the agency head. There a
group of officials and scholars, which eventually included Endō
and Toba, were to organize them for publication. The compilers
planned to proceed in an orderly manner, assembling the documents *han* by *han*, working from north to south until they had
covered the country.

The project began with documents of Tsugaru *han*. The Aomori
prefectural government, which administered the area, hired a
group of elderly residents who could read old documents and were
familiar with local forest terminology to transcribe material in the
prefectural library. Using carbon paper, they made four copies of
each document. The first two were clear, the third marginal, and

the fourth nearly unreadable. The three readable copies were for-
warded to Tokyo, where compilers arranged them for binding. By
the time the Aomori transcribers finished their task, they had
copied material enough to fill 302 handwritten volumes (*kan*).

As sheaves of material poured into Tokyo, it became apparent
that the documentation was much more extensive than anticipated,
and the compilers excluded more and more peripheral records.
To complicate matters further, after two years of work government retrenchment halved the number of compilers. The remaining
workers had to screen materials even more rigorously, and in consequence the documentation from other *han* is much less complete.
In contrast to Tsugaru's 302 *kan*, for example, the source materials
on Morioka fill 121; Akita, 80; Kii and Owari, only 23 each; and
Saga and Kumamoto, 33 and 38, respectively. Moreover, the compilers finally focused upon 41 *han* and the *bakufu*, whose forests were
most important, completely excluding materials from the other
200-odd *han*.

Despite this substantial scaling down of the project, the compilers
produced 1,380 *kan* of 150–250 pages apiece under the title *Nihon
rinseishi chōsa shiryō* [Documents of the investigation into the history
of Japan's forest system]. To assure that their handiwork would
escape the fate of *Sanrin enkakushi*, the three readable copies of the
manuscript were stored separately: one at the ministry; one in a
research library at Tokyo Imperial University; and the other in
the closed archives of the Tokugawa Institute for the History of
Forestry (Tokugawa Rinseishi Kenkyūjo) at Mejiro in northwest
Tokyo.[9]

Upon completion of the basic compilation, further selection during 1930–35 produced *Nihon rinseishi shiryō* [Records of the history
of Japanese forestry] (**165**), a thirty-volume published edition of
documents relating to forest administration. It consists of one
volume on pre-Tokugawa forest management; one on management
by temples, shrines, and nobles; three on *bakufu* forest policy; and
twenty-five volumes that cover thirty-eight *han*.

During the Pacific War the original ministry copy of the 1,380-
kan document was destroyed by American bombers. The other two
copies survived, but neither was complete due to mishaps in the
compiling process and later losses. Together they did constitute a
complete set, however, and following the recovery from the war,

the gaps in each were filled with photocopies from the other. In 1970 the complete work was microfilmed, and copies of the 706-reel version are now available in several locations in Japan but, as of this writing, not in the United States. A guide to the work, which originally appeared in the journal *Sanrin ihō* in 1936, was republished in 1971 by the Tokugawa Institute, with collations for the microfilm edition (**269**). Also in 1971 the thirty-volume published edition of administrative documents was reprinted.

In the decades after the Meiji Restoration many other compilation projects were undertaken. Some of these (**224–27**) included works by Edo-period agronomists such as Miyazaki Antei, Ōkura Nagatsune, Satō Shin'en, and the Okinawan, Sai On, most of whom devoted some attention to forest problems and practices. Since then the most important of the early modern agricultural writings have reappeared periodically in new editions. Prefectural governments have published collections of documents on the history of their areas, and these commonly include materials on forestry. Cities, likewise, have published histories and collections of documents that contain entries on woodland affairs. Towns, villages, and local historical associations from time to time find and reproduce local records pertaining to forests, and lumber-merchant organizations and families have published some of their records. Finally, individual scholars continue to unearth and utilize unpublished documents (**78, 185**).[10] Illustrative of such contributions is Shimada Kinzō's recent book-length study of Edo lumber merchants, which consists of 129 documents plus an interpretive essay on their significance (**186**).[11]

The appearance of these original sources has been crucial to the discipline's development. The original compilation of *Sanrin enkakushi* made possible Shirakawa Tarō's pioneering *Teikoku rinseishi* [A history of the empire's forest system], published in 1902 (**200**). The compilation of documents after 1925 and the publication of *Nihon rinseishi shiryō* underlay the scholarly achievements of the 1930s. The reissue of works by early modern agronomists has been crucial to the study of afforestation and forest thought. And the dramatic maturation of the discipline during the past quarter century has been based directly on the capacity of scholars to obtain and utilize the documents necessary for more detailed analyses of their subjects.[12]

Pre–Pacific War Scholarship

Following Shirakawa Tarō's pathfinding work of 1902, the only notable scholarly works for nearly three decades were a few based on documents of selected *han* (**111, 271, 279**), in particular Tsukii Tadahiro's richly documented study of Akita (Kubota) *han* forestry and Tokugawa Yoshichika's *Kisoyama*, a descriptive ethnography of the mountainous Kiso area.

During the 1930s several more studies of specific *han* appeared. In 1935 Monda Sai, a scholar-official in Kōchi, published *Tosa han rinseishi* (**133**). A year later Tokugawa Yoshichika began reworking his study of Kiso, publishing the results in twenty-two issues of the journal *Goryōrin* (**270**). In 1939 this type of inquiry culminated in Iwasaki Naoto's massive, highly intelligent, exhaustively researched study of forestry in Akita (**90**). Iwasaki described Akita's forest system as a whole and then focused on the *sugi* forests of the Yoneshiro river watershed. He examined the system of forest protection, the overcutting of conifers, *han* responses thereto, the destruction of broadleaf stands, countermeasures that followed, and finally the planting, nurturing, vicissitudes, and marketing of the *sugi* plantations that became established from about 1800 onward.

Broader studies of the early modern forest system also appeared. The most noteworthy was "Tokugawa jidai ni okeru rin'ya seido no taiyō" [An outline of the forest system of the Tokugawa period]. This series of essays, which was the most immediate by-product of *Nihon rinseishi shiryō*, was prepared by Takeda Hisao, a Nōrinshō official involved in the compilation project, and appeared in *Sanrin ihō* between 1934 and 1940. Each essay is a systematic distillation of the main characteristics of forest organization in one of the *han* covered by the published collection. The essays, which in their entirety constitute a summary interpretation of the collected documents, were reproduced in book form in 1954 by the Department of Forestry (Rin'yachō) (**177**).

Two shorter general works of the thirties also owed much to the compilation effort. One was a fine, concise essay on Tokugawa forestry that Toba Masao wrote for the multivolume Iwanami history of Japan published in 1934–36 (**231**). The other was *Ringyō keizai kenkyū* [A study of the economics of forestry], a general work prepared by Hattori Marenobu in 1940, which was in great part a reissue of earlier essays (**49–55**).[13]

Endō Yasutarō, most ambitious of the 1930s scholars, attempted to produce a definitive work on the Tokugawa forest system. He was able to complete only one "section," however, titled *Nihon sanrinshi: Hogorin hen* [A history of Japanese forestry: Protection forests] (**14**). That one "section" is a three-volume work: one volume of narrative, one of illustrations and tables, and one of documents arranged topically. The 908-page narrative volume treats systematically a great variety of early modern forests, including those protecting temples, highways, soil, beaches, and riverbanks, and those maintained for water conservancy, fuel, hunting, sanitation, and aesthetic reasons.

Endō never completed his gigantic project, but he did publish other valuable works (**12–16**), notably an imaginative volume that examines the link between forestry and culture in northeast Japan by exploring the region's forestry and forest life and industry (**15**). He and other scholars, Hattori and Toba in particular (**230, 232, 236, 238**), also wrote shorter pieces on aspects of afforestation and forest administration, economics, protection, and harvesting.

In 1936 the Dai Nihon Sanrinkai (Forest Association of Imperial Japan) published a two-volume collection of biographical sketches of figures noted for their contributions to afforestation (**310**). Volume one has short sketches from a half page to several pages of 142 figures active during the Edo period. Volume two covers figures active after 1868. An earlier companion work contained sketches of figures whose contributions were in the field of shoreline conservancy (**113**).

Valuable studies of Edo-period thought on forests and forestry also began to appear during the thirties. A pioneer essay by Yamamoto Tokusaburō in 1928 examined the writings on forestry of Kumazawa Banzan (**303**). Subsequently, Endō Yasutarō wrote two essays and Tokoro Mitsuo and others one apiece on forest thought (**13, 16, 98, 245, 287**).

The outstanding contributor to this silvicultural history was Tokugawa Muneyoshi. During 1940 he wrote for the journal *Sanrin* a series of ten concise essays discussing ten major Edo-period writers on forestry, and two years later he formulated a general periodization for the development of early modern silvicultural thought (**265, 267**). In 1941 he published his masterpiece, *Edo jidai ni okeru* *zōrin gijutsu no shiteki kenkyū* [A historical study of afforestation techniques in the Edo period] (**266**). It is a lucid exposition of the techniques of vegetative and seedling propagation, examining such topics as seed selection, seedbed preparation, sowing, nurturing, transplanting, rearing, and harvesting. The author based his work on exhaustive scrutiny of the writings of early modern agronomists, family and village records, and government documents. And he brought to it a sound grasp of modern silvicultural insight.

In toto, during the thirties some two or three dozen secondary works—books, articles, and series of articles—examined early modern forest history. Meanwhile, an independent line of scholarship was beginning to converge with this corpus. That was the study of common land (*iriaichi*) and the process of division (*yamawari*) that allotted parcels of it to individual households, thereby giving it some of the attributes of private property and making it more amenable to the long-term management required by plantation forestry.

The study of common land and its division began near the turn of the century as an inquiry into contemporary village problems. An early scholar of note was Nakada Kaoru. His analyses of post-1868 common-land developments were deemed sufficiently valuable to warrant their reissue as a book in 1949 (**148**). Many other scholars also examined *iriaichi* and land division, as Ueda Tōjurō noted early in 1931 (**290**), but they, like Nakada, usually focused on agricultural land and post-1868 patterns. During the thirties, however, as Harada Toshimaru pointed out in 1969 (**38**), scholarly understanding of common land and its division advanced rapidly, becoming inextricably linked to forest history (**195, 288–89**). In the early forties, forested common land (*rin'ya iriaichi*) of the Edo period began receiving attention (**134**).

The major prewar study of *iriai* practices was Kainō Michitaka's *Iriai no kenkyū* (**93**), a sophisticated analysis of both forested and open common land. Kainō focused primarily on post-1868 developments but devoted about a fourth of his pages to the Edo period. With the appearance of his study, which became a key reference work, the main threads of prewar Japanese forest history were in place. After surviving the catastrophic years 1944–46, scholars would pick up again the themes of forest administration and eco-

nomics, afforestation, forest thought, and forests in village life and
build them into the rich subdiscipline that is the contemporary field
of early modern forest history.

Scholarship during the Postwar Decade

For Japanese intellectuals the road back to scholarly vitality was a
long and painful one. In the field of early modern forest history a
decade passed before the discipline regained its prewar level of
quality and quantity. Some writing was done, however, motivated
by two concurrent public tasks. One was the task of repairing
woodland damaged by pervasive overharvesting during the war
and postwar reconstruction. The other was resolution of land-use
disputes, many pertaining to common-land use rights (*iriaiken*), that
accompanied postwar land reform.

    This present-centered interest led scholars of forestry and forest
history to pursue both historical research and the study of current
problems of forestry (**187, 234–35, 300**). To note but one example,
Endō Jiichirō, a scholar-official associated with the Department of
Forestry, was deeply involved in the reform of common-land usage.
He also found time for historical scholarship. In 1947 he published
a book, *Nihon rin'ya iriaiken ron* [Disputes over rights to forested
common land in Japan] (**11**), that reviewed Edo-period *iriai* practices, their reorganization during the Meiji period, and the contemporary situation. A decade later he republished the book with
an appended essay on postwar forest reform.

    The concern to revive Japan's forests inspired the study of
Tokugawa afforestation techniques. The first notable postwar piece
on the subject was completed by Yamanouchi Shizuo in 1949
(**304**). The following year a team of scholars published *Sugi no
kenkyū* [Studies of cryptomeria], a work that zeroed in on Japan's
most valuable timber tree (**181**). It was a multidisciplinary examination of *sugi* culture and use and included an essay by Matsushima
Yoshio that surveyed Japan's long history of *sugi* afforestation
(**125**). In a later piece Matsushima broadened his scope to cover the
history of early modern afforestation in general (**126**). In a short
essay in 1950, and two years later in a book, the professional forester Tanaka Hajime treated the topic in much more detail and with
a more overtly expressed wish to preserve the "spiritual" values of

Japan in the face of overweening "Western materialism" (**228–29**). In 1953 the intellectual historian Kanō Kyōji began publishing in the journal *Ringyō keizai* a series of solid scholarly essays that analyzed the contributions of major early modern writers on forestry.

A few other pre-Meiji topics also received article-length treatment in the early fifties (**95, 99, 135, 171, 185, 198**), and in 1954 the Department of Forestry republished in book form Takeda Hisao's prewar synopses of early modern forest administration (**177**). The subject that commanded the most sustained attention, however, was common land and its division. The postwar debate over *iriaichi* was launched by Furushima Toshio, whose studies, which generally focus on post-1868 trends and patterns, are probably unmatched in both quality and influence. Some of the best have recently reappeared in a new multivolume edition (**27**).

Much of the vast literature on common land, communalism, and land division is not relevant to the study of Tokugawa forestry because it deals with post-1868 agricultural lands and is primarily concerned with village structure and conditions. A few essays of the early fifties, however, did deal with early modern forested common land, examining its organization and use and the changes that accompanied its division among village households (**80, 158, 183, 275**). Major works by Furushima in 1955 and Nishikawa Zensuke in 1957 may be seen as culminating this postwar phase of debate and setting the stage for subsequent scholarly disputes about the cause, character, and consequence of changes in *iriai* arrangements (**29, 161**).

By the time Nishikawa's book appeared, the world of Japanese forest history was entering an era of dramatic growth. In the decades after 1955 new scholars would rise to prominence, and the discipline would acquire unprecedented diversity and sophistication.

Recent Scholarship on Preindustrial Forestry, 1955–80

Since 1955, scholars of preindustrial forest history have been extremely active, but they have not given equal attention to all facets of their subdiscipline. Nearly all research focuses on early modern forestry; only a few pieces examine pre-Tokugawa developments. Within the early modern segment there have been a number of general works, much research on forest administration and industry (*rinseishi* and *ringyōshi*), and extensive study of mountain villages (*sansonshi*). Less effort has been devoted to forest thought (*sanrin shisōshi*), afforestation (*zōrinshi*), and the history of forest technology (*ringyō gijutsushi*), although a few major contributions have been made in those areas. Water conservancy and forest ecology have also received some attention.

Pre-Tokugawa Forest History

The study of pre-1600 forestry received a major boost in 1958 with the appearance of *Meijizen Nihon ringyō gijutsu hattatsushi* [The development of forest technology in pre-Meiji Japan], compiled by Nihon Gakushiin (**153**). It is a masterful, topically organized study that traces the techniques and technology of forest exploitation from prehistory through the nineteenth century. In 1959, 1961, and 1962 Tokoro Mitsuo penned three essays, all titled "Ringyō," that examined forestry in preindustrial Japan (**255–57**). The first ranged broadly from prehistory to the nineteenth century, describing timber and logging technology, land-use rights, and the rites and rituals of forest work. The 1961 piece described the history of lumbering, lumber use, and forest management in the centuries before 1600, and the third focused on logging techniques and the carpenter's arts, especially during the centuries 700–900.

In a series of essays that appeared in *Ringyō keizai* in 1964–67, Yamamoto Hikaru summarized main trends in forestry from prehistory to the seventeenth century, relying on the scholarly work of general historians for much of his information (**295–99, 301–2**). Over the years a few other pieces have appeared that illuminate aspects of pre-Tokugawa forest history (**16, 125, 140–41, 159, 171, 235, 304**). A recent work that suggests the possibilities still present in this field is Toda Yoshimi's essay on aristocratic woodland management in tenth-century Japan (**239**).

General Works on Early Modern Forestry

One of the less satisfying aspects of early modern forest history during the past twenty-five years has been that of general interpretation. So far no scholar has successfully pulled together the several thriving lines of research to present an integrated explanation of how the Tokugawa forest system functioned as a whole.

This situation is not surprising. The great works of compilation that underlay earlier general interpretations consisted primarily of government documents. They conveyed the picture of a forest system operated by *bakufu* and *han* officials in accordance with government regulations. Although the system might seem a nearly incomprehensible labyrinth, it was essentially a unidimensional, government-controlled phenomenon.

The current picture is more complex. Monographic work of recent decades has shown that government, villages, merchants, and village householders all shared in operating woodland. Their relationships and degrees of influence varied tremendously, however, from place to place and time to time. Moreover, the relationships had both conflictive and symbiotic dimensions that were expressed through buying, selling, leasing, and sharing and that encompassed diverse forms of obligation and payment. Successful integration of all these variables has thus far eluded scholars, and the field is characterized by great caution at this level of interpretation.

Nevertheless, the quarter century to 1980 witnessed the appearance of several general essays on the subject. Although most authors focus on the twentieth century, allotting little space to the Tokugawa period, and even less to preceding centuries, a few trace the history from its beginnings. In 1960 Funakoshi Shōji examined the rise of the modern lumber industry as an aspect of emerging Japanese capitalism, devoting forty pages to Edo-period logging before focusing on post-1868 developments (**23**). The same year the Department of Forestry published *Nihon ringyō hattatsushi* [A history of the rise of Japanese forestry] (**176**), which also focused on post-1868 developments. However, its authors opened with a lucid thirty-page description of *bakufu* and *han* forest organization and devoted forty pages to an examination of those districts where entrepreneurial forestry flourished during the late Edo period. The work treated governments as determining forest utilization, with official policy allowing various forms of village participation in the use of forest products.

In 1978 Tsutsui Michio published *Nihon rinseishi kenkyū josetsu* [An introduction to the study of Japanese forest history] (**281**). The sixty pages devoted to Tokugawa forestry are an admirable source of information on *han* policy, notably afforestation, and they also contain a revealing discussion of burnt-field culture. The essay retains, however, the government-centered focus of earlier scholarship and reveals little of the complexity of village and merchant roles in forest usage.

There remains for consideration one other general work, Tokoro Mitsuo's *Kinsei ringyōshi no kenkyū* [Studies in the history of early modern forestry] (**249**). Drawing material freely from his earlier essays, Tokoro opens with a section on pre-1600 forestry and then examines *bakufu* forestry in the Ina and Hida areas and *han* forest operations in Matsumoto, Matsushiro, and Owari. The volume also contains a fifty-page compilation of forest terms based on glossaries of the Edo period that is valuable because the vocabulary of early modern forestry is so different from that of today's as to be inaccessible. The book conveys a sense of the complex interplay of forces in early modern forestry, and while an integrated picture of the system as a whole may not emerge clearly, the volume sums up a lifetime of scholarship. A treasure house of detailed information and valuable insights, it reveals the author's mastery of his subject.

Local forest history has flourished since the sixties. A number of local studies, such as Hirao Michio's book on forestry in Tosa (**58**), fall into the category of general works because their purpose is to describe all major aspects of the forest system and its functioning in a given locality. Several solid essays of this type can be found in the volumes of *Nihon sangyōshi taikei* [An outline of the industrial history of Japan] (**9, 115, 121, 136, 144, 233, 251**), and others have appeared elsewhere (**116, 120, 131, 143, 147, 169, 199, 258**).

Forest Administration (Rinseishi)

Homonyms can obscure useful distinctions. The term *rinsei* can be written in two ways. The first, using the *sei* of *seido* (system, institution, organization) denotes the forest system in formal, static, institutional terms. It entails the identification of organizational structures, rules and regulations, realms of authority, and the fixed procedures of administration. The second *rinsei*, using the *sei* of *seiji* (government, administration, politics) denotes the forest system in dynamic terms of process. It involves description and analysis of how forests are operated, how disputes are settled, how interests interact, and how over time relationships, interests, structures, regulations, and procedures change.

As long as the scholarly study of forest administration was pre-occupied with formal structure, as in Takeda Hisao's essays (**177**), it was possible to draw a clear distinction between *rinsei*, meaning "structural" *rinsei*, and the disciplinary subspecialties of *ringyō* and *zōrin* (forest industry and afforestation). Once basic institutions had been delineated, however, and scholars started scrutinizing the dynamics of the system, the distinctions between *rinsei*, in the sense of "dynamic" *rinsei*, and *ringyō* and *zōrin* began to blur. Further-more, as scholars have scrutinized the dynamics of early modern forestry, the complexity of merchant-village-government relation-ships has become more apparent. This has diminished the analyti-cal utility of the three categories of government, village, and house-hold woodland, causing mountain village history (*sansonshi*) to become thoroughly entwined with the histories of *rinsei*, *ringyō*, and *zōrin*.

Nevertheless, works that can usefully be categorized as *rinseishi* continue to appear (**4, 35, 56, 106, 114, 118, 149, 170, 215, 219, 244, 272, 292, 306**). Even these, however, tend to overlap other fields. Thus, Asai Junko's study of *bakufu* forest administration on Mount Amagi touches on *zōrinshi* by illuminating the regime's afforestation policies (**3**). And an essay by Minemura Hideo uses documents of the forest inspector's office in Suwa *han* to illuminate both the domain's afforestation policy (*zōrinshi*) and its methods of regulating timber harvesting (*ringyōshi*) (**128**).

Some of the best studies of forest administration examine two practices that are particularly interesting from the perspective of woodland preservation: the formation of *buwakebayashi*, or shared-yield forests, and the establishment of *nenkiyama*, or leased forests. The outstanding work on shared-yield forests is Shioya Tsutomu's 654-page *Buwakebayashi seido no shiteki kenkyū* [Historical studies of the shared-forest system] (**197**), which combines detailed study of the practice in individual *han* with integrative essays on the practice in both early modern and post-1868 Japan.

The *nenkiyama* phenomenon initially received attention because historians saw in it a developing capitalist lumber industry and thus an experience illustrative of the elemental dynamics of history. Now the practice is considered too diverse for such a unitary interpretation. As Sawata Takaharu's study of forestry on Awaji island points up (**182**), there were different types of leasing. A fair amount simply entailed granting villagers very short-term access to scrubland to permit harvesting of fertilizer and fuel materials, as Wakabayashi Kisaburō has shown (**293**). Very different, and more important in the development of plantation forestry, was the type of leasing that Kaneiwa Yoshio, Kasai Kyōetsu, and Shimada Kinzō have described (**99, 102, 189–92**).

Forest Industry (Ringyōshi)

Studies of forest industry (*ringyō*), lumbering in particular, form the heart of recent scholarship on Tokugawa forestry.[14] It is a complex area of study because major aspects merge with a host of related subjects, including village history and the history of afforestation as well as shared-yield and forest-leasing practices.

A key economic issue that bears directly on the relationships among governments, merchants, and villagers is the question of who controlled and carried on lumbering. There were two distinguishable but connected types of lumbering in early modern Japan: that under government auspices and that initiated by venture capitalists of merchant or peasant provenance. Nishikawa Zensuke used these categories when he examined the history of forest industry in a series of seminal essays in *Ringyō keizai* in 1959–61 (**159, 160**), and his formulations have underlain subsequent research.

A number of essays, mostly by Tokoro Mitsuo, have examined the roles of lord and merchant in forest exploitation during the years of Hideyoshi and the early Tokugawa rulers (1590–1630) (**196, 241, 243, 250, 254, 262**). Other studies in *ringyōshi* have had a regional focus (**62–63, 127, 129, 179, 240, 261**). Tokoro's research on the Kiso valley (**246, 249, 264**), Iioka Masatake's essays on logging in the Tenryū valley (**81–87**), Takase Tamotsu's analyses of Kaga *han* lumbering (**218–22**), and Fujita Yoshitani's study of logging in the Ōi watershed northwest of Kyoto (**20**) merit special notice.

Getting timber to market was the crux of the logger's task, and most wood went by river and sea. Scholars have examined the development of transportation arrangements, especially rafting.

Fujita Yoshitani's study of Ōi river logging, like some of Iioka's essays, devotes substantial attention to transportation. Tokoro's delightful old study of the log boom at Nishikori on the Kiso (**253**) must also be mentioned. More recent essays by Tokoro, Shimada, Takase, and others have also examined water transport (**123, 142, 194, 216–17, 263, 291**), and an excellent article by Yokoyama Atsumi looks at overland shipment of lumber produced in Matsumoto *han* (**307**).

Many of the works already cited deal with merchant activity, that of Fujita Yoshitani being a major example. Other studies focus on lumber merchants in Osaka (**172, 305**), Kyoto (**132**), or Edo (**157, 186, 188, 308**). The histories of lumbermen's associations tend to deal almost entirely with post-1868 developments (**97, 211**), but for the study of early modern lumbering, one of the most useful is *Shizuoka ken mokuzaishi* [A history of lumbering in Shizuoka prefecture] (**201**), which has a section on pre-Meiji forestry in the Suruga area. The question of how large-scale city merchants related to local merchants, villages, and governments, a question that has important implications for basic interpretations of Japanese history, lies at the heart of the best and conceptually most self-conscious studies in this corpus. Essays by Nishikawa Zensuke (**162**) and Shimada Kinzō (**189, 193**) address the question directly.

Finally, the study of *ringyōshi* has at its periphery the study of several forest products other than lumber. Most important are firewood and charcoal, which often are discussed together, although some works focus entirely on the charcoal industry (**1, 2, 57**). Of the many other forest industries, we can mention for illustrative purposes lacquer and wax (**164, 202**), both of which were derived from trees; pottery and tile (**103**), which needed abundant fuelwood for firing; and mining, which required both mine timbers and smelting fuel.[15]

Forestry and Mountain Villages (Sansonshi)

It is egregiously artificial to remove studies of mountain villages from the context of general village history and to break them off at 1868. Such measures are necessary, however, to make the vast corpus manageable and to identify those works most pertinent to Tokugawa forest history.

Most of the general works on mountain villages, such as Miyamoto Tsuneichi's twenty-volume regionally organized study (**130**), deal primarily with the past century. A few, however, examine villages of the Tokugawa period (**10, 28, 213**) and provide a point of departure for the researcher. The relations between early modern villagers and outsiders, primarily government officials and urban entrepreneurs, were marked by tension and legal conflict. The resulting documentation has provided grist for scholarly research, some of it forest-related (**39, 77, 96, 100, 160, 246, 248**). Other works have dealt more directly with the impact of logging on villages (**21–22, 117, 168, 275**), notably the essays in *Nihon ringyō-rinsei no shiteki kenkyū* [Historical studies of forest industries and administration], edited by Hōjō Hiroshi and Ōta Katsuya (**75**).

The study of common land (*iriaichi*) remains central to the historiography of early modern mountain villages.[16] Because the topic has been tied to modern-day social problems, however, general works on common land, like those on mountain villages, focus on post-1868 developments. This is evident in the works of Hōjō (**71, 73–75**), currently one of the most active students of *iriaichi*, and in the publications of others (**104, 152, 282**).

There is, nevertheless, a considerable literature on early modern wooded common land, notably the works of Hirasawa Kiyondo (**59–67**), who examines village forestry in the Ina district. Other scholars continue this line of inquiry, frequently citing the works of Hirasawa, Furushima, and Nishikawa as seminal in the field. Perhaps the most thorough study since Hirasawa's is Hōjō's recent book on common land near Mount Fuji (**72**). Other studies explore the origin of common woodland, trends during the Edo period, the effect of common-land arrangements on village living conditions and class relations, and the nature and outcome of disputes (**68, 79, 108, 167, 207, 210, 283, 285, 309**).

The other major focus of study in village-forestry relations is upland division (*yamawari*). The topic has commanded attention because it has seemed central to the historical process that destroyed communalism; eroded the Tokugawa system; gave rise to private property rights, parasitic landlordism, and capitalist forest holding; and resulted in the proletarianization of poorer villagers and the creation of an exploitative, authoritarian state order that finally wreaked havoc in Japan, ravaged the rest of Asia, and brought on the catastrophe of 1945. Obviously, this assessment sees *yamawari* as an integral part of a ruinous social process. Other writers, by contrast, find in it themes of human liberation from communal and political oppression, the assertion of individual rights, improved management of natural resources, and increased village productivity.

Taking the works of Furushima, Nishikawa, and Hirasawa as points of departure, several scholars have threaded their way through this explosive intellectual terrain to delineate the significance of *yamawari* during the Edo period. Of the group the most prolific has been Harada Toshimaru, many of whose carefully researched essays were incorporated in his book, *Kinsei iriai seido kaitai katei no kenkyū* [Studies in the decay of the early modern commonland system] (**36–48**). Together with others in the field (**24–26, 203, 206, 214**), Harada has given us a richly documented picture of the changes involved in upland division.

One topic in *sansonshi* that has received rather little attention, perhaps because documentation is scarce, is slash-and-burn agriculture. Its history is closely tied to that of early modern forestry, but the nature of the connection has yet to be thoroughly explored. Furushima Toshio's old essay on the historical character of burnt-field culture in Japan (**31**) is a convenient introduction to the topic and a guide to the slender earlier literature. Subsequent works on the topic also are few.[17] Furushima's work, however, together with the discussion by Tsutsui Michio in his introductory text on forest history (**281**), will serve to sketch out the character, function, and fate of burnt-field culture during the Edo period.[18]

In terms of preindustrial forest history the relevance of these studies of mountain villages is not always apparent. Often it is necessary to read past an author's main themes and infer significance that is not made explicit. Nevertheless, cumulatively they reveal much about forest control and use. They help us explain, for example, why parcels of common land might be abused while nearby "privately held" household land fared better. They help us locate *iriaichi* in the global history of common land and assist our understanding of early modern Japanese entrepreneurial afforestation and wood production.

Forest Thought and Technology; Afforestation;
Water Conservancy

At present the history of forest thought (*sanrin shisōshi*) has all the earmarks of a defunct subspecialty, with only three noteworthy works appearing during the past twenty-five years. In 1963 Kanō Kyōji republished in book form (**101**) his studies that previously had appeared in *Ringyō keizai* of Edo-period intellectuals. Six years later Ōishi Shinzaburō brought out his two-volume edition of *Jikata hanreiroku*, a horticultural treatise prepared by Ōishi Hisayoshi in about 1794 (**166**). In 1974 Tsukamoto Manabu published a thoughtful essay on seventeenth-century attitudes toward "private" holding of forestland (**277**). Until fresh thought and new perspectives are brought to the topic, *sanrin shisōshi* seems unlikely to flourish.

The study of forest technology (*ringyō gijutsu*) and afforestation (*zōrin*) are in nearly as parlous condition. The postwar burst of interest in silvicultural techniques reached its climax in 1959 with the earlier-cited *Meijizen Nihon ringyō gijutsu hattatsushi* (**153**). It contained extensive information on early modern afforestation and protection forestry as well as detail on the technology of wood use. Otherwise, save for a study of afforestation in Yoshino during the Edo period and a review of the use of cuttings in *sugi* regeneration (**89, 124**), the principles and techniques of early modern afforestation have practically ceased to command scholarly attention.

The study of afforestation has gained a new lease on life, however, because scholars have broadened their scope of inquiry, thereby giving it new interpretive capabilities. Rather than simply elucidating techniques and policy theory, they have cast afforestation into the larger context of a basic shift from exploitative to regenerative forestry. Within that framework they now ask what actually was done and by whom, when, why, how, and with what result. In this expanded formulation, which merges *zōrinshi* and *ringyōshi*, the subspecialty is flourishing and fresh studies are shedding light on afforestation practices. For example, some of the multidisciplinary work on the forests of Yamaguni being done by Motoyoshi Rurio and his colleagues at Kyoto University deals with the Edo period (**140–41**). Recent essays by Fujita Yoshihisa bring into focus regional differences in afforestation practices (**17–18**), and Tokoro Mitsuo has placed tree planting in the Kiso valley in the wider context of Owari *han*'s overall forest preservation policy (**247, 260**). Satō Takayuki has posed the critical question of how well government planting initiatives fitted the wishes of villagers (**180**), and essays by several other scholars clarify other aspects of early modern afforestation (**119, 173, 209, 274, 280**).

In early modern tree planting, water conservancy was a major concern. The two key objectives were to prevent flooding and assure a stable supply of water for paddy land. Flooding did occur, however, and riparian works developed to minimize the damage. There is a substantial literature on stream management, but its authors generally assume, rather than examine, the connections between deforestation, forest management, flooding, and riparian policy. Consequently, the literature on this topic is much less useful in the study of forest history than it might be (**5, 32, 107, 146, 174–75, 178, 212, 278**).

There are, finally, two idiosyncratic works that do not fit these historiographical categories but are valuable for any ecologically oriented study of Japan's forest history. They are Chiba Tokuji's *Hageyama no kenkyū* [A study of bald mountains] and *Hageyama no bunka* [The culture of bald mountains], the latter being a radically reorganized version of the former (**7–8**). In these eclectic, insightful studies, Chiba utilizes early modern cases to examine the processes whereby human activity has led to the denuding of mountains. He perceives the process in terms of interacting biological, geological, and social factors. These works can help one understand the achievements—and limits—of early modern Japanese efforts at forest preservation and regeneration.

A Summation

As of 1880 there existed no field of historical study in early modern Japanese forestry. By 1980 it constituted a rich subdiscipline characterized by specialization, diversity, and depth.

Two qualities have characterized the field from its inception to the present. First, there has been an intimate connection between the assemblage and dissemination of original source materials and the production of a secondary literature. Second, the subdiscipline has been inspired by contemporary concerns. Immediate issues relating to forest organization and use rights have figured prominently in much of the scholarship. Larger issues of social justice, national identity, material need, and postulated dynamics of history have been central to other work. And in the recent, relatively affluent years, a socially detached, or at least satisfied, academic curiosity has become more evident.

Two other points deserve note. As the subdiscipline has matured, it has become ever more complex. Begun as the study of organizational structure, it has grown to embrace organizational process, forest industry, forestry thought and techniques, afforestation, and village-forestry relations, to cite only the main research foci. Second, as scholarship has probed more deeply, it has revealed a much more intricate history than earlier studies suggested. The history involves several complexly interacting social groups and is characterized by dramatic growth and change. For all its disciplinary maturity, the study of early modern Japanese forestry has only begun to reveal the dynamics of this phase of forest history. It is an exciting field. The splendid monuments of the past notwithstanding, the best work is yet to come.

Notes

Introduction: An Overview of
Preindustrial Japanese Forest History

1. This introduction is an extensively revised portion of my essay "Forestry in Early Modern Japan, 1650–1850: A Preliminary Survey."

2. The major English-language study of Japanese geography is Glenn Thomas Trewartha, *Japan: A Physical, Cultural, and Regional Geography*. Regarding geological foundations, see Takashi Yoshida, ed., *An Outline of the Geology of Japan*, 3d ed.

3. An authoritative English-language study of Japanese demography is Irene Taeuber, *The Population of Japan*. The more recent study by Susan B. Hanley and Kozo Yamamura, *Economic and Demographic Change in Preindustrial Japan, 1600–1868*, contains an excellent bibliography on the subject.

4. Here I am disregarding the millennia before the last Wisconsin interglacial, circa 40,000–30,000 B.P., although some type of human, perhaps *Homo sapiens neanderthalis*, was present in Japan at the time. See Fumiko Ikawa-Smith, "Current Issues in Japanese Archeology," for a concise report on nearly current understanding of Japan's human prehistory.

5. By "Kinai basin" I mean basically the watersheds of the Yodo and Yamato rivers, which encompass the five "home provinces" of Izumi, Kawachi, Yamato, Yamashiro, and Settsu, plus Ōmi and Iga, and the Ōi watershed in Tanba.

6. We can view Japan's age of regenerative forestry in terms of two phases. The first, lasting from the seventeenth until the late nineteenth century, can be called the era of early modern forestry. The second, dating from the formation of national forests late in the nineteenth, runs to the present and can be called the era of modern forestry. It consists of two periods of overcutting followed by years of recovery. Overcutting in early

Meiji slowed as national forest regulations came into effect, but from the 1930s war-related logging intensified, even consuming trees in city parks. As cities rebuilt after 1945, public forests were scoured for usable timber and landlords hurriedly clearcut woodlots before losing them to land reform. By 1950 Japan's forests were exhausted and the country entered its current state of arboreal rejuvenation.

7. Of course, many wooded areas lying outside those indicated on the map were cut over by regional power holders. For example, a pollen-count study has shown that the maintenance of frontier forts against Ezo tribesmen in the Sendai area produced substantial change in local woodland composition during the eighth century (Yoshinori Yasuda, "Early Historic Forest Clearance around the Ancient Castle Site of Tagajo, Miyagi Prefecture, Japan"). Around the year 1000, forests were cut down in the vicinity of Hiraizumi, about eighty kilometers north of Sendai, when a powerful local family undertook to create a replica of Heian and felled trees enough to build several thousand structures, including scores of temples, shrines, and mansions (Endō Yasutarō, [*Sanrinshi jō yori mitaru*] *Tōhoku bunka no kenkyū* [*ichimei: Tōhoku sanrinshi*], 43). Prior to the early modern predation, forests in Kyushu and elsewhere also felt the ax to satisfy the egos and ambitions of the regionally powerful and to provide timber for eastern China, where forests were severely reduced. (On the early need for reforestation in Kagoshima, for example, see Shioya Tsutomu, "Hansei jidai no rinsei.")

8. Of course, this statement does not apply to Hokkaido. However, that island was not really integrated into Japanese society until the twentieth century and is therefore disregarded in this study.

1. The Ancient Predation, 600–850

1. In its original form this chapter grew out of information in the works of Tokoro Mitsuo, Yamamoto Hikaru, and Nihon Gakushiin, as cited below. To strengthen the argument, I subsequently read more extensively, in the process profiting particularly from the work of William Wayne Farris. I owe a special debt of gratitude to Cornelius Kiley, friend of years too numerous to count. His bibliographical guidance and helpful criticism led me to useful materials and saved me from embarrassing errors. For those flaws that surely remain, only I am accountable.

2. Yamamoto Hikaru, "Waga kuni kodai no ringyō," 18. Yamamoto reports that when fanned with a bellows, hardwood charcoal could generate temperatures of one thousand degrees Fahrenheit.

3. Nihon Gakushiin, comp., *Meijizen Nihon ringyō gijutsu hattatsushi*, 465. To identify tree species, see the Glossary of Vegetation.

4. Iyanaga Teizō, "Ritsuryōsei teki tochi shoyū," 33–78, reports that in regulations of the *ritsuryō* period the common modern Japanese word for forest, *hayashi (rin)*, meant an area hand planted to trees rather than natural woodland. *Hayashi* was, in other words, a product of human intent. Rather similarly, in medieval England "forest" identified an area of land, of whatever vegetation, that had been explicitly defined as crown property subject to forest law. Clarence J. Glacken, *Traces on the Rhodian Shore*, 325–26 n. 122, discusses the term's etymology. J. V. Thirgood, *Man and the Mediterranean Forest: A History of Resource Depletion*, 83 n. 82, suggests that the term "forest" may trace to the medieval Latin phrase *foris stare*, meaning "keep out," which was used by overlords when denying local people rights of exploitation in designated parcels of woodland. In both the Japanese and European cases "forest" was a product of human will, but in the Japanese case it evidently arose from the "positive" policy of tree planting and in Europe from the "negative" policy of restricting use of natural growth.

5. Yazaki Takeo, *Social Change and the City in Japan*, 15.

6. J. Edward Kidder, *Early Buddhist Japan*, 61.

7. Yazaki, *Social Change*, 49, writes that Heian *dairi* "were built according to age-old Japanese architectural styles, with exposed natural lumber and thatched roofs of cypress bark," but he does not refer to the use of sunken pole construction, as he did in an earlier description (35) of the Heijō *dairi*. Kidder, *Early Buddhist*, 46, 54, 57, 61–66, 69–71, 76, 81, 87, 89, 95, 96, 199, 200, has information on the adoption and use of stone bases in seventh- and eighth-century Japanese architecture.

8. The customary explanation for these moves, which tends to lump together the two phenomena of reconstruction and relocation, cites religious principles of pollution that presumably rendered the palace site of a deceased sovereign unfit for the successor. In "Why Leave Nara? Kammu and the Transfer of the Capital," 331–47, Ronald Toby summarizes the debate and argues that political factionalism grounded in imperial genealogy lay at the base of these moves, as evidenced most particularly in the move to Heian.

9. In 1704–10 a major flood-control project rerouted the Yamato river to its modern course, which flows directly west across Kawachi into Osaka bay.

10. Yamamoto, "Waga kuni," 21–22. Robert Treat Paine and Alexander Soper, *The Art and Architecture of Japan*, 2d ed., 195, give a brief description of the capital at Fujiwara.

11. This interpretation has been skillfully developed by Takikawa Masajirō, who argues in *Kyōsei narabi ni tojōsei no kenkyū* that, following the move to Heian, the conscious tradition of "dual capitals" (*baito*) that derived

from China was displaced by the ideal of a single capital. Takikawa contends that the secondary capitals of the dual capital system should not be confused with "detached palaces" (*rikyū*), which were essentially vacation villas.

12. Toby, "Why Leave Nara?" 333–36, and Yazaki, *Social Change*, 46–47, discuss Shōmu's movements. Toby reports "a series of earthquakes" as preceding the imperial decision to return to Heijō. Nihon Gakushiin, *Meijizen*, 15, and Yamamoto, "Waga kuni," 21, mention forest fires near Shigaraki. The *Shoku Nihongi* (henceforth *SN*), in *Shintei zōho kokushi taikei* (henceforth *SZKT*), ed. Kuroita Katsumi, vol. 2, pp. 181–85, carefully reports these natural disasters. Because Chinese cosmology, which enjoyed official support in Heijō, treated natural phenomena as evidence of a ruler's virtue or lack thereof, court records of such phenomena must be regarded as more than merely dispassionate reports of current natural events. But perhaps we may assume they were not fabrications.

13. Takikawa, *Kyōsei*, 352–67, reports on the capital at Hora. Murao Jirō, *Ritsuryō zaisei no kenkyū* (*zōteihan*), 65–87, provides information on the provisioning for Ishiyamadera construction.

14. Toby, "Why Leave Nara?" 332, citing *SN*, date of 788/9/28; Yazaki, *Social Change*, 47.

15. Kidder, *Early Buddhist*, 77.

16. Yamamoto Hikaru, "Heian jidai no rin'ya riyō," 34; Motoyoshi Rurio, "Yamaguni ringyō chitai ni okeru jinkō zōrin no shinten to ikurin gijutsu no hensen," 72; idem, "Yamaguni sugi ni kan suru kenkyū (ichi)," 42–43.

17. For a concise description of Kyoto and its history, see John W. Hall, "Kyoto as Historical Background," 3–38.

18. Yamamoto, "Waga kuni," 20.

19. Tokoro Mitsuo, "Ringyō" (1959), 144–45. According to Nihon Gakushiin, *Meijizen*, 319, citing an unidentified document from the Shōsōin, a cartload of *hiwada* contained thirty-five to forty bundles.

20. High-density tree growth forces rapid, straight stem development, so that lower branches are shaded out, die after a few years, wither, and shortly drop off, leaving only a small knothole that the tree can soon grow over, forming a straight, smooth, uninterrupted bark surface. Such a surface, unlike one that is marred with knotholes, will pull away from the log in one solid piece. When installed on a roof, it will overlap tightly and shed water dependably.

21. Tokoro Mitsuo, *Kinsei ringyōshi no kenkyū*, 4–5. Tokoro seems to be describing the same building as Paine and Soper, *Art and Architecture*, 203–4. For fuller detail on the building, including the raw figures on which Tokoro may have based his calculations, see Sekino Masaru, "Zai

Shigaraki Fujiwara Toyonari itadono kō," 15–38. One *tsubo* equals about thirty-six square feet.

22. Tokoro, "Ringyō" (1959), 122.

23. William H. Coaldrake, "Edo Architecture and Tokugawa Law," 254. Coaldrake uses this document to support a very different thesis regarding government leaders' alleged concern with the physical accoutrements of high status.

24. Tokoro, "Ringyō" (1959), 123. Kidder, *Early Buddhist*, 79–126, furnishes considerable detail on pre-Heian temples.

25. The term "processed lumber" sounds redundant, but it distinguishes *yōzai* from *genboku*. Because large logs were heavy and difficult to move, they usually were reduced to manageable size in the forest by peeling, splitting, or sawing. The resulting pieces, together with logs, were *genboku*, which were further processed into final construction pieces, *yōzai*, at the building site.

26. Tokoro, "Ringyō" (1959), 124; idem, *Kinsei*, 9. One hundred thousand *koku* (about twenty-eight thousand cubic meters) of *yōzai* are equivalent to some 980,000 boards one foot wide by ten feet long. An eighteen-by-twenty-four-foot house contains floor space equal to four six-mat rooms.

27. Tokoro, "Ringyō" (1959), 123; Nihon Gakushiin, *Meijizen*, 5, 285–86; Tokoro Mitsuo, "Ringyō" (1962), 872. Robert Karl Reischauer, *Early Japanese History* (*c. 40 B.C.–A.D. 1167*), 159, cites the 685/10/13 order regularizing the twenty-year alternation of Ise Shrine between two sites. I presume that previous reconstructions had been handled less methodically.

28. Paine and Soper, *Art and Architecture*, 211.

29. Lumber yields vary by species, age, fullness of stand, and quality of site. My figure is based on tables for sixty-year-old *hinoki* stands growing in the Kiso river valley, as given in yield tables of Tōkyō Kyōiku Daigaku Nōgakubu Ringakka, comp., *Jitsuyō ringyō keisan hikkei*, 15. The yield for *sugi* is somewhat higher than that for *hinoki* because *sugi* grows more rapidly. The yield for a number of other conifers is lower because they grow more slowly. See nn. 35 and 46 of chapter 3 for more comments on yield calculations.

30. *Kure* is the term that appears in ancient documents, but some scholars refer to it by the alternative Edo-period term, *kureki*. The wooden walls of the Shōsōin and Tōshōdaiji warehouses consist of long timbers split in the manner of *kure*, that is, in "*mikanwari*" style, through the heart of the log, with the pointed heartwood then cut out to leave a stick with a blunted wedge-shaped cross section. It is sometimes unclear in discussions of *kure* whether the term refers to the log that is to be so split or to the piece

resulting from the splitting. In some instances the former seems to be the case and in others the latter, which suggests that *kure* was an imprecise generic term for wood used in that manner.

31. Toda Yoshimi, "Sekkanke ryō no somayama ni tsuite," 358.

32. These comments on shipbuilding are based on Nihon Gakushiin, *Meijizen*, 286–87, 459–65.

33. Except as noted, the sources for these paragraphs on sculpture are Nihon Gakushiin, *Meijizen*, 8–9, 468–69; Yamamoto, "Waga kuni," 18; and idem, "Heian," 35.

34. *Hinoki* has been described as "strong, elastic, durable, and scented." It is also straight-grained and relatively soft (Natural Resources Section, *Important Trees of Japan* [Report No. 119], 23).

35. Nihon Gakushiin, *Meijizen*, 468, mentions *kaya* and *asunaro* as the main conifers and *sendan, harigiri, keyaki, sakura, kaede,* and *katsura* among the broadleafs used in sculpture.

36. These comments on fuel use derive from Tokoro, *Kinsei*, 3–4, 33; idem, "Ringyō" (1959), 143–44; and Nihon Gakushiin, *Meijizen*, 494–95. Tokoro, *Kinsei*, 4, gives the 90 percent figure for Germany. According to Franz Heske, *German Forestry*, 39, as late as 1850 about 70 percent to 80 percent of total German wood production was fuelwood. And in France, according to Theodore S. Woolsey, Jr., *Studies in French Forestry*, 70, as late as 1920 some 75 percent of French forest yield was fuelwood.

37. Tokoro, "Ringyō" (1959), 144, also reports that in 740, sixty bundles of firewood sold for four hundred *mon*, or about six and a half *mon* per bundle, so a shoulder load likely consisted of two bundles.

38. Tokoro, *Kinsei*, 4, has changed his figure, given here, from the 18,686 *koku* he gave in 1959. My conversion rate assumes these to be maritime *koku* (one by one by ten *shaku*) rather than the agricultural tax *koku* of the Edo period, which is about 40 percent smaller.

39. Toba Masao, *Nihon ringyōshi*, 70–74, exhaustively lists forest products used by Nara-Heian people of all sorts. And on 103–9, he lists by province forest products paid as taxes.

40. Tokoro, "Ringyō" (1959), 126, cites an archeological find, an ancient house uncovered in Akita in 1817. Whether it bears much resemblance to commoner housing in the warmer Kinai region is hard to say.

41. Iyanaga, "Ritsuryōsei," 38. He notes that when such disputes occurred within a province, they would be settled locally. In consequence, they would not show up in court records, and the frequency of such disputes is unknown.

42. Except as noted, this recapitulation of deforestation is based on Yamamoto, "Waga kuni," 21; Yamamoto, "Heian," 37; Nihon Gakushiin, *Meijizen*, 315; and Tokoro, *Kinsei*, 14–15, 21.

43. Murao, *Ritsuryō zaisei*, 70, 74.

44. Tokoro, "Ringyō" (1959), 145. This order of 796/9/26 appeared about six months after new regulations that tightened up the permissible dimensions for official lumber. The document, from *Ruiju sandai kyaku* (henceforth *RSK*), is in *SZKT*, vol. 25, 587–88. The order of 1030 also restricted lower aristocrats in their use of wood in walls (Reischauer, *Early Japanese*, 332).

45. I discuss the techniques and problems of timber provisioning in a separate study.

46. Murao, *Ritsuryō zaisei*, 77–78, 81, fixes clearly on transit cost as a key factor in lumber prices. See also figures cited from the *Engi shiki* by Tokoro, "Ringyō" (1959), 136. On labor cost differentials along the supply line in Edo-period lumber provisioning, see my essay "Logging the Unloggable: Timber Transport in Early Modern Japan."

47. Toba, *Nihon ringyōshi*, 99.

48. William Wayne Farris, *Population, Disease, and Land in Early Japan, 645–900*, 13. Temmu's order of 675/2/15 is reproduced from *Nihon Shoki*, in *Kokushi taikei*, vol. 1, p. 507. (Farris cites the page reference from volume one of *SZKT*, which I was unable to consult while preparing this chapter.)

49. Iyanaga, "Ritsuryōsei," 36–37. Toba, *Nihon ringyōshi*, 158–71, lists forest-related ordinances from 676 to 924, gleaned from primary sources.

50. Quoted in Yamamoto, "Waga kuni," 23. Iyanaga notes that this phrasing had precedent in Chinese law.

51. Farris, *Population*, 76–77. He suggests that the courtiers sought "more land, not more rice paddies" but does not indicate why they wanted it.

52. Toda, "Sekkanke," 329–58, describes *sekkanke* forests and their use.

53. Tokoro, *Kinsei*, 19, 32.

54. Farris, *Population*, 76–77. The documents are reproduced from *SN*, in *SZKT*, vol. 2, pp. 26, 47.

55. Tokoro, *Kinsei*, 19–20; Yamamoto, "Heian," 34–36. In "Shōen tenkai katei ni miru rin'ya seido: Toku ni sono kaisōsei ni chakumoku shite," 18–23, Ōsaki Rokurō examines forest-use rights in *shōen*, but mostly for later centuries.

56. This order of 798/12, from *RSK*, can be found in *SZKT*, vol. 25, 497.

57. Nihon Gakushiin, *Meijizen*, 15; Tokoro, *Kinsei*, 14, 18–20.

58. Farris, *Population*, 111, translates Temmu's notice of 676/5. It is reproduced from *Nihon Shoki*, in *Kokushi taikei*, vol. 1, p. 510. The order of 710/2/29 is cited in Reischauer, *Early Japanese*, 169. It is from *SN* and can be found in *SZKT*, vol. 2, p. 43.

59. Toba, *Nihon ringyōshi*, 163. See, for example, the order of 806/ intercalary 6/8, from *RSK*, in *SZKT*, vol. 25, p. 498.

60. Quoted in Farris, *Population*, 100. He translates somewhat more of the document.

61. Tsuchiya Takao, "An Economic History of Japan," 87–89, lists items sold in the Heian marketplace.

62. Yamanouchi Shizuo, *Nihon zōrin gyōseishi gaisetsu*, 2. Nihon Gakushiin, *Meijizen*, 5, 15, 730, discusses forest fires in ancient Japan.

63. *SN*, in *SZKT*, vol. 2, p. 182. Perhaps the smallpox epidemic of the 730s had so decimated the Kinai populace that arable was abandoned, returning to wild growth, which developed by 745 into highly flammable brushland. See Farris, *Population*, 53–69, for a discussion of the epidemic of 735–37 and its consequences.

64. Quoted from an unidentified source in Nihon Gakushiin, *Meijizen*, 15. However, *SN*, in *SZKT*, vol. 2, p. 183, simply reports that "a thousand people from Ōmi turned out and suppressed a forest fire in the Kōga capital vicinity."

65. Chiba Tokuji, *Hageyama no kenkyū*, 92–96. Chiba reports that *hiratake* requires over 30 percent soil moisture, while *matsutake* thrives on less than 30 percent.

66. This discussion of ancient afforestation measures is gleaned from these sources: Endō Yasutarō, "Suigen kan'yōrin ni tai suru zendai hito no shisō," 93–96; Yamanouchi, *Nihon zōrin*, 4–7; Matsushima Yoshio, "Sugi no zōrinshi," 101–4, 107–10; Nihon Gakushiin, *Meijizen*, 14; and Tokoro, *Kinsei*, 19–20.

2. Forests and Forestry in Medieval Japan, 1050–1550

1. How much and how steadily the population grew are issues of ongoing scholarly debate. For a recent and exciting examination of this topic in English, see William Wayne Farris, *Population, Disease, and Land in Early Japan, 645–900*. For some customary population figures, see my *Japan before Perry*, 15–16 n. 7. For a sharply lower estimate of the population in 1600, see Hayami Akira, "The Population at the Beginning of the Tokugawa Period—An Introduction to the Historical Demography of Pre-industrial Japan." For monographic detail on the Edo period, see Susan B. Hanley and Kozo Yamamura, *Economic and Demographic Change in Preindustrial Japan, 1600–1868*. In n. 2 of the Conclusion I discuss the logic of the figures used in this study.

2. This material on agricultural change comes from the following essays by Yamamoto Hikaru: "Heian jidai no rin'ya riyō," 39; "Kamakura jidai no ringyō," 9, 13; "Nanbokuchō jidai ni okeru sanrin gen'ya no riyō," 30; "Muromachi jidai no ringyō," 30–31; and "Sengoku jidai no ringyō," 35.

3. In English the most thorough investigation of medieval Japanese agriculture is that currently being pursued by Kristina Troost, a graduate student at Harvard. When Troost's work is complete, it will enrich our understanding immensely and probably require modification of some passages in this chapter.

4. Furushima Toshio, "Yakibatake nōgyō no rekishiteki seikaku to sono kōsaku keitai," 40–43.

5. Chiba Tokuji, *Hageyama no kenkyū*, 92–96.

6. Ōsaki Rokurō, "Shōen tenkai katei ni miru rin'ya seido: Toku ni sono kaisō sei ni chakumoku shite," 22; Toba Masao, *Nihon ringyōshi*, 173–80.

7. Jeffrey P. Mass, *The Kamakura Bakufu: A Study in Documents*, 27–28, 72, 106–7.

8. Whereas most of the Muromachi regime's ordinances on pawning goods date from 1441, the first one that concerns pawned lumber appears to date from 1520, and other laws dealing with woodland production do not seem to exist (Kenneth A. Grossberg, *The Laws of the Muromachi Bakufu*, 148).

9. Furushima Toshio, *Kinsei keizaishi no kiso katei: Nengu shūdatsu to kyōdōtai*, 142–45.

10. Toba, *Nihon ringyōshi*, 174–79; Ōsaki, "Shōen tenkai katei," 21–23; Furushima, *Kinsei keizaishi*, 153.

11. This summary of village change is primarily an attempt to sum up the essays by Yamamoto Hikaru. He, in turn, is condensing the analyses of other Japanese scholars (Yamamoto, "Heian," 36–39; idem, "Kamakura," 9–10, 12–13, 15; idem, "Nanboku," 28–30; idem, "Muromachi," 32; idem, "Sengoku," 33–35). See also Nishikawa Zensuke, "Ringyō keizai shiron (2): Mokuzai seisan o chūshin to shite," 15–30, for details on *soma*, especially in the Yamaguni district.

12. Yamamoto, "Heian," 36, 38.

13. Furushima, *Kinsei keizaishi*, 148–151.

14. Yamamoto, "Heian," 34, 36, furnishes an example of this pattern on a parcel of Tōdaiji land in Iga province.

15. Nishikawa, "Ringyō keizai shiron (2)," 26–30; Motoyoshi Rurio, "Yamaguni ringyō chitai ni okeru jinkō zōrin no shinten to ikurin gijutsu no hensen," 74.

16. Furushima, *Kinsei keizaishi*, 151–55, summarizes this development nicely.

17. Yamamoto, "Sengoku," 34–35. The tools were *kamakiri, nata*, and *masakari*.

18. This paragraph is based on Yamamoto, "Kamakura," 10, 13; and idem, "Muromachi," 31–32. Trial by ordeal is discussed in Harada Toshimaru, "Kinsei no Ōmi ni okeru rin'ya no kyōkai sōron to tekka saiban," 81.

19. Akabane Takeshi, "Hokensei ka ni okeru mokutan seisan no tenkai kōzō (1)," 2.

20. Yamamoto, "Kamakura," 11, quoting *Azuma kagami* for 1253/10/ 11. The prices set were 100 *mon* per horse load of charcoal and 100 *mon* per thirty bundles of firewood. A bundle measured "three hands" in circumference; the size of a horse load is unclear. The guidelines also listed these items: 50 *mon* per horse load (eight bundles) of thatch; 50 *mon* per horse load (eight bundles) of straw; and 50 *mon* per horse load of rice bran.

21. Yamamoto, "Heian," 39–40; idem, "Kamakura," 11. My "fifteen feet" derives from fourteen to fifteen *shaku*, and "up to four feet" from four *shaku*.

22. Yamamoto, "Kamakura," 15.

23. Tokoro Mitsuo, *Kinsei ringyōshi no kenkyū*, 15; Nihon Gakushiin, comp., *Meijizen Nihon ringyō gijutsu hattatsushi*, 6.

24. Quoted in Yamamoto, "Kamakura," 15. The date referred to is 1219/9/22. The *Azuma kagami*, or "The Mirror of the East," is a history of the early years of the Kamakura *bakufu*.

25. Yamamoto, "Muromachi," 32.

26. Yamamoto, "Kamakura," 11. See also Toba, *Nihon ringyōshi*, 112. By "foot" I refer to *shaku*, which equals .994 foot. This Kamakura *kureki*, which evidently followed late Heian ("as of old") precedents, was substantially shorter than the twelve-*shaku kureki* of Nara. The seven-*shaku* minimum probably refers to the length between raft-lashing grooves, the notched or eyed places near the ends of sticks where they were lashed together to form rafts.

27. This material on Kinai provisioning is from Nihon Gakushiin, *Meijizen*, 6, 13. Also Yamamoto, "Muromachi," 32–33; idem, "Sengoku," 36–37.

28. Until 1586 the Kiso joined the Nagara just east of Ōgaki.

29. This description of Tōdaiji provisioning derives from information in Nihon Gakushiin, *Meijizen*, 308. Also Yamamoto, "Kamakura," 10–11; Toba, *Nihon ringyōshi*, 51.

30. Even this pick of the Saba stand yielded pillars decidedly inferior to those of the original Tōdaiji. Because they had grown less densely or on a less favorable site, the trees were shorter and the fellers had to take specimens that were about a foot wider at the base in order to obtain the desired height. This meant that when installed the pillers consumed substantially more floor space, resulting in a more crowded, less convenient, and less aesthetically appealing structure. My "eighty to ninety feet" derives from nine to ten *jō* and "about five feet" from five *shaku* four *sun*.

31. Nihon Gakushiin, *Meijizen*, 308. My "twenty miles" derives from three hundred *chō* and "seventeen miles" from seven *ri*.

32. Motoyoshi, "Yamaguni ringyō chitai," 73; Motoyoshi Rurio, "Yamaguni sugi ni kan suru kenkyū (ichi)," 42–43.

33. Yamamoto, "Muromachi," 33. The Tōfukuji's six thousand horse loads formed two hundred rafts. The Nanzenji's one thousand cartloads yielded three hundred raft loads. Assuming equal-sized rafts, one cartload equals about nine horse loads.

34. Even in the great medieval Zen monasteries, which emulated the Karayō architectural style of China, Japanese builders evidently did not attempt to replicate the height of Chinese monasteries. Moreover, in comparison with earlier monastery architecture of Japan, "in place of bold spans and sturdy members, there is a cautious piecing-together of a multitude of small parts" (Robert Treat Paine and Alexander Soper, *The Art and Architecture of Japan*, 2d ed., 243, 245).

35. Yamanouchi Shizuo, *Nihon zōrin gyōseishi gaisetsu*, 5, 10.

36. Yamamoto, "Nanboku," 30; idem, "Muromachi," 33; Sakamoto Kiyozō, *Kitayama daisugi to migaki maruta*, 53–56; Matsushima Yoshio, "Sugi no zōrinshi," 101, 109–110, 115.

37. Matsumura Yasukazu, "Sugisashiki ringyō no gijutsushiteki kōsatsu: Sugi no sashiki ringyō no kenkyū (dai yon)," 144–48. Matsushima, "Sugi no zōrinshi," 99–116, reports on these afforestation efforts.

38. Toba, *Nihon ringyōshi*, 41–42, 47, 51–52.

39. Toba, *Nihon ringyōshi*, 113.

3. Timber Depletion during the Early Modern Predation, 1570–1670

1. The term "shrine" refers to Shintō establishments (*jinja, jingū*). "Temple" and "monastery" refer to Buddhist institutions (*tera*). In Japan Buddhism was originally a religion of monks engaged in the pursuit of enlightenment, but during the medieval period it evolved into a popular religion in which priests ministered to believers. Hence, *tera* evolved from "monasteries" housing monks into "temples" where the faithful participated in religious services.

2. George Elison and Bardwell L. Smith, *Warlords, Artists, and Commoners: Japan in the Sixteenth Century*, 62–63. For a sense of Azuchi's elegance, see especially Carolyn Wheelwright's essay, "A Visualization of Eitoku's Lost Paintings at Azuchi Castle," 87–112.

3. Yamamoto Hikaru, "Azuchi Momoyama jidai no ringyō," 23.

4. Nishikawa Zensuke, "Ringyō keizai shiron (5): Ryōchiteki ringyō chitai," 2. The figures here are changed slightly to be consistent.

5. Nakamura Kōya, *Ieyasuden*, 529–38.

6. Mitsuhashi Tokio, "Yoshino-Kumano no ringyō," 257.

7. Toba Masao, "Sengoku jidai no shinrin keizai to rinsei," 32.

8. Shioya Junji, "Fushimi chikujō to Akita sugi," 48.

9. Yamamoto Hikaru, "Sengoku jidai no ringyō," 36; Shizuoka Ken Mokuzai Kyōdō Kumiai Ren'aikai, *Shizuoka ken mokuzaishi*, 10. Michael P. Birt mentions Hōjō forest policy briefly in his essay "Samurai in Passage: Transformation of the Sixteenth-Century Kantō," 394.

10. Yamamoto, "Sengoku," 36; *Shizuoka ken mokuzaishi*, 11.

11. Miyashita Ichirō, "Takatō han no rinseishi (ichi)," 51–52.

12. *Shizuoka ken mokuzaishi*, 12–13; Yamamoto, "Sengoku," 36; Matsushima Yoshio, "Sugi no zōrinshi," 114.

13. Yamamoto, "Sengoku," 35.

14. Endō Yasutarō, (*Sanrinshi jō yori mitaru*) *Tōhoku bunka no kenkyū* (*ichimei: Tōhoku sanrinshi*), 46.

15. Tokoro Mitsuo, *Kinsei ringyōshi no kenkyū*, 21; Toba Masao, "Toyo taikō to shinrin keizai," 10.

16. Nihon Gakushiin, comp., *Meijizen Nihon ringyō gijutsu hattatsushi*, 315–16.

17. Toba, "Toyo taikō," 10.

18. Tokoro, *Kinsei*, 21–22.

19. Hirao Michio, *Tosa han ringyō keizaishi*, 4.

20. Tsuboi Shunzō, "Kinsei chū-go ki Tenryū ringyō ni tsuite," 20–21.

21. Tokoro, *Kinsei*, 122; Yamamoto, "Azuchi," 25; Tokoro Mitsuo, "Ringyō" (1965), 205.

22. Shioya, "Fushimi," 50–51; Tokoro, *Kinsei*, 24–26.

23. This analysis of Hideyoshi's levy on Akita is from Shioya, "Fushimi," 49–51.

24. The measure stipulated was six *shaku* four *sun* rough measure and six *shaku* three *sun* "net width," a figure evidently allowing for loss from the saw cut or finishing.

25. Mitsuhashi, "Yoshino-Kumano," 243–44.

26. Yamamoto, "Azuchi," 25; Tokoro, "Ringyō" (1965), 211; Tokoro Mitsuo, "Ieyasu kurairichi jidai no Kiso kanjō shiryō," 330–31.

27. Nishikawa, "Ringyō keizai shiron (5)," 12; Yamamoto, "Azuchi," 24.

28. Tokoro, *Kinsei*, 802, 805; Yamamoto, "Azuchi," 24. Raft loads of lumber (mostly *kureki* and *itago*) went down the Kiso along its old channel to the Nagara and then down the Nagara to a landing at Sunomata or further to the Nagara's confluence with the Ibi and up the Ibi to a landing just south of Ōgaki. There the rafts were disassembled and the lumber loaded onto horses or carts for portage along the Nakasendō via Sekigahara to Asazuma on Lake Biwa (just north of Hikone), from whence it went by water to Kyoto and Fushimi.

29. Tokoro Mitsuo, "Suminokura Yoichi to Kisoyama," 8.

30. See my essay "Logging the Unloggable: Timber Transport in Early Modern Japan" for a somewhat fuller discussion of river improvement.

31. Shimada Kinzō, *Edo-Tōkyō zaimoku ton'ya kumiai seishi*, 518. Timber bound for Edo from northeast Japan initally went down the Pacific coast to the mouth of the Tone river at Chōshi in Shimōsa. There, to avoid the dangerous seas at the tip of the Bōsō peninsula, riverboats hauled the pieces up the Tone to where its southern branch forked off to flow south into Edo bay. Later in the century Tōhoku lumber began circling Bōsō, going by sea all the way to the city lumberyards.

32. Yoshida Yoshiaki, *Kiba no rekishi*, 52–53. Suminokura's labor battalions excavated a channel to the east of the Kamo river, running it northward from the Uji river through Fushimi, past the Hōkōji, almost to the site of the new palace, where it tapped into the Kamo for water. It soon filled with rafts and timber-carrying vessels, and along its banks fifteen timber merchants established their offices and lumberyards.

33. Toba Masao, "Edo jidai no rinsei," 11.

34. *Shizuoka ken mokuzaishi*, 14. Ieyasu's Sunpu residences were the "harbor mansion" (*hama goten*) at Shimizu and a villa at Miho. He built the harbor mansion in 1607, the year he settled into semiretirement at Sunpu. He erected the villa on nearby Miho spit two years later. From it he had a breathtaking view of Mount Fuji towering over Suruga bay. The harbor mansion was torn down after his death. Part of the villa was destroyed by a storm in 1611, and it was abandoned after 1619, to be obliterated by an earthquake and tidal wave in 1707.

35. Tokoro, *Kinsei*, 12–13, 117, 257. According to Tokoro, four *koku* of *tachiki* yield two of *genboku* and one of *yōzai*. Admittedly, deriving acreage figures from estimates of lumber usage produces at best unreliable "guesstimates," and I offer them solely to suggest the general magnitude of the impact this construction activity had on woodland. My figures for timber yield derive from the column of figures for thinned plus remaining stem volume in the stand tables of Tokyo Kyōiku Daigaku Nōgakubu Ringakka, comp., *Jitsuyō ringyō keisan hikkei*. Because the tables are based on plantation stands rather than the customarily less well stocked natural growth, I am equating the stem volume figures with *tachiki* (stumpage) rather than *genboku* (modern-day pulpwood, but in the Edo period, timber that had been processed in any of various ways for rafting) in hopes that conversion will give the acreage estimates a bit more validity.

36. Tokoro, "Ieyasu kurairichi," 329–30.

37. Hirao, *Tosa*, 4.

38. Tokoro, "Ringyō" (1965), 205–6.

39. Tokoro, *Kinsei*, 150–51. On occasion Ieyasu took a direct personal interest in the process of lumber selection. Thus, in the spring of 1608, after Sunpu castle burned, he traveled to his large lumber storage facility on the

Tenryū and selected some two thousand pieces of *kureki* for use in the reconstruction (Tokoro, *Kinsei*, 148).

40. Tokoro, *Kinsei*, 543. On p. 615 he gives an alternative figure for this
period of eight hundred thousand pieces of *yōzai* of all sorts annually.

41. Tokoro, *Kinsei*, 604.

42. For illustrations of the splendor of daimyo mansions in Edo, see
William H. Coaldrake, "Edo Architecture and Tokugawa Law," 261–84.

43. Yamamoto, "Azuchi," 24.

44. Matsuki Kan, "Tsugaru no hiba (hinoki)," 150.

45. This material on Matsumoto derives from Tokoro, *Kinsei*, 228–31,
258–60, 267–68, 276–78, 287. The Shinano river is called the Sai in its
upper reaches.

46. Tokoro, *Kinsei*, 257–58. Tokoro estimates that each house had twenty
tsubo (720 square feet) of floor space and that each *tsubo* required three
koku of *yōzai*. A lumber (or maritime) *koku* measures ten cubic *shaku* (9.82
cubic feet or 0.278 cubic meters), so two hundred thousand *koku* is 56,000
cubic meters of *genboku*, which would have required about 111,200 cubic
meters of *tachiki*. The stand table on p. 29 of Tokyo Kyōiku Daigaku
Nōgakubu Ringakka, *Jitsuyō ringyō keisan hikkei*, estimates that fifty-year-
old *akamatsu* in first-grade stands in Nagano prefecture yield 440 cubic
meters of lumber per hectare. If one equates that yield with *tachiki*, to obtain 111,200 cubic meters would have meant clear-cutting 250 hectares
(620 acres) of first-rate plantation or vastly more of natural woodland.

47. Hirao, *Tosa*, 2–5, 138, 140, 163, 164. The neighborhood of Tosa's
lumber storage in Osaka came to be known as Shiragachō, evidently after
the mountain that furnished the timber. The moneylender presumably
was one to whom the *han* was in debt.

48. Hirao, *Tosa*, 164–65.

49. Hirao, *Tosa*, 167–68.

50. Marius B. Jansen, "Tosa in the Seventeenth Century: The Establishment of Yamauchi Rule," 124, 128.

51. *Shizuoka ken mokuzaishi*, frontispiece commentary.

52. Nihon Gakushiin, *Meijizen*, 464–65.

53. *Shizuoka ken mokuzaishi*, 26.

54. Toba, "Edo jidai," 11–12. Shimada, *Edo-Tōkyō*, 524–28, lists the
major Edo fires and their locations.

55. Nishikawa Zensuke, "Edo zaimokushō no kigen: Edo mokuzai
ichibashi josetsu," 14.

56. Yoshida, *Kiba no rekishi*, 52.

57. For a description of the lumber industry, see my essay "Lumber
Provisioning in Early Modern Japan, 1580–1850."

58. Shioya, "Fushimi," 52.

59. Yamamoto, "Azuchi," 26; Tokoro, *Kinsei*, 124, 186; Sekishima Hisao, "Tōyama-ke no keizaiteki haikei (ichi): Musashi kuni Tama gun Ogawa mura Ogawa-ke no Ina mokuzai kiridashi shiryō no shōkai," 42.

60. Tokoro, *Kinsei*, 605, 614; Tokoro, "Suminokura," 8.

61. Tokoro, "Ringyō" (1965), 198. Kumazawa wrote this widely quoted comment in *Usa mondo*. Nishikawa, "Ringyō keizai shiron (5)," 3, reports cutting on Ezo from 1678.

62. See n. 45.

63. Hirasawa Kiyondo, *Kinsei iriai kankō no seiritsu to tenkai: Shinshū Shimo Ina chihō o chūshin ni shite*, 222.

64. Tokoro, *Kinsei*, 124, quoting a report of 1718 that probably was part of the discussions resulting in the reduction of *kureki* dimensions. *Sanbō*, or "three side" measure, is the sum of the exterior and two radial faces of each split piece.

65. Tokoro, "Ringyō" (1965), 214.

66. The figures, from Tokoro, *Kinsei*, 126, are these:

Date and Type	Length (shaku)	Sanbō (sun)	Hara (sun)
1649 ("long *kureki*")	3.6	4.5	3.0
1678 ("short *kureki*")	2.6	4.5	3.0
1718 ("long")	3.3	3.0	1.5
1718 ("short")	2.3	3.0	1.5

Hara is the width of the inside surface of *kureki*, where heartwood has been cut out.

67. Hirasawa, *Kinsei iriai*, 272. The final column of derived figures is my addition to Hirasawa's table.

68. In 1725, to reduce stick losses on the river, the *bakufu* ordered *kureki* bound into rafts at the mouths of branch rivers, whereas they previously had floated loose to a downstream assembly point. See n. 75.

69. Hirasawa, *Kinsei iriai*, 221–22.

70. Tokoro, "Ringyō" (1965), 214. In some cases villagers fought so hard to pay the tax in money because they wished to send lumber into the more lucrative private trade. This suggests that scarcity had driven up the market price of wood enough to assure a profit for anyone with timber to sell. In that case the matter was essentially a contest between government and peasant as to who would profit from the marketing opportunity.

71. Hirasawa, *Kinsei iriai*, 150, 245–46.

72. Iioka Masatake, "Takatōryō 'ohayashi' ni okeru goyōki-uriki no saishutsu: Genroku-Kyōhō ki no 'mokushi sato,'" 447–63, studies this case thoroughly.

73. See my "Logging the Unloggable" for a more general discussion of rafting with details on Kiso river practices.

74. Tokoro, *Kinsei*, 147.

75. Iioka Masatake has studied this matter extensively in two of his closely analyzed essays on Tenryū lumbering: "Enshū Funagira ni okeru bakufu no kureki shobun: Genroku-Shōtoku ki Shinshū Kashio-Ōkawabarayama no motojime shidashi to kanren shite," 117–18; and "Enshū Funagira ni okeru bakufu yōzai no chūkei kinō," 114–16.

76. Nishikawa, "Ringyō keizai shiron (5)," 3.

77. Hattori Marenobu, *Ringyō keizai kenkyū*, 147. See also my *Origins of Japan's Modern Forests: The Case of Akita.*

78. Matsushima Yoshio, "Tokugawa jidai ni okeru zōrin seisaku ni tsuite," 42–43.

79. Morita Seiichi, "Higo no ringyō," 119.

80. Hirao, *Tosa*, 9–10. Figures from Akita tell a similar story in its later stages. The Yoneshiro watershed, heartland of the *han*'s fabled woodland, produced (to cite typical figures) 15,522 cubic meters of lumber in 1717; 7,020 in 1747; and an average of 3,947 in 1812–16 (Iwasaki Naoto, *Akita ken Noshirogawa kami chihō ni okeru sugibayashi no seiritsu narabi ni kōshin ni kan suru kenkyū*, 209).

81. Hirao, *Tosa*, 10.

82. Hirao, *Tosa*, 9.

83. Tokoro, *Kinsei*, 557–59, 655. It is suggestive of the Owari problem that in 1721 some 3,200 hectares of the formerly rich forest area of Tadachi mountain numbered a mere thirty-five conifers of over six inches dbh per hectare (Tokoro Mitsuo, "Kinsei Kiso sanrin no hozoku taisaku," 18). Thirty-five is my extrapolation from Tokoro's figures. Figures on stand density for particular sites are scattered widely through the literature or, more correctly, can be derived from figures so scattered. What they signify in particular cases is not at all clear, but the uniformity of very low figures surely means what it suggests: the forests had been plundered, and few mature trees remained standing.

84. Tokoro, "Suminokura," 15.

85. Tokoro, "Ringyō" (1965), 207–8.

86. Tsutsui Michio, *Nihon rinseishi kenkyū josetsu*, 174.

87. Quoted in Matsuki, "Tsugaru no hiba," 150–51.

88. "Custom" or "tradition" will not do as an explanation of why a situation is as it is; it merely describes "what" is and perhaps the habitual way in which members of that society understand "why" it is.

89. A convenient technical summary of Japan's geological history and character is Takashi Yoshida, ed., *An Outline of the Geology of Japan*, 3d ed., 6–24.

4. The Negative Regimen: Forest Regulation

1. A new and convenient bibliographical guide to further reading on Tokugawa society is John W. Dower, *Japanese History and Culture from Ancient to Modern Times: Seven Basic Bibliographies*. For a concise description of Tokugawa society and its major segments, see Charles J. Dunn, *Everyday Life in Traditional Japan*. For a lucid description of the Tokugawa political system, see John W. Hall, "The Nature of Traditional Society: Japan." For more detail on the *bakufu*, see my *Politics in the Tokugawa Bakufu, 1600–1843*.

2. The classic study of Tokugawa rural society is Thomas C. Smith, *The Agrarian Origins of Modern Japan*. For a recent guide to English-language literature on the Tokugawa peasantry, see my essay "Tokugawa Peasants: Win, Lose, or Draw?"

3. Initially, some forest preserves were maintained as bird and game sanctuaries to provide the rulers with sport hunting, but that interest waned within a few decades as the ruling samurai elite became urbanized. Many sanctuaries evolved into timber preserves, others into protection forests, and some into *iriaichi* or household woodland.

4. Tokoro Mitsuo, *Kinsei ringyōshi no kenkyū*, 235–36. Boundary delineation also facilitated taxation. Thus, in 1686 the *bakufu* ordered a resurvey of land in the Numata area of Kōzuke province, specifying that woodland and waste were to be covered in the survey and that large parcels of household forest were to be taxed "lightly," but small parcels could be ignored (Nōrinshō, comp., *Nihon rinseishi shiryō*, vol. 5, pp. 63–67).

5. During the seventeenth century, before afforestation techniques became established, one factor that surely made government woodland of more interest to villagers than village woodland was to the government was that villagers could easily see how building timber could be reduced to fuelwood, fuelwood to fertilizer material, and much fertilizer to fodder; but even the canniest official would have been hard put to reverse the process except by completely closing woodland to exploitation for decades at a time.

6. Tokoro, *Kinsei*, 243–47, sums up the diversity of *iriaichi* arrangements.

7. "Ownership" essentially seems to be a particular cluster of use rights—the right to acquire, to alienate, and while "owning" to utilize exclusively as one wishes, subject to little or no external constraint—whose value is determined, ideally, by the market. Arrangements very akin to "ownership" did arise during the Edo period, but, particularly for woodland, they were never recognized as a single, indivisible conceptual unit of human relations.

8. Tsutsui Michio, *Nihon rinseishi kenkyū josetsu*, 177–80.

9. Nōrinshō, *Nihon rinseishi*, vol. 5, pp. 54–55.

10. Nōrinshō, *Nihon rinseishi*, vol. 5, pp. 45, 91–92; Toba Masao, "Edo jidai no rinsei," 32.

11. Shioya Tsutomu, *Buwakebayashi seido no shiteki kenkyū: Buwakebayashi yori bunshūrin e no tenkai*, 59.

12. Nōrinshō, *Nihon rinseishi*, vol. 5, pp. 17, 87. The *ken*, now fixed at 1.99 yards (1.82 meters), ranged from about six to seven feet during the seventeenth century, varying regionally and changing as decades passed.

13. Tsutsui, *Nihon rinseishi*, 179. If the builder acquired his own wood, presumably he was allowed to use more.

14. Tsutsui, *Nihon rinseishi*, 178–79.

15. Linking consumption rights to status had the corollary effect of turning the rationing system into an integral part of the status hierarchy. The general pattern of status-linked sumptuary regulation is nicely laid out by Donald H. Shively, "Sumptuary Regulation and Status in Early Tokugawa Japan," 123–64. More recently, architectural aspects of the pattern have been treated in William H. Coaldrake, "Edo Architecture and Tokugawa Law," 235–84. Neither author confronts the tricky question of cause, assuming that the pattern was simply an expression of political ideology. From the outset the Tokugawa regime certainly did envisage a correlation between a person's social status and material standard of living. During the early seventeenth century, however, when the economy was still growing ebulliently, sumptuary legislation was neither extensive nor particularly precise in detail. Not until later in the century, when the broader problem of ecological limits really started to press in on government and society did the rulers begin cranking out ever more elaborate and restrictive consumption edicts. They did so, I submit, not because the edicts gave visible expression to some abstract sense of social propriety but because it seemed an appropriate way, and perhaps the only way they could envisage, to cope with the problems of the moment that resulted from excessive human demand on the ecosystem. That the policy seemed to serve their own interests was, needless to say, one aspect of its perceived appropriateness.

16. The basic outlines of forest administration are given in standard studies, such as Tsutsui, *Nihon rinseishi*; Ringyō Hattatsushi Chōsakai, ed., *Nihon ringyō hattatsushi: Meiji ikō no tenkai katei*; and Nihon Gakushiin, comp., *Meijizen Nihon ringyō gijutsu hattatsushi*. For a highly systematized *han* by *han* description of forest regulatory arrangements, see Rin'yachō, comp., *Tokugawa jidai ni okeru rin'ya seido no taiyō*.

17. Ringyō Hattatsushi, *Nihon ringyō*, 6, 15.

18. Tsutsui, *Nihon rinseishi*, 177–215, and Tōkugawa Muneyoshi, *Edo jidai ni okeru zōrin gijutsu no shiteki kenkyū*, 351–71, provide convenient summaries of the main lines of government forest regulation.

19. Analytical categories can be misleading. The distinction being made here between "protection" and "production" should not obscure the fact that the two were inherently related. In the minds of rulers protection growth was to benefit some sort of production, usually agricultural. And often enough trees originally preserved for protection purposes ended up being harvested.

20. In 1615 Ieyasu assigned the Kiso area to Owari, the domain of his newly married, newly enfeoffed son Yoshinao, but he stipulated that the area must continue providing timber to Edo upon request. By 1630, however, Owari leaders were obstructing such provisioning and keeping the Kiso yield for their own use (Tokoro Mitsuo, "Suminokura Yoichi to Kisoyama," 11–13).

21. Tokoro, *Kinsei*, 97, 104–5, discusses protection forests. The regulations cited in this paragraph can also be found in Nōrinshō, *Nihon rinseishi*, vol. 5, pp. 4–6. The phrasing on careless cutting of trees and bamboo subsequently became routine in directives to officials administering newly reassigned areas.

22. William S. Atwell, "Some Observations on the 'Seventeenth-Century Crisis' in China and Japan," 226.

23. The regulations cited in this paragraph appear in Nōrinshō, *Nihon rinseishi*, vol. 5, pp. 17, 19–20, 22, 23.

24. Nōrinshō, *Nihon rinseishi*, vol. 5, p. 29.

25. Nōrinshō, *Nihon rinseishi*, vol. 5, pp. 33, 38. The injunctions of 1652 can also be found in Ishii Ryōsuke, *Tokugawa kinreikō*, ser. 1, vol. 4, pp. 124–25.

26. Nōrinshō, *Nihon rinseishi*, vol. 5, p. 48. Also quoted in Yamanouchi Shizuo, *Nihon zōrin gyōseishi gaisetsu*, 58.

27. Nōrinshō, *Nihon rinseishi*, vol. 5, pp. 68–69.

28. Nōrinshō, *Nihon rinseishi*, vol. 5, p. 61. Also quoted in Tokoro, *Kinsei*, 97–98. The "other jurisdictions" mostly were daimyo lands.

29. Nōrinshō, *Nihon rinseishi*, vol. 5, pp. 61–62. Also quoted in Tokoro, *Kinsei*, 98–99. The date is 1684/8/13.

30. Toba, "Edo jidai," 32. A notable characteristic of the documentation and scholarship on early modern Japan is that the topics of forest utilization and riparian control exist almost independently of one another even though there is a fundamental causal relationship between the two. The documentary segregation almost surely reflects an administrative particularism and bureaucratic separation that resulted in the creation of separate sets of records. The scholarly segregation probably reflects, in part, the extent to which research is shaped by the documents a scholar uses and, in part, the questions a scholar brings to the documents, questions about production and politics in the case of forests, and engineering and politics in the case of riparian work. The more basic ecological perspective

that sees the inextricable linkage between forest use and river condition does not seem really to have become established in this area of scholarship.

31. Tokoro, *Kinsei*, 99–100.

32. Instances of the *bakufu* urging the opening of land during the early eighteenth century can be found, for example, in Nōrinshō, *Nihon rinseishi*, vol. 5, pp. 135, 138–40, 151, 161. Their effectiveness is not indicated.

33. Nōrinshō, *Nihon rinseishi*, vol. 5, pp. 151–52.

34. Nōrinshō, *Nihon rinseishi*, vol. 5, pp. 155–56. The source cited is *Jikata shūi*.

35. Fukai Masaumi, "Zaimoku (ishi) bugyō narabi ni hayashi bugyō no shūninsha ni tsuite," 207–8.

36. Nōrinshō, *Nihon rinseishi*, vol. 5, p. 27.

37. Nōrinshō, *Nihon rinseishi*, vol. 5, p. 162; Fukai, "Zaimoku bugyō," 208–9.

38. Shioya, *Buwakebayashi*, 52–53.

39. See, for examples, entries in Nōrinshō, *Nihon rinseishi*, vol. 5, pp. 7, 9, 11, 15.

40. Nōrinshō, *Nihon rinseishi*, vol. 5, p. 91. Also quoted in Shizuoka Ken Mokuzai Kyōdō Kumiai Ren'aikai, *Shizuoka ken mokuzaishi*, 21–22.

41. Nōrinshō, *Nihon rinseishi*, vol. 5, pp. 58–59, 109. Also quoted in *Shizuoka ken mokuzaishi*, 21.

42. Nōrinshō, *Nihon rinseishi*, vol. 5, pp. 92–93.

43. Nōrinshō, *Nihon rinseishi*, vol. 5, pp. 101–2, 104–5, 147. The document for 1733 also appears in Ishii, *Tokugawa kinreikō*, ser. 1, vol. 4, p. 146.

44. Shioya, *Buwakebayashi*, 53.

45. Quoted in Tokoro, *Kinsei*, 108–9. The villages appear to be in the foothills north of Gifu. The indicated dates for the removal of trees from the register are my interpretation of sexagenary entries in the record.

46. Diameter at breast height, or dbh, is the standard measure of stem size in modern forest mensuration. Given the relatively short stature of Edo-period Japanese, dbh is reasonably convertible to a common Edo-period measure, circumference at eye level.

47. *Akamatsu* is found throughout Japan, whereas the other noteworthy pines are not. *Kuromatsu* is located along the coast, particularly in the south, and *himekomatsu*, preferring a cooler latitude, is rare in Mino. Moreover, *himekomatsu* is normally identified as such, whereas *akamatsu* is commonly signified as simply *matsu*.

48. Tokoro, *Kinsei*, 110.

49. Tokoro, *Kinsei*, 114–15. All trees in this count are roughly three inches dbh or over. One square *chō* equals 2.45 acres. The last entry of eighty-four *chō* is my calculation for an area recorded as fourteen by five *chō* in linear measure (one *chō* equals 109 meters).

50. Tokoro, *Kinsei*, 110–11. The "ridgeline conifers" probably were trees on the parcel's boundary that were counted separately because their felling normally was forbidden.

51. Tokoro, *Kinsei*, 116; Nōrinshō, *Nihon rinseishi*, vol. 5, pp. 162–63.

52. Except as noted, this material on Amagi derives from Asai Junko, "Ohayashiyama ni okeru bakufu ringyō seisaku: Izu Amagi ohayashiyama ni tsuite," 1–18. In a few particulars the information on Amagi in *Shizuoka ken mokuzaishi*, 22–24, differs slightly.

53. On Amagi "large" trees were, by definition, three *shaku* or more in circumference at eye level. "Small" were one to three *shaku* in circumference, and those under one *shaku* were designated "seedlings" (*naeki*) (Asai, "Ohayashiyama," 12). The large trees that the regime chose not to protect may have been overaged wolf trees. The smaller ones that were protected might have had more potential as timber trees, but they were also more easily felled and slipped surreptitiously into charcoal kilns.

54. A faint echo of this intense concern with fire on Amagi is evident in Dazai Osamu's novel of 1947, *Shayō*, translated by Donald Keene as *The Setting Sun*, 31–38. A refugee from war-ravaged Tokyo moves to the interior of Izu north of Amagi, where she accidentally burns her house down, much to the dismay and outrage of her neighbors, who are unforgiving of her carelessness.

55. *Shizuoka ken mokuzaishi*, 24, 49, mentions the acts of 1762 and 1766.

56. *Shizuoka ken mokuzaishi*, 49.

57. This material on Hida derives from Tokoro, *Kinsei*, 152–60; Niwa Kunio, "Hida 'ohayashiyama' no ichi kōsatsu"; and Nōrinshō, *Nihon rinseishi*, vol. 3, which consists entirely of documents relating to the Hida forests. Tokoro's analysis is grounded in substantial documentation derived from other sources as well.

58. Nōrinshō, *Nihon rinseishi*, vol. 3, pp. 1, 2. Kanamori had designated some uplands *jitōyama* and some *unjōyama*. The former presumably were areas assigned to his vassals; the latter, subject to his direct taxation.

59. Nōrinshō, *Nihon rinseishi*, vol. 3, pp. 34–45, 364–80.

60. Tokoro, *Kinsei*, 95.

61. Reconstruction after the Meireki fire also subjected lumbermen to distressing swings in a boom or bust entrepreneurial marketplace. I discuss that issue briefly in "Lumber Provisioning in Early Modern Japan, 1580–1850."

5. Silviculture: Its Principles and Practice

1. Aspects of this *nōsho* literature are discussed by Thomas C. Smith in "Okura Nagatsune and the Technologists," and his earlier work, *The*

Agrarian Origins of Modern Japan. Jennifer Robertson has discussed the literature in "Japanese Farm Manuals: A Literature of Discovery," and "Sexy Rice: Plant Gender, Farm Manuals, and Grass-Roots Nativism." Smith looks at *nōsho* from an economic perspective; Robertson, from an ethnographic one. The literature is yet to be treated in English from an ecological perspective.

2. These examples are taken from Tokugawa Muneyoshi, *Edo jidai ni okeru zōrin gijutsu no shiteki kenkyū*, 333–34.

3. Tokugawa, *Edo jidai*, 336. *Jikata kikigaki* [Verbatim notes on rural affairs], originally published in two *kan* and filling forty-eight pages of modern text, consists of five parts, one of them dealing with woodland. It provides guidance on administering rural areas, as distinct from administering towns and handling judicial matters. The author is unknown, but references to the work suggest that it was written by a *bakufu* intendant (Kantō *gundai*) or one of his subordinates (*Nihon rekishi daijiten*, vol. 9, pp. 196–97). Pine is generally not a favored fuelwood among North Americans, but it has advantages. Pine trees survive on poor sites and grow comparatively rapidly. The wood is soft for easy harvesting and lighter than most hardwoods to carry. It provides a fast, hot fire and ample Btu's per unit of weight. However, it does not burn long and steadily as good hardwoods do and yields fewer Btu's per volume measure.

4. See Smith, *Agrarian Origins*, 88–89, and Robertson, "Japanese Farm Manuals," 182–84, for a discussion of the *Nōgyō zensho* [Encyclopedia of farming].

5. Here and in what continues I am following Kanō Kyōji, *Edo jidai no ringyō shisō*, 26–29.

6. Kanō, *Edo jidai*, 30–31.

7. Kanō, *Edo jidai*, 51. Probably the most prolific and eclectic scholar of the Edo period, Satō Shin'en (or Nobuhiro) wrote on foreign affairs, society, taxation, defense, geography, astronomy, Shintō, and religion more broadly, as well as on agricultural economics and silviculture. That he has received so little attention among foreign scholars probably reflects the bad press he has received because of the limited political perspective from which his work is viewed.

8. Quoted from Satō's *Keizai yōroku* in Kanō, *Edo jidai*, 57.

9. Kanō describes Satō's thinking at some length in *Edo jidai*, 53–108.

10. Motoyoshi Rurio, "Yamaguni sugi ni kan suru kenkyū (san)," 75–95, contains a discussion of the famous but atypical *daisugi* or *kabusugi* culture of Yamaguni. After a few regenerations coppice loses its vitality, and durable coppice stands must regularly include some new growth derived from seedlings or slips.

11. As the footnotes reveal, this chapter is heavily indebted to Tokugawa, *Edo jidai*. Muneyoshi's book is about as close as we can get to a truly definitive study. Based on a thorough and informed review of the original materials, it is methodically organized in terms of the several facets of silvicultural practice, including seed selection, seedbed preparation and management, slip culture, soil improvement, site selection and preparation, transplanting techniques, aftercare, and coppice management. Muneyoshi was born in 1897, a direct descendant of the Tokugawa daimyo line at Mito. He received his doctorate in agriculture from Tokyo Imperial University and served as an instructor there and as a middle school principal. He enjoyed a distinguished career as a national legislator and government official. He served as director of the Agency for Land Planning (Kokudo Keikakukaichō), director of the Association of Japanese Museums (Nihon Hakubutsukan Kyōkaichō), and assistant director of the Japan Forest Association (Nihon Sanrinkai Fukukaichō). This book is his best-known piece of scholarship, but during 1940, as the bibliography indicates, he also published in the journal *Sanrin* [Forestry] a number of concise essays on individual forestry commentators of the Edo period.

12. This material on seedling culture derives from Tokugawa, *Edo jidai*, 6–270. It constitutes the heart of his study.

13. This section on cuttings is based on material derived from Tokugawa, *Edo jidai*, 81–91, 229–41.

14. Quoted in Tokugawa, *Edo jidai*, 295.

15. This material on aftercare derives from Tokugawa, *Edo jidai*, 287–91, 295–303, 306–14, 317–24.

16. Tokugawa, *Edo jidai*, 317.

17. Muneyoshi's study reveals both the spread of silviculture and its refinement. It is also clear from his study, however, that there were no fundamental changes in the basic understanding of silviculture during the Tokugawa period. The improvements that took place occurred within a stable conceptual frame of reference.

18. When viewed through the prism of Muneyoshi's work, this Tokugawa silviculture seems particularly instructive even today. One reason, no doubt, is that Muneyoshi was a trained silviculturist who organized and assessed materials in terms of his own fund of professional knowledge. Hence, despite the great difference in levels of technical sophistication, his presentation of Tokugawa forestry bears a striking resemblance to silvicultural material as it appears in modern texts. See, for example, the pertinent sections of Grant W. Sharpe, Clare W. Hendee, and Shirley W. Allen, *Introduction to Forestry*, 4th ed.; and Theodore W. Daniel, John A. Helms, and Frederick S. Baker, *Principles of Silviculture*, 2d ed.

6. Plantation Forestry:
Economic Aspects of Its Emergence

1. This chapter is a revised version of my essay "Plantation Forestry in Early Modern Japan: Economic Aspects of Its Emergence."

2. I explore this issue in the essay "Lumber Provisioning in Early Modern Japan, 1580–1850."

3. Protection forests, such as those established on coastal sand dunes facing the Sea of Japan, derived from more complex considerations, but production forests, rather than protection stands, are the focus of our attention.

4. Fujita Yoshitani, *Kinsei mokuzai ryūtsūshi no kenkyū: Tanbazai ryūtsū no hatten katei*, 116. I discuss Akita practices in *The Origins of Japan's Modern Forests: The Case of Akita.*

5. Tokoro Mitsuo, "Saishu ringyō kara ikusei ringyō e no katei," 19–20.

6. Hattori Marenobu, "Hitoyoshi han ni okeru ikuseiteki ringyō: Toku ni buwakebayashi no ringyōshiteki igi," 76, 78.

7. Motoyoshi Rurio, "Yamaguni sugi ni kan suru kenkyū (san)," 48–49, 55–57, 77.

8. Matsumura Yasukazu, "Mito han ringyō no kiban to sono gijutsu-teki tenkai," 8.

9. Ringyō Hattatsushi Chōsakai, ed., *Nihon ringyō hattatsushi: Meiji ikō no tenkai katei*, 28. Alternatively, they were known as "Osaka seedlings" or "Ikeda seedlings," according to Toba Masao, "Kinsei no shinrin keizai to kamikata jūmyō (jō)," 1.

10. This description of Ikeda nursery activity is based on Toba, "Kinsei (1)," and his similarly titled essay, "Kinsei (2)." Toba reports that besides *sugi*, the Ikeda nurseries furnished many other species, notably *hinoki*, *matsu*, *kashi*, *hiba*, and various bamboo.

11. The figure of 300,000 assumes that a pole load is two baskets of 100 to 200 seedlings apiece. The amount of 100 to 200 comes from Tokugawa Muneyoshi, *Edo jidai ni okeru zōrin gijutsu no shiteki kenkyū*, 112, and refers to bundles of seedlings in general, not to those from Ikeda specifically. Nurserymen in Osaka paid the city government annual license fees of "ten silver pieces" each for their monopoly rights. If these "pieces" were *momme*, it was a token fee rather than an extortionate levy (Toba, "Kinsei (1)," 17–19).

12. Motoyoshi Rurio, *Senshin ringyō chitai no shiteki kenkyū: Yamaguni ringyō no hatten katei*, 254, 257. For comparison, in December 1985 in Tokyo stores, first-grade rice was selling for 550 to 580 yen per kilogram, depending on brand name reputation. Two gallons of water weigh about 7.27 kilo-

grams; rice weighs somewhat less, and so today the rice that would have cost about three silver *momme* in the mid-Edo period would cost roughly 3,500 yen.

13. To illustrate price fluctuation, Tsu *han* bought 135,500 *sugi* seedlings for 107 *ryō* (about five *momme* per hundred) in 1793. The next year it paid 93 *ryō* for 329,392 (about two *momme* per hundred). Seedling age is not indicated, though it certainly should have affected the price (Toba, "Kinsei (1)," 21).

14. This material on Mito is from Matsumura Yasukazu, "Mito han rinseishi josetsu," 148–51, and "Mito han gotateyama seido ni kan suru ichi kōsatsu," 85–86.

15. Tokoro Mitsuo, *Kensei ringyōshi no kenkyū*, 102–3. *Bakufu* wages in Hida were comparatively high because tree planting served in part as a form of government work-relief for impoverished villagers.

16. Tsutsui Michio, *Nihon rinseishi kenkyū josetsu*, 200. He cites information from Akita, Shinjō, Morioka, Mito, Hikone, Tsu, Hiroshima, and Kumamoto between the 1780s and 1850s. At the time, reports Tsutsui, one hundred *mon* of *zeni* generally would buy approximately 1.5 to 3 *shō* (about three to six quarts) of rice, depending on the location. Nakajima Akira, "Maebashi han no rin'ya seido: Ohayashi o chūshin ni shite," 15, reports that in Maebashi *han* in the 1860s, villagers received two *zeni* per forty-five seedlings they planted and two *zeni* for every one hundred *tsubo* (331 square meters) of area they cleared of weeds and brush. Perhaps the coin was *momme* of silver rather than *zeni* of copper, which were worth about 1/120 of a *momme*.

17. Kurotaki Hidehisa, "Kinsei ni okeru mokuzai ryūtsū no kōzō: Hirosaki han ni okeru mokuzai ishutsu o jirei to shite," 66.

18. Matsushima Yoshio, "Tokugawa jidai ni okeru zōrin seisaku ni tsuite," 48–49, mentions the various ways of paying for planting. Asai Junko, "Ohayashiyama ni okeru bakufu ringyō seisaku: Izu Amagi ohayashiyama ni tsuite," 15–17, describes practices in *bakufu* lands on the Izu peninsula. Hattori, "Hitoyoshi," describes nicely the methods of afforestation in Hitoyoshi *han*.

19. Tsutsui, *Nihon rinseishi*, 192–207, attempts to assess the fiscal worth of forests in several *han*, most especially Tsu. He reports that the labor expense for planting in Tsu was commonly two or three times the original seedling cost. Total cost normally worked out to five or more *momme* per hundred planted, which puts normal seedling cost at about one to two *momme* per hundred. That figure is well below those of the Ikeda nurseries, suggesting that a significant portion, perhaps half, of the real seedling cost in Tsu was being absorbed by villages and forest users. And yet, this regenerative forestry was still not cost-effective, at least not in the short term

of one or two decades. On p. 207 Tsutsui presents the following data, which reveal the considerable variation in acknowledged costs of seedling culture. The right-hand column, with *momme* figured at sixty per *ryō*, is my own derivation from the other figures.

Planting Activity	Seedlings as % of Total Cost	Labor, Etc., as % of Total Cost	Total Cost (ryō)	Seedlings per Ryō	Momme per 100 Seedlings
3,400 sugi	43.9	56.1	$3\frac{1}{4}$	1,130	5.74
211,514 seedlings	18.6	81.4	$59\frac{1}{4}$	3,584	1.68
189,414 sugi					
21,000 hinoki					
100 sakura					
1,000 hiba					
192,493 sugi and hinoki	31.6	68.4	$174\frac{1}{2}$	1,106	5.44
498,252 sugi and hinoki	25.2	74.8	$560\frac{1}{2}$	889	6.75
379,292 sugi and hinoki	33.0	67.0	$324\frac{1}{4}$	1,170	5.13
75,397 sugi and hinoki	10.3	89.7	$204\frac{1}{4}$	369	16.25

20. Motoyoshi Rurio, "Yamaguni ringyō chitai ni okeru jinkō zōrin no shinten to ikurin gijutsu no hensen," 83. The other 437 *momme* of cost is not identified but probably included rent, tax fees, and other overhead. See also n. 40 below for another instance of concealed labor costs.

21. Fujita Yoshihisa, "Kinsei ni okeru ikurin gijutsu taikei no chiiki-sei," 110. Tokugawa, *Edo jidai*, 81, lists seventeen types of trees sometimes reproduced by cuttings.

22. Matsumura Yasukazu, "Sugisashiki ringyō no gijutsushiteki kōsatsu: Sugi no sashiki ringyō no kenkyū (dai yon)," 145–51.

23. Matsumura, "Sugisashiki," 150–51, 154; Ringyō Hattatsushi, *Nihon ringyō*, 538. The two sources give slightly different information.

24. This description of *tokozashi* technique derives from Matsumura, "Sugisashiki," 149–53. Ringyō Hattatsushi, *Nihon ringyō*, 526, 535, briefly describes slip culture in the Chizu and Kitayama areas west and north of Kyoto.

25. Morita Seiichi, "Higo no ringyō," 116.

26. Shioya Tsutomu and Sagio Ryōshi, *Obi ringyō hattatsushi*, 32–33.

27. Regulations issued in 1776 in Hitoyoshi *han* (which lay between Kumamoto and Obi and which relied heavily on *sugi* cuttings and customarily had corvée laborers plant them) excused villagers from corvée duty if they paid 24 *mon* in copper for every cutting of their obligation. This rate of substitution converts (at 120 copper *mon* per silver *momme*) to a fee of twenty *momme* per hundred cuttings. It is a rate appreciably higher than that for afforestation with seedlings, which suggests that the rate was designed to discourage such substitution (Hattori, "Hitoyoshi," 80–81).

28. Asai, "Ohayashiyama," 13; Matsumura, "Sugisashiki," 150–51.

29. The figures in this paragraph derive from Asai, "Ohayashiyama," 13, and Satō Takayuki, "Kinsei chūki no bakufu zōrin seisaku to murakata no taiō: Hōreki-An'ei ki Hokuen chihō o jirei to shite," 174–75, 178–79, 181, 182.

30. Tokugawa, *Edo jidai*, 286–329, discusses aftercare in detail.

31. Fujita, *Kinsei mokuzai*, 123.

32. This summary of Mito aftercare is from Matsumura, "Mito han ringyō," 8–10.

33. Tsutsui Michio, "Akita han ni okeru ringyō ikusei seisan soshiki to gyōsei no hōhō," 19.

34. Asai, "Ohayashiyama," 17.

35. Ōsaki Rokurō, "Ohayashi chiseki kakutei katei no ichi kenshō: Kōzuke kuni (Gumma ken) Tone gun o taishō to shite," 26.

36. Matsumura, "Mito han gotateyama," 86. These Mito *yamamori* also received various supplemental rewards.

37. Mitsuhashi Tokio, "Yoshino-Kumano no ringyō," 252, reports a 5 to 10 percent salary rate; Ringyō Hattatsushi, *Nihon Ringyō*, 510, reports 1.5 to 5 percent.

38. Fujita, *Kinsei mokuzai*, 123.

39. Nakajima, "Maebashi," 16. The *nōbiban* of table 2 were on duty from the beginning of the twelfth month to the end of the third month during the fire-prone winter months.

40. Matsumura Yasukazu, "Kinsei Ōme ringyō no seiritsu oyobi hat-

ten ni kan suru rekishi chirigakuteki kenkyū (shōroku)," 16–17. Matsu-mura's figures seem to reveal partial concealment of labor costs. The *sugi* seedlings themselves cost 3 *ryō*, but the six planters only cost 0.75 *ryō* (three *bu*), or about 46 *momme*. The 3 *ryō* could have bought about six thousand seedlings for original and replacement planting. Setting six thousand out would have required roughly sixty man-days of labor or, if remunerated in silver at some 2 *momme* per man per day, some 120 *momme*, rather than 46.

41. Motoyoshi, "Yamaguni sugi," 79.

42. Nihon Gakushiin, comp., *Meijizen Nihon ringyō gijutsu hattatsushi*, 451–52.

43. This discussion of "brand name recognition" is based on data in Ringyō Hattatsushi, *Nihon ringyō*, 27 (general comments), 506 (on Yo-shino), and 531 (on Obi).

44. It may be more correct historically to say that by a process of "natural economic selection" optimally located plantations ended up as flourishing entrepreneurial enterprises.

45. Matsumura Yasukazu, "Ōme no ringyō," 196.

46. I have examined transportation costs in "Logging the Unloggable: Timber Transport in Early Modern Japan." On *yamaotoshi* see particularly 186, 191. The plantation grower may have faced a greater investment burden at harvesttime insofar as he had an even-aged stand that he may have clear-cut, incurring full cost before recouping, whereas the feller of uneven-aged natural stands might spread his felling costs over several years, recovering them as he went along.

47. Motoyoshi, "Yamaguni ringyō chitai," 86.

48. Ringyō Hattatsushi, *Nihon ringyō*, 515.

49. Katō Morihiro, "Nishikawa ringyō hasseishi ni kan suru ichi kōsatsu," 171, 178; Motoyoshi, "Yamaguni ringyō chitai," 78; Asakawa Kiyoei, "Kinsei Suwa-gun ni okeru hayashi aratame to hayashi kenchi," 125–66.

50. Iwanaga Yutaka, "Edo-Meiji ki ni okeru Yoshino ringyō no ikurin gijutsu," 14–23.

51. Motoyoshi, "Yamaguni ringyō chitai," 95.

52. Quoted in Tsuboi Shunzō, "Kinsei chū-go ki Tenryū ringyō ni tsuite," 23.

7. Land-Use Patterns and Afforestation

1. Parts of this chapter first appeared in my essays "Land-Use Patterns and Afforestation in the Edo Period" and "From Exploitation to Planta-tion Forestry in Early Modern Japan."

2. Here "multiple use" pertains to specific parcels of woodland, not, as

in the U.S. Forest Service's definition, to an entire forest system, in which the single use of specific tracts may be normative. The key paragraph of the Forest Service's definition, which is a world-class example of committee writing and interest-group accommodation, is quoted in Grant W. Sharpe, Clare W. Hendee, and Shirley W. Allen, *Introduction to Forestry*, 4th ed., 46–47.

3. Hirasawa Kiyondo, *Kinsei iriai kankō no seiritsu to tenkai: Shinshū Shimo Ina chihō o chūshin ni shite*, 46–53.

4. Hirasawa, *Kinsei iriai*, 226–27.

5. The material on Maebashi *han* is from Rin'yachō, comp., *Tokugawa jidai ni okeru rin'ya seido no taiyō*, 233–41.

6. The material on Tsugaru is from Matsuki Kan, "Tsugaru no hiba (hinoki)," 152–59.

7. Tokoro Mitsuo, "Kinsei Kiso sanrin no hozoku taisaku," 9–12.

8. Tokoro Mitsuo, "Kiso no gomen shiraki," 24–26.

9. Minemura Hideo, "Hayashi metsuke no kiroku yori mita Suwa han no sanrin seisaku," 395.

10. Ōsaki Rokurō, "Ohayashi chiseki kakutei katei no ichi kenshō: Kōzuke kuni (Gumma ken) Tone gun o taishō to shite," 23.

11. Asakawa Kiyoei, "Kinsei Suwa-gun ni okeru hayashi aratame to hayashi kenchi," 133.

12. Matsumura Yasukazu, "Mito han rinseishi josetsu," 138; and idem, "Mito han gotateyama seido ni kan suru ichi kōsatsu," 88–89.

13. Murai Hideo, *Akita han rin'yashi kenkyū josetsu: Okachi gun Akinomiya o chūshin to suru rin'ya shoyū narabi ni riyō no jittai*, 58.

14. Katō Morihiro, "Nishikawa ringyō hasseishi ni kan suru ichi kōsatsu," 175.

15. An influential pioneer study of *shakuchi ringyō* in Yoshino is Kasai Kyōetsu, *Yoshino ringyō no hatten kōzō*. Fujita Yoshihisa, "Yoshino ringyōshi ni okeru 'shakuchi ringyō' no saikentō ni tsuite," 120–46, carefully refutes Kasai, using the same source materials. He does so by defining *shakuchi ringyō* literally as "land rental," whereas Kasai defined it loosely and included a wide variety of sale and leasing practices. The issue is not merely a semantic quibble, however: Kasai used the data to show that urban merchants employed *shakuchi ringyō* to reduce the Yoshino mountain peasantry to servitude, but Fujita contends that trends in forest-use rights did not lead to that outcome.

16. A major source of information on *wariyama* is Harada Toshimaru, *Kinsei iriai seido kaitai katei no kenkyū: Yamawari seido no hassei to sono henshitsu*. Furukawa Sadao and Kanai Kiyotoshi have also written on *wariyama* in recent years. Furushima Toshio is perhaps the dean of scholars of *iriai* studies, and Nishikawa Zensuke a major interpreter. The *wariyama* system

has been the subject of extensive study by historians interested in the development of capitalism, landlordism, and accompanying social stratification in rural Japan. In consequence, most of the literature draws no distinction between communal areas of tillage, pasture, scrubland, and woodland, and much of the analysis is marginal for a study of forest history. Philip Brown's recent work on *warichi* examines a related phenomenon, but one that in a sense is quite opposite in its implication: practices whereby villages continued exercising some degree of communal control over plots of arable that were nominally assigned to individual households but which in fact were redivided among villagers from time to time.

17. In general, *yamawari* appears to have resulted in better-managed village uplands, in part because it reduced demand on the areas allotted to most households, forcing poorer villagers to concentrate their search for fertilizer and fuel in the remaining parcels of *iriaichi*. Chiba Tokuji, *Hageyama no kenkyū*, 112–13, cites suggestive materials on this matter.

18. Shōji Kichinosuke, "Kinsei ni okeru tochi oyobi sanrin no bunkatsu: Minami Aizu gun Kanaizawa mura no mura yakujō monjo o chūshin ni," 22–23. Rather than say that villagers imposed these regulations on themselves, it might be more correct to say that those villagers with more woodland, who generally were more wealthy and influential, persuaded their neighbors to accept regulations that restricted the use rights of less well endowed neighbors.

19. Shōji, "Kinsei," 23–34.

20. Nōrinshō, comp., *Nihon rinseishi shiryō*, vol. 5, pp. 94–95.

21. Harada Toshimaru, "Yamawari seido to sono hensen," 179–80. *Satsuyama*, or "tagged forests," were areas in which use was restricted by specific government orders applied to the particular site. I discuss *satsuyama* briefly in *The Origins of Japan's Modern Forests: The Case of Akita*, 25–26.

22. Harada Toshimaru, "Muramochi sanrin no hogo to yamawari seido," 26.

23. This description of Yoshino practice follows the analysis in Fujita, "Yoshino ringyōshi." For another useful account see Mitsuhashi Tokio, "Yoshino-Kumano no ringyō."

24. An early study of Tenryū *nenkiyama* is Kaneiwa Yoshio, "Tenryū ringyō chitai ni okeru sugiyama nenki uriwatashi nado ni kan suru kenkyū." Shimada Kinzō has published essays on the subject in the 1977–81 issues of *TRK Kenkyū kiyō*. In the first of these essays he discusses briefly the pertinent historiography of Yoshino forestry.

25. Shimada Kinzō, "Kinsei Tenryū ringyōchi ni okeru nenkiyama baibai," 35. Kaneiwa, "Tenryū ringyō," reproduces sixty-seven of these contracts, which reveal the great variety of particular arrangements in even one locality.

26. Shimada Kinzō, "Kinsei Tenryū ringyōchi ni okeru shikin ryūtsū katei," 66–67.

27. The major work on shared-yield forests is Shioya Tsutomu, *Buwakebayashi seido no shiteki kenkyū: Buwakebayashi yori bunshūrin e no tenkai.*

28. Shioya, *Buwakebayashi*, 251–549, discusses the practice *han* by *han*, ranging over Tōhoku, Kyushu, and selected areas in between.

29. Shioya Tsutomu and Sagio Ryōshi, *Obi ringyō hattatsushi*, 30, 34–36.

30. Shioya, *Buwakebayashi*, 508.

31. Tokoro Mitsuo, "Saishu ringyō kara ikusei ringyō e no katei," 18.

32. Satō Takayuki, "Kinsei chūki no bakufu zōrin seisaku to murakata no taiō: Hōreki-An'ei ki Hokuen chihō o jirei to shite," describes the failure of *bakufu* afforestation in north Tōtōmi in the 1760s and 1770s.

33. Tokoro Mitsuo, *Kinsei ringyōshi no kenkyū*, 102–3, 159. Niwa Kunio, "Hida 'ohayashiyama' no ichi kōsatsu," 85–93, examining one locality up to the 1840s, offers a less sanguine conclusion.

34. Minemura, "Hayashi metsuke," 380–85. I presume the twenty liters of seed were mixed with chaff; no seed count is available.

35. Morita Seiichi, "Higo no ringyō," 117. The "Annual Rate" figures are my calculations, and they suggest that the original figures are, in part at least, estimates.

36. Matsushima Yoshio, "Sugi no zōrinshi," 135.

37. Fujita Yoshihisa, "Kinsei ni okeru ikurin no seiritsu jiki to sono chiikisa ni tsuite," 144.

38. Fujita Yoshihisa, "Kinsei ni okeru ikurin gijutsu taikei no chiikisei," 120.

39. Fujita, "Kinsei ni okeru ikurin gijutsu," 105–6.

40. Ringyō Hattatsushi Chōsakai, ed., *Nihon ringyō hattatsushi: Meiji ikō no tenkai katei*, 28.

41. Matsuki, "Tsugaru," 156.

42. Kurotaki Hidehisa, "Kinsei ni okeru mokuzai ryūtsū no kōzō: Hirosaki han ni okeru mokuzai ishutsu o jirei to shite," 75.

43. Shioya and Sagio, *Obi ringyō*, 23–24. Although unspecified, this figure likely refers to *genboku*.

44. Morita, "Higo no ringyō," 116.

45. Matsumura Yasukazu, "Ōme no ringyō," 196.

Conclusion

1. An earlier version of this conclusion appeared in my "Forests of Tokugawa Japan: A Catastrophe That Was Avoided."

2. In adopting these population figures, I am following Kristina Troost (see n. 3 in chapter 2), who is versed in the most recent work of Japanese

medievalists. The more traditional figure of 18 million for 1600, which I have used in earlier writings, is an arbitrary choice derived from a tax-based estimate of 18 million *koku* of agricultural output for the country as a whole. The number is treated as a population statistic on the assumption that one person requires about one *koku* of agricultural yield per year to survive. Needless to say, the lower figure of 12 million is more convenient for my thesis that explosive growth in human consumption of biomass during the seventeenth century was a major cause of the overcutting and damaging of Japan's woodland, which in turn led to the rise of regenerative forestry. The lower figure also meshes nicely with the contention in chapter 2 that medieval demand on forests was generally not excessive.

The last figure, 120 million, is anomalous. The earlier population figures are estimates of the numbers of humans being supported by the archipelago's biosystem; the present-day figure is the number of humans who happen to be resident in the archipelago but who are supported by the global ecosystem as manipulated through techniques available to an industrial society. Glenn Thomas Trewartha, *Japan: A Physical, Cultural, and Regional Geography*, 134, reports that in 1960 only Belgium, the Netherlands, and Java-Madura had a greater density per total area than Japan.

3. Information conveyed by Tokoro Mitsuo, 26 May 1982. Tokoro, as the bibliographical essay reveals, has devoted a lifetime to monographic study of Edo-period forestry, concentrating on the Kiso river area.

4. By the eighteenth century scarcity of green fertilizer evidently had driven up its cost enough to permit substitution of fish meal, night soil, and other commercial fertilizer materials, at least around cities and towns. Since most land clearing, especially in the areas where commercial fertilizers were used most intensively, had been accomplished before their use became widespread, they evidently served not to facilitate the opening of more land but to sustain and enhance the productivity of land already under cultivation. In part their use constituted a more efficient utilization of terrestrial biomass and in part an extension of human exploitation beyond the coast, so that sea life rather than forest life paid the price for enhanced human well-being. Whether substitution reduced the level of pressure on woodland, or simply allowed expanded human consumption without increasing that pressure, is probably impossible to determine in the absence of price figures whose meaning in terms of real costs of production can be determined. But any reduction likely was modest because most of the other signs of scarcity—social conflict, substitution, rationing, deterioration of physical plant, and government manipulation—persisted.

5. *Hageyama no bunka* by Chiba Tokuji is a readable and insightful historical study of the process of forest soil degradation in central Japan.

6. The difficulty of linking the great falloff in temple construction during

the Heian period to any decline in religiosity should also be noted. What seems to have declined was organized religion's connection to anyone with sufficient will to overcome the growing obstacles to temple building.

7. See Theodore W. Daniel, John A. Helms, and Frederick S. Baker, *Principles of Silviculture*, 282–91, for a discussion of forest dynamics, and plant succession in particular.

8. During the seventeenth century, moreover, rulers who were more concerned to assure food and fuel supplies than timber stands encouraged brushy broadleaf growth. In Akita, for example, where cold winters required a great deal of fuel for heating, *han* leaders of the mid-seventeenth century encouraged the removal of low-quality *sugi* to make room for broadleafs, which provided superior fuel (Iwasaki Naoto, *Akita ken Noshirogawa kami chihō ni okeru sugibayashi no seiritsu narabi ni kōshin ni kan suru kenkyū*, 249). Later, as timber became more scarce, rulers more consistently promoted conifer growth, in the process colliding with villagers. But even then, as noted in chapter 7, governments sometimes sacrificed timber stands to fodder-fertilizer-fuel production.

9. According to Constantine Nomikos Vaporis, "Overland Communication in Tokugawa Japan," 1, "carts were kept off the principal roads as part of a conscious policy to maintain the roads in good condition for pedestrian traffic." Vaporis (64) adds that although he has seen "no documentary evidence for a statutory ban on the use of carts on the Gokaidō, such a ban may nevertheless have been in effect." The reasons for such a ban, he indicates, were not only an official desire to preserve smooth roads but also "the opposition of post horse operators to carts, which threatened their livelihood."

10. Information conveyed by Iioka Masatake, 12 February 1982. Iioka was referring to the situation in central Japan, but in Akita as well saws were not used for felling until the 1820s.

11. In this discussion of the conservation ethic I obviously am avoiding two intriguing questions: why and how. To explain why this ethic arose quickly enmeshes one in philosophical speculation about the dynamics of the formation of human values, which is far beyond the boundary of our task here. To explain the mechanisms of the diffusion and maintenance of those values would entail a far simpler foray into social history that touches the political structure, the schooling and writing system, kinship and village organization—territory already well explored in English by other scholars and other studies.

12. Tsukii Tadahiro, *Akita han rinsei seishi*, 2.

13. "Parasites" of the homocentric biological community in Japan could be said to include, for example, those species of mosquitoes that flourish in paddy land and other creatures that live off the collaborating

biota, as well as the rats, mice, cockroaches, flies, intestinal parasites, and so on that commonly come to mind.

14. From a twentieth-century perspective, in which Hokkaido (Ezo) seems an indivisible part of Japan, it may appear strange that Japanese of the Edo period made no sustained effort to log the island. The probable reasons are fairly complex but can be boiled down. For reasons of diplomacy and internal politics, leaders in Edo opposed any intrusions on the island most of the time. One of the few major efforts by *bakufu* leaders to develop Ezo was undertaken by Tanuma Okitsugu in the 1760s, and it came to naught because of political complications. Moreover, the daimyo who controlled access to the island discouraged visits by outsiders lest his sources of wealth be threatened. Finally, the island was regarded as so distant, forbidding, and alien that few people wished to go there for any reason, and the idea that timber from there could be a boon seems never to have gained currency, and consequently no pressure group arose to challenge the island's de facto closure.

15. To propose that "intensifying constraints" were the root cause of population limitation does not, of course, predetermine the mechanisms of such a limitation. Whether the numbers were held in check by famine, war, disease, malnutrition, contraception, abortion, infanticide, delayed pregnancy, or whatever is not the issue. Here the point is that none of these mechanisms would have become operative if the Tokugawa populace had been able to satisfy its wants without resort to (or being subjected to) them. But absent an industrial revolution or program of conquest and emigration, as gross human numbers approached thirty million, satisfying basic wants became increasingly difficult. Even after mechanisms and rationales of population control became established, the constraints evidently did not disappear: population stability seems to have persisted, at least until circa 1840. When population began growing again from about that time, may that not have been in part because of the success of reforestation projects that relaxed the basic limitations imposed by the biosystem? See my article "Tokugawa Peasants: Win, Lose, or Draw?" for a guide to relevant books and articles in English and a brief exploration of the issues of population growth and standards of living among commoners, in which I adopt a position somewhat at odds with the currently preferred one of many, perhaps most, economic historians.

16. Vaporis, "Overland Communication," 65, reports that in the city of Edo humans replaced animals in cartage.

17. Although long-term trends are unclear, the dog population may have peaked about 1700 and subsequently declined, freeing caloric yield for other uses. See Donald H. Shively, "Tokugawa Tsunayoshi the Genroku Shogun," 95–96.

Bibliographical Essay:
Scholarship on Preindustrial
Japanese Forestry, 1880–1980

1. The earliest English-language piece on the topic, a concise and useful introduction, is Masako M. Osako, "Forest Preservation in Tokugawa Japan."

2. An earlier, abbreviated version of this essay is my "Century of Scholarship on Early Modern Japanese Forestry, 1880–1980."

3. This essay does not examine the institutional dimensions of this disciplinary development. The origins, purpose, personnel, vicissitudes, and accomplishments of the various forestry-related scholarly organizations are disregarded. Notable organizations include Dai Nihon Sanrinkai (Forest Association of Imperial Japan), Nihon Ringakkai (Forestry Research Association of Japan), Nihon Ringyō Chōsakai (Commission to Investigate Japanese Forestry), Nihon Ringyō Gijutsu Kyōkai (Society for Japanese Forest Technology), Ringyō Hattatsushi Chōsakai (Society for Research on the Development of Forestry), Ringyō Keizai Kenkyūjo (Institute for Research on Forest Economics), and Tokugawa Rinseishi Kenkyūjo (Tokugawa Institute for the History of Forestry). The forest-research arrangements of the nation's universities are not examined here. Nor does the essay treat the history of relevant government organs, such as the Sanrinkyoku and its successor, the Rin'yachō, or the many business and local organizations and the various, often transitory, publishing organs that constitute the subdiscipline's skeleton.

4. Although writings are scattered widely, certain journals are particularly valuable. Before the Pacific War, *Sanrin ihō* carried many useful essays. Since the war, *Ringyō keizai*, particularly on economic aspects of modern forestry, and *Shinano*, on essays relating to that heavily forested province (modern Nagano prefecture), have been strong. The thick annual issues of the Tokugawa Rinseishi Kenkyūjo's *Kenkyū kiyō* regularly carry historical studies of early modern and modern forestry by the finest scholars of Japanese forest history, making it the preeminent journal in the field.

5. For example, I have been unable to locate a copy of a commonly cited classic, *Shinrin to bunka* by Toba Masao, published in Tokyo in 1943, at the height of World War II. I estimate that the 300-odd scholarly books and articles on which this essay is based probably comprise over 80 percent of the works written between 1880 and 1980 that deal primarily with Japan's preindustrial forestry.

6. In "The Japanese Experience with Scarcity: Management of Traditional Common Lands," Margaret A. McKean describes concisely the

main attributes of early modern *iriai* practice. A splendid examination of early modern *iriaichi* is "Common Losses: Transformations of Common-land and Peasant Livelihood in Tokugawa Japan, 1603–1868," by Karen [Lewis] Wigen.

7. The boldface numbers in parentheses are those by which works are listed in the bibliography.

8. In 1930 Endō Yasutarō reported in "Aizu han no zōrin seido oyobi sono jigyō ni kan suru ichi kōsatsu," no. 1, p. 13, that a partial copy of *Sanrin enkakushi* survived the quake, apparently because it was in the house of the official who had prepared it, and this was later turned over to the Sanrinkyoku.

9. I am indebted to Professor Tokoro for providing much of this detail on the preparation of *Nihon rinseishi chōsa shiryō*, in a conversation of 26 May 1982.

10. One project that deserves special note, despite its post-1868 focus, is the large series of usually slender, handwritten, paperbound volumes published during the 1950s and 1960s by Ringyō Hattatsushi Chōsakai (Society for Research on the Development of Forestry), whose guiding figure was Shimada Kinzō, a professor of forest economics at the University of Tokyo. The individual volumes generally consist of collected documents accompanied by an interpretive essay, and they mostly deal with developments in the forestry of selected localities or with statistical series or other specialized topics.

11. The documents that Professor Shimada analyzes were brought to his attention by Yoshida Yoshiaki, who used them in his readable study, *Kiba no rekishi*.

12. Two major forestry reference works deserve mention even though they are marginal to the study of preindustrial forest history. One is the one-volume *Ringyō hyakka jiten* [Encyclopedia of forestry], put out by Nihon Ringyō Gijutsu Kyōkai, which has a sprinkling of historical terms among its descriptions of forest vegetation, outlines of forest production in the prefectures of modern Japan, explanations of modern technical terminology, and descriptions of wood products. The other work is the five-volume *Ringyō gijutsushi* [A history of forestry techniques] by the same society, which, its title notwithstanding, has two volumes on regional forestry in the important timber areas of modern Japan, two volumes on technical aspects of forestry, and one volume on the industrial uses, processes, and chemistry of wood products.

13. Hattori's work reveals especially well the scholarly concern with the contemporary problems of Japan's forests and the people whose lives depended on them, which was so characteristic of this forestry scholarship.

14. *Ringyōshi* is essentially industrial history, and in this book I have purposely avoided it lest it so dominate the analysis as to sabotage my attempt to treat the human-forest relationship as a problem in environmental history. I have adumbrated aspects of the topic in two essays, "Logging the Unloggable: Timber Transport in Early Modern Japan," and "Lumber Provisioning in Early Modern Japan, 1580–1850."

15. The mining industry was a big consumer of wood. Being a major industry, however, it has been studied as an independent topic, and I have omitted references to it in this bibliography.

16. The boundary of early modern forest history is especially difficult to delineate in works dealing with *iriaichi*. In this survey I have attempted to include *iriai* studies if the common land under consideration appeared to be forested but have omitted them if the nature of the study was such that the character of vegetation was irrelevant. Wigen, "Common Losses," 28–49, *passim*, contains a very thoughtful discussion of topics imbedded in common-land history.

17. In "Shifting Cultivation and Land Tenure in Shirakawa-go: Changes from the 1690s to the 1880s," Professor Mizoguchi Tsunetoshi of the College of Liberal Arts at Toyama University has compiled a helpful bibliography on the literature of early modern slash-and-burn cultivation, with particular reference to the Hida vicinity.

18. In late 1944, as Japan's domestic situation grew desperate, Yamaguchi Yaichirō published a 238-page study of slash-and-burn agriculture, *Tōhoku no Yakibata kankō*. Ostensibly written to help his country prepare for the terrible years of semiarboreal subsistence that seemed in store, his work provides valuable insight into the customs and techniques of burnt-field culture as practiced in 1930s Japan. Doubtless, many of the techniques were also characteristic of early modern slash-and-burn culture.

Glossaries

General Glossary

akiyama	明山	lord's forest
amado	雨戸	sliding rain door
azukaridokoro	預かり所	land held in trust
azukariyama	預かり山	lord's forest held in trust
baito	倍都	dual capital system
bakufu	幕府	shogunate; military regime
bu	分	a coin or unit of monetary value
buwakebayashi	部分林	shared-yield forests
chisan chisui	治山治水	management of mountains and waters
chō	町	a measure of distance or acreage
chōbu	町歩	a measure of acreage
daibutsuden	大仏殿	main (Buddha) hall of a temple
daikan	代官	intendant
daimyō	大名	regional military leader; major feudal lord
dairi	内裏	imperial residence

daisugi	台杉	coppice cryptomeria
doi	土居	short split pieces
dosha kata yakusho	土砂方行所	office of erosion control
fuchimai	扶持米	rice paid as per diem wages
fushin bugyōsho	普請奉行所	office of construction
fushin yaku	普請役	construction office personnel
genboku	原木	unprocessed (felled) timber, such as logs or *kureki*
gen'ya	原野	wasteland
gimmiyaku	吟味役	comptroller
gogyō	五行	the five elements
goyō shōnin	御用商人	merchant quartermaster
goyōki	御用木	lord's wood
gundai	郡代	intendant
gun'yaku	軍役	military obligation
hageyama	禿げ山	bald mountain
hama goten	浜御殿	"harbor mansion"
han	藩	early modern baronial domain
haniwa	埴輪	protohistoric clay figurine
hara	腹	inner surface of split piece
hatamoto	旗本	lesser shogunal retainer
hayashi	林	forest
hayashi bugyō	林奉行	forest (mountain) magistrate
hinoki bugyō	桧奉行	timber magistrate
hiwada	桧皮	cypress bark
hiyō	費備	day laborer; wage laborer
honbyakushō	本百姓	tax-paying landholder
hyakushō yama	百姓山	household woodland

hyakushōdai	百姓代	peasant representative; village official
iriai; iriaichi	入会；入会地	communal land
iriaiken	入会権	common-land use rights
itabuki	板葺	shingle roofing
itago	板子	planking; board stock
jikatasho	地方書	farm manual
jikizashi	直挿し	in situ slip culture
jinja	神社	Shintō shrine
jingū	神宮	major Shintō shrine
jitō	地頭	land steward; land-holding samurai
jitōyama	地頭山	steward's upland
jō	丈	a measure of land
kabusugi	株杉	coppice cryptomeria
kadomatsu	門松	New Year's decorative pine tree
kaibutsu	開物	enhancing productivity
kama	鎌	sickle
kama	釜	kettle, cauldron
kama	窯	kiln, stove, oven
kama	竈	oven, hearth
kamakiri	鎌切り	sickle
kan	貫	a unit of money
kanjō bugyō	勘定奉行	superintendent of finance
kanjōsho	勘定所	finance office
karasuki	唐鋤	a Chinese plow
karidono	仮殿	secondary shrine building
karō	家老	senior councillor of a daimyo

kawaragi	瓦木	roof shingles
ken	間	a linear or cubic measure
kofun	古墳	ancient burial mound
kojōya	小庄屋	village headman
koku	石	a measure of volume
kokudaka	石高	putative agricultural yield
kōri bugyō	郡奉行	intendant
kōtan	荒炭	industrial-use charcoal
koya	小屋	bunkhouse
koyamamori	小山守	village forest overseer
kumi	組	work crew; unit of personnel
kumigashira	組頭	neighborhood chief
kure; kureki	榑；榑木	split timber; split pieces
kuwa	鍬	long-bladed hoe
machi bugyō	町奉行	city magistrate
masakari	鉞	ax; broadax
midori no rettō	緑の列島	''the green archipelago''
mikanwari	蜜柑割り	tangerine-like sectioning
miteyama	御手山	lord's forest
momme	匁	a coin or unit of coinage
mon	文	a coin or unit of coinage
myōga	冥加	a thanksgiving to one's lord
myōji taitō	名字帯刀	the right to sword and surname
myōshu	名主	freeholder
naeki	苗木	seedling
nanushi	名主	village notable; headman
nata	鉈	hatchet; machete
nenkiyama	年季山	forest under fixed-term lease

nobiban	野火番	field fire patrols
norimono	乗り物	palanquin
nōsho	農書	farm manual
ōga	大鋸	heavy-duty saw
ohayashi	御林	lord's forest
ohayashi bugyō	御林奉行	forest magistrate
ohayashi daichō	御林台帳	forest register
ohayashi mamori	御林守り	forest overseer
ohayashikata	御林方	forest overseer
ohayashiyama	御林山	lord's forest
ojikiyama	御直山	lord's forest
ōjōya	大庄屋	headman of several villages
okuyama	奥山	lord's forest
omotoyama	御本山	lord's forest
otateyama	御立山	reserved forest
otomebayashi	御留め林	reserved forest
oyama	御山	lord's forest
ōyamamori	大山守	regional forest overseer
ri	里	a measure of distance
rikyū	離宮	detached palace
ringyō	林業	forest industry; forestry
ringyō gijutsushi	林業技術史	history of forest technology
ringyōshi	林業史	history of forest industries
rinseishi	林政史；林制史	history of forest administration
rōjū	老中	senior councillors of the shogun
ryō	両	a unit of gold coinage
sake	酒	rice wine

samurai	侍	warrior
sanbō	三方	three-sided measure of split pieces
sankin kōtai	参勤交代	"hostage" system for daimyo
sanrin bugyō	山林奉行	forest warden
sanrin shisōshi	山林思想史	history of forest thought
sansonshi	山村史	history of mountain villages
satsuyama	札山	restricted-use forest parcel
seiki	精気	arboreal vital fluids
sekkanke	摂関家	major Fujiwara households
shaku	尺	a measure of length
shakuchi ringyō	借地林業	rental forestry
shakujime	尺メ	a cubic measure
shikakurayama	鹿蔵山	lord's forest [lit. deer preserve]
shiraki	白木	peeled wood
shō	升	a unit of volume measure
shōen	荘園	ancient estate land
shōya	庄屋	village headman
soma	杣	professional logger or woodsman
soma yaku	杣役	woodcutting duty and right
suai	すあい	planting stick
sun	寸	a measure of length
tachiki	立木	stumpage
takamochi hyakushō	高持ち百姓	taxable peasant
tamazashi	玉挿	balled cutting
tan	反	a measure of area
tatami	畳	sedge mat flooring

tatebayashi	立林	stocked (planted) forest
tateyama	立山	stocked forest
tedai; *tetsuki*	手代；手付き	assistant
teiri	手入り	plantation aftercare
tenshukaku	天守閣	castle donjon
teppō ashigaru	鉄砲足軽	foot soldiers with firearms
tera	寺	Buddhist monastery or temple
tobimatsu	飛び松	wind-seeded pine trees
tokozashi	床挿	cutting-bed slips
tomeki	留め木	reserved trees
tomeyama	留め山	forest preserve
tsubo	坪	a measure of floor space
uekikata	植木方	forester
uji	氏	tribe
uji no kami	氏の守	tribal ruler
ukeyama	請山；受山	lord's forest held in trust
unjō	運上	tax payment; contract fee
unjōyama	運上山	taxed upland
usuita	薄板	thin (ceiling) board
warichi	割地	divided land
wariyama	割山	divided forest or upland
watan	和炭	domestic-use charcoal
yamaban	山番	forest warden
yama bugyō	山奉行	forest (mountain) magistrate
yama daikin	山代金	upland tax
yamakata bugyō	山方奉行	forest magistrate
yamamawari	山回り	forest warden
yamamori	山守	forest warden; forester

yamamori be	山守部	forest warden
yama nengu	山年貢	upland tax
yamaotoshi	山落し	working logs downhill
yamate; yamateyaku	山手；山手役	upland tax
yamawari	山割	assigning upland to households
yamayaku	山役	upland tax
yōzai	用材	processed lumber
zaimoku bugyō	材木奉行	timber magistrate or superintendent
zatsuboku	雑木	(*see* zōki)
zeni	銭	copper coinage
zōki	雑木	miscellaneous or weed trees
zōrinshi	造林史	history of afforestation

Glossary of Vegetation

Mainly based on Kitamura Siro 北村四郎 and Okamoto Syogo 岡本省吾. *Gensoku Nihon jumoku zukan* 原色日本樹木図鑑 [Colored illustrations of the trees and shrubs of Japan] (Tokyo: Hoikusha, 1959).

akamatsu	赤松	Japanese red pine	Pinus densiflora
asunaro	羅漢柏	Japanese cedar	Thujopsis dolabrata
biwa	枇杷	Japanese medlar	Eriobotrya japonica
buna	橅	Siebold's beech	Fagus crenata
byakudan	白檀	sandalwood	Santalum album
chigaya	茅	a reed	Imperata cylindrica
enoki	榎	Chinese nettle tree	Celti sinensis
fuji	藤	wisteria	Wisteria spp.
harigiri	針桐	?	Kalopanax septemlobus
hazenoki	櫨の木	sumac; wax tree	Rhus succedanea

hiba	桧葉	false arborvitae	Thujopsis dolabrata, var. Hondai Makino
himekomatsu	姫小松	Japanese white pine	Pinus pentaphylla
hinoki	桧	Japanese cypress	Chamaecyparis obtusa
hiratake	平茸	agaric (a fungus)	Agaricus subfunereus
kaede	楓	maple	Acer spp.
kaki	柿	persimmon	Diospyros kaki
karamatsu	唐松	larch	Larix leptolepis
kashi	樫	evergreen oak	Quercus spp. (mainly subgen. Cyclobalanopsis)
kashiwa	柏	white oak	Quercus dentata
katsura	桂	katsura	Cercidiphyllum japonicum
kaya	茅	(*see* chigaya)	
kaya	榧	a torreya nut tree	Torreya nucifera
keyaki	欅	zelkova	Zelkova serrata
kiri	桐	paulownia	Paulownia tomentosa
konara	小楢	white oak	Quercus serrata
kōyamaki	高野槙	umbrella pine	Sciadopitys verticillata
kōzo	楮	paper mulberry	Broussonetia kazinoki
kunugi	櫟；椚	oak	Quercus acutissima
kuri	栗	Japanese chestnut	Castanea crenata
kurobe	黒部	(*see* kurobi)	
kurobi	黒桧	Standish arborvitae	Thuja standishii
kuromatsu	黒松	Japanese black pine	Pinus thunbergii
kusunoki	楠；樟	camphor tree	Cinnamomum camphora

maki	槇	podocarp	Podocarpus spp.
matsu	松	pine	Pinus spp.
matsutake	松茸	a mushroom	Armillaria edodes
momi	樅	white or silver fir	Abies firma
momo	桃	peach	Prunus spp.
nara	楢	white oak	Quercus spp.
nire	楡	elm	Ulmus spp.
sakura	桜	cherry	Prunus spp.
sasa	笹	(*see* sasagaya)	
sasagaya	笹茅	dwarf bamboo	Microstegium japonica
sawara	花柏	Sawara cypress	Chamaecyparis pisifera
sendan	栴檀	Bead tree	Melia azedarach, var. subtripinnata
sugi	杉	cryptomeria	Cryptomeria japonica
todomatsu	椴松	white fir	Abies sachalinensis
togasawara	栂花柏	Douglas fir	Pseudotsuga japonica
tsuga	栂	Northern Japanese hemlock	Tsuga diversifolia
tsuki	槻	(*see* keyaki)	
tsuta	蔦	Japanese ivy	Parthenocissus tricuspidata
tsuzura	葛	(*see* tsuzurafuji)	
tsuzurafuji	葛藤	arrowroot	Sinomenium acutum (and similar vines)
ume	梅	plum	Prunus mume
urushi	漆	lacquer tree	Rhus verniciflua
warabi	蕨	fernbrake; a bracken	Pteridium aquilinum, var. japonicum
yanagi	柳	willow	Salix spp.

Bibliography

Works in English

Armson, K. A. *Forest Soils: Properties and Processes*. Toronto: University of Toronto Press, 1977.

Atwell, William S. "Some Observations on the 'Seventeenth-Century Crisis' in China and Japan." *Journal of Asian Studies* 45, no. 2 (February 1986): 223–44.

Birt, Michael P. "Samurai in Passage: Transformation of the Sixteenth-Century Kantō." *Journal of Japanese Studies* 11, no. 2 (Summer 1985): 369–99.

Coaldrake, William H. "Edo Architecture and Tokugawa Law." *Monumenta Nipponica* 36, no. 3 (Autumn 1981): 235–84.

Daniel, Theodore W., John A. Helms, and Frederick S. Baker. *Principles of Silviculture*. 2d ed. New York: McGraw-Hill, 1979.

Dazai, Osamu. *The Setting Sun* (*Shayō*, trans. Donald Keene). New York: New Directions, 1956.

Dower, John W. *Japanese History and Culture from Ancient to Modern Times: Seven Basic Bibliographies*. New York: Marcus Weiner, 1986.

Dunn, Charles J. *Everyday Life in Traditional Japan*. Rutland, Vt.: Tuttle & Co., 1972.

Elison, George, and Bardwell L. Smith. *Warlords, Artists, and Commoners: Japan in the Sixteenth Century*. Honolulu: University of Hawaii Press, 1981.

Farris, William Wayne. *Population, Disease, and Land in Early Japan, 645–900*. Cambridge: Harvard University Press, 1985.

Glacken, Clarence J. *Traces on the Rhodian Shore*. Berkeley: University of California Press, 1967.

Grossberg, Kenneth A. *The Laws of the Muromachi Bakufu*. Tokyo: Monumenta Nipponica, 1981.

Hall, John W. "Kyoto as Historical Background." In *Medieval Japan: Essays in Institutional History*, ed. John W. Hall and Jeffrey P. Mass, 3–38. New Haven: Yale University Press, 1974.

————. "The Nature of Traditional Society: Japan." In *Political Modernization in Japan and Turkey*, ed. Robert E. Ward and Dankwort A. Rustow, 14–41. Princeton: Princeton University Press, 1964.

Hanley, Susan B., and Kozo Yamamura. *Economic and Demographic Change in Preindustrial Japan, 1600–1868*. Princeton: Princeton University Press, 1977.

Hayami, Akira. "The Population at the Beginning of the Tokugawa Period—An Introduction to the Historical Demography of Preindustrial Japan." *Keio Economic Studies* 4 (1966–67): 1–28.

Heske, Franz. *German Forestry*. New Haven: Yale University Press, 1938.

Ikawa-Smith, Fumiko. "Current Issues in Japanese Archeology." *American Scientist* 68, no. 2 (1980): 134–45.

Jansen, Marius B. "Tosa in the Seventeenth Century: The Establishment of Yamauchi Rule." In *Studies in the Institutional History of Early Modern Japan*, ed. John W. Hall and Marius B. Jansen, 115–29. Princeton: Princeton University Press, 1968.

Kidder, J. Edward. *Early Buddhist Japan*. London: Thames and Hudson, 1972.

Mass, Jeffrey P. *The Kamakura Bakufu: A Study in Documents*. Stanford: Stanford University Press, 1976.

McKean, Margaret A. "The Japanese Experience with Scarcity: Management of Traditional Common Lands." *Environmental Review* 6, no. 2 (Fall 1982): 63–91.

Mizoguchi, Tsunetoshi. "Shifting Cultivation and Land Tenure in Shirakawa-go: Changes from the 1690s to the 1880s." Paper presented at the Workshop on Population Change and Socioeconomic Development in the Nobi Region, Stanford University, 15–18 March 1987.

Natural Resources Section. *Important Trees of Japan (Report No. 119)*. Tokyo: General Headquarters, SCAP, 1949.

Osako, Masako M. "Forest Preservation in Tokugawa Japan." In *Global Deforestation and the Nineteenth-Century World Economy*, ed. Richard P. Tucker and J. F. Richards, 129–45. Durham: Duke University Press, 1983.

Paine, Robert Treat, and Alexander Soper. *The Art and Architecture of Japan*. 2d ed. London: Penguin Books, 1974.

Reischauer, Robert Karl. *Early Japanese History (c. 40 B.C.–A.D. 1167)*. Princeton: Princeton University Press, 1937.

Robertson, Jennifer. "Japanese Farm Manuals: A Literature of Discovery." *Peasant Studies* 11, no. 3 (Spring 1984): 169–94.

————. "Sexy Rice: Plant Gender, Farm Manuals, and Grass-Roots Nativism." *Monumenta Nipponica* 39, no. 3 (Autumn 1984): 233–60.

Sharpe, Grant W., Clare W. Hendee, and Shirley W. Allen. *Introduction to Forestry*. 4th ed. New York: McGraw-Hill, 1976.

Shively, Donald H. "Sumptuary Regulation and Status in Early Tokugawa Japan." *Harvard Journal of Asiatic Studies* 25 (1964–65): 123–64.

————. "Tokugawa Tsunayoshi, the Genroku Shogun." In *Personality in Japanese History*, ed. Albert M. Craig and Donald H. Shively, 85–126. Berkeley: University of California Press, 1970.

Smith, Thomas C. *The Agrarian Origins of Modern Japan*. Stanford: Stanford University Press, 1959.

————. "Okura Nagatsune and the Technologists." In *Personality in Japanese History*, ed. Albert M. Craig and Donald H. Shively, 127–54. Berkeley: University of California Press, 1970.

Taeuber, Irene. *The Population of Japan*. Princeton: Princeton University Press, 1958.

Thirgood, J. V. *Man and the Mediterranean Forest: A History of Resource Depletion*. New York: Academic Press, 1981.

Toby, Ronald. "Why Leave Nara? Kammu and the Transfer of the Capital." *Monumenta Nipponica* 40, no. 3 (Autumn 1985): 331–47.

Totman, Conrad. "A Century of Scholarship on Early Modern Japanese Forestry, 1880–1980." *Environmental Review* 9, no. 1 (Spring 1985): 34–53.

————. "Forestry in Early Modern Japan, 1650–1850: A Preliminary Survey." *Agricultural History* 56, no. 2 (April 1982): 415–26.

————. "The Forests of Tokugawa Japan: A Catastrophe That Was Avoided." *Transactions of the Asiatic Society of Japan*, 3d ser., no. 18 (1983): 1–15.

————. "From Exploitation to Plantation Forestry in Early Modern Japan." In *History of Sustained-Yield Forestry: A Symposium*, ed. Harold Steen, 270–80. Forest History Society, 1984.

————. *Japan before Perry*. Berkeley: University of California Press, 1981.

————. "Land-Use Patterns and Afforestation in the Edo Period." *Monumenta Nipponica* 39, no. 1 (Spring 1984): 1–10.

————. "Logging the Unloggable: Timber Transport in Early Modern Japan." *Journal of Forest History* 27, no. 4 (October 1983): 180–91.

————. "Lumber Provisioning in Early Modern Japan, 1580–1850." *Journal of Forest History* 31, no. 2 (April 1987): 56–70.

————. *The Origins of Japan's Modern Forests: The Case of Akita*. Honolulu: University of Hawaii Press, 1985.

————. "Plantation Forestry in Early Modern Japan: Economic Aspects of Its Emergence." *Agricultural History* 60, no. 3 (Summer 1986): 23–51.

————. *Politics in the Tokugawa Bakufu, 1600–1843.* Cambridge: Harvard University Press, 1967.

————. "Tokugawa Peasants: Win, Lose, or Draw?" *Monumenta Nipponica* 41, no. 4 (Winter 1986): 457–76.

Trewartha, Glenn Thomas. *Japan: A Physical, Cultural, and Regional Geography.* Madison: University of Wisconsin Press, 1965.

Tsuchiya, Takao. "An Economic History of Japan." *Transactions of the Asiatic Society of Japan*, 2d ser., no. 15 (1937): 1–268.

Vaporis, Constantine Nomikos. "Overland Communications in Tokugawa Japan." Ph.D. diss., Princeton University, 1987.

Wheelwright, Carolyn. "A Visualization of Eitoku's Lost Paintings at Azuchi Castle." In *Warlords, Artists, and Commoners: Japan in the Sixteenth Century*, ed. George Elison and Bardwell L. Smith, 87–112. Honolulu, University of Hawaii Press, 1981.

Wigen, Karen [Lewis]. "Common Losses: Transformations of Commonland and Peasant Livelihood in Tokugawa Japan, 1603–1868." Master's thesis, University of California at Berkeley, 1985.

Woolsey, Theodore S., Jr. *Studies in French Forestry.* New York: John Wiley & Sons, 1920.

Yasuda, Yoshinori. "Early Historic Forest Clearance around the Ancient Castle Site of Tagajo, Miyagi Prefecture, Japan." *Asian Perspectives* 19, no. 1 (1978): 42–58.

Yazaki, Takeo. *Social Change and the City in Japan.* Tokyo: Japan Publications, 1968.

Yoshida, Takashi, ed. *An Outline of the Geology of Japan.* 3d ed. Kawasaki: Geological Survey of Japan, 1975.

Works in Japanese

Note: *TRK Kenkyū kiyō* = Tokugawa Rinseishi Kenkyūjo *Kenkyū kiyō.*

1. Akabane Takeshi. "Hokensei ka ni okeru mokutan seisan no tenkai kōzō (1)" [The development of charcoal production within Japanese feudalism (1)]. *Ringyō keizai* 22-11, no. 253 (November 1969): 1–14.

2. Asai Junko. "Bakufu ohayashiyama ni okeru ringyō seisan: Izu Amagi goyōtan nenki ukeoi seitan ni tsuite" [Forest production in shogunate forestland: The production of government charcoal by fixed-term contractors on Amagi in Izu]. *Shiryōkan kenkyū kiyō* 3 (March 1970): 89–142.

3. ————. "Ohayashiyama ni okeru bakufu ringyō seisaku: Izu Amagi ohayashiyama ni tsuite" [Shogunate forest policy on government woodland: Woodland on Mount Amagi in Izu]. *Nihon rekishi* 351 (August 1977): 1–18.

4. Asakawa Kiyoei. "Kinsei Suwa-gun ni okeru hayashi aratame to hayashi kenchi" [Forest delineation and surveys in Edo-period Suwa in Shinano]. *TRK Kenkyū kiyō* 55 (1980): 125–66.

5. Asanaga Keiichirō. "Edo jidai no mizu mondai ni tsuite" [The problem of water in the Edo period]. *Kokushigaku kenkyū* (of Ryūdani Daigaku). *Sōkangō* no. 1 (March 1975): 26–36.

6. Chiba Tokuji. "Chūsei ni okeru Kyōto kimbō no shinrin ni tsuite" [The woodland surrounding medieval Kyōto]. *1954 shunki taikai kōen yōshi* (of Nihon Chiri Gakkai).

7. ———. *Hageyama no bunka* [The culture of bald mountains]. Tokyo: Gakuseisha, 1973. 233 pp.

8. ———. *Hageyama no kenkyū* [A study of bald mountains]. Tokyo: Nōrin Kyōkai, 1956. 237 pp.

9. Chihōshi Kenkyū Kyōgikai, ed. *Nihon sangyōshi taikei* [An outline of the industrial history of Japan]. 8 vols. Tokyo: Tōkyō Daigaku Shuppankai, 1959–60.

10. Dōshisha Daigaku Jinbun Kagaku Kenkyūjo, comp. *Ringyō sonraku no shiteki kenkyū: Tanba Yamaguni ni okeru* [Historical studies of forest villages: The Yamaguni district of Tanba prefecture]. Kyoto: Mineruva Shoten, 1967. 537 pp.

11. Endō Jiichirō. *Nihon rin'ya iriaiken ron* [Disputes over rights to forested common land in Japan]. Tokyo: Kōyū Rin'ya Chōsakai Rin'ya Kyōzaikai, 1947: 200 pp.; 1957: 477 pp.

12. Endō Yasutarō. "Aizu han no zōrin seido oyobi sono jigyō ni kan suru ichi kōsatsu" [A study of the afforestation system of Aizu domain and its accomplishments]. *Sanrin ihō* 25, nos. 1–5 (1930): 12–20; 10–19; 12–26; 12–18; 63–75.

13. ———. "Kinsei ni okeru ringyō bunken no gaikan" [An overview of the Edo-period literature on forestry]. *Nihon ringakkai shi* 17, no. 12 (1935): 64–71.

14. ———. *Nihon sanrinshi: Hogorin hen (jō, ge, shiryō)* [A history of Japanese forestry: Protection forests (vols. 1, 2, documents)]. Tokyo: Nihon Sanrinshi Kankōkai, 1934, 1936. 908, 420, 956 pp.

15. ———. *(Sanrinshi jō yori mitaru) Tōhoku bunka no kenkyū (ichimei: Tōhoku sanrinshi)* [A study of Tōhoku culture: Viewed from the history of its forests (also titled: A history of Tōhoku forests)]. Tokyo: Nihon Sanrinshi Kenkyūkai, 1938. 391 pp.

16. ———. "Suigen kan'yōrin ni tai suru zendai hito no shisō" [The thought of earlier generations on watershed forestry]. *Sanrin ihō* 26, nos.

3–4; 27, nos. 1–3; 28, no. 1 (1931–33): 93–96; 60–65; 5–9; 141–43; 68–71; 1–4.

17. Fujita Yoshihisa. "Kinsei ni okeru ikurin gijutsu taikei no chiikisei" [The regional character of the organization of forest technology in the Edo period]. *TRK Kenkyū kiyō* 55 (1980): 98–124.

18. ———. "Kinsei ni okeru ikurin no seiritsu jiki to sono chiikisa ni tsuite" [Regional variation in the emergence of tree plantations in the Edo period]. *TRK Kenkyū kiyō* 54 (1979): 136–58.

19. ———. "Yoshino ringyōshi ni okeru 'shakuchi ringyō' no saikentō ni tsuite" [A reexamination of so-called forest leasing in Yoshino forest history]. *TRK Kenkyū kiyō* 56 (1982): 120–46.

20. Fujita Yoshitani. *Kinsei mokuzai ryūtsūshi no kenkyū: Tanbazai ryūtsū no hatten katei* [A study of the history of Edo-period lumber distribution: The development of lumber distribution from Tanba]. Tokyo: Ōhara Shinseisha, 1973. 668 pp.

21. Fujiyoshi Nobuhiro. "Hōkenteki ringyō keiei to koyō rōdōsha no sonzai keitai" [Feudal forest management and the living conditions of forest wage laborers]. *TRK Kenkyū kiyō* 42 (1967): 101–32.

22. ———. "Kiso no ringyō ni okeru shōya to shidashi gentei: Kiso Ōtakimura Matsubara-ke no ringyō keiei" [A village head and the control of production in Kiso forestry: The forest operation of the Matsubara family in Ōtaki village in Kiso]. *TRK Kenkyū kiyō* 43 (1968): 70–102.

22a. Fukai Masaumi. "Zaimoku (ishi) bugyō narabi ni hayashi bugyō no shūninsha ni tsuite" [The successive appointees to the offices of timber (stone) and forest magistrates]. *TRK Kenkyū kiyō* 61 (March 1987): 207–20.

23. Funakoshi Shōji. *Nihon ringyō hattenshi* [The development of lumbering in Japan]. Tokyo: Chikyū Shuppansha, 1960. 296 pp.

24. Furukawa Sadao. "Hōreki-ki no bakufu zōchōsaku to hyakushō wariyama" [Shogunate tax collection policy and the division of peasant mountain land during the 1760s]. *Shinano* 26, no. 10 (October 1974): 37–50.

25. ———. "Kita Shinano ni okeru ohayashi to wariyama" [Mountain division and "lord's forest" in northern Shinano]. *TRK Kenkyū kiyō* 49 (1974): 18–48.

26. ———. "Shinshū Iiyama-ryō ni okeru kinsei zen-chūki no hyakushō wariyama" [Peasant mountain division of the early and middle Edo period in Iiyama fief in Shinano]. *TRK Kenkyū kiyō* 47 (1972): 52–95.

27. Furushima Toshio. *Furushima Toshio chosakushū* [The collected works of Furushima Toshio]. 6 vols. Tokyo: Tōkyō Daigaku Shuppankai, 1975.

28. ———. *Kinsei keizaishi no kiso katei: Nengu shūdatsu to kyōdōtai* [Basic patterns in early modern economic history: Tribute exploitation and the folk community]. Tokyo: Iwanami Shoten, 1978.

29. ————. *Nihon rin'ya seido no kenkyū: Kyōdōtaiteki rin'ya shoyū o chūshin ni* [A study of the Japanese forest system: Communal forest possession practices]. Tokyo: Tōkyō Daigaku Shuppankai, 1955. 274 pp.

30. ————. *Sanson no kōzō* [The structure of mountain villages]. Tokyo: Nihon Hyōronsha, 1949; Ochanomizu Shoten, 1952. 304 pp.

31. ————. "Yakibatake nōgyō no rekishiteki seikaku to sono kōsaku keitai" [The historical character of swidden agriculture and its tillage patterns]. *Nōgyō keizai kenkyū* 16, no. 1 (1940): 34–69.

32. Gotō Shigemi. "Edo makki ni okeru mura to suiri fushin" [Villages and irrigation construction in the late Edo period]. *Seiji keizai shigaku* 113 (October 1975): 1–13.

33. Handa Ryōichi, Morita Manabu, and Yamada Tatsuo. "Yoshino ni okeru shakuchi ringyō no keisei to tenkai" [The character and development of rental forestry in Yoshino]. *Kyōdai enshurin hōkoku* 39 (1967).

34. Haneyama Hisao. "Katsuura-gun Setsumura ni okeru yakibatake to ohayashi" [Swidden and government forests in Setsu village in Tokushima]. *Shisō* (of Tokushima Chihōshi Kenkyūkai) 6 (February 1976): 52–59.

35. Harada Eiko. "Kaga han no yamamawari yaku" [The mountain patrols of Kaga domain]. *Shiron* (of Tokyo Joshi Daigaku Rekishigaku Kenkyūshitsu) 8 (1960): 542–48.

36. Harada Toshimaru. "Echizen Hinogawa ryūiki no yamawari ni tsuite" [Mountain division on land along the Hino river in Echizen]. *TRK Kenkyū kiyō* 44 (1969): 59–74.

37. ————. "Kinsei Gōshū yamawari jirei shūi" [A selection of examples of mountain division in early modern Ōmi]. *Shiga daigaku keizai gakubu fuzoku shiryōkan kenkyū kiyō* 1 (March 1968): 51–64.

38. ————. *Kinsei iriai seido kaitai katei no kenkyū: Yamawari seido no hassei to sono henshitsu* [Studies in the decay of the early modern common-land system: Development and degeneration of the mountain division system]. Tokyo: Hanawa Shoten, 1969. 456 pp.

39. ————. "Kinsei no Ōmi ni okeru rin'ya no kyōkai sōron to tekka saiban" [Forest boundary disputes and trial by ordeal in early modern Ōmi]. *TRK Kenkyū kiyō* 46 (1971): 79–88.

40. ————. "Kinsei no yamawari seido ni okeru bunkatsu no hōhō to kikan ni tsuite" [The manner and timing of division in the early modern mountain division system]. *Shiga daigaku keizai gakubu fuzoku shiryōkan kenkyū kiyō* 2 (March 1969): 29–39.

41. ————. "Muramochi sanrin no hogo to yamawari seido" [The protection of village forests and the mountain division system]. *Hikone ronsō* 68 (July 1960): 20–30.

42. ————. "Ōmi Gokashō ni okeru yamawari seido" [The mountain division system of Gokashō in Ōmi]. *Hikone ronsō* 43 (May 1958): 38–55.

43. ———. "Ōmi Kinomoto chihō no yamawari seido" [The mountain division system of the Kinomoto area in Ōmi]. *Hikone ronsō* 65–67 (combined issue; June 1960): 34–46.

44. ———. "Ōmi Kōga chihō ni okeru yamawari seido" [The mountain division system in the Kōga district of Ōmi]. *Hikone ronsō* 70–72 (combined issue; October 1960): 33–45.

45. ———. "Ōmi Kowaki sato no yamawari ni tsuite" [Dividing mountains in Kowaki village in Ōmi]. *Hikone ronsō* 119–20 (combined issue; August 1966): 78–85.

46. ———. "Ōmi Kuchikidani no yamawari ni tsuite" [Mountain division in the Kuchiki valley in Ōmi]. *TRK Kenkyū kiyō* 53 (1978): 82–95.

47. ———. "Yamato ni okeru kinsei no yamawari shiryō" [Records of mountain division in early modern Yamato]. *TRK Kenkyū kiyō* 45 (1970): 137–44.

48. ———. "Yamawari seido to sono hensen" [The mountain division system and its changes]. *Kyūshū daigaku Kyūshū bunkashi kenkyū kiyō* 8–9 (combined issue; March 1961): 179–91.

49. Hattori Marenobu. "Akita han no buwakebayashi seido" [The shared-forest system of Akita domain]. *Keizaishi kenkyū* 17, no. 5 (May 1937): 15–42.

50. ———. "Akita han no rinsanbutsu senbaisei" [The forest products monopoly system of Akita domain]. *Keizaishi kenkyū* 18, no. 3 (September 1937): 14–31.

51. ———. "Akita han no shinrin riyō seigensaku" [Akita domain's policy for restricting the use of forests]. *Keizaishi kenkyū* 19, no. 5 (April 1938): 53–70.

52. ———. "Hitoyoshi han ni okeru ikuseiteki ringyō: Toku ni buwakebayashi no ringyōshiteki igi" [Plantation forestry in Hitoyoshi domain in Kyushu: Especially its significance in the history of the shared-forest system]. *Keizaishi kenkyū* 19, no. 2 (February 1938): 75–101.

53. ———. "Nanbu han no toriwakebayashi ni tsuite" [The divided forests of Nanbu]. *Nihon ringakkai shi* 19, no. 12 (December 1937): 744–51.

54. ———. *Ringyō keizai kenkyū* [A study of the economics of forestry]. Tokyo: Nishigahara Kankōkai, 1940. 260 pp. Chikyū Shuppansha, 1967. 262 pp.

55. ———. "Tokugawa jidai ni okeru hoanrin seido no tokushoku" [Special features of the Edo-period forest preserve system]. *Keizaishi kenkyū* 16, no. 2 (August 1936): 67–83.

56. Hayashi Tadakazu. "Kinsei Kiso ni okeru sanrin settō [Lumber theft in early modern Kiso]. *Shinano* 9, no. 8 (1957): 479–90.

57. Higuchi Kiyoyuki. *Nihon mokutanshi (keizai hen)* [A history of Japanese charcoal (volume on economics)]. Comp. Nihon Mokutanshi Hensan Iinkai. Tokyo: Zenkoku Nenryō Kaikan, 1960. 1,229 pp. Republished in 2 vols.: Kōdansha, 1978.

58. Hirao Michio. *Tosa han ringyō keizaishi* [An economic history of Tosa forestry]. Kōchi: Kōchi Shimin Toshokan, 1956. 230 pp.

59. Hirasawa Kiyondo. "Chizuki iriai no kōsaku shita iriaichi no mo-kuzai bassai ni tsuite no funsō ichirei" [An example of disputes over logging in communal lands that are mixed with communal parcels assigned to designated households]. *TRK Kenkyū kiyō* 42 (1967): 157–72.

60. ———. "Ina gun no kurekiyama no suii" [The evolution of split-piece timber areas in Ina district of Shinano]. *Shinano* 14, nos. 5–6, 12 (May, June, December 1962): 22–43; 33–46; 19–35.

61. ———. "Ina ni okeru kurekiyama no iriai to chiso kaisei" [Split timber common lands and land tax reform in Ina district]. *TRK Kenkyū kiyō* 44 (1969): 75–97.

62. ———. "Ina no 'kureki bugyō' 'kurekiyama' kō" [A study of the "split-timber magistrate" and "split-timber mountains" of Ina district]. *TRK Kenkyū kiyo* 46 (1971): 89–102.

63. ———. "Ina no 'kureki narimura' kō" [A study of the "split-timber-producing villages" of Ina district]. *TRK Kenkyū kiyō* 43 (1968): 125–69.

64. ———. "Iriaiyama no tachiki no shobun ni tsuite: Shinshū Ina gun chihō no baai" [The disposal of standing timber on communal land: The case of Ina district in Shinano]. *TRK Kenkyū kiyō* 41 (1966): 85–120.

65. ———. *Kinsei iriai kankō no seiritsu to tenkai: Shinshū Shimo Ina chihō o chūshin ni shite* [The formation and evolution of Edo-period common-land customs: The Shimo Ina area of Shinano province]. Tokyo: Ochanomizu Shobō, 1967. 292 pp.

66. ———. "Kinsei ni okeru iriai kakuritsu katei: Mura yūrin no keiei seikō no en'in (ikō)" [The establishment of early modern communal land: The basic causes of success in handling village forests (a posthumous essay)]. *TRK Kenkyū kiyo* 48 (1973): 123–35.

67. ———. "Kinsei Shinshū Ina gun no iriai kankō ni okeru jimoto—iriaikata—irikata ni tsuite" [Abutting, participating, and admitted parties in common-land practices in early modern Ina district]. *TRK Kenkyū kiyō* 45 (1970): 85–96.

68. Hirayama Kōzō. "Kanbun jūsan nen Kishū Ito gun iriai sōron ezu narabi ni aishōmon" [A general map and verbal declarations in delibera-tions regarding common lands in Ito district of Kii in 1673]. *TRK Kenkyū kiyō* 46(1971): 124–33.

69. Hirose Makoto. "Kurobe okuyama to Kaga han: Sono batsurin jigyō o megutte" [The inner mountains of the Kurobe river and Kaga domain: Logging activity there]. *Shinano* 17, no. 1 (1965): 38–50.

70. ———. "Tenpō kyūnen no Kurobe okuyama bassai jigyō to sono zasetsu o megutte" [Frustrating a logging venture in the Kurobe mountain area in 1838]. *Shinano* 26, no. 10 (October 1974): 25–36.

71. Hōjō Hiroshi. "Kanrin no seiritsu to shoki kanrin seisaku" [The establishment of Meiji government forests and the initial Meiji forest policy]. *TRK Kenkyū kiyō* 52 (1977): 144–73.

72. ———. *Kinsei ni okeru rin'ya iriai no shokeitai* [The several configurations of forest commons in the Edo period]. Vol. 5, *Sonraku shakai kōzōshi kenkyū sōsho.* Tokyo: Ochanomizu Shobō, 1978. 506 pp.

73. ———. *Rin'ya iriai no shiteki kenkyū (jō)* [Historical studies of common lands (1)]. Tokyo: Ochanomizu Shobō, 1977. 684 pp.

74. ———. "Rin'ya riyō ni okeru kanshū" ["Custom" in forestland usage]. *TRK Kenkyū kiyō* 48 (1973): 25–82.

75. Hōjō Hiroshi and Ōta Katsuya, eds. *Nihon ringyō-rinsei no shiteki kenkyū* [Historical studies of forest industries and administration]. Tokyo: Tachibana Shoin, 1980. 282 pp.

76. Hosoi Junshirō. "Kinsei sonraku no seikaku keisei to ikuseirin no tenkai ni kan suru yōin: Tōtōmi kuni Okawa mura o jirei ni" [Essential factors in the formation of early modern village character and plantation forestry: The.case of Okawa village in Tōtōmi province]. *Rekishi chirigaku kiyō* 20 (1978).

77. Hosokawa Hayato. "Yamatodome ikken" [An incident of mountain closure]. *Shinano* 12, no. 4 (1960): 40–44.

78. Ichinomiya Masasuke. "Harunayama tachiki ni kan suru kiroku (ichi, ni, san)" [Records relating to the timber on Mount Haruna in Gumma (pts. 1, 2, 3)]. *Gumma bunka* 157, 158, 159 (December 1974; January, February 1975): 10–12; 18–19; 12–15.

79. Igeta Yoshiharu. "Hōken shakai ni okeru sonraku kyōyū sanrin to sonraku kōzō: Yakuyama-myōshūyama-toshiyoriyama ni kan suru ichi shiryō" [Village communal forests and village structure in Japanese feudal society: A historical record pertaining to three forms of local woodland holding]. *Dōshisha hōgaku* 63 (1961): 353–419.

80. ———. "Muranaka iriai no seiritsu" [The establishment of village common land]. *Dōshisha hōgaku* 18 (1953): 135–40.

81. Iioka Masatake. "Enshū Funagira ni okeru bakufu no kureki shobun: Genroku-Shōtoku ki Shinshū Kashio-Ōkawabarayama no motojime shidashi to kanren shite" [Handling government split timbers at Funagira in Tōtōmi: The case of a lumber merchant working in Kashio and Ōkawabarayama, circa 1688–1715]. *TRK Kenkyū kiyō* 50 (1975): 101–19.

82. ———. "Enshū Funagira ni okeru bakufu yōzai no chūkei kinō" [The operation of the government's tax-lumber transfer station at Funagira in Tōtōmi]. *TRK Kenkyū kiyō* 52 (1977): 95–117.

83. ———. "Kinsei chūki ni okeru 'goyōki' shidashi: Shinshū Ina gun

Ōkawabarayama no baai" [Getting out government lumber in the mid-Edo period: The case of Ōkawabarayama in Ina district]. *TRK Kenkyū kiyō* 54 (1979): 72–97.

84. ———. "Kinsei chūki no yōzai seisan shihō to saiunhi: Shinshū Kashio-Ōkawabarayama de no Genbun-Kanpō ki shidashi o chūshin ni" [Logging procedures and shipping costs of government lumber in the mid-Edo period: The output of the Kashio-Ōkawabarayama area of Shinano, circa 1736–43]. *TRK Kenkyū kiyō* 51 (1976): 107–24.

85. ———. "Shinshū Inadani ni okeru nengu kure no daizaimokunō: Chimura Heiuemon azukaridokoro no kōnō hōhō no henkaku" [Substitute payments for split-timber taxes in the Ina valley in Shinano: The process of tax reform in the trust lands of Chimura Heiuemon]. *TRK Kenkyū kiyō* 53 (1978): 96–116.

86. ———. "Takatōryō 'ohayashi' ni okeru goyōki-uriki no saishutsu: Genroku-Kyōhō ki no 'mokushi sato'" [The taking out of government and market lumber from government forests in Takatō domain: So-called logging villages circa 1700–30]. *TRK Kenkyū kiyō* 47 (1972): 447–63.

87. ———. "Tenryūgawa Funagira watashiba ni okeru goyō kure no 'kaeriki'" [The "returned lumber" in government split lumber at the Funagira transfer point on the Tenryū]. *TRK Kenkyū kiyō* 55 (1980): 207–16.

88. Ishii Ryōsuke. *Tokugawa kinreikō* [Regulations of the Tokugawa shogunate]. Ser. 1, vol. 4. Tokyo: Sōmonsha, 1959.

89. Iwanaga Yutaka. "Edo-Meiji ki ni okeru Yoshino ringyō no ikurin gijutsu" [The afforestation technology of Yoshino forests during the Edo-Meiji periods]. *Ringyō keizai* 23-1, no. 255 (January 1970): 14–23.

90. Iwasaki Naoto. *Akita ken Noshirogawa kami chihō ni okeru sugibayashi no seiritsu narabi ni kōshin ni kan suru kenkyū* [Research on the establishment and revitalization of cryptomeria forests in the upper Noshiro river area of Akita prefecture]. Tokyo: Kōrinkai, 1939. 605 pp.

91. Iyanaga Teizō. "Ritsuryōsei teki tochi shoyū" [Landholding in the ancient Japanese polity]. In *Iwanami kōza Nihon rekishi (kodai 3)* [Iwanami's history of Japan (ancient period, vol. 3)], 33–78. Tokyo: Iwanami Shoten, 1962.

92. Izumi Eiji. "Edo jidai ni okeru Yoshino ringyō no mokuzai ryūtsū kikō" [The organization of Yoshino lumber transport during the Edo period]. *Kyōdai enshurin hōkoku* 45 (1973).

93. Kainō Michitaka. *Iriai no kenkyū* [A study of common land]. Tokyo: Nihon Hyōronsha, 1943. 496 pp.

94. Kanai Kiyotoshi. "Kinsei chūki no sōbyakushō wariyama: Minochi gun Jindai-Nakao mura no baai" [The dividing of peasant mountain land in the mid-Edo period: The case of Jindai and Nakao villages in Minochi district of Shinano]. *Shinano* 76, no. 3 (May 1976): 11–28.

95. Kanamaru Heihachi. "Shiyūrin ni kan suru shiron: Hitoyama jinushi no seitai ni tsuite" [A sketch of private woodland: The life-style of a forest landlord]. *Mita gakkai zasshi* 47, nos. 1–2 (1954): 71–90; 38–52.

96. ——. "Shiyūrin o meguru sōron no ichirei: Shimozuke kuni Tsuga gun Ōkubomura" [An example of the disputes surrounding private woodland: Ōkubo village in Tsuga district of Shimozuke]. *Mita gakkai zasshi* 49, no. 2 (1956): 18–25.

97. Kanaya Masayuki. *Okayama mokuzaishi* [A history of lumbering in Okayama]. Okayama: Okayama Mokuzai Kyōdō Kumiai, 1964. 650 pp.

98. Kanayama Katsuyuki. "Ninomiya Sontoku no sanrinkan" [Ninomiya Sontoku's views on forestry]. *Sanrin* 629 (April 1935): 93–96.

99. Kaneiwa Yoshio. "Tenryū ringyō chitai ni okeru sugiyama nenki uriwatashi nado ni kan suru kenkyū" [A study of the advance marketing of cryptomeria stands in woodland along the Tenryū river]. *Shizuoka daigaku nōgakubu kenkyū hōkoku* 5 (1955): 162–88.

100. Kanno Toshisaku. "Haneirin no keiei to shoyū no kōzō" [The administration and ownership of domanial forests]. *Tochi seido shigaku* 6 (January 1960): 44–54.

101. Kanō Kyōji. *Edo jidai no ringyō shisō* [Forestry thought in the Edo period]. Tokyo: Gannandō, 1963; 1967. 485 pp.

102. Kasai Kyōetsu. *Yoshino ringyō no hatten kōzō* [The development of forestry in Yoshino]. In *Gakujutsu hōkoku tokushū 15*. Utsunomiya: Utsunomiya Daigaku Nōgakubu, 1962. 113 pp.

103. Katō Eiji. "Tōgyō to rin'ya: Tōkai-Owari tōgyō chiiki ni okeru shigen ritchi o rei to shite" [The pottery industry and woodland: Raw material sites in the Tōkai-Owari pottery area]. *Ritsumeikan bungaku* 422/423 (September 1980): 57–90.

104. Katō Masao et al. "Rin'ya iriai ni kan suru jakkan no mondai" [Problems relating to forested common lands]. *Dōshisha hōgaku* 40, 42 (1956, 1957): 161–98; 130–51.

105. Katō Morihiro. "Nishikawa ringyō hasseishi ni kan suru ichi kōsatsu" [An examination of the beginnings of forestry in the Nishikawa area]. *TRK Kenkyū kiyō* 56 (1982): 165–96.

106. Katō Yasushi. "Hayashikata bugyōsho to Mizuno daikansho" [The offices of the forest magistrate and intendant for the Mizuno vicinity in Owari]. *Rekishi kenkyū* (of Aichi Kyōiku Daigaku) 19 (March 1972): 43–46.

107. Kiryū Katsumi. "Kyōho-ki ni okeru chisui seisaku no tenkan katei" [The changes in riparian policy during the early eighteenth century]. *Hōsei shigaku* 7 (March 1980): 54–70.

108. Koganezawa Toshio. "Sanrin no sonzai keitai (jō, ge): Yagunzan iriai o chūshin to shite" [Living conditions in forestland (1, 2): Communal land in the Yagun mountain area of Shinano]. *Shinano* 14, nos. 5–6 (May, June 1962): 2–21; 13–32.

109. *Kokushi taikei* [The classics of Japanese history]. Vol. 1, *Nihon shoki*. Tokyo: Keizai Zasshisha, 1906.

110. Kuroita Katsumi, ed. *Shintei zōho kokushi taikei* [The classics of Japanese history, revised and enlarged]. Vols. 2, 25. Tokyo: Yoshikawa Kōbunkan, 1935.

111. Kuromasa Iwao. "Okayama han no rinsei" [Forestry in Okayama domain]. *Nōgyō keizai kenkyū* 1, no. 3 (1925): 527–54.

112. Kurotaki Hidehisa. "Kinsei ni okeru mokuzai ryūtsū no kōzō: Hirosaki han ni okeru mokuzai ishutsu o jirei to shite" [Timber shipping in the Edo period: Timber exports from Hirosaki domain]. *Nōkei kenkyū hōkoku* (of Tōkyō Nōgyō Daigaku) 13 (February 1982): 63–83.

113. *Kyōdo o sōzō seshi hitobito* [The people who created our home villages]. Tokyo: Dai Nihon Sanrinkai, 1934. 246 pp.

114. Matsuda Koretoshi. "Matsushiro han no 'otedashi' ni tsuite" [The "lord's involvement" in woodland of Matsushiro domain]. *TRK Kenkyū kiyō* 44 (1969): 98–112.

115. Matsuki Kan. "Tsugaru no hiba (hinoki)" [The false arborvitae, commonly called *hinoki*, of Tsugaru]. In *Nihon sangyōshi taikei*, ed. Chihōshi Kenkyū Kyōgikai, vol. 3, 149–59. Tokyo: Tōkyō Daigaku Shuppankai, 1960.

116. Matsumura Yasukazu. "Kinsei Ōme ringyō no seiritsu oyobi hatten ni kan suru rekishi chirigakuteki kenkyū (shōroku)" [An historicogeographical study of the establishment and evolution of forestry in Ōme during the Edo period (a summary)]. *Tōkyō gakugei daigaku kenkyū hōkoku* 16, no. 9 (1964): 1–22.

117. ———. "Kinsei Tamagawa keikoku no kyōson to ohayashi (dai 4 hō)" [A border village and shogunate forest in the Tama river valley during the Edo period (report no. 4)]. *Tōkyō gakugei daigaku kenkyū hōkoku* 7 (1955): 397–403.

118. ———. "Mito han gotateyama seido ni kan suru ichi kōsatsu" [A study of the government forest system in Mito domain]. *TRK Kenkyū kiyō* 52 (1977): 78–94.

119. ———. "Mito han ringyō no kiban to sono gijutsuteki tenkai" [The basis of Mito domain forestry and its technical development]. *Ibaragi kenshi kenkyū* 38 (February 1978): 1–11.

120. ———. "Mito han rinseishi josetsu" [An introduction to the history of forestry in Mito domain]. *TRK Kenkyū kiyō* 42 (1967): 133–56.

121. ———. "Ōme no ringyō" [The forest industry of the Ōme vicinity]. In *Nihon sangyōshi taikei*, ed. Chihōshi Kenkyū Kyōgikai, vol. 4, 183–99. Tokyo: Tōkyō Daigaku Shuppankai, 1959; 1970.

122. ———. "Ōme ringyō chiiki ni okeru rin'ya no riyō to shoyū: Kinsei Tamagawa keikoku Ryūjuji mura no baai" [The use and possession of forestland in the Ōme area: The case of Ryūjuji village in the Tama river gorge during the Edo period]. *Chirigaku hyōron* 30, no. 5 (May 1957): 34–48.

123. ———. "Ōme ringyō ni okeru okada" [Rafting in Ōme lumbering]. *Jinbun chiri* 7, no. 5 (1955): 14–33.

124. ———. "Sugisashiki ringyō no gijutsushiteki kōsatsu: Sugi no sashiki ringyō no kenkyū (dai yon)" [A study in the history of afforestation techniques using cryptomeria cuttings: Research on afforestation with cryptomeria cuttings (report no. 4)]. *TRK Kenkyū kiyō* 41 (1966): 140–72.

125. Matsushima Yoshio. "Sugi no zōrinshi" [A history of cryptomeria afforestation]. In *Sugi no kenkyū*, ed. Satō Yatarō, 95–143. Tokyo: Yōkendō, 1950.

126. ———. "Tokugawa jidai ni okeru zōrin seisaku ni tsuite" [Afforestation policy in the Edo period]. *Kyōto daigaku enshūrin hōkoku* 22 (June 1953): 41–57.

127. Michishige Tetsuo. "Hansei goki ni okeru hanyō mokuzai no seisan kōzō" [The structure of lumber production for government use in the late Edo period]. *Geibi chihōshi kenkyū* 78 (1969): 1–10.

128. Minemura Hideo. "Hayashi metsuke no kiroku yori mita Suwa han no sanrin seisaku" [The forest policy of Suwa domain as seen in records of the forest inspector]. In *Nihon shakai keizaishi kenkyū* (*Kinsei* vol.), comp. Hōgetsu Keigo Sensei Kanreki Kinenkai, 369–98. Tokyo: Yoshikawa Kōbunkan, 1967.

129. Mitsuhashi Tokio. "Yoshino-Kumano no ringyō" [Lumbering in Yoshino and Kumano]. In *Nihon sangyōshi taikei*, ed. Chihōshi Kenkyū Kyōgikai, vol. 6, 241–66. Tokyo: Tōkyō Daigaku Shuppankai, 1960.

130. Miyamoto Tsuneichi. *Sanson shakai keizaishi sōsho* [Essays on the social and economic history of mountain villages]. Tokyo: Kokudosha, 1973. 333 pp.

131. Miyashita Ichirō. "Takatō han no rinseishi (ichi, ni, san, shi)" [The history of forest affairs in Takatō domain (1, 2, 3, 4)]. *Shinano* 14, nos. 5–8 (May, June, July, August 1962): 51–61; 47–57; 48–59; 47–58.

132. Mizutani Seizō. "Kinsei Kyōto no mokuzai yusō (jō, ge): Umezu o chūshin to shita sankasho nakama no rekishi chiriteki kōsatsu" [The movement of lumber in Edo-period Kyoto: A historicogeographical examination of the monopoly merchants of the "three places," especially Umezu (pts. 1, 2)]. *Ritsumeikan bungaku* 181, 183 (1960, 1961): 43–61; 53–77.

133. Monda Sai. *Tosa han rinseishi* [A history of Tosa domain's forest system]. Kōchi: Kōchi Eirinkyoku, 1935. 95 pp.

134. Mori Kahyōe. "Kyū Nanbu han ni okeru sanson iriaiken no kenkyū: Ōu sanson kenkyū no ichibu" [A study of mountain village common-land rights in former Nanbu domain: A fragment from research on mountain villages in Ōu province]. *Shakai Keizai shigaku* 12, no. 2 (May 1942): 19–66.

135. Morita Seiichi. "Higo han rinsei no seikaku ni tsuite" [The character of the Higo domain forest system]. *Kumamoto shigaku* 5 (1953): 6–15.

136. ———. "Higo no ringyō" [Forestry in Higo]. In *Nihon sangyōshi taikei*, ed. Chihōshi Kenkyū Kyōgikai, vol. 8, 106–22. Tokyo: Tōkyō Daigaku Shuppankai, 1960.

137. Motoyoshi Rurio. "Kinseiki-Meiji shoki ni okeru rinsei to rin'ya riyō ni kan suru shomondai" [Issues in forest systems and use during the eighteenth and nineteenth centuries]. *Kyōto furitsu daigaku enshūrin hōkoku* 18 (1973).

138. ———. "Oku Mikawa chihō ni okeru ringyō no shiteki hatten ni kan suru kenkyū" [A study of the historical development of forest industry in the interior of Mikawa province]. *Kyōto furitsu daigaku enshūrin hōkoku* 20 (1976).

139. ———. *Senshin ringyō chitai no shiteki kenkyū: Yamaguni ringyō no hatten katei* [A historical study of an advanced area of forest industry: The development of the Yamaguni forest industry]. Tokyo: Tamagawa Daigaku Shuppanbu, 1983. 454 pp.

140. ———. "Yamaguni ringyō chitai ni okeru jinkō zōrin no shinten to ikurin gijutsu no hensen" [The development of afforestation and changes in silviculture in the Yamaguni forest area]. *TRK Kenkyū kiyō* 55 (1980): 72–97.

141. ———. "Yamaguni sugi ni kan suru kenkyū (ichi, ni, san, shi, go)" [Studies of cryptomeria in the Yamaguni area of Tanba (pts. 1–2, 3, 4–5)]. *Kyōto furitsu daigaku enshūrin hōkoku* 12, 13, 14 (1968, 1969, 1970): 41–52 and 53–66; 39–81; 1–26 and 27–44.

142. Mukōyama Masashige. "Shinshū Tōyama chihō no kawagari" [River shipping of lumber in the Tōyama area in Shinano]. *TRK Kenkyū kiyō* 46 (1971): 134–55.

143. Murai Hideo. *Akita han rin'yashi kenkyū josetsu: Okachi gun Akinomiya o chūshin to suru rin'ya shoyū narabi ni riyō no jittai* [An introduction to the study of Akita forestland history: The actual situation of forest possession and use, focusing on Akinomiya in the Okachi district]. Akita: Kikuchi Kōhansha, 1959. 88 pp.

144. Murai Hideo and Takahashi Hideo. "Akita no sugi" [The cryptomeria of Akita]. In *Nihon sangyōshi taikei*, ed. Chihōshi Kenkyū Kyōgikai, vol. 3, 130–48. Tokyo: Tōkyō Daigaku Shuppankai, 1960.

145. Murao, Jirō. *Ritsuryō zaisei no kenkyū (zōteihan)* [A study of the ancient fisc (expanded edition)]. Tokyo: Yoshikawa Kōbunkan, 1961. 597 pp.

146. Murata Michitō. "Kinsei Setsu-Kawa ni okeru kassen shihai no jittai to seikaku" [The character and state of river administration in early modern Settsu and Kawachi provinces]. *Hisutoria* 85 (December 1979): 56–77.

147. Nagamata Kiyotsugu. *Akita sugi e no kyōshū* [Recollections of the cryptomeria of Akita]. Tokyo: Tōhoku Shikō Kabushiki Kaisha, 1969. 228 pp.

148. Nakada Kaoru. *Mura oyobi iriai no kenkyū* [Studies of villages and communal lands]. Tokyo: Iwanami Shoten Kankō, 1949. 331 pp.

149. Nakajima Akira. "Maebashi han no rin'ya seido: Ohayashi o chūshin to shite" [The forest system of Maebashi: The lord's forest]. *Gumma bunka* 93 (October 1967): 2–20.

150. Nakamura Kōya. *Ieyasuden* [A biography of Ieyasu]. Tokyo: Kōdansha, 1965. 719 pp. text, 232 pp. chronology.

151. Nakano Masao. "Tokugawa jidai ni okeru sanron no ichirei: Iga Okugano mura yama ni okeru iriaiken no hensen" [An example of Edo-period woodland disputes: Changes in rights to common land in the mountains of Okugano village in Iga]. *Shakai keizai shigaku* 4, no. 10 (1935): 71–78.

152. Nakao Hidetoshi. *Iriai rin'ya no hōritsu mondai* [Legal problems of forest common lands]. Tokyo: Keisō Shobō, 1969; 1977. 391 pp.

153. Nihon Gakushiin, comp. *Meijizen Nihon ringyō gijutsu hattatsushi* [The development of forest technology in pre-Meiji Japan]. Tokyo: Nihon Gakujutsu Shinkōkai, 1959; Nōkan Kagaku Igaku Kenkyū Shiryōkan, 1980. 753 pp.

154. *Nihon rekishi daijiten* [Dictionary of Japanese history]. Vol. 9. Tokyo: Kawade Shobō Shinsha, 1961.

155. Nihon Ringyō Gijutsu Kyōkai. *Ringyō gijutsushi* [A history of forestry techniques]. 5 vols. Tokyo: Nihon Ringyō Gijutsu Kyōkai, 1972–75.

156. ———. *Ringyō hyakka jiten (shinpan)* [Encyclopedia of forestry (new edition)]. Tokyo: Maruzen Kabushiki Kaisha, 1979. 1,168 pp.

157. Nishikawa Zensuke. "Edo zaimokushō no kigen: Edo mokuzai ichibashi josetsu" [The origins of Edo lumber markets: An introduction to the history of the Edo lumber marketplace]. *Ringyō keizai* 169 (November 1962): 4–17.

158. ———. "Iriai bunkatsu to sonraku kōzō: Kiso Kaida mura Nishino no jirei" [The dividing of common lands and the structure of villages: The case of Nishino in Kaida village in Kiso]. *Shakaigaku hyōron* 2, no. 2 (August 1951): 43–62.

159. ———. "Ringyō keizai shiron (1, 2, 3, 4): Mokuzai seisan o chūshin to shite" [A treatise on the economics of forestry (1, 2, 3, 4): Lumber production]. *Ringyō keizai* 134, 135, 137, 138 (1959–60): 4–13; 15–30; 16–31; 6–27.

160. ————. "Ringyō keizai shiron (5, 6, 7, 8, 9): Ryōchiteki ringyō chitai" [A treatise on the economics of forestry (5, 6, 7, 8, 9): Areas of feudal forestry]. *Ringyō keizai* 148, 149, 151, 152, 154 (1961): 1–12; 7–23; 28–44; 12–21; 12–21.

161. ————. *Rin'ya shoyū no keisei to mura no kōzō: Iriaiken no jisshōteki kenkyū* [Village structure and the formation of forest ownership: A monographic study of common-land rights]. Tokyo: Ochanomizu Shobō, 1957. 402 pp.

162. ————. "Ryūtsū ichiba kara mita mokuzai shōhin seisan no hatten" [The development of commercial lumbering as seen from the marketplace]. *Shakai keizai shigaku* 27, no. 1 (1961): 1–24.

163. Niwa Kunio. "Hida 'ohayashiyama' no ichi kōsatsu" [A study of the "lord's forest" in Hida]. *TRK Kenkyū kiyō* 56 (1982): 69–94.

164. Noguchi Kikuo. "Kinsei ni okeru hazenoki saibai gijutsu no seiritsu to tenkai" [The establishment and development of the art of cultivating wax trees (*Rhus succedanea*) in the Edo period]. *Kyūshū bunkashi kenkyūjo kenkyū kiyō* 15 (March 1970): 45–76.

165. Nōrinshō, comp. *Nihon rinseishi shiryō* [Records of the history of Japanese forestry]. Vol. 3, *Edo bakufuryō, jō* [Shogunal domain, pt. 1]; vol. 5, *Edo bakufu hōrei* [Regulations of the shogunate]. Tokyo: Nozokawa Shoten, 1971.

166. Ōishi Hisayoshi. *Jikata hanreiroku* [An exegesis on practical affairs]. Ed. Ōishi Shinzaburō. 2 vols. Tokyo: Kondō Shuppansha, 1969; 1980.

167. Oka Mitsuo. "Iriai rin'ya no riyō keitai to sonraku kōzō: Nōminsō no kōsei to no kanren" [The pattern of communal woodland use and village structure: Its relationship to the composition of the peasant class]. *Shigaku zasshi* 65, no. 2 (February 1956): 26–45.

168. ————. "Shiyūrin ni okeru ichiba no tenkai to shōgyō shihon: Yoshino gun Kawakami sato Takahara mura no shiryō o chūshin to shite" [The development of marketing and merchant capital in private forestland: From documents of Takahara village in Kawakami town in Yoshino district of Nara prefecture]. *Nōgyō keizai* (of Hyōgo Nōgyō Daigaku) 3 (1958): 1–34.

169. Okinawaken Nōrin Suisanbu. *Okinawa no ringyōshi* [A history of Okinawa forestry]. Naha: Okinawaken Nōrin Suisanbu, 1972. 125 pp.

170. Ōsaki Rokurō. "Ohayashi chiseki kakutei katei no ichi kenshō: Kōzuke kuni (Gumma ken) Tone gun o taishō to shite" [A study of the standardizing of lord's forest surveys: The Tone district of Kōzuke]. *Ringyō keizai* 119 (1958): 19–32.

171. ————. "Shōen tenkai katei ni miru rin'ya seido: Toku ni sono kaisōsei ni chakumoku shite" [The forest system as viewed in terms of change in the estate system: With particular attention to class structure]. *Ringyō keizai* 4, no. 1 (1951): 18–23.

172. Ōta Katsuya. "Kinsei chūki no Ōsaka zaimoku ichiba: Torihiki kiyaku to 'ton'ya' no nakama gitei no kentō o chūshin ni" [The Osaka lumber market in the mid-Edo period: An examination of the trading agreements and monopoly arrangements of "wholesale" merchants]. *TRK Kenkyū kiyō* 50 (1975): 69–100.

173. Ōta Saburō. "Kaidō kōtsūshi ni okeru namiki matsu no ichi kōsatsu" [A study of the lines of roadside pine trees in the history of highway commerce]. *Gifu shigaku* 70 (October 1979): 19–36.

174. Ōtani Sadao. "Bunka-Tenpō ki no chisui seisaku" [River conservation policy, 1804–44]. *Kokushigaku* 109 (October 1979): 1–27.

175. ———. "Hōei ki no kawa fushin joyaku ni tsuite" [The assistant chief of riparian construction, circa 1705]. *Kokugakuin zasshi* 80, no. 11 (November 1979): 273–83.

176. Ringyō Hattatsushi Chōsakai, ed. *Nihon ringyō hattatsushi: Meiji ikō no tenkai katei* [A history of the rise of Japanese forestry: Its development since the Meiji Restoration]. Tokyo: Rin'yachō, 1960. 779 pp.

177. Rin'yachō, comp. *Tokugawa jidai ni okeru rin'ya seido no taiyō* [An outline of the forest system of the Tokugawa period]. Ed. Takeda Hisao. Tokyo: Rin'ya Kyōzaikai, 1954. 771 pp.

178. Saitō Yōichi. "Kazusa-kuni Nishihara mura no yōsui sōron" [Riparian disputes in Nishihara village in Kazusa province]. *Chibaken no rekishi* 10 (August 1975): 25–32.

179. Sakamoto Kiyozō. *Kitayama daisugi to migaki maruta* [The coppice cryptomeria of Kitayama and polished-log timbers]. Tokyo: Dai Nihon Sanrinkai, 1970. 177 pp.

180. Satō Takayuki. "Kinsei chūki no bakufu zōrin seisaku to murakata no taiō: Hōreki-An'ei ki Hokuen chihō o jirei to shite" [Mid-Edo period shogunate afforestation policy and its accommodation by villagers in northern Tōtōmi, circa 1750–80]. *TRK Kenkyū kiyō* 55 (1980): 167–200.

181. Satō Yatarō, ed. *Sugi no kenkyū* [Studies of cryptomeria]. Tokyo: Yōkendō, 1950.

182. Sawata Takaharu. "Awaji ni okeru ukeyamasei sanrin keiei: Kinsei shoki Mihara gun Anaga mura ni okeru Yamaguchi ke to ukeyamagyō ni tsuite" [The administration of leased-land forests on Awaji: The leased-land business of the Yamaguchi family in Anaga village in the early Edo period]. *Hyōgo ken no rekishi* 13 (July 1975): 14–31.

183. Seki Jun'ya. "Kinsei ni okeru iriai rin'ya no seikaku: Mōri han–Kameyama han nado o chūshin to shite (ichi, ni)" [The character of Edo-period communal woodland: The domains of Mōri and Kameyama

(1, 2)]. *Yamaguchi keizaigaku zasshi* 4, no. 7/8, 4, no. 9/10 (1954): 52–66; 60–72.

184. Sekino Masaru. "Zai Shigaraki Fujiwara Toyonari itadono kō" [A treatise on Fujiwara Toyonari's plank mansion at Shigaraki]. *Hōun* 20 (August 1937): 15–38.

185. Sekishima Hisao. "Tōyama-ke no keizaiteki haikei (ichi): Musashi kuni Tama gun Ogawa mura Ogawa-ke no Ina mokuzai kiridashi shiryō no shōkai" [The economic background of the Tōyama lineage (1): An introduction to the logging record in the Ina district of the Ogawa family of Ogawa village in Musashi]. *Seiji keizai rondan* 13 (November 1953): 41–58.

186. Shimada Kinzō. *Edo-Tōkyō zaimoku ton'ya kumiai seishi* [An authoritative history of the lumbermen's association of Edo-Tokyo]. Tokyo: Doi Ringaku Shinkōkai, 1976. 596 pp.

187. ———. *(Kaitei) rinseigaku gaiyō* [An outline of the study of forest administration (revised)]. Tokyo: Chikyū Shuppan, 1953. 272 pp. Original edition, 1948.

188. ———. "Kawabe ichibangumi kōton'ya kumiai monjo to Edo zaimoku ichiba" [The records of the former first riverside merchant's association and the Edo lumber market]. *TRK Kenkyū kiyō* 51 (1976): 37–62.

189. ———. "Kinsei Tenryū ringyōchi ni okeru nenkiyama baibai" [Woodland leasing in early modern Tenryū timber country]. *TRK Kenkyū kiyō* 52 (1977): 23–77.

190. ———. "Kinsei Tenryū ringyōchi ni okeru nenkiyama no gensho keitai" [The original types of woodland leasing in early modern Tenryū forest areas]. *TRK Kenkyū kiyō* 56 (1982): 36–68.

191. ———. "Kinsei Tenryū ringyōchi ni okeru nenkiyama no kanri keiei: Nenkiyama kōchō ni yoru kaiseki" [The administration of leased woodland in early modern Tenryū: Researched from records of legal appeals]. *TRK Kenkyū kiyō* 54 (1979): 23–71.

192. ———. "Kinsei Tenryū ringyōchi ni okeru nenkiyama no kanri keiei: Tamura nenkiyama kōchō ni yoru kaiseki" [The administration of leased woodland in early modern Tenryū: Researched from records of legal appeals concerning other villages' leased woodland]. *TRK Kenkyū kiyō* 55 (1980): 28–71.

193. ———. "Kinsei Tenryū ringyōchi ni okeru shikin ryūtsū katei" [The pattern of capital circulation in early modern Tenryū timber country]. *TRK Kenkyū kiyō* 53 (1978): 29–81.

194. ———. *Ryūbatsu ringyō seisuishi: Yoshino-Kitayama ringyō no gijutsu to keizai* [A history of the vicissitudes of lumber rafting: The forest technology and economics of Yoshino-Kitayama]. Tokyo: Doi Ringaku Shinkōkai, 1974. 183 pp.

195. ———. *Shinrin kumiairon: Buraku kyōyūchi no jissō kenkyū o moto to shite*

[A thesis on forest guilds: With a foundation in research on the actual conditions of hamlet common lands]. Tokyo: Iwanami Shoten, 1941. 495 pp.

196. Shioya Junji. "Fushimi chikujō to Akita sugi" [The construction of Fushimi castle and the cryptomeria of Akita]. *Kokushi danwakai zasshi* (of Tōhoku Daigaku Bungakubu Kokushi Kenkyūjo), vol. titled *Toyoda-Ishii ryōsensei taikan kinengō* (February 1973): 47–54.

197. Shioya Tsutomu. *Buwakebayashi seido no shiteki kenkyū: Buwakebayashi yori bunshūrin e no tenkai* [Historical studies of the shared-forest system: The development from shared forest to divided forest]. Tokyo: Rin'ya Kyōzaikai, 1959. 654 pp.

198. ———. "Hansei jidai no rinsei" [Forestry during the Edo period]. In *Kagoshima ken nōchi kaikakushi*, comp. Kagoshima Ken, 121–34. Tokyo: Kondō Shuppansha, 1954.

199. Shioya Tsutomu and Sagio Ryōshi. *Obi ringyō hattatsushi* [A history of the development of forestry in Obi district]. Nichinan: Hattori Rinsan Kenkyūjo, 1965. 134 pp.

200. Shirakawa Tarō. *Teikoku rinseishi* [A history of the empire's forest system]. Tokyo: Yūrindō, 1902. 265 pp.

201. Shizuoka Ken Mokuzai Kyōdō Kumiai Ren'aikai. *Shizuoka ken mokuzaishi* [A history of lumbering in Shizuoka prefecture]. Shizuoka: Shizuoka Ken Mokuzai Kyōdō Kumiai Ren'aikai, 1968. 804 pp.

202. Shōji Kichinosuke. "Aizu no urushi to rō" [The lacquer and wax of Aizu]. In *Nihon sangyōshi taikei*, ed. Chihōshi Kenkyū Kyōgikai, vol. 3, 160–76. Tokyo: Tōkyō Daigaku Shuppankai, 1960.

203. ———. "Kinsei ni okeru tochi oyobi sanrin no bunkatsu: Minami Aizu gun Kanaizawa mura no mura yakujō monjo o chūshin ni" [The division of land and forest in the Edo period: Records of village contracts in Kanaizawa village in southern Aizu]. *Tōhoku keizai* 38 (October 1962): 1–35.

204. Sunaga Akira. "Kinugawa jōryūiki ni okeru ringyō chitai no keisei" [The establishment of forests in the upper Kinugawa area]. *Tochigi kenshi kenkyū* 22 (December 1981): 1–32.

205. Suzuki Hideo. *Rinseishi zuihitsu: Akita sugi (kyū Akita han rinseishi nyūmon no shiori)* [Writings on forest history: The cryptomeria of Akita (a guide to the forest history of Akita domain)]. 2 vols. Kanagawa: Suzuki Hideo, 1979.

206. Tachibana Matsuhisa. "Mito han ni okeru bunzukeyama no tenkai katei" [The development of divided mountain land in Mito domain]. *Ibaragi kenshi kenkyū* 40 (1979): 24–39.

207. ———. "Mito han ni okeru iriai kankō no seiritsu to tenkai" [The emergence and evolution of the custom of communal land in Mito domain]. *Ibaragi shirin* 7 (May 1978): 1–18.

208. Tachiishi Tomoo. "Hansei jidai ni okeru Shōnai sakyū no sabō shokusai (1, 2)" [Sand-control planting on the Shōnai dunes during the domanial period (1, 2)]. *Nihon daigaku shizen kagaku kenkyūjo kiyō* 11, 12 (1976).

209. ———. "Nihonkai hokubu kaigan sakyū ni okeru sabō shokusai" [Sand-control planting on the sand dunes of the northern Sea of Japan coast]. *TRK Kenkyū kiyō* 51 (1976): 150–80.

210. Takagi Masatoshi. "Ushū Murayama chihō ni okeru iriai kankō to sanron, toku ni Yamaguchi mura o chūshin ni" [Disputes over forest common-land usage in the Murayama area of Dewa, focusing on Yamaguchi village]. *Hōsei shiron* 7 (March 1980): 71–89.

211. Takahashi Takashi. *Ōsaka mokuzaigyō gaishi* [An unofficial history of the Osaka lumber business]. Osaka: Ōsaka Mokuzaigyō Kumiai, 1957. 352 pp.

212. Takamaki Minoru. "Bakuhan ryōshū no chisui seisaku to rinchū" [Government riparian policy and polder land]. In *Bakuhansei kokka seiritsu katei no kenkyū* [Studies in the formation of the Tokugawa state], ed. Kitajima Masamoto, 447–76. Tokyo: Yoshikawa Kōbunkan, 1978. 705 pp.

213. ———. *Bakuhansei kakuritsuki no sonraku* [Villages at the time the Tokugawa system was established]. Tokyo: Yoshikawa Kōbunkan, 1973. 589 pp.

214. ———. "Kinsei Hida no iriaichi bunkatsu ni tsuite" [The division of communal land in Edo-period Hida]. *Nihon rekishi* 164 (February 1962): 57–67.

215. ———. "Mino ni okeru Bunroku no yama aratame-no aratame ni tsuite" [The inquest of mountains and fields in Mino in the early 1590s]. *TRK Kenkyū kiyō* 45 (1971): 65–84.

216. Takase Tamotsu. *Kaga han kaiunshi no kenkyū* [Studies in the history of Kaga domain's maritime transport]. Tokyo: Yūzankaku, 1979. 599 pp.

217. ———. "Kaga han no Matsumae-Tōhoku chihō kara no mokuzai inyū—Hida tenryōka igo ni tsuite" [Lumber imports from Matsumae and Tōhoku by Kaga domain following the conversion of Hida to shogunate control]. *Kaijishi kenkyū* 27 (October 1976): 43–62.

218. ———. "Kaga han no tateyama ni okeru rinsan shigen no kaihatsu" [The exploitation of timber resources on restricted-use woodlands by Kaga domain]. *TRK Kenkyū kiyō* 51 (1976): 534–56.

219. ———. "Kaga han rinsei no seiritsu ni tsuite" [Establishing a system of forestry in Kaga domain]. *TRK Kenkyū kiyō* 54 (1979): 519–34.

220. ———. "Kaga han shoki no Hishū kitakata zai chōdatsu ni tsuite: Shutoshite Etchū Shōgawa no baai" [The provision of north Hida lumber in the early years of Kaga domain: In particular the case of the Shō river in Etchū]. *TRK Kenkyū kiyō* 47 (1972): 427–46.

221. ———. "Kinsei ni okeru Hida goyōki no motokiri to unsō" [The felling and transporting of government timber in Edo-period Hida]. *Chihōshi kenkyū* 22, no. 6 (December 1972): 1–24.

222. ———. "Tenryō igō no Hida kitakata zai no shūsan ni tsuite" [The assembly and dispersal of north Hida lumber after Hida became a shogunal domain]. *TRK Kenkyū kiyō* 49 (1974): 394–416.

223. Takikawa Masajirō. *Kyōsei narabi ni tojōsei no kenkyū* [Studies of capitals and urban bastions]. Tokyo: Kadokawa Shoten, 1967. 513 pp.

224. Takimoto Seiichi. *Nihon keizai sōsho* [Collected writings on the Japanese economy]. 36 vols. Tokyo: Nihon Keizai Sōsho Kankōkai, 1914–17.

225. ———. *Nihon keizai taiten* [An encyclopedia of the Japanese economy]. 54 vols. Tokyo: Keimeisha, 1928–30.

226. ———. *Satō Shin'en kagaku zenshū* [Collected writings of Satō Shin'en]. 3 vols. Tokyo: Iwanami Shoten, 1927.

227. Takimoto Seiichi and Mukai Shikamatsu. *Nihon sangyō shiryō taikei* [Collected historical records of industry in Japan]. 12 vols. Tokyo: Chūgai Shōgyō Shinpōsha, 1926–27.

228. Tanaka Hajime. *Kinsei zōrin gijutsu* [Afforestation techniques of the Edo period]. Tokyo: Nihon Ringyō Gijutsu Kyōkai, 1954. 450 pp.

229. ———. "Kyūhan jidai no zōrin gijutsu" [Silvicultural techniques of the Edo period]. *Ringyō keizai* 5, no. 4 (1952): 26–31.

230. Toba Masao. "Edo bakufu no shinrin keizai seisaku ni oite" [The shogunate's forest economic policy]. *Gakushikai geppō* 509 (1930): 1–7.

231. ———. "Edo jidai no rinsei" [The Edo-period forest system]. In *Iwanami kōza Nihon rekishi*, vol. 7, pt. 9, pp. 1–38. Tokyo: Iwanami Shoten, 1934.

232. ———. "Kinsei no shinrin keizai to kamikata jūmyō (jō, ge)" [Early modern forest economics and tree nurseries in the Osaka vicinity (1, 2)]. *Keizaishi kenkyū* 31, 32 (May, June 1932): 1–21; 32–53.

233. ———. "Minami Kyūshū no ringyō" [The forest system of southern Kyushu]. In *Nihon sangyōshi taikei*, ed. Chihōshi Kenkyū Kyōgikai, vol. 8, 123–29. Tokyo: Tōkyō Daigaku Shuppankai, 1960.

234. ———. *Nihon no ringyō* [Forestry in Japan]. Tokyo: Yūzankaku, 1948. 265 pp.

235. ———. *Nihon ringyōshi* [A history of Japanese forestry]. Tokyo: Yūzankaku, 1951. 238 pp.

236. ———. "Sengoku jidai no shinrin keizai to rinsei" [Forestry and forest economics in the sixteenth century]. *Shakai keizai shigaku* 3, no. 9 (1934): 25–37.

237. ———. *Shinrin to bunka* [Forests and civilization]. Tokyo: Dai Nihon Shuppansha Hōbunsō, 1943. 382 pp.

238. ———. "Toyo taikō to shinrin keizai" [Hideyoshi and the forest economy]. *Rekishi Nihon* 2, no. 4 (1943): 8–11.

239. Toda Yoshimi. "Sekkanke ryō no somayama ni tsuite" [The timber land of the major Fujiwara estates]. In *Nihon kodai no kokka to shūkyō (ge)* [State and religion in ancient Japan (pt. 2)], comp. Inoue Kaoru Kyōju Taiken Kinenkai, 327–58. Tokyo: Yoshikawa Kōbunkan, 1980.

240. Tokoro Mitsuo. "Chiiki ringyō ni okeru ryōshūteki seisan: Matsumoto ryō ringyō no baai" [Daimyo production in regional forestry: The Matsumoto forest industry]. *TRK Kenkyū kiyō* 41 (1966): 1–26.

241. ———. "Edo bakufu shoki no eirin jigyō: Shinshū Ina sanrin no baai" [Forest industry in the early Edo period: The forests of Ina in Shinano]. *TRK Kenkyū kiyō* 51 (1976): 1–36.

242. ———. "Edojō nishimaru no saiken to yōzai" [Lumber supplies and the reconstruction of Edo castle's western enceinte]. *TRK Kenkyū kiyō* 48 (1973): 1–24.

243. ———. "Hideyoshi-Ieyasu ryō jidai no Kisozai saiun shiryō" [Records of lumbering in Kiso during the tenure of Hideyoshi and Ieyasu, 1589–1615]. *TRK Kenkyū kiyō* 43 (1968): 399–438.

244. ———. "Ieyasu kurairichi jidai no Kiso kanjō shiryō" [Financial records of Kiso as Ieyasu's warehouse land]. *TRK Kenkyū kiyō* 42 (1967): 309–34.

245. ———. "Kanbunhan *Jikata bunsho* ni tsuite" [The 1668 edition of *Jikata bunsho*]. *Shakai keizai shigaku* 9, no. 2 (1939): 73–96.

246. ———. "Kinsei Kiso ringyō no kiban: Kyōhō kaikaku ki o chūshin to shite" [The basis of the early modern forest industry in Kiso: Focusing on the Kyōhō reform period]. *TRK Kenkyū kiyō* 55 (1980): 1–27.

247. ———. "Kinsei Kiso sanrin no hozoku taisaku" [The Edo-period preservation policy in Kiso forests]. *TRK Kenkyū kiyō* 52 (1977): 1–22.

248. ———. "Kinsei no rin'ya funsō to kōsai: Kōshū Hirano mura to Sōshū Setsuki mura no sanron no rei" [Edo-period forest disputes and their formal settlement: The dispute between the villages of Hirano in Kai and Setsuki in Sagami]. *TRK Kenkyū kiyō* 50 (1975): 1–38.

249. ———. *Kinsei ringyōshi no kenkyū* [Studies in the history of early modern forestry]. Tokyo: Yoshikawa Kōbunkan, 1980. 858 pp.

250. ———. "Kinsei shoki no shōnin ni yoru yōzai seisan" [Lumber production by merchants early in the Edo period]. *TRK Kenkyū kiyō* 45 (1970): 1–22.

251. ———. "Kiso-Hida no ringyō" [The lumber industry in Kiso and Hida]. In *Nihon sangyōshi taikei*, ed. Chihōshi Kenkyū Kyōgikai, vol. 5, 389–415. Tokyo: Tōkyō Daigaku Shuppankai, 1960.

252. ———. "Kiso no gomen shiraki" [The plain wood allotted to the intendant and villagers of Kiso]. *TRK Kenkyū Kiyō* 56 (1982): 7–35.

253. ———. "Nishikori tsunaba ni tsuite: Kuchie kaisetsu" [The log boom at Nishikori: An introductory explanation]. *Shakai keizai shigaku* 2, no. 12 (1933): 101–18.

254. ———. "Ōkubo Iwami no kami Nagayasu to Shinano" [Ōkubo Nagayasu, and Shinano]. In *Chihō kenkyū rongyō*, 181–223. Nagano-shi: Isshi Shigeki Sensei Kanreki Kinenkai, 1954.

255. ———. "Ringyō" [Forestry]. In *Nihon kagaku gijutsushi*, 863–85. Tokyo: Heibonsha, 1962.

256. ———. "Ringyō" [Forestry]. In *Nihon minzokugaku taikei*, vol. 5, 121–45. Tokyo: Asahi Shinbunsha, 1959.

257. ———. "Ringyō" [Forestry]. In *Nihon sangyōshi taikei (sōron hen)* [Summary volume], ed. Chihōshi Kenkyū Kyōgikai, 135–62. Tokyo: Tōkyō Daigaku Shuppankai, 1961.

258. ———. "Ringyō" [Forestry]. In *Taikei Nihonshi sōsho: Sangyōshi dai 3*, vol. 11, 198–223. Tokyo: Yamakawa Shuppansha, 1965.

259. ———. "Rinseishi" [The historiography of Japanese forestry]. *Shakai keizai shigaku* 10, no. 9/10 (1941): 83–106.

260. ———. "Saishu ringyō kara ikusei ringyō e no katei" [The route from exploitation to regenerative forestry]. *TRK Kenkyū kiyō* 44 (1969): 1–26.

261. ———. "Shihan 'ohayashi' no riyō keitai: Matsushiro han Kutsuno ohayashi no baai" [The utilization of a domain lord's woodland: The case of Kutsuno forest in Matsushiro domain]. *TRK Kenkyū kiyō* 49 (1974): 1–17.

262. ———. "Suminokura Yoichi to Kisoyama" [Suminokura Yoichi and the Kiso mountains]. *TRK Kenkyū kiyō* 43 (1968): 1–26.

263. ———. "Unzai chūkei kichi to shite no Inuyama: Kisogawa unzai-shi no issetsu" [Inuyama, a connecting point in lumber shipping: A chapter in the history of Kiso lumber transport]. *TRK Kenkyū kiyō* 42 (1967): 1–34.

264. ———. "Ura Kisoyama no yōzai seisan" [Lumber production in the Ura Kiso mountains]. *TRK Kenkyū kiyō* 47 (1972): 1–29.

265. Tokugawa Muneyoshi. "Edo jidai ni okeru ringyō shisō (sono 1–10)" [Forestry thought in the Edo period (pts. 1–10)]. *Sanrin* 686–95 (January–October 1940): 68–72; 107–10; 114–18; 62–68; 85–90; 110–17; 65–75; 58–65; 62–85; 67–76.

266. ———. *Edo jidai ni okeru zōrin gijutsu no shiteki kenkyū* [An historical study of afforestation techniques in the Edo period]. Tokyo: Nishigahara Kankōkai, 1941. 373 pp.

267. ———. "Kyōhō jidai zengo no Yoshimune o chūshin to suru rin-gyōron" [Forestry thought, particularly of Yoshimune, around the 1720s]. *Ringyō keizai seisaku shiryō* 7 (March 1942): 111–22.

268. ———. "Meiji shoki no ringyō bunken" [Works on forestry of the early Meiji period]. *Sanrin* 662 (1938): 84–94.

269. Tokugawa Rinseishi Kenkyūjo. "*Nihon rinseishi chōsa shiryō*" sōmo-

kuroku [A general table of contents to "Documents of the investigation into the history of Japan's forest system"]. Tokyo: Yūshōdō Shoten, 1971. 171 pp.

270. Tokugawa Yoshichika. "Kiso rinseishi 1–22" [The history of forestry in Kiso, pts. 1–22]. *Goryōrin* 101–73 (1936–38, 1941–42): 101 = 45–67; 102 = 60–70; 103 = 59–72; 105 = 76–104; 106 = 25–37; 108 = 45–54; 110 = 46–65; 112 = 74–94; 116 = 73–96; 119 = 46–60; 121 = 2–17; 122 = 15–37; 123 = 11–26; 125 = 2–18; 126 = 45–61; 156 = 23–37; 158 = 26–43; 159 = 28–39; 161 = 25–36; 171 = 13–30; 172 = 13–23; 173 = 14–31.

271. ———. *Kisoyama* [The Kiso mountains]. Tokyo: Dōrōsha, 1915. 401 pp.

272. ———. "Kisoyama kafū to Kiso no nengu" [The supplemental fief of Kiso and its taxes]. *TRK Kenkyū kiyō* 43 (1968): 367–72.

273. Tōkyō Kyōiku Daigaku Nōgakubu Ringakka, comp. *Jitsuyō ringyō keisan hikkei* [Manual of applied forest mensuration]. Tokyo: Shōkōdō, 1955.

274. Tsuboi Shunzō. "Kinsei chū-go ki Tenryū ringyō ni tsuite" [Tenryū forestry in the middle and late Edo period]. *Chihōshi Shizuoka* (of Shizuoka Kenritsu Chūō Toshokan) 9 (November 1979): 20–33.

275. Tsugawa Masayuki. "Kinsei ni okeru Yamato Kitayama sato no sonraku kōzō to ringyō (ichi, ni)" [The village structure and forest industry of Edo-period Kitayama village in Yamato (1, 2)]. *Keizai ronshū* (of Kansai Daigaku) 5, nos. 3, 5 (June, August 1955): 116–46; 71–112.

276. ———. "Kinsei no Kitō ringyō" [Early modern forest production of the Kitō district]. *Keizai ronshū* (of Kansai Daigaku) 6, no. 5 (1956): 50–91.

277. Tsukamoto Manabu. "Meisan ōsawa fuhō ron ni tsuite" [The discourse on the phrase "famous mountains and great swamps are not restricted"]. *TRK Kenkyū kiyō* 49 (1974): 245–72.

278. ———. "Owari han no mizu shihai kikō ni tsuite" [The water management system of Owari domain]. *TRK Kenkyū kiyō* 45 (1970): 159–86.

279. Tsukii Tadahiro. *Akita han rinsei seishi* [A true record of Akita domain forestry]. Akita: Kiki Kappansho, 1905. 334 pp.

280. Tsutsui Michio. "Akita han ni okeru ringyō ikusei seisan soshiki to gyōsei no hōhō" [The organization of afforestation activity and trends in its administration in Akita domain]. *Tōkyō daigaku nōgakubu enshūrin hōkoku* 53 (1957): 1–26.

281. ———. *Nihon rinseishi kenkyū josetsu* [An introduction to the study of Japanese forest history]. Tokyo: Tōkyō Daigaku Shuppankai, 1978. 227 pp.

282. Tsutsui Taizō. "Chiso kaisei ki ni okeru iriaiken funsō: Nagano ken Iidashi seibu sanchi no rei" [Disputes over common-land rights at land tax reform time: The example of hill land west of Iida in Nagano]. *TRK Kenkyū kiyō* 46 (1971): 103–23.

283. ———. "Kinsei ni okeru yamanaka no shinden mura seiritsu to iriai mura aida no funsō: Shinshū Ina gun Taiheizan no baai" [Disputes among villages with communal lands and the formation of new mountain villages in the Edo period: The case of Mount Taihei in Ina district in Shinano]. *TRK Kenkyū kiyō* 45 (1970): 98–122.

284. ———. "Shinshū Iida han ryō ni okeru shiyūrin no seiritsu katei" [The formation of private forest holdings in Iida domain in Shinano]. *TRK Kenkyū kiyō* 48 (1973): 105–22.

285. Uchida Tokuhei. "Shinshū Ina gun Noguchi mura sawayama kusaba iriai sōron" [Disputes over communal use of marshy uplands in Noguchi village in Ina district in Shinano]. *Shinano* 28, no. 11 (November 1976): 1–14.

286. ———. "Shinshū Ina no chizukiyama ni okeru sakikari to atogusa iriai" [Prior-cutting and leftover-grass common land in woodland attached to arable in Ina district in Shinano]. *Shinano* 29, no. 7 (July 1977): 16–34.

287. Ueda Tōjurō. "Okinawa no senkakusha Sai On" [Sai On, pioneer intellectual of Okinawa]. *Keizaishi kenkyū* 25, no. 5 (May 1941): 27–43.

288. ———. "Ōmi kuni Ishibechō ni okeru yamawari seido" [The mountain division system in Ishibe town in Ōmi]. *Keizaishi kenkyū* 25, no. 3 (March 1941): 37–44.

289. ———. "Tango Kami Sanō mura ni okeru yamawari seido" [The mountain division system in Kami Sanō village in Tango]. *Keizaishi kenkyū* 25 (November 1931): 90–96.

290. ———. "Tango no jiwari seido" [The land division system in Tango]. *Keizaishi kenkyū* 16 (February 1931): 25–49.

291. Uesugi Mutsuhiko. "Kita Kantō kasen ryūtsū ni okeru mokuzai ichiba no tenkai: Kinugawa jōryū no ikada sōron o chūshin to shite" [The development of lumber marketing by north Kantō waterways transportation: Focusing on disputes over rafts in the upper Kinu river]. *Tochigi kenshi kenkyū* 6 (November 1973): 3–24.

292. Wakabayashi Kisaburō. "Kaga han no ohayashiyama to tomeyama: Oku Noto jiryōnai tomeyama bassai negai o chūshin to shite" [The lord's forests and forest preserves of Kaga domain: Focusing on requests to fell trees in temple-land forest preserves of inner Noto]. *TRK Kenkyū kiyō* 54 (1979): 98–114.

293. ———. "Kinsei ni okeru issaku ukeyama kankō ni tsuite: Oku Noto Terayama mura no baai o rei to shite" [The Edo-period practice of single-season mountain leasing: The case of Terayama village in inner Noto]. *TRK Kenkyū kiyō* 51 (1976): 203–28.

294. Yamaguchi Yaichirō. *Tōhoku no yakibata kankō* [Burnt-field customs in the northeast]. Tokyo: Kōshunkaku, 1944. 238 pp. Republished in *Yamaguchi Yaichirō senshū*, vol. 3. Tokyo: Sekai Bunko, 1972. 546 pp.

295. Yamamoto Hikaru. "Azuchi Momoyama jidai no ringyō" [Forestry in the Azuchi-Momoyama period]. *Ringyō keizai* 226 (August 1967): 20–28.

296. ———. "Heian jidai no rin'ya riyō" [Forest use in the Heian period]. *Ringyō keizai* 205 (November 1965): 33–40.

297. ———. "Kamakura jidai no ringyō" [Forestry in the Kamakura period]. *Ringyō keizai* 214 (August 1966): 8–16.

298. ———. "Muromachi jidai no ringyō" [Forestry in the Muromachi period]. *Ringyō keizai* 220 (February 1967): 30–39.

299. ———. "Nanbokuchō jidai ni okeru sanrin gen'ya no riyō" [Forest and wasteland use in the era of dual courts]. *Ringyō keizai* 217 (November 1966): 26–32.

300. ———. *Ringyō oyobi rinsanbutsu* [Forestry and forest products]. Tokyo: Sangyō Zusho, 1954. 219 pp.

301. ———. "Sengoku jidai no ringyō" [Forestry in the warring states period]. *Ringyō keizai* 222 (April 1967): 32–40.

302. ———. "Waga kuni kodai no ringyō" [Forestry in the ancient period]. *Ringyō keizai* 193 (November 1964): 17–25.

303. Yamamoto Tokusaburō. "Kumazawa Banzan no sanrinron shiken" [A personal perspective on Kumazawa Banzan's writings on forestry]. *Dai Nihon sanrin kaihō* 542 (January 1928): 50–62.

304. Yamanouchi Shizuo. *Nihon zōrin gyōseishi gaisetsu* [A historical introduction to the administration of afforestation in Japan]. Tokyo: Nihon Ringyō Gijutsu Kyōkai, 1949. 148 pp.

305. Yasuoka Shigeaki. "Tokugawa chūki Ōsaka maki ichiba no kōzō" [Structure of the Osaka firewood market in the mid-Edo period]. *Ōsaka daigaku keizaigaku* 7, no. 3 (1957): 104–45.

306. Yokoyama Atsumi. "Azusagawadani ni okeru Matsumoto han no motogiriyama to shidashiyama-unjōyama (ichi, ni)" [Three types of forest administration in the Azusagawa valley in Matsumoto domain (1, 2)]. *Shinano* 16, nos. 6–7 (June, July 1964): 33–40; 33–43.

307. ———. "Shiraki kō: Chūbu sangoku chitai ni okeru seisan to ryūtsū" [A treatise on "plain wood": Its production and transport in the Chūbu mountain district]. *TRK Kenkyū kiyō* 55 (1980): 542–62.

308. Yoshida Yoshiaki. *Kiba no rekishi* [A history of lumberyards]. Tokyo: Shinrin Shigen Sōgō Taisaku Kyōgikai, 1959. 280 pp.

309. Yumoto Tatsuyasu. "Kinsei sonraku ni okeru kasō nōmin no iriaiken kakudai katei: Shinshū Takai gun Akaiwa mura no baai" [The broadening of lower-class peasant common-land rights in Edo-period villages: The case of Akaiwa village in Takai district of Shinano]. *Shinano* 32, no. 10 (October 1980): 66–77.

310. *Zōrin kōrōsha jiseki (kyūhan jidai)* [Distinguished figures in the field of afforestation (Edo period)]. 2 vols. Tokyo: Dai Nihon Sanrinkai, 1936. 250 pp.

Index

Key Entries: with pertinent subtopics listed

Afforestation
Agriculture
Commoner forest use
Daimyo
Deforestation
Exploitation forestry

Forest administration
Political process
Regenerative forestry
Urban forest use
Use rights
Villages and woodland

Compositor:	Asco Trade Typesetting Ltd.
Text:	11/13 Baskerville
Display:	Baskerville
Printer:	Braun-Brumfield, Inc.
Binder:	Braun-Brumfield, Inc.
Maps:	Eureka Cartography